Writing Travel
Series Editor, Jeanne Moskal

Writing Travel
Series Editor, Jeanne Moskal

The series publishes manuscripts related to the new field of travel studies, including works of original travel writing; editions of out-of-print travel books or previously unpublished travel memoirs; English translations of important travel books in other languages; theoretical and historical treatments of ways in which travel and travel writing engage such questions as religion, nationalism/cosmopolitanism, and empire; gender and sexuality; race, ethnicity, and immigration; the history of the book, print culture, and translation; biographies of significant travelers or groups of travelers (including but not limited to pilgrims, missionaries, anthropologists, tourists, explorers, immigrants); critical studies of the works of significant travelers or groups of travelers; and pedagogy of travel and travel literature and its place in curricula.

Other Books in the Series
Maria Graham's Journal of a Voyage to Brazil, ed Jennifer Hayward and M. Soledad Caballero (2010)
Au Japon: The Memoirs of a Foreign Correspondent in Japan, Korea, and China, 1892–1894, Amédée Baillot de Guerville, ed. by Daniel C. Kane (2009)
Sarah Heckford: A Lady Trader in the Transvaal, ed. by Carole G. Silver (2008)
Vienna Voices: A Traveler Listens to the City of Dreams, Jill Knight Weinberger (2006)
Eating Europe: A Meta-Nonfiction Love Story, Jon Volkmer (2006)

Nellie Arnott's Writings on Angola, 1905–1913

Missionary Narratives Linking Africa and America

Sarah Robbins and Ann Ellis Pullen

Parlor Press
Anderson, South Carolina
www.parlorpress.com

Parlor Press LLC, Anderson, South Carolina, USA

© 2011 by Parlor Press
All rights reserved.
Printed in the United States of America

SAN: 254-8879

Library of Congress Cataloging-in-Publication Data

Robbins, Sarah.
  Nellie Arnott's writings on Angola, 1905-1913 : missionary narratives linking Africa and America / Sarah Robbins and Ann Ellis Pullen.
     p. cm. -- (Writing travel)
  Includes bibliographical references and index.
  ISBN 978-1-60235-141-7 (pbk. : alk. paper) -- ISBN 978-1-60235-142-4 (hardcover : alk. paper) -- ISBN 978-1-60235-143-1 (adobe e-book)
  1. Angola--Description and travel. 2. Angola--Church history. 3. Darling, Nellie Jane Arnott, 1873-1963--Travel--Angola. 4. Missionaries--Travel--Angola. 5. Women missionaries--Travel--Angola. 6. Congregational churches--Missions--Angola. 7. Americans--Travel--Angola. I. Pullen, Ann Ellis, 1943- II. Darling, Nellie Jane Arnott, 1873-1963. III. Title.
  DT1282.R63 2011
  266'.02373067092--dc22
  [B]
                                2010046852

Cover design by David Blakesley.
Cover illustration: Postcard, map and group photograph from a scrapbook and album prepared by Nellie Arnott Darling. Nellie Jane Arnott Darling Papers, 1905–1943. Courtesy of The Bancroft Library, University of California, Berkeley.

Printed on acid-free paper.

Parlor Press, LLC is an independent publisher of scholarly and trade titles in print and multimedia formats. This book is available in paper, cloth and Adobe eBook formats from Parlor Press on the World Wide Web at http://www.parlorpress.com or through online and brick-and-mortar bookstores. For submission information or to find out about Parlor Press publications, write to Parlor Press, 3015 Brackenberry Drive, Anderson, South Carolina, 29621, or e-mail editor@parlorpress.com.

Contents

Abbreviations	vi
Illustrations	vii
Acknowledgments	ix
Introduction: Missionary Authorship as Network-Building	xiii
Part I: Contexts for Reading Nellie Arnott's Writing	1
1 Nellie Arnott Darling: Traveler in Mission Service	3
2 Mission Service in National and Transnational Contexts	21
3 Writing on Multiple Journeys	69
Part II The Public Writings of Nellie J. Arnott (Darling)	135
4 Traveling to Portuguese West Africa	139
5 Woman's Work at a Highlands Mission Station	183
6 Cultivating Networks of Influence	217
Appendix 1: Mission Publications' Editing of Arnott's Writing	271
Appendix 2: ABCFM Missionaries in Angola	279
Appendix 3: Image Citations and Explanatory Context	289
Bibliography	299
Index	325
About the Authors	337

Abbreviations

ABCFM	American Board of Commissioners for Foreign Missions, Nellie Arnott's governing organization during foreign mission service
NJADP	Nellie Jane Arnott Darling Papers (The Bancroft Library, University of California, Berkeley)
AMA	American Missionary Association, sponsor of Nellie Arnott's "home" mission service in the southern U.S.
WBM	Woman's Board of Missions, headquartered in Boston
WBMI	Woman's Board of Missions of the Interior, headquartered in Chicago; Arnott's sponsoring group for Angola service

Illustrations

All illustrations come from these sources: The Bancroft Library, University of California, Berkeley, or family collection of Mary Darling Caris. See Appendix 3 for more detailed information about the illustrations.

Figure 1: Scenes from Kamundongo, Arnott's station.	xiv
Figure 2: Arnott (center) in Angola.	xxviii
Figure 3: "Now I Lay Me Down to Sleep" in Umbundu, from one of Arnott's letters to her grandchildren.	5
Figure 4: Arnott Family, about 1898.	8
Figure 5: Page from Arnott's Photo Album: Angola maps and postcard.	22
Figure 6: Scenes of Woman's Conference at Bailundu, 1911.	43
Figure 7: Arnott's circular letter notebook for 1905.	73
Figure 8: Arnott (left, in a tepoia) and Mrs. [Elisabeth] Ennis in a bush-cart.	78
Figure 9: Arnott's official ABCFM photograph.	81
Figure 10: Four Photographs from Ocileso.	169
Figure 11: Missionary delegates at Ohualondo Conference, 1907.	185
Figure 12: Camping scenes, 1911.	206
Figure 13: Marriage license of Nellie Arnott and Paul Darling.	242
Figure 14: Cipuku and Nakalu, with Arnott's notation: "My Girls, 1905–1912."	246
Figure 15. 1937 Christmas card from Means School.	253
Figure 16: Page of English-Umbundu Hymnal.	275
Figure 17: Photo album page with Bailundu (Bailundo) scenes and missionary photos.	280
Figure 18: Dr. and Mrs. Sanders, Marshall and Danforth, 1912.	285

Acknowledgments

This project has had many generous sponsors and supporters.

We must thank, first of all, the energetic and generous staff of the Bancroft Library at the University of California Berkeley for introducing us to the Nellie Jane Arnott Darling collection in all its rich complexity. Through multiple visits to the library over many years, we found the entire team at the Bancroft to be a model of collegial support; we especially thank Susan Snyder, a true colleague in the archival recovery process.

Once our initial research had uncovered the basic outline of Nellie Arnott's experiences as an African missionary, we needed to find the beloved grandchildren who were referenced so often in her papers. After a series of dogged but unsuccessful attempts to track down these family members, we were close to giving up when our marvelous student assistant, Marty Lamers, made contact with the two Darling grandchildren, now, of course, adults with extended families of their own. Mary Darling Caris and Christopher (Truman) Darling gave us access to a wide range of family materials and personal stories that deepened our understanding of their grandmother's life. Mary and Chris were patient and encouraging during our long process of research and writing. We appreciate their willingness to contribute to the project.

From the outset, we received important support from Kennesaw State University (KSU). The KSU Foundation and the Faculty Incentive Grant program assisted our initial research, including funds for student assistants who learned about archival work by doing it with us. Our first-round team of student assistants included Allyson Manning and Jamie Spears, and toward the end of our manuscript preparation, Kathryn Jonell brought fresh eyes to the material. Original research team member Margie Hendrix remained with the project through the end of her undergraduate program and into graduate work. Margie took on a series of roles funded by such programs at KSU as the Graduate Research Assistants program and the Student Assistance for Leadership in Teaching initiative. Later on, KSU graduate student Kenzie Freeman brought her incisive and careful editing skills to our manuscript. KSU administrators and faculty colleagues were unfailingly supportive throughout our years of research and writing. In particular, we want to recognize Griselda Thomas and Cherif Diop for providing important input into the revision of our introduction, and we thank Sam Abaidoo for an especially helpful discussion of mission schools in Ghana.

The body of materials Arnott left behind was far more vast and complex than one might imagine a single missionary could produce, and partly for that reason, we began to recognize the benefits of using the Web to make her diaries—the most personal record of her experiences—available along with records from other missionaries who served in Angola. In anticipation of potentially producing such a website, we assembled a team to assist our planning. Special thanks, therefore, go to the following advisory board members: Akanmu Adebayo, Gatsinzi Basaninyenzi, Shirley Brown, Harvey Hill, Kathy Matthews, Barbara McCaskill, Laura McGrath, Laura Micham, Jean Pfaelzer, Liz Rohan, Karen Sanchez-Eppler, Ann Smith, Laura Wexler, and Sandra Zagarell. Meanwhile, one audience we were especially eager to reach through our study of Arnott has been schoolteachers, so we thank Traci Blanchard, Michelle Goodsite, Scott Kent, Deb Schmalholz, and Dave Winter for serving as advisors from secondary school settings.

Beyond her work on our advisory board, we thank Liz Rohan for her generosity in sharing her own research materials on Janette Miller, another missionary serving in Angola.

Though our work began in one outstanding library, the Bancroft, we quickly found that we needed to draw upon numerous other collections. We thank the staffs at the Houghton Library at Harvard University and the Pitts Theological Library at Emory University for their invaluable assistance. The interlibrary loan team at Kennesaw State University, especially Amy Thompson, patiently tracked down sources. Staff members at several other facilities welcomed us, particularly the St. Louis Public Library and the New Hampton (Iowa) Public Library. Camille Chesley, a talented student at Oberlin College, helpfully located some of Arnott's correspondence in the collection there.

Acknowledgments

For documenting Nellie Arnott's youth in Iowa, the assistance of Jere Keenan Brands and Harold Brands was invaluable as they drove around Chickasaw County locating sites mentioned in Nellie Arnott Darling's letters and made introductions to others with knowledge of the area. Staff members in the deed room at the Chickasaw County Courthouse were especially helpful. Reverend Robert Treichel of the Nashua First Congregational Church, United Church of Christ, facilitated research in the records of the church that the Arnott and Darling families attended for many years.

Scholars and affiliates of the mission movement supported us with conversations about their work, with several granting us extended interviews and/or emailing with us on topics ranging from the Umbundu language to life in a mission station. We especially thank the late Muriel (Ki) Henderson, Nancy Henderson James, Kathleen Henderson Ashley, Joyce Myers-Brown, Patricia R. Hill and Frank Collins. Muriel (Ki) Henderson generously provided records from the files of her husband, missionary and author Lawrence Henderson, and shared her own materials from their time in Angola, as did her daughters, Kathleen H. Ashley and Nancy Henderson-James.

Audiences at numerous venues gave us feedback during various stages of our process. Of particular importance was the 2006 conference "Competing Kingdoms: Women, Mission, Nation, and American Empire, 1812–1938" held at the Rothermere American Institute, Oxford University. Conference organizers Kathryn Kish Sklar, Rui Kohiyama, Barbara Reeves-Ellington, and Connie Shemo pushed our thinking about imperialism and world missionary activity. International scholars at the 2002 conference "The State of the Art(s): African Studies and American Studies in Comparative Perspective," University of Cape Coast, Ghana, provided insightful critique of an early presentation from our research. Other audiences included conferences of the American Studies Association (ASA), Conference on College Composition and Communication (CCCC), American Literature Association (ALA), Society for the Study of American Women Writers (SSAWW), the Modern Language Association (MLA), and groups at several universities in the U.S. and abroad.

Jeanne Moskal, who manages the "Writing Travel" Parlor Press series in which this book appears, guided us to a focus on Arnott's published writing and a positioning of this study within the broader context of travel writing. Professor Rhonda Semple was a generous and knowledgeable outside reader of our manuscript during its review. David Blakesley, Parlor Press's chief editor, answered our countless requests with unfailing grace and insight.

Our collaboration on this project built upon many years of shared work, including team teaching in women's studies, grant writing, and shared experiments with new technologies for scholarship and teaching. These sustained enterprises—like the work on this book—were enabled in large part by our family members, who cheerfully took trips to do research with us, read draft materials, and accepted our need for long phone conversations and email communications—sometimes to the detriment of family time. Thanks, then, to George Pullen and John Robbins for their patience and their enthusiasm for our work. A special thanks to George and to Patty Robbins and Margaret Robbins for assisting with transcriptions of Arnott's writing. Many other friends, family members, and students have contributed ideas to our project's unfolding progress over the years. Thanks to you all.

Introduction: Missionary Authorship as Network-Building

"A native house was set on fire about midnight[,] and as the wind was very strong another house was set from it. We hardly think our enemies will dare to set fire to any Mission property, and we hope all fires will soon cease." Thus wrote Nellie Jane Arnott in a September 1905 letter sent home to the U.S. as she arrived in the Angola highlands. Having hinted at the challenges she faced as an American Protestant mission teacher in a Catholic Portuguese colony, she moved immediately to an idyllic description of the station's surroundings: "I wish you might see all our beautiful orange trees," and "We also have plenty of bananas, guavas, strawberries and all garden vegetables."

Such shifts in tone and content were typical in the writing produced by Nellie Arnott and other foreign missionaries of her era. Charged with carrying out Protestant service in faraway lands, missionary women were also expected to generate sustained support—especially funds—by writing about their work. Maintaining stakeholders' involvement at a time when many worthy causes competed for white middle-class women's attention necessitated holding readers' interest in the foreign locales where missionaries labored. Accordingly, these authors dispatched their texts to a much larger audience than family and friends. In this case, for example, Nellie Arnott's report may have been composed initially as a letter and directed to a limited circle of readers, but by April of 1906, a version of this narrative also appeared as an article in *Mission Studies*, a popular publication of the American women's foreign mission movement.[1]

Mission Studies was certainly not the only publication that disseminated her writing. Though hardly a household name today, at the turn of the previous century the byline of Nellie J. Arnott would have been easily recognized by the niche group of readers who followed Congregational foreign mission service in periodicals such as *Missionary*

Herald and *Life and Light*. She would have been even better known—indeed, viewed as a close personal friend in Christian service—by the smaller community of mission movement activists who read the reports she regularly posted to her sponsoring organization and the less formal "circular letters" she sent to a cadre of dedicated colleagues. Nellie Arnott's writing for these venues, like her magazine accounts, was self-consciously public. So, Arnott's publications provide not an objective record of foreign missionaries in action or an unfiltered account of her personal perceptions but rather one example of how the movement *represented* itself in a specific historical moment for a well-defined audience. Keeping that rhetorical context in mind, in this book we examine Arnott's public writing about her experiences at a highlands mission station in Portuguese West Africa between 1905 and 1912, her subsequent return to the U.S. on furlough, and her marriage.

Figure 1: Scenes from Kamundongo, Arnott's station. Courtesy of The Bancroft Library, University of California, Berkeley.

Gendered Writing on Foreign Mission Service

Travel to faraway places became increasingly available to white middle-class women in the early years of the twentieth century, and one major route to such experiences was through the American women's foreign mission enterprise. Whether journeying to an overseas posting themselves or reading about evangelical activities in a distant locale, American women (especially white middle-class Protestants) used mission literature to explore cultures very different from their own.[2]

Like other women actively engaged in the movement at its peak, Nellie Jane Arnott was a prolific writer and an enthusiastic reader of missionary texts. Growing up in Iowa, Arnott had become fully invested in Christian service. Her personal role in the mission enterprise expanded considerably over the years from its beginning in midwestern Protestant church culture, to teaching assignments in the U.S. South at American Missionary Association (AMA) schools, to service in Africa in the early twentieth century. Across that span of involvement, one constant was her use of shared literacy practices to connect with the movement's far-flung network and, eventually, to memorialize her own career.[3]

In the late nineteenth and early twentieth centuries, missionary periodicals claimed a dedicated readership and provided an important opportunity for women writers to hone their rhetorical skills.[4] Similarly, although historians have made relatively limited use of the official reports from such women and have concentrated instead on the more visible male leaders, writing like Nellie Arnott did for the American Board of Commissioners for Foreign Missions (ABCFM) and its affiliated women's groups helped shape those institutions.[5] When we read the correspondence she sent to supporters, we can see how women like Arnott used their writing to blur the lines between the domestic settings where many foreign mission enthusiasts spent their entire lives and the international stage to which the movement's texts provided imaginative access. Taken together, these texts offer valuable insight into a key site of American culture-making in her day.

The white middle-class women engaged in the mission endeavor during its heyday recognized that their leadership roles would be constrained by gender. However, they did capitalize on accessible dimensions of women's work to accrue social power. Consistent with gendered approaches to cultural work in nineteenth- and early twentieth-century settings (such as the suffrage and temperance campaigns), these women used collaboration as a major tool. Arnott's authorial career certainly exemplifies this trend. Writers like Arnott, assigned to far-off stations, sent letters to friends and family and to mission organizations. In both cases, the first recipients were intermediaries collaborating with the writers to pass texts along to others, whether by sharing pieces in a parlor reading group, studying these stories in Sunday school, or editing them for more extensive formal circulation in printed form. When Arnott transmitted writing from her foreign station, she knew her reports would pass through multiple stages of readership and that her initial audience would be locating her work within a broader institutional context.[6]

The women who were Arnott's first readers for circular letters and magazine stories would have seen themselves as her colleagues partnering in gendered labor for the mission movement. Male administrators who received Arnott's formal reports to the ABCFM adopted a less collaborative and more supervisory stance, and she positioned her authorial voice toward them accordingly. In either situation though, Arnott portrayed herself and her particular duties overseas in ways consistent with idealized middle-class women's work in U.S. domestic settings. Within the writing itself, she used genre features already closely associated with women's authorship, such as sentimental appeals to emotion and story lines linked to moral uplift—of her students in Africa and of her readers at home.

If we revisit Arnott's oeuvre with her original readers in mind, we recognize how much of her writing was highly public in conception and execution, in contrast with her more private compositions. Because she left behind diaries for all but one of her years in Africa, we know that her personal, interior reflections about mission service on any particular day could be quite different from the portrait she painted for readers at home. While a specific diary entry might express a fear that her teaching might never win her students over to Christianity, a public report prepared on the same day was likely to be far more upbeat. Still, through such common features as Biblical allusions, both Arnott's diaries and her more public writings demonstrate her strong commitment to her work and its firm grounding in Protestant religious training. Altogether, her ongoing literacy practices exemplify the powerful hold the foreign mission enterprise exercised over its participants and the role that reading and writing played in sustaining that commitment.

In light of the consistent worldview evident in both her personal and her published writing, some might question the distinction we draw between Arnott's "private" and "public" texts. We do affirm the feminist principle that everything personal has a political dimension, and we agree with Fredric Jameson's view "that there is nothing that is not social and historical—indeed, that everything is 'in the last analysis' political" (6). However, after extensive review of the currently retrievable archive of Arnott's public writing, we have identified core traits there more closely aligned with the social dimensions of the movement than with her personal needs. In that regard, we follow another aspect of Jameson's study of narrative writing as a social and political act—his view that "Genres are essentially literary *institutions*, or social contracts between a writer and a specific public, whose function is to specify the proper use of a particular cultural artifact."[7] Thus, we take as one aim of our study to examine how the literary institution of gendered narratives composed for the American foreign mission movement shaped Arnott's writing—especially how her texts addressed the implied contract anticipated by that particular public. Conversely, we will show how she resisted those expectations at times. Overall, we will demonstrate that study of one woman writer composing for the early twentieth-century mission movement sheds light on a larger literacy network and on a major cross-cultural enterprise.

Although Arnott's public writing is rhetorically sophisticated, affiliating with genre patterns and beliefs familiar to her readers, her voice and style are also quite distinctive. Attending to the details she selects to depict her own activities over time and to interpretations she knits into those descriptions, we can track her personal growth by noting significant shifts in her thinking and in her priorities for mission work itself. For example, writing produced early in her African service exhibits a tentative stance as she questions her ability to face such challenges of mission teaching as learning the local language. By the end of her career, in contrast, she is confident enough in the knowledge she has acquired through foreign service to take male administrators in the U.S. to task on certain issues. On a parallel track, we can retrace some notable changes in her attitudes toward the Umbundu people. Although her writing consistently reflects assumptions about the superiority of American Christian culture, we see Arnott beginning to blend her persistent critiques of some local social practices (such as local men having multiple wives) with more sensitive appreciation of others (such as women's skill at corn cultivation). In addition, she employs a growing number of words from the Umbundu language to convey concepts unavailable to her in American English—a strong sign of acculturation.

Such shifts in her writing help us realize that her personal journey had more than geographic dimensions. The trajectory of her evolving intercultural skills is uneven and inconsistent, nonetheless. Thus, we need to deploy several tools to interpret her texts. Below, we outline three of those frameworks. One involves analyzing relationships between the missionary enterprise in Arnott's day and European empire-building in Angola. A second examines how Arnott's authorial agency was both constrained and enabled by her gendered personal standpoint. Third, we will describe what we are calling "discursive gaps" in Arnott's public writing. These discursive gaps mark spaces between her lived experience among the Umbundu people and her genre-guided representations of that experience, as well as between the cultural lenses for interpreting African social life that she brought with her from America, versus her evolving perceptions based on sustained cross-cultural exchanges at the mission site.

Imperialism, Colonialism, and Colonial Discourse

To situate Arnott's writing within the context of the American women's foreign mission movement, we must examine how that vast enterprise was bound up in the international politics of her era. Especially in light of Protestant evangelism's casting Christianity as essential to an enlightened life, we should note how a determined cultural hierarchy comes into play in Arnott's writing. At the same time, we should recognize that the particular Protestant missionary stations founded by Arnott's organization—the ABCFM—were generally perceived by the imperial political power in that region—the Portuguese—as *undermining* European efforts to control West Africa in the first years of the twentieth century. For instance, local Portuguese officials were highly suspicious of missionaries' efforts to learn the local language and to provide literacy skills (both reading *and* writing) to the students in mission schools. After all, as activists like Paulo Freire have repeatedly argued, acquisition of literacy can help foster a more critical consciousness, one very likely to promote political assertiveness.[8]

In this contested local space within the larger landscape of early twentieth-century West Africa, some terms are especially important for our analysis. Key concepts include *imperialism, colonialism*, and *colonial discourse*. In this study, we use *imperial, imperialism*, and *empire-building* when referring to the imposition of direct political rule by an outside force, in this case by the Portuguese on Angola. We use *colonialism* and *colonizing* to refer to a broader, ongoing enterprise focused (in the context of Arnott's experience) in the late nineteenth and early twentieth centuries as European and Euro-American groups sought comprehensive social power in areas of Africa and Asia, based in part on patterns of action established earlier in imperial campaigns in the Americas.[9] We also adopt *colonial* and *colonizing* to reference sustained cultural practices growing out of those historical periods and their aftermath (and continuing even today in various forms of *neocolonialism*). In that sense, we will point to ways in which Arnott's writing participates in colonial discourse, even though her stance eventually makes some tentative moves away from cultural hierarchy, and even though the white American colleagues with whom she worked in Angola were not members of the imperial force seeking to govern Angola in political terms.

In characterizing Arnott's writings and her daily work as contributing to a colonial enterprise, we affiliate our project with views of colonialism not only as exhibiting recurring traits across multiple geographic spaces and eras but also as taking on diverse characteristics in different locations and times. For example, in *Colonialism's Culture*, Nicholas Thomas has pointed out that "Colonialism needs to be analysed and theorized because its pervasive and enduring ramifications are all too evident," but he has also explained that "there is an impasse, in much current writing, that arises from too dogged an attachment to 'colonialism' as a unitary totality, and to related totalities such as 'colonial discourse,' 'the Other,' Orientalism and imperialism." Following Thomas, we agree that "localized theories and historically specific accounts" offer a productive route beyond the impasse, particularly through a focus on cultural (rather than only political, military and economic) actions. Other scholars are issuing similar calls to avoid casting colonialism in monolithic terms, to instead aim for "plural and particularized" views.[10]

Frederick Cooper advocates carefully differentiated study of colonialism in specific times and geographic settings. Cooper declares, "The possibilities for organizing colonial societies could shift sharply in particular conjunctures," so that "the scramble for Africa" played out differently than "the American recolonization of the Philippines and Puerto Rico" or "the clash of a growing Japanese imperialism." Urging researchers to focus not only on the ways in which "circuits" of "personnel, commodities, and ideas" were set in place to support colonialism but also on how such circuits were "vulnerable to redirection" (53), Cooper anticipates our efforts to analyze the complex relationship between the circuits of political control Portuguese officials attempted to establish in Angola's highlands and the often conflicting networks of discourse the ABCFM missionaries developed for quite different purposes. Cooper draws a distinction particularly salient for our study of Arnott's writing and its rhetorical aims. "Among colonizing elites," he notes, "even if they shared a conviction of superiority—tensions often erupted between those who wanted to save souls or civilize natives and those who saw the colonized as objects to be used and discarded at will" (24). Invoking Cooper's point in the context of Arnott's ABCFM mission group in the Angolan highlands, we can see that they certainly sought to impose Westernized social practices in an African colonized space, but she and her colleagues there were often viewed by the Portuguese imperial power as undercutting the very processes of management typically associated with colonization.[11] In this regard, Arnott's allusion to "our enemies" in the passage opening this chapter is significant; clearly, she is not referencing the Africans living in Kamundongo but the Portuguese settlers.

At the same time, as scholars like David Spurr have emphasized, "the essential confrontation of cultures marking the colonial situation extends beyond" imperial governance itself. Rhetoric, or using language as a social tool, has played a notable part in colonialism's lingering influence, especially if we adopt Spurr's suggestion to examine colonialism as a form of hegemony—"the power of ruling ideas which continue to hold sway outside the historical and institutional limits of direct domination."[12] In this sense of claiming social influence through discourse versus political intervention, Arnott's writing qualifies as *colonial* (though, as we will show, inconsistently so).

To signal ways in which her mission teaching and her writing about that work participated in colonialism's sustained social enterprise, we can invoke work by postcolonial authors—both in literature and in postcolonial theory. In twentieth-century fiction depicting missionaries in Africa, such as Ngũgĩ wa Thiong'o's *The River Between*, as well as in memoirs like Eva Chipenda's, we find powerful testimony about the connections between missionary teaching and colonial impulses.[13] Along related lines, Aimé Césaire's *Notebook of a Return to the Native Land* presents a searing critique of colonialism as imposing pervasive long-term constraints upon the people it controls. Referencing both his birth home of the Caribbean and by extension the broader suppression of transnational black communities he and other leaders of the Négritude movement sought to reclaim, Césaire characterized colonialism's systems as leaving its victims "domesticated and Christianized," "inoculated" into "degeneracy" and a "collective trembling." From Césaire's perspective, the coercive systems of colonialism —especially as exercised through public discourse and education—left blacks, in particular, caught in its network, incapable of meaningful resistance.[14]

Césaire's *Discourse on Colonialism*, along with books by his influential student Frantz Fanon, played a seminal role in establishing arguments of postcolonial theory that are central to our own project. In a voice full of anger often veering into sarcasm, Césaire assaulted what he cast as the hypocritical claims of colonizers to be bringing civilization to the colonized through avenues such as teaching and evangelizing: "the chief culprit in this domain is Christian pedantry, which laid down the dishonest equations *Christianity = civilization, paganism = savagery*, from which there could not but ensue abominable colonialist and racist consequences, whose victims were to be the Indians, the Yellow peoples, and the Negroes" (33). Thus, Césaire posited, "between *colonization* and *civilization* there is an infinite distance" (34). *Discourse on Colonialism* placed particular emphasis on the power of language and ideas and on the oppressive work of such figures as historians, journalists, religious leaders, ethnographers and educators in carrying out colonialism's mandate, offering as one strong example a representative missionary figure, Reverend Tempels (54–64).

Echoing and extending Césaire's work, texts like Albert Memmi's *The Colonizer and the Colonized*, Frantz Fanon's *The Wretched of the Earth*, and Ngũgĩ wa Thiong'o's *Decolonising the Mind* have demonstrated that we cannot assume a neat separation between the political work of imperial governance and the less violent, less overt forms of cultural control associated with colonialism.[15] Ngũgĩ's work is especially vital to take into account when considering the careers of teachers like Arnott and her colleagues since he emphasizes that African colonizers' management of education and other culture-shaping institutions was crucial to maintaining social power. Ngũgĩ argues that "the most important area of domination [within colonialism] was the mental universe of the colonized, the control, through culture, of how people perceived themselves and their relationship to the world" (16).

Our study of Arnott's writing highlights elements that affiliated her work with a pedagogical type of colonizing—one her first readers would have actually viewed as admirable, even necessary, and one they would have envisioned as generalizable across a range of geographic spaces, including, as Césaire would later observe, enforced education programs for Native Americans and Chinese immigrants within the U.S. As a determined advocate of Protestant Christianity, and in terms of postcolonial criticism such as Ngũgĩ's, Arnott and her mission station colleagues were seeking to colonize the minds of her students. As active promoters of Americanized social practices (including using sanitation approaches at odds with local traditions), the ABCFM's women missionaries in Angola in Arnott's era aimed to colonize local women's and children's domestic spaces. By striving to have the local people adopt norms consistent with Protestant orthodoxy and inconsistent with local mores (such as monogamy versus polygyny), these same teachers were also, in Césaire's terms, enacting the *Christianity = civilization* fallacy.

Still, any moves these missionaries made to redirect the social practices and belief systems of the people around Kamundongo, Angola, were carried out within the constrained context of the Portuguese ruling power and, partly due to the relative remoteness of the station, within a day-to-day situation that encouraged the American women there to place immediate practical needs such as assisting with childbirth and sickness ahead of their evangelical goals. Both these features of the ABCFM situation in the highlands during Arnott's posting there tended to align the local Umbundu people and the missionaries as allies, if not equals, thus undoing, at least somewhat, the cross-cultural hierarchy generally associated with colonialism. One key factor contributing to social relations atypical for a colonial locale was the two groups' shared use of the Umbundu language. In contrast, Ngũgĩ has asserted that, in other settings, imposing European language on colonized peoples played a decisive part in maintaining dominance. Speaking of growing up in Kenya, Ngũgĩ classifies the enforced use of English in schools as a form of "systematic suppression" of local language and culture, including not only traditions of orature but also perceptions of self-value and cultural identity (*Decolonising*, 12–13).

Overall, it is crucial to distinguish between what we here classify as the Portuguese imperial agenda operating in Angola at the time of Arnott's service there—a political intervention certainly far more punitive for the local Africans than for Arnott but one limiting the American missionaries, nonetheless—and the cultural interventions the ABCFM was trying to enact on the scene. Along related lines, Dana Robert notes, "In practice, missionary work tended to be pragmatic and responsive to the immediate needs of the particular context." Further, she points out, both the U.S.-based ABCFM (Arnott's sponsoring organization) and the British Church Missionary Society (CMS) had in the mid-nineteenth century formulated a vision of mission work that aimed to build up indigenous leaders—a stance consistent with these groups' intellectual links to the abolitionist movement.[16] In addition, whereas Roy Bridges has pointed to ways in which, during high imperialism, British missionaries often came into regular contact with fellow countrymen who were engaged in colonial administration and has speculated that shared social class identification between these groups would have led to some blurring of their roles and attitudes, such a situation was not consistent with Arnott's ABCFM group in Angola. Indeed, in an interview with later-generation missionary wife Muriel ("Ki") Henderson, who served for decades with her husband Lawrence, one of the most striking anecdotes we heard was Mrs. Henderson's account of regularly being excluded from the rich social scene of European administrative officials and their families because of the ABCFM representatives' ongoing egalitarian interactions with the local people.[17]

Though Arnott and her ABCFM colleagues often criticized Umbundu people living around her mission station for an array of faults (including drinking, uncleanliness, and acceptance of "witchcraft"), her same American group also forcefully critiqued Portuguese colonials, who were Catholic rather than Protestant and (especially in the interior) often from lower economic classes. Meanwhile, as we shall see in Chapter 2, the highlands region where Arnott was stationed—far removed from the more Europeanized coastal sites—was itself in a highly fluid, contested state as the Portuguese sought throughout her stay there to increase control through strategies such as building a railroad to the interior.[18]

In that vein, although this site of cross-cultural contact may (seem to) have disempowered the local Umbundu people far more than it did

Arnott, we must recognize the purposeful strategies available to—and used by—colonized societies. According to Andrew Porter, indigenous people "took advantage of missionary resources, not in any abject or desperate surrender to an imposed set of values and conditions, but positively as their chosen and most effective strategy for communal survival." Arnott's writings from Angola reveal Umbundu men and women doing just what Porter suggests; they used missionaries to help navigate the contingencies of Portuguese imperial power. Her experience bears out Porter's observation that any assessment of mission impact must take into account "the likelihood that local peoples would find value for themselves in the Christianity preached to them."[19]

One scholar who has helpfully emphasized the agency of indigenous people living in mission-influenced settings is Fiona Bowie. Bowie's interviews with Bangwa living in an area of Cameroon served by missionaries have demonstrated ways in which local colonized groups made distinctions between the cultural influences missionaries were trying to exercise and such practical, mission-provided benefits as medical and educational services. Thus, Bowie noted, missionary activity could be constraining and empowering at the same time.[20] Drawing on Bowie's observations, we will show that Arnott's ABCFM organization was neither officially aligned with the imperial political power operating around Arnott's station nor free of its influence. Arnott's public texts and her interactions with Umbundu society reflect complex cross-cultural exchanges whereby her teaching offered avenues of action that local people could adapt for their own purposes, even as she depicted that process for readers at home as enacting a Christian agenda.

Finally, when considering the connections between Arnott's work in the Angolan highlands and the imperial enterprise there, we must take gender into account. Partly through texts crafted by her mission magazine editors, readers at home encountered a version of Arnott as an active messenger for Christianity, radically redefining the social space of her mission station. (See Chapter 3.) In actuality, as an American woman living in a setting governed by a European power and carrying out a role constrained by the male-dominated structure of the ABCFM, Arnott cannot be classified as exercising the same version of colonizing as the men working in the region at the same time. Male ministers like Reverend Sanders were the authority figures at mission stations. Arnott and her colleague Sarah Stimpson would sometimes chafe under that authority, but they could not escape it entirely, even during temporary assignments to mission outstations located several days' walk away from Kamundongo. While the male missionaries preached, directed building programs, and even went on hunting expeditions, the women taught school, provided nursing care, and took only limited trips beyond the station after securing approval.[21] Though there were occasional lapses in this division of labor at Arnott's station, the pattern held overall. To conceptualize her position vis-à-vis the colonial context of mission work, we should remember that her ability to effect new social practices among the local people and thereby to colonize their homes and minds was limited by constraints associated with maintaining expectations for middle-class American womanhood, even while living in West Africa.

SITUATING ARNOTT'S AUTHORIAL AGENCY

Up to now, our introduction has focused on various constraints guiding Nellie Arnott's authorship as she crafted public writing about her mission service. We have noted ways in which her gender limited her authority within the ABCFM, whose home-based administrators and on-site leaders were male. While stressing that Arnott's gender did enable her to affiliate with white middle class women readers, we have also emphasized that this audience brought particular expectations to their reading, thereby shaping numerous dimensions of her texts—including content, tone, theme, structure, and diction. We have noted how the ABCFM in Angola in the early twentieth century was itself constrained by virtue of being an American enterprise situated in a Portuguese colony. Taken altogether, this focus on the specific institutional location for Arnott's writing could seem to deny her any meaningful rhetorical agency. However, one goal of our project is to identify ways in which she did exercise authorial choice in line with her own evolving understanding of her context. In this aspect of our analysis, here and in later chapters we will be drawing upon feminist readings of Foucault and feminist standpoint theory. This section of our introduction will explain how our interpretation of Arnott's authorial agency will weave together these two threads.

The first of these threads addresses Foucauldian views on agency. Foucault's emphasis on institutional culture as disciplining the individual is central to our work as suggested in the preceding sections. But we also assert, with Jana Sawicki, that even the most powerful organizational and political cultures do leave room for individual choice, particularly in creating discourse. With Sawicki, we affirm the Foucauldian principle that an individual "does not control the overall direction of history, but is able to choose among the discourses and practices available to [her] and to use them creatively." Furthermore, we concur with Sawicki's interpretation of Foucault as showing how an individual "is able to reflect upon the implications of [her] choices as they are taken up and transformed in a hierarchical network of power relations," potentially even "suspend[ing] adherence to certain principles and assumptions, or to specific interpretations of them, in efforts to invent new ones." Applying this reading of Foucault to Arnott as a writer, we hope to show that she was neither fully autonomous nor wholly constrained, that while she was not "the originator of the discourses and practices" that she used to write about her foreign mission experience, she did have room to reshape those patterns in response to her own shifts in perspective over time in Angola. Our reading of Arnott's oeuvre suggests that her ability to "reflect upon the implications of [her] choices," in Sawicki's terms, remained limited. But we have identified multiple instances where her writing moves beyond the standard genre features of missionary discourse, resisting some stereotypes, redesigning familiar themes, and claiming enhanced social agency for herself and for (at least some of) the Umbundu people with whom she worked.[22]

A second element in our approach for interpreting Arnott's authorial agency comes from feminist standpoint theory, particularly examinations of situations where a woman is attempting to "speak for" others, as Arnott often tries to do when writing about Umbundu girls and women. Linda Alcoff argues that the growing appreciation of how important one's standpoint is for any epistemology should be supplemented by an equally important maxim: "certain privileged locations are discursively dangerous" (99). For Alcoff, a standpoint like Arnott's would clearly qualify for this "dangerous" category since the missionary's stance positions her as "speaking for or on behalf of less privileged persons," a situation that "has actually resulted (in many cases) in increasing or reinforcing the oppression of the group spoken for." Alcoff warns that, in reading such discourse, we must (1) recognize that the texts themselves are only representations ("fictions" versus reliable reports); (2) understand that these representations nonetheless "have very real material effects" on those they depict, including potentially reinscribing hierarchical power relations; and (3) remember that the operation of particular texts attempting to "speak for" others will be mediated by particular contexts of production and consumption (100–01). When applying these principles to particular occasions of "speaking for," Alcoff suggests we should shift our sense of the site of meaning from the text itself to a larger field that includes its contexts of creation and use. In addition, we should be vigilant in ascertaining how those complex contexts potentially undermine "the truth-value or epistemic status" of the writing.[23]

Drawing on Alcoff's formulation, we will continue to highlight the role of the mission movement and its literary genres as institutional coauthors of Arnott's texts. We will remember that Arnott's efforts to speak for Umbundu people cannot be taken at face value. And we will move beyond describing the content of Arnott's writing to characterizing what we can infer about its impact in her own day. To construct necessarily tentative suggestions about that impact, we again draw on Alcoff, who suggests that "We cannot simply look at the location of the speaker or her credentials to speak; nor can we look merely at the propositional content of the speech; we must also look at where the speech goes and what it does there." In Arnott's case, we need to consider not only *what* she says about her work in Angola when communicating with readers at home but also how those texts situate themselves within the ongoing conversation of discourse being produced by the ABCFM and related groups. In that regard, we will show that Arnott's writing does progress toward a more informed and empathetic view of the people she "speaks for." At the same time, however, following Alcoff, we note that "Though the speaker may be trying to materially improve the situation of some lesser-privileged group, one of the effects of her discourse is to reinforce racist, imperialist conceptions and perhaps also to further silence the lesser-privileged group's own ability to speak and be heard."[24]

Based on her mission station's locale and time period, Arnott herself was a liminal figure in a fluid social space. No wonder her writing reflects inconsistent self-positionings in relation to local people and the mission enterprise. Affiliating in some ways with the West Africans and in other ways with the Portuguese, Arnott was also, at different times and in different contexts, distancing herself from both groups rhetorically and socially. Even in her personal relationships with the other missionary women working in the highlands, Arnott's position was somewhat tenuous. For example, she was not married like Mrs. Sanders, and her diary shows that she resisted some efforts by Sarah Stimpson to carve out a more intimate connection than Arnott wished to develop.[25] Homesick for her family and especially for Paul Darling when she first arrived in Angola, by the midpoint in her sojourn in Africa she had written him to break off their engagement and accepted long separations from family as essential to her career. Her strongest affiliation during her time in Africa may well have been with the women supporters of foreign mission service to whom she wrote so faithfully. Seeking to maintain that link, she would sometimes struggle in her writing to reconcile new experiences and shifting perceptions based on her own lived experience in the Angolan highlands with her deep understanding of what her home-based colleagues would be expecting her to do, believe, and write.

Figure 2: Arnott (center) in Angola. Courtesy of The Bancroft Library, University of California, Berkeley.

Discursive Gaps in Arnott's Writing

One important framework for studying Arnott's authorial career emerges around the distinction between her daily experience and representations of it that she and others created for readers at home.[26]

It would certainly be inaccurate to say that her writing masked personal attitudes directly at odds with her published portrayals of Africa, Umbundu people, and cross-cultural interactions. However, as noted above, Arnott's personal standpoint was fluid, and this position influenced her writing. Literary genre conventions, the practical need for fundraising, and the attitudes of station leaders from earlier generations prompted her to portray her work in language more aligned with colonial ideology than her day-to-day life—in close, often collaborative situations with Umbundu students—would have encouraged. Therefore, we need to be attentive to what we are calling *discursive gaps* because they are places where this experience/representation tension appears directly in the text itself, often as a site of rhetorical inconsistency. Also, when we do see shifts in Arnott's stance toward a local social practice or questions about the local culture that suggest she is also interrogating her own background, these moments bear close scrutiny. At those points in her texts, we can note subtle signs of cultural change with implications beyond Arnott herself as an individual since her public writing was certainly intended to teach others at home.

In pinpointing these discursive gaps, it is helpful to recognize Arnott's authorial enterprise as shaped by social forces beyond her personal standpoint—and even in some ways at odds with the mission movement's traditions. One crucial example of such tension is that between the egalitarian views espoused by the ABCFM in an earlier era and the increasingly compelling influence of pseudoscientific racial hierarchies gaining currency later in the nineteenth century. Indeed, Andrew Ross contrasts the assertions of Enlightenment-oriented beliefs in Africans being equal with Euro-American whites, as expressed by ABCFM leaders in the middle of the nineteenth century, with the shifts in discourse emerging once the values of racial hierarchy held sway in common parlance in subsequent decades, during Arnott's period of service.[27] Arnott's own views were ambiguous with her published language exhibiting an inconsistent stance and her incorporation of others' terms (as in her scrapbooks) ranging from seeming acceptance of racial hierarchies to a more egalitarian perspective.

Keeping such larger contexts in mind, one of the most striking ways to highlight discursive gaps in Arnott's writing, as we shall outline more fully in Chapter 3, is to contrast it with texts by other missionary movement authors—including U.S.-based figures reporting on her mission station's activities. In others' portraits of Arnott at work, for instance, we can identify a far greater tendency to fall into the stereotypes associated with colonial discourse. One example of a gap between Arnott's language and that of her U.S.-based counterparts appears in "West Central Africa," an account within the 1907 Woman's Board of Missions of the Interior (WBMI) report on foreign missions. Incorporating a number of extended quotations from Nellie Arnott's letters, the framing passages created by a Miss A. G. Marchant paint a far more negative picture of Kamundongo and the local people there than does Arnott's own language. Arnott praises the capabilities of a local widower who, having been converted, volunteers to be a traveling preacher. Marchant juxtaposes that optimistic portrait with this add-on observation: "The work in this part of the Dark Continent is slower and results are less apparent than in some of our older missions, where the people are more developed intellectually." Similarly, a 1908 *Mission Studies* account, "At Kamundongo," begins with the promise to describe "something of the work of your own missionary in Africa, Miss Nellie Arnott." Stereotyping local people while chronicling the struggles of an earlier missionary in Africa, the U.S.-based author notes, "He told them about God, their Father, but you know in Africa they do not know what it is to have kind, loving fathers, and so that did not help them much." Arnott, in contrast, came to celebrate the strong family ties among Umbundu people.[28]

However, Arnott's own representations of the local people with whom she worked never entirely rejected the negative stereotypes associated with colonial discourse about indigenous populations in her day. Indeed, even in the late stages of her service, she could fluctuate within the same text between affiliating with individuals from the Umbundu communities where she worked and categorizing others as "heathen." One example of this pattern is in a March 1911 circular letter to women supporters in the U.S., which later appeared as a *Mission Studies* article in August of the same year. (See Circular Letter 7, "The Beginning of a Boarding School in West Central Africa," in Chapter 6.) Arnott described efforts to establish a girls' boarding school, a project that she limned as a cooperative enterprise involving local Umbundu families. Housing nine girls at the time of this report, Arnott portrayed herself as highly encouraged by the support of Umbundu parents, a number of whom had already donated food and/or "spoken to [Arnott] about taking their daughters." In addition, she documented the efforts of local men who helped with "first digging over of the garden," which she hoped the girls themselves would eventually be able to use as the main source of food for the school. Near the end of her text, however, Arnott shifted her stance from one of collaborating with Umbundu partners to invoking old stereotypes and associated hierarchies: "I believe the earlier we can separate the children from their own homes, villages, and heathen influences, the better and stronger Christian men and women we will have." Even if we assume this language is pitched to the expectations of her anticipated audience, such discursive gaps are barriers against any argument we might (wish to) make about a fundamental change in Arnott's personal standpoint and her worldview. At the same time, the repeated references elsewhere in the letter/article to local girls' agricultural skills and to the positive efforts of parents to ensure learning opportunities for their children mark a change in stance from her early writing about Angolan people in the highlands.

Another sign of textual tension emerges in a letter dated 1912, as she began her journey home for a furlough. In diction recalling her mixed feelings about leaving friends and family as she crossed the Atlantic back in 1905, Arnott cast herself as now reluctant to depart Angola. Describing her leave-taking from the village, she noted: "when I reached the women, girls and children on the road the crying began, and they followed a long way. It was very hard indeed to leave them all." Stopping at Ciyaka on an April Sunday to visit the Ennises, a missionary couple, she "[a]ttended service and took [i.e., taught] the women in Sunday School." Again expressing reluctance to loosen her ties with the local culture, Arnott declared: "It is the last Umbundu teaching I am likely to do until my return. I do hope I will not forget the language."

Such self-portraits are striking in part because they reflect Arnott's growing identification with the place where she worked. On the one hand, Ngũgĩ might point out, even in her by-then-confident use of the local language, she was teaching Sunday school and Bible lessons, not sharing folktales from the reservoir of Umbundu cultural texts. On the other hand, by choosing to present such positive depictions of her interactions with local people and by affirming the value of the local language for maintaining those ties, she substantially distances her 1912 view of Angola from the perspective with which she had begun her foreign mission service in 1905. Though she never achieved a full intercultural awareness, discursive gaps like these do mark her increasing efforts to convey a positive image of Umbundu culture to her readers at home.

TITLE, SUBTITLE, AND ORGANIZATIONAL STRUCTURE

To title this book, we have kept our aim of historically focused rhetorical analysis in mind. Having compared Arnott's writing with that of other missionaries, we are convinced that her work merits its own edition. In that vein, our title, *Nellie Arnott's Writings on Angola, 1905–1913*, acknowledges her significance as an author producing memorable texts about a specific locale during a particular era. At the same time, we view Arnott's writing as evidence of a much larger phenomenon: the efforts of American foreign missionaries and their stakeholders at home in the U.S. to maintain a literacy-based social network supporting their endeavor. In Arnott's case, this network connected her personal experiences in Africa not only with a gendered group of readers in America but also with the more broadly conceived mission enterprise. Our subtitle, *Missionary Narratives Linking Africa and America*, locates Arnott's texts within that overarching frame.

That much of her writing took the form of narratives was far from accidental. Storytelling was a necessary skill for foreign missionaries like Arnott. Written narratives brought readers at home into imaginative identification with missionary work abroad. Oral storytelling in cross-country fundraising campaigns like the one Arnott carried out during her furlough was also a crucial tool. As Rhonda Semple has noted in research on British counterparts to Arnott, missionaries relied on strong communication skills—and not just in foreign fields.[29] Arnott's notable abilities for crafting missionary narratives like those referenced in this book's subtitle give her writing a lingering power today, even in a time when religious rhetoric is often suspect. Situating her accounts within their original networks of circulation, meanwhile, underscores that globalization is hardly a new phenomenon. Linking constituents at home to work abroad, writers like Arnott were early practitioners of global communications bound up with both nation-enhancing and transnational social goals.

Given such a multifaceted context, in choosing terms to name the particular spaces of cross-cultural contact central to this book, we have sought to balance historical awareness with sensitivity to current usage patterns. In our book's subtitle we invoke "Africa" and "America" without today's emphasis on precision (e.g., around "the United

States" versus other "American" spaces). We highlight links between "Africa" and "America," the place names that Arnott's own readership would have been very likely to use. In the title we use "Angola," actually only one of the designations employed by missionaries like Arnott during her era. Thus, while we may seem at times to utilize "Angola," "West Central Africa," and "Portuguese West Africa" interchangeably, we have tried to signal an understanding of how different Euro-Americans would have deployed different terms on varying occasions. For instance, in their own publications, the ABCFM designated Arnott's assigned locale as the "West Central Africa Mission." Arnott herself sometimes referred to the entire geographic area as Angola but often in her letters simply listed a city name followed by "Africa." For example, her circular letter of June 22, 1905, uses the header "Benguella, Africa," yet later in this same communication she references her visit to "Loanda," the "capital of Angola." Others' contemporary accounts during the period of her stay might have been more likely to say "Portuguese West Africa." In naming and describing the indigenous population with whom Arnott worked in Angola, we have followed missionary Gladwyn Childs, who explains that *Ovimbundu* (singular *Ocimbundu*) is "the name of the people" of the Angolan highlands, while "*Umbundu* is the name of the language, of the culture, and the form of the descriptive adjective."[30]

The inclusive dates in our book's title—1905-1913—represent the time period when Nellie Arnott (Darling) was composing texts for publication by and circulation within the official networks of the American women's foreign mission movement. Certainly, as the biographical sketch in Chapter 1 will demonstrate, Arnott had a keen interest in foreign missions long before her overseas posting in 1905, and she continued to follow the movement's progress (particularly in West Africa) in the years after she married and settled in California. Thus, she created texts (including letters and multimedia pieces, as in her scrapbooks) about foreign mission work for a far longer period than our book's title delineates—i.e., both before and after 1905-1913. In selecting materials for this edition, we have focused on her professional career as a foreign missionary because a central aim of this book is to examine her rhetorical choices for writing aimed at mission movement supporters and leaders in the U.S. Therefore, we begin with writing she generated at the start of her journey to her overseas posting in Portuguese West Africa, and we end with the last of her published narratives about that work—i.e., with magazine stories she produced around the time of her marriage in 1913 (though the periodicals' extended publishing schedules meant some of that writing first appeared in print in 1914).

The first half of this book builds upon this introduction to provide guidance for reading Arnott's writing with critical awareness today. These three chapters (forming Part I) offer a series of interpretive lenses: biographical (Chapter 1), historical (Chapter 2), and literary-rhetorical (Chapter 3). Chapter 1 gives a sketch of Arnott's life. Chapter 2 presents a historical backdrop for reading Arnott's writing not only in the context of trends in American women's history (such as the growing influence of social organizations for white middle-class women) but also in light of international issues (such as conflicts in the U.S. over territorial expansion). Chapter 3 relates Arnott's public texts to scholarship on gendered travel writing and mission literature.

Our work on Part I has been highly collaborative. Consistent with differences in our disciplinary training, Ann took the lead in preparing Arnott's biographical sketch (Chapter 1) and the historical background discussion (Chapter 2). Besides assuming the major responsibility for this introduction, Sarah focused on Chapter 3's literary and rhetorical evaluation of Arnott's published writing. We each provided editorial feedback for the other: raising questions, suggesting additional commentary, and assisting revision.

Although we expect many readers may want to begin with the "Contexts" chapters, others may prefer to dive into Arnott's own texts first. As in Part I, our work on Part II allowed us to bring different skills to the project and to collaborate. We have both done extensive archival research to assemble the primary materials. Finding Arnott's widely dispersed publications, organizing them into a meaningful sequence, and preparing explanatory notes were tasks of such complexity that it would be impossible, at this point, to distinguish individual contributions with precision.

At the beginning of Part II, we describe our editorial method. Then, the three chapters within Part II show how Arnott's public missionary writing moved through three stages. Chapter 4 presents public texts about her initial journey from the U.S. to Africa. Included there are a number of Arnott's circular letters, many of which she wrote in a copy book with multiple sheets of carbon paper to facilitate distribution to literally dozens of readers. Chapter 5 focuses on magazine stories from the middle period in Arnott's overseas experience, when she had settled into her teaching role. At this stage, she wrote primarily to make her daily work appealing to supporters. In some cases, we can see purposeful variations across the different periodical venues where Arnott's texts appeared; a few pieces, for instance, are aimed primarily at Sunday school teachers and children, whereas others are clearly pitched to potential women donors.[31] Chapter 6's entries come from the final stage of Arnott's formal career as a foreign missionary, when she had become an experienced professional. Some of these texts appeared in periodicals, but others are drawn from her formal letters to mission officials.

Appendices extend our examination of Arnott's public writing. Appendix 1, prepared by Sarah, offers examples of how editors affected her authorship. Appendix 2, assembled by Ann, provides biographical sketches of other missionaries serving in Angola. Appendix 3 provides contextual information about the illustrations in this edition. Our bibliography identifies primary and secondary texts used in our research.

Overall, this book examines the public oeuvre and social context of one foreign mission author as a step toward understanding how the transnational networks of American women's missionary writing operated in her era. Our goal has embraced valuing the important contribution her texts make to women's history and literature while also highlighting the limits inherent in her own and her colleagues' understanding of their cultural work. We have not attempted to provide a definitive interpretation of the ABCFM's far-reaching and sustained activities in Angola or even to tell "the" full story of Arnott's own life as a missionary. We recognize, in particular, that much more interpretation remains to be done around what we have called *discursive gaps*—including not only the distance between Umbundu life as experienced by the local people in the highlands and Arnott's ability to report on it but also the gap between Arnott's own increasing understanding of Angolan culture and the expectations of her reading audience. Furthermore, given the vast array of under-examined materials associated with the women's mission movement work in Africa both in Arnott's own day and in later years, there is still much more textual recovery work ahead in the archives, including, potentially, around Arnott herself. Similarly, while we make references to missionary activity in a range of African settings involving diverse mission organizations, our study is not meant to be systematically comparative. Rather, we see this project as answering calls for studies focused on particular locations, periods, and individuals. We hope our work will lay a foundation for additional scholarly explorations of mission-affiliated travelers and the complex social influence their writing exercised.

NOTES

1. Nellie J. Arnott, "Kamundongo, West Central Africa," *Mission Studies*, April 1906, 103–05. The explosion of print culture in England and the United States beginning in the nineteenth century helped fuel the publishing process in which Arnott's articles took part. As John MacKenzie has noted in a British-focused study, developments in printing as a mass medium included new production processes that reduced costs and therefore enhanced capacities for broad circulation. *Propaganda and Empire: The Manipulation of British Public Opinion, 1880–1960* (Manchester: Manchester Univ. Press, 1984), 17–18.

2. William R. Hutchison, who marks 1880–1930 as the heyday for the foreign mission movement, notes that "missionaries were the chief interpreters of remote cultures for the people at home, and as such played a central role in the shaping of American public attitudes." *Errand to the World: American Protestant Thought and Foreign Missions* (Chicago: Univ. of Chicago Press, 1987), 1.

3. One family memento signaling a view of Arnott's African service as part of a sustained commitment to mission work is a 1952 copy of a newsletter called the *Friendship Messenger*, published by the California church to which she belonged by then. Describing Arnott (then Mrs. Paul Darling) as a church member others should get to know, the newsletter indicates that she "was a missionary for sixteen years," including "five years as a home missionary in the South, two years at Moody's Bible Institute in Chicago; church missionary in Youngstown, Ohio, for two years and seven years in the Foreign Missionary field at Angola, Africa." *Friendship Messenger* 4, no. 2 (Pasadena: November 1952): 4, in the papers of Mary Darling Caris.

4. On the important place that mission magazines held in the personal and spiritual lives of their writers and readers, see Sarah Robbins, "*Woman's Work for Woman:* Gendered Print Culture in American Mission Movement Narratives," in *Women in Print: Essays on the Print Culture of American Women from the Nineteenth and Twentieth Centuries*, ed. James P. Danky and Wayne A. Wiegand, 251-80 (Madison: Univ. of Wisconsin Press, 2006).

5. Foundational texts highlighting the significance of U.S. women's role in foreign missions include Patricia R. Hill, *The World Their Household: The American Woman's Foreign Mission Movement and Cultural Transfor-*

mation, 1870–1920 (Ann Arbor: Univ. of Michigan Press, 1985) and Jane Hunter, *The Gospel of Gentility: American Women Missionaries in Turn-of-the-Century China* (New Haven: Yale Univ. Press, 1984). For an example of a scholar who has focused on American missionaries in Africa, see Sylvia M. Jacobs, "African-American Women Missionaries and European Imperialism in Southern Africa, 1880–1920," *Women's Studies International Forum* 13, no. 4 (1990): 381–94 and "Three African-American Women Missionaries in the Congo, 1887-1899," in *Competing Kingdoms: Women, Mission, Nation, and the American Protestant Empire, 1912-1960*, ed. Barbara Reeves-Ellington, Kathryn Kish Sklar and Connie A. Shemo, 318-41 (Durham: Duke Univ. Press, 2010).

6. Deborah Brandt's work on later twentieth-century "sponsors of literacy" has influenced our interpretation of how the institutional context of the early twentieth-century ABCFM and its active literacy network shaped Arnott's writing. See *Literacy in American Lives* (Cambridge: Cambridge Univ. Press, 2001), 26.

7. Fredric Jameson, *The Political Unconscious: Narrative as a Socially Symbolic Act* (Ithaca: Cornell Univ. Press, 1981), 20, 106. Jameson's argument that "cultural artifacts" are actually "socially symbolic acts" (20) would apply to Arnott's mission texts. Writing for other movement affiliates, she crafted pieces addressing a shared social agenda that, today, is recoverable in part through such "artifacts" as her publications.

8. Paulo Freire, *Education for Critical Consciousness* (New York: Seabury Press, 1973). Richard Elphick has noted that evangelical English preachers in the Cape Colony in the first half of the nineteenth century were often at odds with the Dutch settlers, who resisted efforts by missionaries to provide equal education to blacks and to recognize conversions among the indigenous and mixed-race groups as equivalent with Christianity among the whites. See "Evangelical Missions and Racial 'Equalization' in South Africa, 1890–1914," in *Converting Colonialism: Visions and Realities in Mission History, 1706–1914*, ed. Dana Robert (Cambridge: William B. Eerdmans, 2008), 112–16.

9. Ania Loomba notes that "Colonialism and imperialism are often used interchangeably," but that making distinctions between the two is important. Her treatment of "colonialism" references the OED's emphasis on "settlement in a new country" but also the point that, historically, such efforts at "'forming a community'" have not occurred in empty land. Therefore, colonial settlers are often bound up in an "imperial" enterprise. For Loomba, imperialism (and neo-imperialism) can be understood as "the phenomenon that originates in the metropolis, the process which leads to domination and control. Its result, or what happens in the colonies as a consequence of im-

perial domination, is colonialism or neo-colonialism" (12). See *Colonialism/ Postcolonialism*, 2nd ed. (New York: Routledge, 2005; orig. pub. 1998).

10. Nicholas Thomas, *Colonialism's Culture: Anthropology, Travel and Government* (Princeton: Princeton Univ. Press, 1994), ix, x, and xi. Julie Evans, Patricia Grimshaw, David Philips and Shurlee Swain have produced a comparative study of British colonialism's interactions with indigenous people in Canada, Australia, and South Africa, emphasizing that the process was always "unfolding in specific fields of struggle" and "responsive to variable and shifting balances of power." *Equal Subjects, Unequal Rights: Indigenous Peoples in British Settler Colonies, 1830–1910* (Manchester: Manchester Univ. Press, 2003), 2.

11. Frederick Cooper, *Colonialism in Question: Theory, Knowledge, History* (Berkeley: Univ. of California Press, 2005). Nancy C. Lutkehaus also observes: "We are beginning to acknowledge that the mission of missionaries has sometimes put them at cross-purposes with colonial officials, plantation owners, traders, and, in some instances, other missionary organizations." See "Missionary Maternalism: Gendered Images of the Holy Spirit Sisters in Colonial New Guinea," in *Gendered Missions: Women and Men in Missionary Discourse and Practice*, ed. Mary Huber and Nancy C. Lutkehaus (Ann Arbor: Univ. of Michigan Press, 1999), 208.

12. David Spurr, *The Rhetoric of Empire: Colonial Discourse in Journalism, Travel Writing, and Imperial Administration* (Durham: Duke Univ. Press, 1993), 6. See also Spurr's discussion of the "colonizer's traditional insistence on difference from the colonized" leading to "a notion of the savage as *other*, the antithesis of civilized value" (7, emphasis in original). Cooper argues that colonialism has aimed for more systematic and sustained control than straightforward political management—that it has included "cultural work" as well as administrative, with the effort "to define hierarchies" and "subordination of particular people" through application of many institutional practices being a key part of the colonizing process (*Colonialism in Question*, 27, 26).

13. See Ngũgĩ wa Thiong'o, *The River Between* (Berkshire: Cox & Wyman for Heinemann, 1965); Eva de Carvalho Chipenda, *The Visitor: An African Woman's Story of Travel and Discovery* (Geneva, Switzerland: World Council of Churches, 1996). The first of these writers has a growing body of influential fiction set in postcolonial Africa; the second, Eva Chipenda, records her own educational experiences, including mission-sponsored education in Angola and study abroad. See Chapter 3 for more on Chipenda.

14. Aimé Césaire, *Notebook of a Return to the Native Land*, trans. Clayton Eshleman and Annette Smith (Middleton: Wesleyan Univ. Press, 2001), 33, 32. Asking sarcastically, "Look, am I humble enough?" Césaire depicts himself, as a metonym for all those victimized by colonial domestication (41,

40). See too Jamaica Kincaid, *A Small Place* (New York: Farrar, Straus and Giroux, 2000). Kincaid critiques such signs of colonialism's intellectual oppression as curricular mandates in schools and institutions like the main library in her native Antigua—full of books from British culture. For Césaire's explanation of the Négritude movement as growing up in Paris to celebrate a shared black history and culture situated in Africa, see René Depestre and Aimé Césaire, "An Interview with Aimé Césaire," in *Discourse on Colonialism,* trans. Joan Pinkham (New York: Monthly Review Press, 2000), 81–94, especially 91–92. For an explanation of Négritude that stresses its commitment to restoring dignity to blackness and to countering black diaspora, but that also points to ways in which the use of the French language undermined its force, see Manthia Diawara, "Reading Africa through Foucault: V. Y. Mudimbe's Reaffirmation of the Subject," in *Dangerous Liaisons: Gender, Nation, and Postcolonial Perspectives,* ed. Anne McClintock, Aamir Mufti, and Ella Shohat (Minneapolis: Univ. of Minnesota Press, 1997), 456–67, especially 458.

15. Albert Memmi, *The Colonizer and the Colonized* (Boston: Beacon Press, 1991; reprint of 1965 edition); Frantz Fanon, *The Wretched of the Earth* (New York: Grove Press, 2005; reprint edition); Frantz Fanon, *A Dying Colonialism* (New York: Grove Press, 1965); Ngũgĩ wa Thiong'o, *Decolonising the Mind: The Politics of Language in African Literature* (Portsmouth: Heinemann, 1986). *The Colonizer and the Colonized* argued in the 1950s that the former as well as the latter paid a high personal and social price for participating in the colonial enterprise. Memmi's recent work, *Decolonization and the Decolonized,* trans. Robert Bononno (Minneapolis: Univ. of Minnesota Press, 2004), addresses challenging questions about the failure of many former colonies to foster empowered citizenship in their postcolonial eras.

16. Dana Robert, introduction to *Converting Colonialism,* ed. Dana Robert, 6, 13, 14–15. Though shifting British attitudes about racial hierarchy and an increasing commitment to empire brought pressure on missionaries to shift to a "trustee" model, Robert explains, individual English missionaries and particular mission sites varied in the degree to which their work veered away from the tradition of egalitarianism. (The "trustee" model assumes the necessity for whites' ongoing supervision of Christianized Africans' own churches and schools.)

17. See Roy Bridges, "The Christian Vision and Secular Imperialism: Missionaries, Geography and the Approach to East Africa," in *Converting Colonialism,* ed. Dana Robert, 45–46. Bridges points to the Royal Geographic Society as one site of social interaction between missionaries and agents of imperialism. Henderson's comment in this case refers to her family's extended service in Lobito, a port town where many European adminis-

trators lived. Interview with Muriel ("Ki") Henderson in Chapel Hill, North Carolina, on August 31, 2005.

18. Here we follow work by Nancy Rose Hunt and others in their anthology of essays on African colonialisms (noting, in particular, the plural form). Hunt explains: "[T]he social action in colonial and post-colonial Africa cannot be reduced to such polarities as metropole/colony or colonizer/colonized or to balanced narrative plots of imposition and response or hegemony and resistance." Instead, Hunt asserts, we should explore "multiple and distinct colonialisms," avoiding binaries and examining specific contexts. Nancy Rose Hunt, introduction to *Gendered Colonialisms in African History*, ed. Nancy Rose Hunt, Tessie P. Liu, and Jean Quataert (Oxford: Blackwell, 1997), 4. Meanwhile, as Juliana Makuchi Nfah-Abbenyi has observed, the tendency to overgeneralize colonial situations has a parallel in postcolonial "totalizations," so that "the term 'post-colonial' ends up being a monolithic term that ignores historical specificity." See "Gender, Feminist Theory, Post-Colonial Writing" in *African Gender Studies—A Reader*, ed. Oyèrónké Oyěwùmí (New York: Palgrave, 2005), 261–62.

19. Andrew Porter, "'Cultural Imperialism' and Protestant Missionary Enterprise, 1789–1914," in *Journal of Imperial and Commonwealth History*, 25, no. 3 (1997): 374–76. E.A. Ayandele notes that where British missionaries worked in Nigeria, "indigenous peoples adopted only the aspects of mission teaching that suited their circumstances," since "traditional customs and institutions still exerted the greater appeal." *The Missionary Impact on Modern Nigeria: A Political and Social Analysis* (London: Longman, 1966), 245, 340. Terence Ranger similarly observes how, among the Tswana, "the cultural initiative lay with Tswana chiefs and elders rather than with missionaries." "Europeans in Black Africa," *Journal of World History* 9, no. 2 (1998): 262.

20. Bowie explains that, while "missionary journals and academic studies by missionaries tend to emphasize the positive side of mission activity," residents of "missionized countries" tend to produce more variable responses, ranging from critiques like Ngũgĩ wa Thiong'o's to celebrations of individuals who exhibited loving care for indigenous people (11, 3). "Introduction: Reclaiming Women's Presence," in *Women and Missions: Past and Present. Anthropological and Historical Perceptions*, ed. Fiona Bowie, Deborah Kirkwood and Shirley Ardener (Providence: Berg Publishers, 1993).

21. Ann Laura Stoler notes that European women living in colonial sites encountered "the cleavages of racial domination and internal social distinctions very differently than men precisely because of their ambiguous positions, as both subordinates in colonial hierarchies and as active agents of imperial culture in their own right." She argues, "European women who left for the colonies in the late nineteenth and early twentieth centuries con-

fronted profoundly rigid restrictions on their domestic, economic, and political options, more limiting than those of metropolitan Europe at the time and sharply contrasting with the opportunities open to colonial men" (344). See "Making Empire Respectable: The Politics of Race and Sexual Morality in Twentieth-Century Colonial Cultures," in *Dangerous Liaisons,* ed. Anne McClintock, Aamir Mufti, and Ella Shohat, 344–73.

22. Jana Sawicki, *Disciplining Foucault: Feminism, Power, and the Body* (New York: Routledge, 1991), 103–04. Like Sawicki's points about Foucault's openness to authorial choice in managing discourse, her emphasis on his discomfort with authority will come into play throughout our analysis. As Sawicki explains, Foucault "was sensitive to the fact that oppositional discourses often unwittingly extend the very relations of domination that they are resisting" (102). In Arnott's case, some of the writing that she produced around a theme of resisting the local society's constraints on women served, at least in part, to replace one kind of domination (little to no freedom in choosing a mate or a time to marry, for instance) with another (living in a "protected" but closed-off setting within a mission-sponsored school). At the same time, however, Sawicki's brand of "Foucauldian feminism" allows for potential challenges to "hegemonic power structures," including by local indigenous girls and women, since it envisions "a form of incrementalism in which the distinction between reform and revolution is collapsed" (8–9).

23. Linda Alcoff, "Speaking for Others," in *Who Can Speak? Authority and Critical Identity,* ed. Judith Roof and Robyn Wiegman, 97–119 (Urbana: Univ. of Illinois Press, 1995). Alcoff explains that "speaking for others does nothing to disrupt the discursive hierarchies that operate in public spaces," leading to critiques of "authors who speak on behalf of the oppressed" being mounted by "members of those oppressed groups" (99). Alcoff classifies this critique as merited. While she does not directly invoke postcolonial theorists, we can see links between her arguments and those of Ngũgĩ and others. For instance, Ngũgĩ points out that even missionaries who adopted local languages for their work maintained control of what discourse was produced using their resources. "African languages were still meant to carry the message of the bible. Even the animal tales derived from orature, which were published by these presses in booklets, were often so carefully selected as to make them carry the moral message and implications revealing the unerring finger of a white God in human affairs" (*Decolonising the Mind,* 67).

24. Alcoff, "Speaking for Others," 113. See too Chandra Talpade Mohanty, "Under Western Eyes: Feminist Scholarship and Colonial Discourses," in McClintock, Mufti, and Shohat, *Dangerous Liaisons,* 255–56, 273.

25. One of the themes in Arnott's diaries that merits its own research project is the complicated interpersonal relationships among the American women working for the ABCFM in Angola. For instance, Arnott confided

in diary entries that she longed for more privacy. However, whenever one of the missionary women did go on furlough, those remaining behind certainly suffered from the separation—as well as from the increased workload.

26. Edward Bruner draws "a distinction between the trip as lived: as it actually happened, the reality; the trip as experienced: consisting of the images, feelings, desires, thoughts, and meanings that emerge in individual consciousness; and the trip as told: usually a story, but possibly a series of photographs or other forms of expression" (19). *Culture on Tour: Ethnographies of Travel* (Chicago: Univ. of Chicago Press, 2005).

27. As an example of the egalitarian viewpoint stronger among earlier missionaries, Ross cites this passage from John Philips of the London Missionary Society in an 1851 report: "'So far as my observation extends, it appears to me that the natural capacity of the African is nothing inferior to that of the European. At our schools, the children of Hottentots, or Bushmen, or Caffrres and of the Bechuanas [terms used for local groups with whom the LMS was working], are in no respect behind the capacity of those of European parents: and the people at our missionary stations are in many instances superior in intelligence to those who look down upon them.'" "Christian Missions and Mid-Nineteenth Century Change in Attitudes to Race: The African Experience," in *The Imperial Horizons of British Protestant Missions, 1880–1914*, ed. Andrew Porter (Cambridge: William B. Eerdmans, 2003), 86.

28. Miss A. G. Marchant, "Africa: West Central Africa," in *39th Annual Report of the Women's Board of Missions of the Interior* (Chicago: WBMI, 1907), 50. L.L., "At Kamundongo," *Mission Studies*, August 1908, 251. For additional examples of Arnott's U.S.-based editors reshaping material she submitted from overseas, see "Benguella" and the WBMI Annual Report for 1907 in Appendix 1.

29. Having an "ability to express complex ideas and feelings to a number of audiences was perhaps what made a successful missionary; one who could communicate difficult messages to their co-workers, the mission society, mission supporters, and their mission constituency." Rhonda Anne Semple, *Missionary Women: Gender, Professionalism, and the Victorian Idea of Christian Mission* (Rochester: Boydell Press, 2003), 18.

30. Lawrence Henderson explains that the name Angola "had its origin in the Kimbundu word *jingola*," referencing a piece of iron used as "an emblem of political authority among the Kimbundu. *Ngola* then was used as the royal title in the region from Luanda to the Malanje highland and the Portuguese referred to it as the kingdom of Ngola." According to Henderson, this "kingdom was not a united political entity and had no recognizable boundaries." The Portuguese government, seeking to exercise control over the region, "referred vaguely to the coastal area of West Central Africa . . .

as the kingdoms of Kongo, Angola, and Benguela." Lawrence Henderson, *The Church in Angola: A River of Many Currents* (Cleveland: Pilgrim Press, 1992), 5. Use of the terms "Ovimbundu" and "Umbundu" is explained in Gladwyn Murray Childs, *Umbundu Kinship & Character, Being a Description of the Social Structure and Individual Development of the Ovimbundu of Angola, with Observations Concerning the Bearing on the Enterprise of Christian Missions of Certain Phases of the Life and Culture Described* (London: Oxford Univ. Press, 1949), xi.

31. While a growing body of scholarship is emerging on women's participation in the foreign mission movement through reading and writing, we hope to see more work on children's place in this literacy network. One helpful model comes from J. S. Bratton, who examined the role that narratives played in teaching imperialist ideology to young British boys. There may be parallels to girls' reading of missionary stories in the U.S. J. S. Bratton, "Of England, Home and Duty: The Image of England in Victorian and Edwardian Juvenile Fiction," in *Imperialism and Popular Culture*, ed. John M. MacKenzie (Manchester: Manchester Univ. Press, 1986), 75–76.

Part I: Contexts for Reading Nellie Arnott's Writing

1 Nellie Arnott Darling: Traveler in Mission Service

The American women's foreign mission movement and, particularly, the opportunities for travel associated with its work were central elements in Nellie Arnott's life history. A clear view of these connections is recoverable in part because, years after becoming Mrs. Paul Darling, Arnott was still actively engaged with the movement through her own reading and writing. She continued to save her mission diaries and created a collection of scrapbooks using mementos of her work as a teacher in Portuguese West Africa.

Other evidence of the movement's hold on her imagination emerges from the series of six small, numbered, autobiographical letters she wrote for her grandchildren. The sketch below draws extensively upon those letters.[1] In their organization, careful visual formatting, and distinctive voice, they demonstrate her skill as a writer—especially the storytelling techniques she had honed over years of writing reports and magazine articles for mission supporters back home. Overall, they mark Nellie Arnott Darling's intense belief in the importance of her foreign mission service. They also reveal her early enthusiasm for travel to locales different from her native Midwest U.S. Synthesizing these and other sources, we can reconstruct a picture of her travels as a mission movement participant—both her literal trips to multiple locations linked to her work and her imaginative revisiting of those experiences as she added to her multimedia memoirs over the years.

As a nine-year-old growing up in Iowa, Nellie Arnott was already envisioning a missionary career for herself—one that would take her beyond her small hometown. Her mother, ill after the birth of a third son, read parts of Harriet Beecher Stowe's *Uncle Tom's Cabin* to Nellie, who was enthralled by the novel. "One day I said to her," she wrote to her grandchildren years later, "'when I am big I am going to be a teacher & missionary to the negro[e]s.' I never let go of that desire."[2]

Reading such an anecdote with an awareness of Nellie Arnott Darling's purpose for writing to her grandchildren later in her life, we see several themes consistent with her mission-based publications years earlier. When Arnott's mission service took her, first, to the southern U.S., and, later, to a remote foreign station, her view of Christian evangelism cast this work in terms consistent with Protestant middle-class gender roles of her day. By linking her mission activity to a domestic reading of *Uncle Tom's Cabin* so many years before, "Grandma Darling" emphasized connections between her public career as a foreign "teacher & missionary to the negro[e]s" and her learning as a child. This bond, by extension, prompted her to instill a similar social commitment in her grandchildren (Mary and Chris [Truman] Darling, the audience Nellie Arnott Darling originally anticipated for her autobiographical letters). In positioning herself as a child acquiring spiritual responsibility through shared domestic literacy, Arnott anticipated a similar scenario for her grandchildren and at the same time situated herself as teaching them, as her mother had done in a previous generation. The biography we can assemble for Nellie Arnott Darling today, therefore, is very much shaped by what she chose to say to Mary and Chris—by how she cast the various journeys of her life in an activist Protestant context aligned with gendered, race- and class-based ideals.

Born November 16, 1873, in Hennepin County, Minnesota, Nellie Jane Arnott was the first child of Philander Arnott and Martha Patten Arnott. When writing in her seventies for her grandchildren, she described her religious training and family life, indicating that even as a young girl she was already committed to a life of service. Growing up, she lived near her maternal grandparents, whom she often visited on the weekends. "Grandpa Patten" read to Nellie from his "big Bible" and saw that she and her cousins attended Sunday School.[3]

When Arnott was eleven, she and her family made the first of many moves that would eventually carry them to the west coast of the U.S. In each case, she drew on her religious background for social connections and stability in her new home—a strategy that would prove quite useful later in life once she embraced even more far-flung travels in mission service. In her preteen years, the family's move was not too radical: the Arnotts relocated within the same region to Chickasaw County, Iowa, in rural Deerfield Township. Nonetheless, Nellie

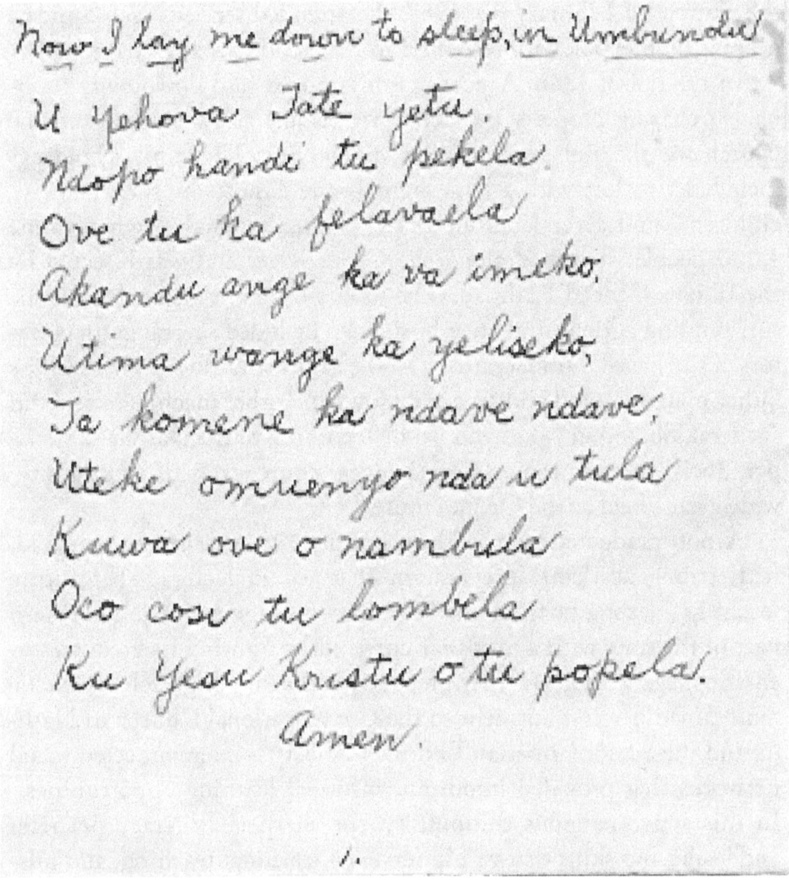

> Now I lay me down to sleep, in Umbundu
> U yehova Tate yetu.
> Ndopo handi tu pekela.
> Ove tu ha felavaela
> Akandu ange ka va imeko,
> Utima wange ka yeliseko,
> Ja komene ka ndave ndave,
> Uteke omuenyo nda u tula
> Kuwa ove o nambula
> Oco cosi tu lombela
> Ku Yesu Kristu o tu popela.
> Amen.
>
> 1.

Figure 3: "Now I Lay Me Down to Sleep" in Umbundu, from one of Arnott's letters to her grandchildren. Courtesy of Mary Darling Caris, San Francisco, CA.

regretted leaving the Pattens, whom she never saw again, but whose inscribed album of Bible verses she would treasure (thereby cultivating a collecting habit she would maintain throughout her life). In Deerfield, she attended a local country school, impressing her teachers with her ability; indeed, one of her former teachers proudly came to hear her speak many years later when Arnott returned from Africa and went on a cross-country fundraising tour.[4]

In the fall of 1886, Arnott's family relocated again—this time near Nashua. Led by Reverend Luther N. Packard, Nellie took an active part in Sunday school, church, and Junior Christian Endeavor meetings at the First Congregational Church. Even before formally uniting with the church on February 20, 1887, she attended services each Sunday, keeping a notebook with responses to Reverend Packard's sermons.[5]

In the fall of 1888, Arnott's family moved into downtown Nashua, purchasing property on Cedar Street, just a few blocks from the church and the high school Nellie was entering. The family's holdings included two lots with a large home—the Arnotts by then had five children—and several outbuildings. Nashua, a small town of some 1,000 people, stretched along the Cedar River and was bisected by the Illinois Central Railroad. The town's economy depended on the surrounding agricultural area; businesses included several grain elevators, a stockyard, lumberyards, a woolen mill, and flour mills. Nellie's father manufactured and repaired plows and other machinery and did "general jobbing in wood and iron," according to the Nashua newspaper. Social life was centered in the local churches, with community-wide events held at the Opera House.[6]

Arnott graduated from high school in 1893, at nineteen years old, with strong academic preparation that would facilitate her future teaching. Nashua boasted one of only two programs in the northern part of the state with a four-year curriculum allowing its graduates to enter college without further preparation. During high school, Nellie maintained her commitment to the Congregational Church in Nashua and the Senior Christian Endeavor Society—interconnected social networks that provided important informal learning opportunities.[7] In this active religious community, she sharpened literacy practices and leadership skills that would serve her learning, teaching, and mission movement aspirations throughout life.

The interdenominational Christian Endeavor Society's principles for its young members included a disciplined, self-reflective religious commitment coupled with active Christian service. Arnott took these tenets seriously. In one of her letters to her grandchildren, she copied her Christian Endeavor (C.E.) Pledge, which she had signed and dated April 3, 1890. As an adolescent, Arnott often attended C.E. meetings at the Bradford Church, the "Little Brown Church in the Vale," where her close friend Edna Heald was a member. Nellie and Edna frequently sang duets at Friday night C.E. meetings, which Reverend Packard organized in local country schoolhouses. Arnott fondly recalled the winter "bob-sleigh" rides Reverend Packard arranged for Christian Endeavor members. She also recounted his teaching techniques, including discussion of *Pilgrim's Progress* (a text Arnott later taught in

Angola) and reading aloud chapters of Charles Monroe Sheldon's *In His Steps: What Would Jesus Do?*, printed as a serial in the C.E. society's magazine.[8] Concerned about "children [who] did not go to Sunday School," Arnott arranged Sunday afternoon services for them. Soon adults were coming as well, and she recruited some to attend the First Congregational Church. She also taught a girls' Sunday school class.[9] Overall, Arnott's involvement with her local church, and particularly its active Christian Endeavor society, helped nurture leadership skills that would later carry over into her missionary role.[10]

This period of Arnott's life also brought her initial contact with Paul Darling, who, over twenty years later, would become her husband. In the summer of 1890, the family of Oscar Nelson Darling moved next door to the Arnotts. The family included Paul, then fifteen years old; his brother, Truman; and his sister, Josephine. "We were soon together daily like one big family," Nellie recalled, attending school and church as a group. Paul's mother, Harriet (called Hattie), played the organ, while Nellie and Paul sang in the choir. By 1893 Paul had moved to Julien, Iowa, apparently to work as a railroad telegraph operator.[11]

After Arnott completed high school, she taught a year in the primary school in Nashua. She was not happy, however, recalling to her grandchildren that "deep in my heart I wanted to be a home missionary and teach the negro children."[12] By the summer of 1894, she and her friend Edna Heald had been accepted to teach in American Missionary Association (AMA) schools, Nellie in Savannah, Georgia, and Edna in Marion, Alabama. The *Weekly Nashua Post* reported that the "best wishes of a host of friends went with these two estimable young ladies" as they left for their teaching assignments.[13]

As the first of her numerous travel experiences linked to mission service, Nellie Arnott's posting to Georgia took her into a region very different from her Midwest family home yet one where she could draw on her familiar Protestant religious practices and her past teaching for stability. In Savannah, Arnott taught first and second grades at Beach Institute with about sixty students in her classroom. She lived next door to the school. On Saturdays she visited the homes of the students, inviting the children and their parents to church. After a trip to Nashua in the summer, when she lectured at the district Christian Endeavor meeting in Osage, she returned to Savannah for the 1895 school year.[14]

Figure 4: Arnott Family, about 1898. Courtesy of Mary Darling Caris, San Francisco, CA.

Recognizing her enthusiasm for seeing the world beyond Iowa—a sentiment evident in her written reminiscences of this period—is crucial to understanding the appeal missionary work held for young middle-class women in her day. Similar to her time in Africa later, Arnott's mission teaching assignment in the southern U.S. provided exciting travel opportunities as well as spiritually uplifting work. For instance, at the end of the 1895 session, Arnott went by steamer to New York, remembering years later "the thrill I had when we sailed into New York harbor and I had my first view of our Statue of Liberty." From New York, she went to Philadelphia to visit relatives and even had her "first experience in ocean bathing" in a trip to Atlantic City. Her enthusiasm for travel continued throughout her lifetime.[15]

After her "two happy years" in Savannah, Arnott was transferred to the AMA school in Meridian, Mississippi, where she remained for three more years. There she met Sarah (Sadie) Stimpson of Massachusetts, who left Mississippi to join the West Central African mission of the ABCFM. Sarah encouraged Nellie to come to Africa. To prepare, Arnott resigned from her AMA position and moved to Chicago in 1899 to study at the Moody Bible Institute, already well known as a training center for foreign missionaries.[16]

Despite concerns about her father's opposition, ABCFM officials accepted Arnott for service in West Africa, believing that her experience teaching "among the colored people" in the South had been solid preparation.[17] To her extreme disappointment, however, the ABCFM postponed her departure due to a health problem that the organization's examining physician described as an abnormality of the uterus. Though the condition evidently caused Arnott no meaningful problems, Board members were reluctant to confirm her assignment given the lack of medical care available in Angola. Evidently seeing no other way to be approved, Arnott opted for corrective surgery at a clinic in Clifton Springs, New York, in September of 1903.[18] In the meantime, she stayed active in religious service. She moved to Youngstown, Ohio, where her brother Charles lived, and became the pastor's assistant at the First Presbyterian Church, developing organizational and secretarial skills that would serve her well in Angola.[19]

Arnott continued to hope for a posting to Africa, and, like women supporters all over the U.S., she maintained a strong affiliation with the foreign mission movement through reading and writing. She was active in the Woman's Board of Missions of the Interior (WBMI), a Chicago-based association founded in 1868 and affiliated with the ABCFM. The WBMI funded female missionaries and managed several publications promoting interest in the foreign mission enterprise. Eventually, the WBMI would be Arnott's primary sponsor for her African service.[20]

Before leaving for Angola, Arnott also established links with a group of Congregational women based in Auburndale, Massachusetts, called the "Substitute Circle," who were writing round-robin letters and raising money for a woman to serve in West Central Africa. These women would remain a significant social network while she lived overseas and even after her return. From her station in Kamundongo, she would send multiple copies of letters to the circle members along with instructions for an order to be followed in passing along the texts so that everyone in the group could receive them. Later, after a typewriter replaced her carbon-sheeted tablets, she continued this correspondence, which also aided her multi-step transformation of some diary reflections into magazine articles, with letters to the circle often acting as a step in between.

By 1904, Arnott's physician at Clifton Springs, Dr. Joseph A. Sanders, granted her a health certificate so that she could finally go to West Africa, where her old friend Sarah Stimpson was still eagerly awaiting support. Meanwhile, as extra preparation for teaching very young children, Arnott enrolled in the Kindergarten Training School at Oberlin College.[21]

In addition to her medical difficulties, another challenge involved funding. Partly because of her family's declining fortunes, Arnott found her finances severely strained as she prepared to go to Africa. In a tragic accident, her brother James (Jimmie), with whom she was especially close, had died on December 31, 1898, after being kicked by one of the family's horses. Within a few months of his death, the Arnotts sold their home in Nashua and moved to the nearby town of New Hampton, where Philander Arnott had a business manufacturing farm implements. Although the family purchased a home there, the Arnotts were unable to meet their mortgage payments, and the property was foreclosed in 1902. Soon afterward, Mr. and Mrs. Arnott relocated for awhile to Cuba, where they joined Arnott's brother Ed for several years. By 1905, while Nellie Arnott was at last planning her departure from the U.S., her parents and younger sister Myrtle were making a fresh start in Campbell, California, where their friends the Darlings had previously moved. Arnott, who had depleted her savings on the Oberlin course, had insufficient funds to visit California until some mission movement friends stepped in. She would worry over her family's finances throughout her time in Africa.[22]

Movement leaders supported her trek back across the U.S. to Boston, where she embarked in the spring of 1905. These backers also covered costs for the series of sea passages to Angola itself. Like other women in foreign mission service, Arnott realized that she was expected to compensate such donors by keeping them informed about her work. Indeed, maintaining the enthusiasm of home-based movement affiliates was so crucial that Arnott was already writing energetic reports for them while crossing the Atlantic. (See Chapter 4.) Some of these texts circulated round-robin to her Substitute Circle supporters; some also fed into official reports in ABCFM publications or even stood alone as published narratives. Once in Angola, though she shared the task of written reporting with others at her station, she devoted substantial time and effort to this work.

Arnott's motivations for service in Angola were complex. The exotic setting certainly provided a chance for adventure. Mission teaching itself represented an opportunity for a fulfilling career.[23] But these factors alone cannot explain her perseverance despite enduring an elective surgery, disregarding the objections of her father and brother, and turning down a proposal of marriage from Paul Darling. Arnott had clearly believed early in her life that God was calling her to teach descendants of freed slaves; what greater vocation than to serve in a country where slavery still existed, like Angola?[24] Determined to go, she was nonetheless ambivalent about her departure, confiding to her diary shortly after sailing from Boston, "Do not feel satisfied with my own heart. The love of the last few weeks, I fear is taking from me the hearty spirit I had in going. I do want to do God's will & I want to love to do it, but human love draws my heart the other way."[25]

Arnott served in Portuguese West Africa until 1912, when, following the normal pattern for foreign missionaries, she went on furlough.[26] She left Kamundongo apparently with every expectation of returning for another seven years. She had been pushing to found a boarding school for girls at the mission. Consistent with that expectation, she traveled home to the U.S. by way of South Africa, where she visited model institutions, such as Inanda Seminary. Arnott thus seemed poised to return to Angola after her furlough to establish the school there.[27]

Arriving in Boston, she met with ABCFM personnel to discuss plans for the school. Heading west, she put her numerous stops to good use by fundraising. She made appearances at church-related conferences, soliciting donations. Arnott even felt confident enough in her leadership role to propose a name for the school since, as she noted, "it is left to me to raise this money the best way I can."[28] Once she reached her family's home in Campbell, California, her busy speaking schedule continued for some months.

By February of 1913, however, she had reconnected with Paul Darling, and on May 1, they married. Intriguingly, she had stopped corresponding regularly with Paul in 1907 when she wrote him that she intended to devote her life to service in Africa and that she viewed their engagement as ended. After her rather sudden marriage in 1913, Arnott turned much of her energy to homemaking and, eventually, to mothering her son, Paul Junior. She and her husband, a real estate broker, settled in the Los Angeles area.[29]

Still, her wedding did not end her mission commitment. She and her husband repeatedly debated the possibility of traveling to West Africa as a missionary couple—a model Arnott had admired among others (such as the Bell, Ennis and Sanders couples) stationed in Angola during her tenure there. Her diaries reflect some frustration over Paul's reluctance to take on a role she found so appealing. Nonetheless, she maintained strong ties with the movement herself. Especially in the early stages of her marriage, Arnott wrote articles for the periodicals so central to the foreign mission enterprise. In an April 1914 *Mission Studies* article, for instance, she presented "The Need of a Girls Boarding School in West Central Africa," seeking support for the endeavor she had originally planned to lead herself. (See Chapter 6.) She also hoped that her son might become a missionary. One family memento is a copy of the "Hannah's Prayer" commitment she made to dedicate his life to such Christian service.[30]

Ultimately, she was the only one from her family to choose foreign mission service. Though unable to win others over to the work, she continued to mark its influence over her own life in the records she developed at home. The scrapbooks she left behind not only embody one account of her own experience overseas, but they also demonstrate ways that she used personal literacy to stay connected with the movement. Layering on new mementos and commentary over time, she signaled an enduring affiliation with the role of mission teacher. In the back of one scrapbook, for example, she pasted a membership list for the Woman's Home Mission Union of Southern California, which recorded that she—Mrs. P.L. Darling of 1358 La Brea Ave, Hollywood—served on the executive committee. For decades afterward, she would regularly add photographs of the missionaries with whom she had served, using newly dated margin notes to track their activities in Africa, their visits to the U.S. on furlough, their retirements, and, eventually, their deaths. She pasted in mission magazine articles about the projects going on at her former station and throughout West Africa, often penciling in comments to describe connections between the printed details and her own earlier experiences. Clearly, she kept on traveling in memory to her overseas posting even though she would never return in person.

Paul Darling died on February 10, 1953; Nellie's death came on March 16, 1963, fifty years after her marriage and almost sixty years after her journey from California to West Africa.[31] One legacy she left was the multifaceted archive of her foreign mission experience—the publications, diaries, letters, and scrapbooks that have made her story at least partially retrievable. Despite the decades that had passed since her time in the Angolan highlands, and despite the importance of other gendered social roles she assumed afterward, the missionary records she assembled underscore how much that experience as a cross-cultural traveler remained at the heart of her self-image and personal values.

Notes

1. Keeping in mind that first-person accounts are never fully reliable, we have corroborated the key facts in the letters through documents such as local newspapers from the Arnotts' Iowa homeplace. Accuracy questions aside, we recognize the great benefit of having such a direct source available.

2. Nellie Arnott Darling [Grandma Darling] to Mary and Truman [Mary Darling Caris and Truman Christopher Darling], n.d., Series of 6, Letter #1, private collection. These letters are in the possession of Mary Darling Caris, San Francisco, CA, who dated them as having been written in the late 1940s or early 1950s. Subsequent references will refer to individual letters from this set by number based on the sequence in which Arnott apparently wrote them.

Arnott was not unique in linking her work as a "teacher & missionary to the negro[e]s" to her reading of *Uncle Tom's Cabin*. Referencing an earlier generation of AMA teachers in the American South, Jacqueline Jones points out that many of them had read Stowe's novel and even drew at times on the characters to describe the people they were serving. See *Soldiers of Light and Love: Northern Teachers and Georgia Blacks, 1865–1873* (Chapel Hill: Univ. of North Carolina Press, 1980), 154 and 250 n. 36. In personal writing and in popular culture representations of whites' interactions with blacks during the post-Civil War decades, we see both the lingering power of Stowe's writing as an inspiration for sincere uplift efforts and, unfortunately, its role as a promoter of racist stereotypes. See Sarah Robbins, Chapters 4 and 5 in *Managing Literacy, Mothering America: Women's Narratives on Reading and Writing in the Nineteenth Century* (Pittsburgh: Univ. of Pittsburgh Press, 2004).

3. Nellie Arnott Darling to Mary and Truman, Letter # 1. Based on data in the 1870 U.S. Census, Arnott's grandfather seems to have been James R. Patten of Minneapolis, Hennepin County, Minnesota. "Jas. R.

Patten," Year: 1870. Census Place: Minneapolis Ward 4, Hennepin, Minnesota. Roll: M593_5; Page: 551; Image: 600. Ancestry.com. 1870 United States Federal Census [database on-line]. Provo, UT, USA: The Generations Network, Inc., 2003. Original data: 1870. http://www.ancestrylibrary.com/search/.

4. Nellie Arnott Darling to Mary and Truman, Letter #2; Arnott, Diary, October 26, 1912; "Mr. Arnott of Deerfield Was in Town," *Weekly Nashua (IA) Post*, September 23, 1886, p. 8. See details on Arnott's cross-country speaking tour in Chapter 6.

5. Nellie Arnott Darling to Mary and Truman, Letter#2 and Letter #3; "Record Book of First Congregational Church UCC," Nashua, Iowa, 41. Arnott would maintain personal notebooks and diaries throughout her time in Africa, with references to scripture and reflections on spiritual questions two of her recurring content elements.

6. Nellie Arnott Darling to Mary and Truman, Letter #3; Town Lot Deed Book N-47 and Town Lot Mortgage Record, J-437, Chickasaw County, Iowa; "P. Arnott Was in Town," *Weekly Nashua Post*, October 28, 1886, p. 8; "Plat Map of Nashua," 1892, *Atlas of Chickasaw County, Iowa, Containing Maps, Plats of the Townships, Rural Directories, Pictures of Farms and Families, Articles about History*. The original records are in the Chickasaw County Courthouse, New Hampton, Iowa.

7. Anne Ruggles Gere has described these types of learning sites as the "extracurriculum," supplementing what is formally studied in school. See "Kitchen Tables and Rented Rooms: The Extracurriculum of Composition," *CCC: College Composition and Communication* 45 (February 1994): 75–92. Nellie Arnott Darling to Mary and Truman, Letter#4 and Letter #5; Vane A. Pattison, "History of Education in Chickasaw County, Iowa" (master's thesis, Univ. of Iowa, 1939), 84.

8. On the popularity of Sheldon's narrative in Arnott's day, see Gregory S. Jackson, "'What Would Jesus Do?': Practical Christianity, Social Gospel Realism, and the Homiletic Novel," *PMLA* 121, no. 3 (May 2006): 641–61. Nellie Arnott Darling to Mary and Truman, Letter #3 and Letter #4.

9. Nellie Arnott Darling to Mary and Truman, Letter #4 and Letter #5. On principles of the Christian Endeavor Society, see Christopher Lee Coble, "Where Have All the Young People Gone? The Christian Endeavor Movement and the Training of Protestant Youth, 1881–1918" (DTh diss., Harvard Divinity School, 2001), 89–105. Arnott comments in one of her autobiographical letters that the "families who lived near the river" failed to send their children to Sunday School, and the 1892 "Plat Map of Nashua" indicates that along the river close to the Arnott home there was a neighborhood of very small lots, likely inhabited by poorer families.

10. The Christian Endeavor society claimed a central place in the lives of many middle-class Protestant women during Arnott's youth. Christopher Coble has outlined the role societies like Christian Endeavor played in an effort Protestant denominations were making then to bridge the period between Sunday school for children and adult church membership. With about 56,000 members by the dawn of the twentieth century, C.E. was one of the largest and most active of these groups. Strategies of the C.E. program included teaching such skills as leading prayer meetings and organizing community service; emphasizing ties to the revival tradition (as in the pledge Arnott signed); and channeling youthful energy (otherwise potentially problematic) into church-sponsored activities. For young women, Coble argues, C.E. societies provided opportunities for leadership growth, despite the groups' ties to conservative Protestant values. "The Role of Young People's Societies in the Training of Christian Womanhood (and Manhood), 1880–1910," in *Women and Twentieth-Century Protestantism*, ed. Margaret Lamberts Bendroth and Virginia Lieson Brereton, 74–92 (Urbana: Univ. of Illinois Press, 2002).

11. Nellie Arnott Darling to Mary and Truman, Letter #5; "Paul Darling Came Home Saturday," *Weekly Nashua Post*, June 2, 1893, p. 8 and "Paul Darling of Julien," *Weekly Nashua Post*, August 4, 1893, p. 8. Although Paul Darling was clearly an active church member while in Iowa, after their marriage years later he would resist Nellie's attempts to interest him in a shared mission posting to Africa.

12. Nellie Arnott Darling to Mary and Truman, Letter #5. In the late nineteenth and early twentieth centuries, affiliates of the Protestant mission movement drew distinctions and connections between "home" and "foreign" mission work that were important to Nellie Arnott's sense of her religious calling. Home missions served people living in the United States and were typically construed in socioeconomic or racial terms—aiding the worthy poor or teaching the former slaves and their descendants. Foreign missions included work at overseas stations like the one in Africa where Arnott served, as well as work within the U.S. that served "foreigners" such as Native American tribes on western reservations and Chinese immigrants in California. Magazines such as *Woman's Work for Woman* made this distinction clear by positioning reports from mission workers at those latter sites within the foreign section of the periodical. Significantly, it was also possible to serve the foreign mission movement at home in the U.S. by studying the geography, culture, and evangelical activities of religious workers in faraway postings. See Sarah Robbins, "*Woman's Work for Woman*," 251–80.

13. "Our Field Workers: Georgia," *American Missionary*, February 1895, 54, 77; Nellie Arnott Darling to Mary and Truman, Letter #6; "Nellie Arnott and Edna Heald Left Monday Evening for Savannah," *Weekly Nashua Post*, September 27, 1894, p. 8. Benevolent societies like the AMA,

the American Freemen's Union Commission (AFUC), the American Baptist Home Missionary Society (ABHMS), and the Freedmen's Aid Society (FAS) worked collaboratively after the Civil War with the government-sponsored Freedmen's Bureau to educate former slaves and their children in the American south. In fact, while the war was still in progress, efforts to educate the "contrabands" had already begun, as in the Port Royal experiment in which Charlotte Forten Grimké participated. Although Reconstruction officially ended as a government-led enterprise in 1877, the benevolent educational organizations of the north continued to fund a number of schools for African Americans throughout the south. Jacqueline Jones has observed that Georgia AMA teachers were typically "from a segment of the New England and Midwest population best described as the literate (and literary) self-conscious Protestant middle class, the group primarily responsible for the creation and support of evangelical reform movements in the antebellum period" (*Soldiers of Light and Love*, 31). Jones also notes that the "'typical'" AMA teacher of the 1860s and 1870s "was white, in her late twenties when she first applied for a commission, a member of a Congregational church, well educated, single, and experienced as a common-school teacher," and she had grown up in a small-town environment (30–31). Nellie Arnott certainly fit the pattern Jones has identified.

14. Nellie Arnott Darling to Mary and Truman, Letter #6; "Our Field Workers: Georgia," *American Missionary*, February 1896, 45, 70.

15. Nellie Arnott Darling to Mary and Truman, Letter #6. Jacqueline Jones has pointed to the appeal opportunities for travel and adventure had for Reconstruction-era teachers who had journeyed to the south just after the Civil War. See *Soldiers of Light and Love*, 40, 46.

16. Nellie Arnott Darling to Truman and Mary, Letter #6; "Our Field Workers: Mississippi," *American Missionary*, March 1898, 20, 29; "Recruit for Africa," *Missionary Herald*, June 1905, 267. Arnott studied at Moody Bible Institute from July 1899 to March 1901 and from December 1901 to April 1902 (Millie Benson, Moody Alumni Association, e-mail message to Ann Pullen, April 11, 2005). Evangelist Dwight L. Moody established the Bible Institute for Home and Foreign Missions in Chicago in 1889. Under the direction of Reuben A. Torrey, the Bible Institute provided training in Christian education for students desiring to become pastors' assistants, urban workers, foreign missionaries, or Bible teachers. See Lyle W. Dorsett, *A Passion for Souls: The Life of D.L. Moody* (Chicago: Moody Press, 1997), 307–10.

17. Nellie J. Arnott to Miss [Sarah] Pollock, December 12, 1899; Sarah Pollock to C.H. Daniels, February 12, 1900, in American Board of Commissioners for Foreign Missions Archives (hereafter cited as ABCFM Archives), ABC 6, Candidate Department, Vol. 75, 1900–1919: Papers of Accepted

Candidates, Vol. I. "Record of Candidates for Missionary Appointment, Number 70, Miss Nellie J. Arnott," Houghton Library, Harvard University. Materials from the ABCFM Archives included throughout this edition are used by permission of the Houghton Library, Harvard University, and by Wider Church Ministries of the United Church of Christ. Pollock, who strongly endorsed Arnott's appointment to a post in Africa, was on the staff of the WBMI.

18. Nellie J. Arnott to C.H. Daniels, April 5, 1900, and medical report of Thomas E. Roberts, M.D. (April 4, 1900) and Roberts to C.H. Daniels, April 2, 1900, in "Record of Candidates . . . Miss Nellie Arnott," ABCFM Archives. Dr. Roberts indicated that she suffered from "retrovansion" (probably meaning "retroversion") of the uterus. Today's medical stance apparently views such abnormalities of the uterus as little, if any, cause for concern, with one online source noting that "Retroversion of the uterus is common and is found to be the normal uterine position in about 20% of all women," that "Uterine retroversion by itself almost never causes any symptoms," and that "Treatment is usually not necessary," since "Usually this condition does not cause problems." See Medical Encyclopedia Online, "Retroversion of the uterus," at the Web site for Medline Plus, U. S. National Library of Medicine and the National Institutes of Health," http://www.nlm.nih.gov/medlineplus/ency/article/001506.htm. Arnott recalled her time at Clifton Springs in a diary entry, January 29, 1906. A strong constitution was a requirement for mission teaching, whether in the U.S. or abroad. Since many mission schools were in remote areas, health care was not easily available and, in any case, the work was quite demanding physically. Rhonda A. Semple comments on the health issue in relation to British female missionaries, who, to secure an assignment, had to provide evidence that "their health could withstand the 'rigours' of a tropical climate." Semple notes that physicians began to evaluate candidates' medical records more exactingly by the late nineteenth century. *Missionary Women*, 28, 31.

19. Nellie J. Arnott to James L. Barton, September 26, 1912, Papers of the American Board of Commissioners for Foreign Missions, ABC 15.1, Western Africa, Vol. 19: Africa Mission 1910–1919, Vol. 2, Letters A-M, Part I, A-E, reel 168, Pitts Theological Library, Emory University (hereafter cited as ABCFM Papers, Pitts Library, with Volume number and reel). Original documents in this microfilm collection are at Harvard University and are used throughout this edition by permission of the Houghton Library, Harvard University, and by Wider Church Ministries of the United Church of Christ.

20. Grace T. Davis, *Neighbors in Christ: Fifty-Eight Years of World Service by the Woman's Board of Missions of the Interior* (Chicago: [WBMI], 1926), 8–9, and 212. The WBMI's purpose was to generate interest in the ac-

tivities of its foreign missionaries, disseminate information about them, and raise funds for their support. The ABCFM, rather than the WBMI, handled recruitment and assignment of missionaries to foreign fields (9).

21. Nellie J. Arnott to Judson Smith, [December, 1904]; January 2, 1905; and January 28, 1905, ABCFM Papers, Pitts Library, Vol. 15, reel 164. Circular Letter of Arnott, May 3, 1905, Nellie Jane Arnott Darling Papers, BANC MSS 92/901 z. Bancroft Library, Univ. of California, Berkeley, hereafter cited as NJADP. Dr. J.A. Sanders was the brother of Rev. William Sanders, whom Arnott accompanied to Angola.

22. "A Fatal Accident," *Weekly Nashua Post*, January 12, 1899, p. 1; James Henry Arnott, *Death Index and Record* (Chickasaw County, IA), Book 2, 1880–1918, p. 3; Arnott, Diary, December 31, 1906; Town Lot Deed Book, R-461 and R-466; Town Lot Mortgage Book O-272; Sheriff's Deed Record, X-627 (Chickasaw County, IA); "Additional Locals," *Nashua Reporter*, April 5, 1900, p. 6, http://www.ancestry.com/; "Home and Abroad," *Nashua Reporter*, October 16, 1902, p. 8, http://www.ancestry.com/; Nellie Arnott to Judson Smith, January 28, 1905, and February 7, 1905, ABCFM Papers, Vol. 15 reel 164. A typical entry reflecting Arnott's concerns about her family's financial situation is in her Diary, June 8, 1906. Arnott recalled that "Jimmie," unlike her father, supported her mission service and told her, "I shall be proud of my sister, if God calls her to Africa" (Diary, August 4, 1906).

23. Arnott's motivations and ambiguous feelings were similar to those of British women that Rosemary Seton studied in "Open Doors for Female Labourers: Women Candidates of the London Missionary Society, 1875–1914," in *Missionary Encounters: Sources and Issues*, ed. Robert A. Bickers and Rosemary Seton (Richmond, Surrey: Curzon Press, 1996), 57–58. Seton found that many female candidates of the LMS could trace their desire to become missionaries back to childhood and that they demonstrated a "sense of calling" even though they often felt conflict between their love of family and friends and their desire to serve in a foreign field.

24. Although slavery was not technically legal in Portuguese West Africa during Arnott's overseas service, reports of abuses of the contract labor system were circulating in Europe and the U.S., leading some human rights activists to campaign against the practice as de facto slavery. (See Chapter 2.) As Adam Hochschild has shown in his study of colonial interventions in the Belgian Congo, not far north of where Arnott would work, local Africans were often forced to harvest rubber under slavery-like conditions—for example, to secure the release of kidnapped family members. See *King Leopold's Ghost: A Story of Greed, Terror, and Heroism in Colonial Africa* (Boston: Houghton Mifflin, 1998), 1–3, 164–66, 180. Arnott herself compared the

contract labor system to slavery in one of her early circular letters. See Chapter 4, circular letter #5, July 11, 1905.

25. Arnott, Diary, April 29, 1905. In her personal writings, Arnott often underscored words for emphasis. We signal those choices by underlining, as in one word of this diary passage.

26. Arnott's trip home is covered in her diary of 1912. See also "Miss Nellie Arnott left for New Hampton Saturday," *Weekly Nashua Post*, October 31, 1912, p. 1 and "Miss Arnott Tells of Work," *New Hampton* (IA) *Gazette*, October 31, 1912, p. 1.

27. Arnott, Diary, March 2, 1912 and Arnott, Diary, April 22–June 13, 1912; [William H. Sanders], "Kamundongo Report, 1910," ABCFM papers, Vol. 18, Africa Mission, 1910–1919: Documents, reel 167; Nellie Arnott to James L. Barton, December 9, 1912, ABCFM papers, Pitts Library, Vol. 19, reel 168. John T. Tucker, *A Tucker Treasury: Reminiscences and Stories of Angola, 1883–1958, Selected and Prepared by Catherine Tucker Ward* (Winfield, British Columbia: Woodlake Books, 1984), 199. The ABCFM founded Inanda Seminary in 1869 to educate the daughters of African Christians. (See Chapter 6.)

28. Arnott recommended calling the institution the Means Memorial School, in honor of Jane Means, an influential mission movement booster who had recently died. Nellie J. Arnott to Dr. James L. Barton, December 9, 1912, and Nellie Arnott, "To the Friends of Mrs. Jane Means, n.d. ABCFM papers, Pitts Library, Vol. 19, reel 168.

29. Numerous entries in Arnott's diaries comment upon her relationship with Paul Darling during her years in Angola. For example, see November 17–18, 1906; April 17, 1907; December 31, 1907. For her reunion with Paul, her agonizing decision to leave mission service and an account of her marriage, see diary entries February 20, 1913, through her wedding day, May 1, 1913. Paul, Jr. was born on September 18, 1916. "Paul L. Darling," Ancestry.com. *California Birth Index, 1905–1995* [database on-line]. Provo, UT, USA: The Generations Network, Inc., 2005. Original data: State of California. *California Birth Index, 1905–1995.* Sacramento, CA, USA: State of California Department of Health Services, Center for Health Statistics. http://www.ancestrylibrary.com/search/.

30. Mary Darling Caris interview with Sarah Robbins, November 23, 2003. Almost 40 years old when she married and with a history of gynecological problems, Arnott must have felt a special connection with the Biblical Hannah, mother of Samuel, who was unable to have children (I Samuel: 1). Hannah prayed that if God gave her "a man child, then I will give him unto the LORD all the days of his life" (v. 11). After Samuel's birth, Hannah declared: "For this child I prayed. . . . [A]s long as he liveth, he shall be

lent to the LORD" (v. 27–28). Arnott's diary entry for November 26, 1913, describes her wish that Paul might agree to go to Angola with her "to do a service for God & the African."

31. Death Certificate of Nellie Jane Darling, Los Angeles (CA) County, 7069–412; "Paul L. Darling," Ancestry.com. *California Death Index, 1940–1997* [database on-line]. Provo, UT, USA: The Generations Network, Inc., 2000. Original data: State of California. *California Death Index, 1940–1997.* Sacramento, CA, USA: State of California Department of Health Services, Center for Health Statistics. http://www.ancestrylibrary.com/search/.

2 Mission Service in National and Transnational Contexts

After "saying the last goodbyes we moved forth from our dear native land. We waved until we lost sight of all & then lifted our hearts to God to give us all the grace we needed in parting with those most dear." So wrote Nellie Arnott in a circular letter (May 3, 1905), exhilarated yet anxious as she departed for a seven-year term of service in Angola, many thousands of miles from "those most dear." She carried with her complex perceptions growing out of her midwestern background, her education and her religious beliefs. Though she did not see herself as a political person, both national and international politics influenced her mission service. Arnott served in Angola between 1905 and 1912, a highly dynamic period when American women's roles were changing and issues linked to U.S. expansionism interacted with questions about social activism's goals. Educational and career options for middle-class women were improving, with foreign mission work one of the most attractive choices. When female missionaries, many single, dispersed to foreign sites, they became caught up in the local politics of their assigned postings and had to cope with unfamiliar customs. In Arnott's case, Portugal's imperial policies played a major role in the lives of the Ovimbundu and missionaries with whom she served.[1] Arnott's decision to join a Congregational mission in Angola thus raises several questions: How did the women's foreign mission movement inspire individuals like Arnott to abandon familiar surroundings for lengthy overseas appointments, and how did her sponsoring organizations guide her work? How did her teaching in American Missionary Association (AMA) schools, her education at Moody Bible Institute, and her conservative religious beliefs shape her experience in Angola? How did public arguments over expansion of U.S. territory influence her time in Africa? How did being an American Protestant missionary in a Catholic Portuguese colony affect her work? How did her background shape her relationships with Umbundu women and children, about whom she wrote frequently but whose own voices are largely absent from the stories she left behind? Definitive answers to such questions are elusive, but posing them illuminates the range of forces that affected her mission work and her writing.

Figure 5: Page from Arnott's Photo Album: Angola maps and postcard. Courtesy of The Bancroft Library, University of California, Berkeley.

Social Activism and the Mission Movement

Arnott began procedures for a missionary appointment in 1899, in a time period characterized by labor strife, racial unrest, political dissension, progressive social reform, and the extension of American territorial holdings. Arnott's extant letters make no comment upon such political matters as the rise of the Populist Party, so strong in her native Midwest. But she was well aware, from her experiences in social outreach, of many issues shaping political debate. As one who "conducted women's meetings and meetings in the jail among the older boys" during her study at Chicago's Moody Bible Institute, she was clearly acquainted with problems of the urban poor.[2] As a teacher in AMA schools in Savannah, Georgia, and Meridian, Mississippi, for five years in the 1890s, she was well aware of the ongoing oppression of African Americans—and the prejudice toward whites who worked with them.

It would be erroneous, however, to present Arnott as an advocate of the emerging Social Gospel movement, which sought reform of social ills through the political system. Rather, her beliefs fit a traditional mold in line with the Congregational Church's Commission Creed of 1883. According to John Von Rohr, this framework was basically conservative, emphasizing personal salvation, "original sin, Christ's atoning death, and everlasting punishment." Arnott reiterated these beliefs in a statement on "Doctrinal Questions" when applying to the ABCFM, declaring, "I believe the Bible is the Word of God and is the only infallible rule for faith and practice," and continuing "I believe in the universal sinfulness of man and that salvation comes only through repentance and belief in Christ." She anticipated "a day appointed in which God will raise the dead and judge the world; that the wicked shall enter everlasting punishment and the righteous into life eternal." Influenced by the teachings of Dwight L. Moody and Reuben A. Torrey, superintendent of the Moody Bible Institute, Arnott was a premillennialist. She believed that Christ's second coming was imminent; therefore, in her view, drawing souls to Christ and personally living a Christian life were more appropriate activities than seeking political reform at home or sweeping social changes in the mission field.[3] As she departed for Africa, her diary reflects these priorities. Her entry for May 14, 1905, provides one example: "May God through His love make me more loving to those to whom I go. . . . Oh! That I might make known such a Saviour to His little ones is my earnest prayer."

The ABCFM, under whose auspices Arnott went to Angola, espoused similar beliefs at the time when she submitted her application for an assignment to Africa. Formed in 1810, the ABCFM originally included Congregational, Presbyterian, and Dutch Reformed members, but by the early twentieth century, Congregationalists led the

Board. From its headquarters in Boston, the Board sponsored missionaries throughout the world.[4] The ABCFM's chief goal in its early years was the "preaching of the Gospel" to save souls; social work was subordinate to evangelism.[5] The organization first established an African mission in 1836 in Natal. By the 1870s, the society was ready to open other missions in the interior of the continent. In 1880, the ABCFM sent three missionaries, including Reverend William Henry Sanders, to Angola, stirred by the call of influential ABCFM member John O. Means to help atone for slavery through evangelizing an area where the institution still existed.[6]

During the 1890s and early 1900s, the goals of the ABCFM in its mission fields shifted to place more emphasis on social needs. Specifically, the organization wrestled with the degree to which humanitarian service, as opposed to evangelism, should be valued. The Board voted in 1897 to give "missionary" status to those engaged in medical work. Though elementary education was generally a part of mission programs, sponsorship of higher education was a controversial topic for the ABCFM in the early twentieth century. Arnott herself faced similar issues—but from the perspective of a missionary in the field who sought the most effective strategies to meet the needs, as she understood them, of the women and children of Angola. Was teaching the Bible sufficient? Or were medical assistance and increased educational opportunities equally important? While she remained convinced that her most important task was to educate students who could contribute to the development of indigenous churches, she increasingly saw health-based initiatives and a "girls' boarding school" (to provide a place of safety as well as of education) as indispensable adjuncts to church development.[7] Evangelization nonetheless remained paramount for Arnott as she nurtured outstation schools in small settlements near Kamundongo, not only teaching children but also assisting male Umbundu preachers in preparing sermons.[8]

The ABCFM's religious values and mission management strategies forcefully shaped Arnott's experience in Africa, but another sponsoring connection also influenced her work. Like many of her female colleagues engaged in foreign mission service, Arnott was sustained by backers of the American women's foreign mission movement, who provided both financial and moral support. Specifically, as indicated in Chapter 1, a Substitute Circle of women mission enthusiasts raised money for her passage and continued to contribute funds throughout her service while her primary support came from the WBMI in Chicago. Within the ABCFM, a Woman's Board of Missions (WBM) coordinated women's work in the East, while the WBMI coordinated this work in the "interior" (the Midwest). These organizations were part of the larger community of middle-class women in the U.S. who devoted time, energy, and funds to foreign mission activities.

The American women's foreign mission movement was one of the most active organizational endeavors of the nineteenth and early twentieth centuries. As Patricia Hill has pointed out, by "1915, there were more than three million women on the membership rolls of some forty denominational female missionary societies," and interdenominational involvement "was substantially larger than [in] any of the other mass woman's movements of the nineteenth century." Like other large-scale enterprises attracting middle-class women in the early 1900s, the movement capitalized on women's eagerness to join in organized cultural work related to important social causes. According to Dana Robert, one reason that missions "occupied the central spot in women's hearts" was because the movement provided "opportunities for leadership" in Protestant denominations. Home and foreign mission societies attracted donations which were, at the turn of the twentieth century, generally dispensed by women's boards, providing a female counterpart within churches to the male-dominated ministry. The motto of the women's foreign missionary movement, "Woman's Work for Woman," offered a gender-based rationale for foreign service, albeit one grounded in Euro-American middle-class cultural assumptions. "Woman's Work for Woman" encompassed not only evangelization but also education and medical care that could help to improve the lives of women who were perceived to be trapped in "oppressive, patriarchal societies."[9] Mission service, with its promise of engaging in such vital work, thus offered a fulfilling career for many women.

Meanwhile, for supporters at home, reading about and contributing to the movement allowed access to significant social service in an appealing spiritual context. Liz Rohan, in her study of Angolan missionary Janette Miller, demonstrates that missionaries like Miller and Arnott promoted an "imagining of communions between individuals and cultures, and particularly between women authors and women readers," as they "translated" African culture for home supporters through their public and private writings.[10] Arnott clearly enjoyed communicating with home readers even as she recognized the importance of the task; her work might be in jeopardy unless her letters and articles presented Umbundu women and children as worthy of study and funding.

Serving in West Africa between 1905 and 1912, Arnott was stationed overseas during the women's foreign mission movement heyday, both in terms of its ability to raise funds for the cause and in terms of the level of personal engagement among supporters.[11] Much of the movement's strength during that time was based in what Patricia Hill has described as "the hold that foreign missions had on the female imagination," a powerful connection that was made possible in part by women's increasing access to advanced educational opportunities.[12] As their school curricula became more rigorous, women became better able to claim entrée into various professional-managerial roles and corresponding activities within the mission movement, such as paid editorships of the publications that had earlier been run by volunteers. In foreign mission service, this same trend was crucial in a shift from the attitude that women should serve overseas *only* as unpaid adjuncts supporting their husbands to the acceptance of single women like Nellie Arnott as professionals with their own distinctive responsibilities and monetary compensation.[13]

When first seeking her posting to Portuguese West Africa during this pivotal time period, Arnott worried that her study at Moody Bible Institute and her kindergarten training course at Oberlin might not provide sufficient educational background for foreign mission work. Writing to the WBMI in 1899, she explained that she had acquired what today would be called experiential learning that suited her for African service: "For a long time I felt that I could not enter foreign work at all, because of lack of preparation, but now I feel, having [taught in the] south, that perhaps I have a preparation suitable for Africa." Mission officials concurred that "her experience in Christian work in the South . . . is easily the equivalent" of "some portion" of a college program.[14] Overall, it is evident from Arnott's drawn-out selection process that the ABCFM chose single female applicants carefully. Having zeal for foreign missions was actually less important by the turn of the century than demonstrating skills for teaching and the personal qualities that would forecast successful service in challenging daily circumstances.[15]

Nonetheless, while much of Arnott's work addressed basic literacy acquisition goals and social services such as health care, its core focus was on Christianizing her students. The ABCFM's mission efforts were but one of a number of ongoing efforts to disseminate American Protestant culture internationally during this era, and its program of "uplift" must be evaluated in that context. As we have seen, Arnott was a committed member of Christian Endeavor, which, according to the movement's founder, Francis E. Clark, by 1906 had expanded into nineteen foreign countries, including South Africa. The temperance movement, with which both Christian Endeavor and the ABCFM had strong ties, found an international voice through the worldwide Women's Christian Temperance Union (WCTU), which fought against the manufacture and distribution of alcoholic beverages in African colonies, among other places. The temperance effort overseas condemned both alcohol introduced by colonial rulers and native drink, falsely arguing that westerners were inducing a taste for alcohol that had not existed before. In many areas, the struggle over indigenous brews centered on their use in non-Christian religious ceremonies; their renunciation became a "symbol of Christian commitment." Though Arnott may never have joined WCTU, she was a forceful opponent of alcohol.[16] Like her belief in premillennialism, her commitment to temperance would shape her interactions with Umbundu men and women—relationships that were also influenced by the politics of expansion among U.S. and Portuguese leaders.

Protestant Missions, Race and Cultural Change

Leaders of the ABCFM and its missions were representative of many Americans whose concept of their own identities was closely bound up with what Susan K. Harris has called "the national Christian." That is, they saw their work in Africa and other foreign locations as an extension of the "errand in the wilderness" role for American manhood that had first been formulated by the Puritan New England founders, then extended through the establishment of the new nation as operating under God's guidance, and later expanded further through arguments associated with Manifest Destiny. The work of foreign missions was consistent with American national ideals for social leadership grounded in Protestant religious values and with ideas about racial essentialism.[17]

Such views permeated American politics, especially foreign policy. Social Darwinist views of Anglo-Saxon racial superiority filled debates over annexation of Hawaii and the Philippines, for example. Building on the long tradition of anti-Catholicism in both England and America, public discourse frequently equated Protestantism with civilization. Catholic countries such as Portugal were sometimes denigrated in racial as well as religious terms. As Eric Love explains, one point in the debate over Hawaii centered on whether or not Portuguese laborers there should be counted as "white."[18] The Spanish-American War inflamed anti-Catholic sentiments as newspapers detailed atrocities that Catholic Spain allegedly visited upon their hapless subjects.[19] A victory over Spain and the opportunity to spread Protestant teachings to "a childlike people such as the Filipinos" seemed divinely ordained, according to Lyman Abbott, a leading Congregational minister; in his view, the U.S. should undertake a "new" type of imperialism, "the imperialism of liberty." Pro-annexationists thus adopted arguments based on Protestant and social Darwinist discourse when they spoke of uplifting nonwhite, sometimes Catholic peoples whom they judged to be inferior.[20]

Elements of this debate over extension of U.S. territory provide a framework for understanding attitudes of Protestant missionaries in a colony governed by Portuguese Catholics. Not surprisingly, Congregationalists in Angola were often at odds with Catholic officials. Arnott herself believed that Catholicism as practiced in Portugal was in "a very degraded condition," as she noted in her circular letter of June 6, 1905. Though she admired the culture of the wealthy Portuguese in Lisbon, the colonial settlers and traders whom she encountered in Angola were often uncouth frontier types. Anti-Catholic sentiments no doubt played a role in mission opposition to Portuguese colonial policies, but resistance to their treatment of Umbundu peoples did as well. Portuguese authorities regarded the Congregationalists as favoring the Ovimbundu in disputes over land and labor. Mission personnel in Angola were on several occasions embroiled in political confrontations with colonial administrators and were scarcely anxious to see any extension of Portuguese power. In Angola, Congregational mission leaders viewed increasing numbers of settlers and traders as dangerous to mission goals because the colonials sought Umbundu men and women for contract labor and enticed students away from mission stations with offers of rum. Overall, Congregational missionaries in Angola in the early twentieth century were suspicious of Portuguese authorities rather than complicit in their imperial agenda.[21]

It is also important to note that while debates about extension of U.S. territorial holdings frequently invoked arguments based on "scientific racism," missionaries in Angola did not commonly employ such terminology. Certainly they were often paternalistic in articulating their perceptions of the superiority of Western Christian culture; Arnott herself clearly held this view. She did not hesitate to condemn certain groups or individuals as "heathens," especially if they trusted "spirits and superstitions." But she stressed to her home readers that although Umbundu people were unfortunate to have been born far from "the blessings that surround our lives in America," they "are just as dear to the Father as any one of us" and she felt "joy for the privilege" of working among them.[22]

Missionaries such as Arnott tended to equate a Western lifestyle with Christianity, and they sought to change some local lifestyle practices as well as beliefs. Congregationalists encouraged Umbundu men and women to embrace new ideas ranging from accepting a monogamous system of marriage to adopting Western dress and sanitary practices. Even the landscape of a Christian community, with its neatly laid-out square houses, looked different from a traditional Umbundu family settlement (*epata*), in which houses for wives surrounded the husband's.[23] In the view of Arnott and her colleagues, such arrangements with their small wattle-and-daub structures were chaotic, with "pigs, goats and chickens running here and there" and much noise and confusion. In a traditional setting, the men's community house or *onjango* (frequently a thatched-roof open structure) was the center; men ate here and discussed political and other matters while women and children joined them in the evening to listen to stories and folktales. In contrast, in an established Christian settlement, adobe houses systematically laid out on streets were more prevalent, with flower gardens and fruit trees. A worship center took the place of the traditional community house; residents still came together to discuss community matters, but Bible stories were a prominent feature of the evening's activities.[24]

We might well view this effort to re-form communal space as central to missionaries' wishing to reform local culture, in Angola and elsewhere. Anthropologists such as John Comaroff argue that the "civilizing colonialism" of the missionaries (in South Africa, in his study) sought to transpose their European world into "a coherent model for Africa" in which indigenous peoples were led "along the high road to refinement." He identifies missionary goals for cultural change that were similar to those in Angola: banishing "superstition," encouraging "healthily clad bodies," replacing "crude, dirty huts" with "square, neatly bounded residences," and converting local rulers to Christianity. In both of these sites of Protestant mission activity in Africa, the intent was to overcome "heathen" aspects of society.[25]

But efforts at cultural reorganization often included some liberating dimensions. African historian Lamin Sanneh argues that whatever forms of "invasive interference" missionaries initiated and intended, literacy introduced through vernacular translations of the Bible and other materials gave local people in colonies like Angola a tool that helped "excite local ambition and fuel national feeling." Just such responses led the Portuguese colonial government in the 1920s to forbid teaching in Umbundu, lest it further indigenous nationalism. Sanneh points out that "disallowing the vernacular because it incites mother tongue aspirations concedes its power," a power that colonial authorities feared and Umbundu speakers came to recognize.[26]

Similar to Sanneh, Ryan Dunch argues that while "missionary condescension" could be "a galling experience for indigenous Christians or mission school students" in various areas of the world, instruction in the vernacular led students and adult readers to fashion their own understandings and uses for these teachings. In settings such as Angola, where missionaries taught in the native language, including creating translations of the Bible and other materials, students inevitably grafted their own cultural views onto foreign concepts. The resulting "fusion of language and ideas," according to Andrew Porter, "produced a complexity of influences which is at odds with the simplicities of 'cultural imperialism.'" Attitudes of missionaries thus were often somewhat beside the point, for local societies evolved on their own, not necessarily in response to or in accordance with missionary entreaties. As a consequence, missionaries' efforts to modify indigenous lifestyles based on Western views were often ineffective.[27]

Furthermore, though missionaries' emphasis on conversion to Christianity implied a religious hierarchy, we need to realize that the American field-workers themselves would have been affected through cultural interaction. Missionaries who learned to use vernacular languages, as Arnott worked so long and hard to do, faced translation challenges ultimately shaping their own perspectives. On one side, many concepts and social practices in the host community would have no equivalent in the missionary's own language, and, on the other side, ideas and values the missionary wanted to teach might have no direct correspondent in the local language. Even beyond developing a new, sometimes hybrid vocabulary within such spaces of cognitive dissonance, the missionary had to hone skills for both oral and print communication with local people. In his article "'Cultural Imperialism' and Protestant Missionary Enterprise," Andrew Porter argues that translation was thus "essentially a two-way process" in which missionaries struggled to explain the "Gospel's meaning in local terms." In Porter's view, this shared language-building meant that many missionaries were in a far less hierarchical relationship with local populations than a straightforward cultural colonialism model would assume, for missionaries were "frequently unable to set the terms of their discussions with local people, and in such circumstances the employment or transmission of a 'colonial discourse' is hard to imagine" (378–79). In acquiring the host country's language, a missionary like Arnott would also have been absorbing different ways of thinking not accessible to the kind of governmental administrators who simply sought to impose a colonizer's language on a colonized people.

In the case of the ABCFM work in Angola during Arnott's tenure, we can document the central role that translation was playing in the enterprise. The Bible had been translated in the early years of the mission, but work was ongoing in developing new materials. In 1911, for example, Nellie Arnott wrote of Reverend Sanders's efforts to revise the Umbundu Vocabulary, a project that involved several months of "collecting and proving words." Arnott and others assisted his wife, Sarah Sanders, in arranging, typing, and printing the 600-page book on the press at Kamundongo. By the 1920s, ABCFM missionaries had translated or written a wide variety of Umbundu books; in addition to the Bible and religious texts, there were spelling and arithmetic books, nature readers, vocabularies, grammar texts, and proverb collections. These translations, especially of the Bible, required give-and-take discussions about meaning and understanding between missionaries and native speakers of a language, leading to the incorporation of vernacular terminology only after complex cultural interchanges.[28] So this ongoing two-way process helped ensure that both native speakers of Umbundu and ABCFM mission workers would have been absorbing new ways of viewing the world and new possibilities for social action.

In examining interactions between indigenous peoples and missionaries in the Angola highlands, we must recognize Umbundu communities as vibrant and dynamic on their own terms. Disputes over politics, economics and society often caused internal rivalries that would have led to change even without foreign contact. The Portuguese presence was accelerating societal changes that would likely have occurred had no missionaries been present. Umbundu society in the early twentieth century was unstable rather than static, as traditional kingdoms redefined themselves based on internal dynamics as well as on interactions with both Portuguese and missionaries. Contests over land and power between Umbundu factions overlapped with contests among Portuguese administrators and settlers, Catholics and Protestants. Missionaries' work was only one of many factors reshaping the culture of the highlands.[29]

The role of Congregationalists in early twentieth-century Angola thus defies simplistic description. They generally opposed Portuguese political and economic imperialism in the highlands. On a social level, they sought to change certain practices (though not others). They introduced literacy in the vernacular, which helped develop a regional Umbundu identity. They could be paternalistic but encouraged development of indigenous churches and schools. Their activities can only be understood as part of a continuum, neither allied with the Portuguese, at one extreme, nor neutral observers immune from a belief in the primacy of Western civilization on the other.

Like the Umbundu peoples in the highlands, missionaries faced many challenges dealing with cross-cultural exchange. As the region saw increased efforts by the Portuguese to claim political control, the social context of mission work would grow even more complex. Therefore, we must turn now to an overview of Portuguese rule in Angola in the late nineteenth and early twentieth century and of its interactions with the ABCFM missions in the interior of the colony.

MISSIONARIES AND PORTUGUESE POLITICAL POWER IN ANGOLA

During the seven years of Nellie Arnott's service in Angola, the highlands were very much a contested space with Portuguese administrators attempting to extend political control, settlers hoping to profit from trade in slaves or commodities, missionaries seeking to preach and educate, and Umbundu men and women looking for ways to benefit from societal and economic changes. The highlands formed a frontier area not yet under firm colonial management. Lines of authority between Portuguese and Ovimbundu were ill-defined with missionaries often navigating disputes between the two.[30] Nellie Arnott and her Congregational colleagues perceived themselves as agents for positive change. In actuality, they were often caught in crosscurrents as the interior of the colony changed economically, socially and politically.

When the ABCFM first established a mission in the region in the 1880s, its Board chose the Angola highlands based upon a report indicating the climate was healthy and the local Umbundu people communicative. Far inland, at an elevation of some 5000 feet, this area was an arduous 300 or so miles from the coast where the Portuguese had first established their presence in the late fifteenth century. Though the Portuguese claimed the highlands and a few traders operated there, there was no administrative control in the early 1880s. Umbundu communities seemingly provided an opportunity to spread the Protestant version of the gospel without undue interference. Eventually settling at Bailundu, by 1905 the ABCFM had established other mission stations in the highland states: Kamundongo in Bié, Sakinjimba (eventually moved to Chilesso in Andulu), and Sacikela, also known as Elende or Ciyaka, in Bailundu.[31] The Canadian Congregational Foreign Missionary Society worked through the ABCFM as well; their station, under the direction of Walter T. Currie, was at Cisamba in Bié.[32]

Aside from the ABCFM, other Protestant and Catholic missions operated in the highlands. Two other Protestant mission stations in the Bié area, Chilonda and Hualondo, were under the auspices of Christian Churches in Many Lands, more commonly known as the Plymouth Brethren.[33] The ABCFM and Brethren mission staffs communicated regularly with each other; to some extent they also stayed in contact with Methodist missionaries in and around Luanda despite the considerable distance separating their stations.[34] Annual meetings, in which ABCFM, Plymouth Brethren and occasionally Methodist missionaries participated, contributed to a shared vision for their work. The ABCFM had little communication with Catholic religious figures, however. Though there was a thriving Catholic mission to the Ovimbundu at Caconda founded in 1882, it was many miles from the Protestant missions in the interior. Indeed, Catholic efforts to establish a presence in Bailundu were frustrated by the influence of the Protestants among the local population, and a permanent Catholic mission only opened there in 1895.[35]

Realizing the economic and strategic importance of the highlands and concerned that the missionaries harbored covert political motives, the Portuguese began seeking means to extend control over the area not long after the missionaries arrived. As a result of diplomatic maneuvering in the wake of the Berlin Conference of 1884–1885, Portugal had given up its dream of retaining claims to territory between Angola on the west coast and Mozambique on the east. Fears of German, British, and Belgian designs on the highlands in Angola meant that Portugal must demonstrate "effective occupation" or risk losing claim to that area as well. The Portuguese thus expanded activities in Bié in the early 1890s with a successful military expedition and the construction of a new fort near Kamundongo at Belmonte. Extending into Bailundu as well, they seized the capital settlement (*ombala*) of the Umbundu ruler there and made it into a fort.[36]

The pacification effort involved administrative and economic initiatives as well as military ones. Traditional Umbundu trading ventures made the Portuguese task of implementing administrative and economic control over the highlands difficult. In the early 1900s, Umbundu traders were rather well off economically due to their trade in wild ("red") rubber, ivory and beeswax. Many thousands of Umbundu men, and to a far lesser degree women, participated in trading caravans that journeyed from the interior to the coast. Consequently, a state priority was the development of infrastructure to lessen dependence on human porters; under a British concession, construction began in 1902 on the Benguela railroad, designed to run through central Angola to Katanga in the Congo.[37]

To further administrative control in the late 1800s, the Portuguese tried when possible to install pliant rulers of royal lineage (*sobas*, in Umbundu *olosoma*) in the highlands area. The Portuguese civil/military leader, the *capitão-mor*, lent the protection of his office to Portuguese traders and settlers. As was typical in frontier areas, traders were generally rough adventurers who did not hesitate to force Umbundu men and women to work in their fields or serve as their porters. In any dispute, the trader was far more likely to receive a favorable judgment than was a native African. As a result, many indigenous locals in the highlands fled to the Protestant mission stations or otherwise sought missionaries' protection. In the Portuguese view, the missionaries were taking the side of the Africans and came under increasing suspicion.[38]

In 1902, the "Bailundu Revolt" broke out, ostensibly as a result of a disagreement between a Portuguese trader and one of the Umbundu leaders. The real issues, however, were long-standing local grievances over trade and sovereignty, coupled with the Portuguese desire to extend control over the Bailundu area once and for all. Umbundu fighters were no match for Portuguese soldiers with their superior weaponry, numbers, and organization. Indeed, not all members of the eight rebellious Umbundu kingdoms supported the uprising; some collaborated with the Portuguese. Missionaries in the Bailundu area did not directly participate, contrary to Portuguese authorities' assertions. Although some of them communicated with Umbundu leaders, they had mixed feelings about the revolt and actually provided Portuguese settlers who took refuge in the Bailundu fort with food and medical assistance. In general, the missionaries were reluctant to do anything to anger the Portuguese, whose permission remained necessary for the work in Angola.[39]

In the aftermath of the Bailundu Revolt, the Portuguese determined to extend secure enough control over the interior to prevent further uprisings. Convinced of missionary collusion with the rebels, Portuguese authorities began to take official action against ABCFM activities in the highlands. The *capitão-mor* of Bié questioned the legality of the missions; the ABCFM responded that the Berlin Act of 1885 and the Anglo-Portuguese Treaty of 1891 both presumably guaranteed religious toleration. The governor-general of the colony argued, however, that the highlands were not covered in these treaties and that the teaching of religions other than Catholicism was accordingly forbidden there. Local Portuguese authorities more than ever turned a blind eye to anti-mission activities on the part of settlers and traders. In 1904, therefore, the West Central Africa Mission sent William H. Sanders and Dr. Frederick Wellman home to Boston to confer with the Board of the ABCFM.[40]

This was the volatile situation awaiting Nellie Arnott when she departed for West Africa, joining Reverend Sanders and his wife as they returned from their furlough to the U.S. With matters still unresolved between the ABCFM and the Portuguese, Sanders carried instructions that the mission stations should continue in their work, disregarding the governor-general's stance. Even though Arnott did not express detailed concerns about political matters, her writing reflects the myriad ways in which mission personnel and their Umbundu neighbors were affected by conflict with the Portuguese. Arnott may have had little understanding initially of the degree to which Angola was undergoing profound social and economic change.[41] But, during the period in which she was a mission teacher, events set in motion by the Bailundu Revolt often led the missionaries to be caught in the middle of Ovimbundu-Portuguese strife.

One of the most hotly contested issues between missions and Portuguese was that of contract labor, an issue that had far-reaching implications outside Angola. By a Portuguese law passed in 1899, all natives in overseas colonies were obligated to work. Using this legislation as an excuse, Portuguese and Umbundu traders bargained for Africans to send as "contract" laborers (*serviçaes*) to plantations on the Portuguese islands of São Tomé and Príncipe, which had grown wealthy through the cultivation of cocoa. This system was nothing more than a thin disguise for slavery. As Arnott herself explained, in a circular letter written from the port at São Tomé, "Under the Portuguese law each one is asked if he will go to St. Thomas & work for seven years. He puts a cross for his name & is given a number which is tied about his neck," she noted. "If any live the seven years[,] the contract is renewed," she continued, because they were "too ignorant to know when the time is up or what the renewal means."[42]

Angola was only one African area in which slavery was still practiced; in both Britain and the U.S., reformers were engaging in a variety of strategies to expose slavery and other atrocities in the Congo. Edmund D. Morel, Secretary of the Congo Reform Association (CRA) in England, came to the U.S. late in 1904 and, among other activities, met with President Theodore Roosevelt. Morel encouraged formation of an American CRA, which Samuel L. Clemens joined as a vice president. In 1905, Clemens, writing under his familiar pseudonym of Mark Twain, published a satirical pamphlet, *King Leopold's Soliloquy*, which was highly popular, passing through multiple printings; he donated royalties from the work to the CRA.[43]

In 1904, hoping to capitalize on public interest in the slavery issue, editors of *Harper's Monthly Magazine* commissioned British journalist Henry W. Nevinson to go to Angola to investigate the rumors that the slave trade continued there, though, ostensibly, reforms after the Bailundu Revolt had mitigated some of its worst abuses. Traveling throughout Angola itself as well as São Tomé and Príncipe in late 1904 and early 1905 (shortly before Arnott's arrival), Nevinson visited highland mission stations of the ABCFM and Plymouth Brethren and gathered much of his information from their staffs. His findings, published in book form in 1906 as *A Modern Slavery*, revealed the sham of the "contracts" that laborers signed.[44] Upon his return to England, Nevinson did his best to publicize the abuses going on in Angola. Rumors had earlier reached the owners of Cadbury Brothers Ltd. that the São Tomé and Príncipe plantations from which they bought cocoa were using slave labor. Skeptical that the Portuguese government's 1903 promise of labor reform was genuine, William Cadbury himself organized an expedition to São Tomé and Príncipe to investigate. His findings corroborated Nevinson's, eventually leading English cocoa buyers to boycott Portuguese cocoa.[45] Cadbury also funded the 1908–1909 investigation carried out by Charles Swan, a Plymouth Brethren missionary in Angola. Swan visited Congregational and Brethren mission stations in the highlands, interviewing their staffs and taking photographs as he went. His findings, published without his interviewees' names, came out in 1909 as *The Slavery of Today*.[46]

International agitation over the contract labor issue increased Portuguese distrust of ABCFM personnel, though missionaries had been careful not to speak out publicly on the issue. Mission stations became vulnerable, as indicated by a series of mysterious fires at Arnott's Kamundongo station. "It is generally believed that the buildings are set on fire by the slaves of the Portuguese," Arnott wrote in her circular letter of June 22, 1905; "as soon [as] they [the Portuguese] see any prosperity in the Station then there is the effort to hinder the work if possible." According to Nevinson, an appeal to authorities at nearby Fort Belmonte would have been "useless," for the administrators were themselves too weak to oppose the traders.[47]

The contract labor dispute was only one of several critical issues affecting the highlands in the years after the Bailundu Revolt. Umbundu political and economic institutions saw continued change as Portuguese administrators pursued taxation and labor policies that favored European settlers. In 1906, the government imposed a "hut tax," which fell especially hard on men with several wives or dependents living in their own houses. As the Benguela Railroad extended into the highlands, authorities conscripted Umbundu laborers to work on its construction and on improving surface roads in its vicinity. With the coming of rail transport, reliance on Umbundu caravans for inland trade declined. Rum and other enticements awaited those who would agree to till fields of the European settlers. Once the traditional trade system began to wither away, local political elites lost their power base, for the system had served to reinforce networks of alliances and extended families upon which their authority depended. Extension of the railroad, crucial to the extraction of resources from the interior, further undermined the local rulers' autonomy. They found it difficult to protect their fields from imperial expansion, their labor from Portuguese appropriation, and their resources from seizure for colonial taxes.[48]

After the Revolt, newly established Portuguese administrators in the highlands continued to destabilize the authority of indigenous leaders. In traditional Umbundu society, the main "kingdoms" included clusters of villages under royal leaders (*olosoma*); each such ruler lived in an *ombala* with his dependents and retainers. *Olosoma* enjoyed many privileges, including taxes in kind or, in the case of larger kingdoms, yearly tribute. The freeborn population, much more numerous than the ruling group, lived in village clusters of households related by kinship or marriage and ruled by an elected elder (*sekulu*). In either case, the villages were subsidiary to royal personages, who held their position through diplomacy, kinship and economic domination fostered through trade relations. *Olosoma* served as judges in disputes in the traditional Umbundu system. As Umbundu caravan trade declined and Portuguese administrative units extended into the interior in the early twentieth century, this function increasingly devolved upon the Portuguese administrator (the *capitão-mor*, later called the *chefe*). Building upon pre-revolt administrative changes, the Portuguese sought to maintain the appearance of local sovereignty, while in reality the *chefe* handpicked both royal and freeborn leaders to maintain control of the local population.[49] For many Umbundu people, consequently, affiliation with a Protestant mission and its outlying Christian settlements offered a buffer against Portuguese settlers and administrators. For others, a tacit link with Portuguese administrators or Catholic missions seemed to offer more security. The question facing Umbundu leaders was how to maneuver in these new political realities to garner the greatest long-term communal benefits.[50]

The period of Nellie Arnott's service in Angola, 1905 to 1912, saw continued unrest between Portuguese and Protestants, though in the wake of Anglo-American censure over the contract labor issue, the Portuguese generally did not want to provoke more criticism. To some extent, the colonial government saw value in the missionaries' work as well. Mission policies helped to calm traditional lineage enmity through the establishment of new Christian communities, whose residents proved reliable in paying taxes. Both traders and administrators alike appreciated the skill of mission physicians. But when Umbundu Protestants became numerous, they might also overcome time-honored rivalries and unite in opposition to the Portuguese, a fact that was never far from the minds of colonial administrators.[51] Several incidents during Arnott's years in Africa demonstrate Portuguese officials' concern about ABCFM leaders in the region. For example, authorities banned missionary Wesley Stover from his station from 1908–1910 under the claim that he was interfering with colonial labor codes and had helped to plan the Bailundu Revolt. In another case that spanned several of Arnott's years in Angola, Kanjundu, who was *soma* (royal leader) of Ciyuka district and the first influential Umbundu leader to become a Christian, faced harassment and eventually imprisonment based on false accusations of a Portuguese trader. He eventually won his freedom due in part to the missionaries' intervention. Upon *Soma* Kanjundu's death, he named missionary John Tucker as co-executor of his sizeable estate rather than designating the local *chefe*, whereupon Tucker was denounced for taking over duties reserved to colonial officials.[52] Portuguese administrators clearly meant these events to remind Protestant missionaries that they were guests in Angola. During the years of Arnott's service, however, Portuguese authority was not yet entrenched in the highlands. Protestant missionaries' role in the spread of literacy in Umbundu, as well as their support of leaders such as *Soma* Kajundu, gave them considerable influence.[53]

Overall, it would be inaccurate to label the early twentieth century ABCFM missionaries who were working in Angola as "political imperialists." Their relationships with Portuguese authorities were often antagonistic rather than cooperative. Angola's situation in the first two decades of the twentieth century demonstrates that missionaries' connections to colonialism were both geographic- and time-specific. Conditions in Angola's highlands were distinct from those in other locales in Africa as well as from Luanda or colonial coastal cities in Angola. Furthermore, conditions in Arnott's day were different from those of the 1920s, when Portuguese policies drew the missions closer in line with governmental goals.[54] In addition, we should make clear distinctions between the American missionaries situated in Africa and those laboring in other locales where the U.S. was involved in its own imperial enterprise, as in the Hawaiian Islands. In contrast with other groups in different time periods and places, the particular team Arnott joined in Angola during the first part of the twentieth century was intent on distinguishing its endeavor from that of political and economic empire-building.[55]

Nonetheless, though ABCFM workers assigned to Angola were not promoting the imperial power's policies, everyday interactions between mission personnel and Umbundu men and women involved a cultural brand of colonialism. Missionaries did promote reforms in daily social practices. It was changes like these that scholars such as John and Jean Comaroff had in mind when they noted that the "colonial encounter . . . was first and foremost an epic of the ordinary." The careers of women like Arnott are particularly important to recover in this context since their work was closely tied to the everyday life of the people they sought to serve—and to convert—in the politically, economically and socially unstable setting of her mission station.[56]

Umbundu Social and Educational Life in Arnott's Day

Assessing the cultural transformations that Arnott sought requires a multifaceted interpretation, for Arnott's attitudes and motives, sometimes predictably Western, were not always so. Sometimes she sought modifications because she deemed them necessary for a Christian lifestyle; in other instances she thought they were essential to protect the lives and health of young women. Arnott's detailed writing about individuals provides one way to examine this contested space of Umbundu social practices, especially those of the women and young girls with whom she worked most closely.

While an informed reading of Arnott's published texts requires knowledge of Umbundu society, providing such a history faces the perennial challenge of lacking substantial written records from the perspective of the local people themselves.[57] Therefore, we are left with an inherently challenging situation: using the records of ABCFM missionaries, who were certainly biased in their viewpoints, to attempt a portrait of the Umbundu communities where they worked. Despite their limitations, missionaries' accounts can be illuminating, especially if we keep in mind that they reveal as much about the authors as about their subjects. Arnott, for example, was in daily contact with the local men, women, and children about whom she wrote. She encountered many students in her schools and often had young girls boarding in her home. From time to time she lived in rural settlements, teaching in those schools for several weeks or even months at a time; on occasion, she was the only white person in residence. So she did have firsthand knowledge of Umbundu life, though from a standpoint very different from the locals with whom she worked.

We must read missionaries' accounts of indigenous life very carefully, for their misunderstandings of local culture were inevitable. As Trinh T. Minh-ha has warned in her critique of western-oriented anthropologists, when depicting natives from other cultures, members of such empowered groups typically construct "a perfect reflection" of themselves rather than a portrayal fully acknowledging the complexity of others' lives. Meanwhile, Trinh notes, in such texts native people often remain "the handicapped who cannot represent themselves," so that "they are entrapped in a circular dance where they always find themselves a pace behind the white saviors." Consistent with this critique, we should recognize that voices of the Umbundu women themselves are generally missing from Nellie Arnott's accounts, so we can only infer how they reacted to her work.[58]

In assessing mission records as sources for African history, however, J. D. Y. Peel argues that "missionaries were among the first outsiders to make sustained contact with indigenous peoples, and their writings frequently contain accounts of local culture and society, oral traditions, etc., which, whatever their deficiencies, have an indispensable documentary value precisely for standing right at the beginning of modern cultural change." In his view, mission records should not be dismissed but used with critical evaluation; missionaries fluent in indigenous languages, in particular, often had valuable insights into cultural practices.[59] In the case of Arnott and other missionaries in Angola, their records of economic and social practices among Umbundu women can provide valuable historical sources, if interpreted with care, despite their having "a specific evangelical agenda."[60]

In at least a few instances, mission records provide glimpses into Umbundu women's activities from both written and visual perspectives, even if not from the women themselves. One notable example is that of yearly Woman's Conferences held among the mission stations in Angola. These meetings, the first of which occurred in 1903, included Umbundu delegates chosen to represent the stations with which they were associated. These women often traveled long distances by foot, according to Arnott, carrying their children on their backs and baskets on their heads, with those containers holding "a little food for the road, a clean cloth and shirt, and [their] books." Missionary John Tucker observed that at the conferences, female mission staff might guide study themes, "but Africans themselves extensively [took] part in the exercises." Typical discussion topics centered on "the Christian life, the care of the home, the training of children and infants' welfare." In the women's absence, Tucker explained, their husbands often cared for their "children and fields." Upon returning home, women relayed newly acquired information to their own churches. In her scrapbook, Arnott carefully labeled two photographs of the 1907 meeting and four of the 1911 conference; pictures of Umbundu delegates show that sixty or more indigenous women attended each gathering. A report on the 1912 conference by missionary Emma Woodside noted that some 300 Umbundu delegates and carriers were present and joined in evening meetings open to all. Along with daytime discussions in which both missionary and Umbundu women participated, indigenous delegates held their own sessions, which, Woodside noted, were led by a "native woman." Reports by missionaries such as Arnott, Tucker and Woodside, supplemented by photographic records, not only reveal the popularity of such conferences but also indicate that indigenous women delegates were fully engaged in the gatherings and subsequent dissemination of the knowledge generated there. Without recorded accounts by Umbundu women, however, we cannot adequately assess the value such meetings held for them.[61]

If we are careful to recognize the limitations of mission accounts, synthesizing details from Arnott's writings about the Ovimbundu themselves can illuminate the local context for her personal mission experience. To build a framework for understanding her environment, we tracked Arnott's portrayals of one Umbundu family through the broad range of genres—both private and personal—in which she wrote during her sojourn in Africa. Assembling a portrait from these scattered records (which are sometimes supplemented by photographs in Arnott's scrapbook collection), we can track Arnott's relationships with that family, especially its women, to examine her own assumptions about Umbundu life; we can also use this family history to illustrate points of conflict between Umbundu values and mission ambitions.[62]

Figure 6: Scenes of Woman's Conference at Bailundu, 1911. Courtesy of The Bancroft Library, University of California, Berkeley.

While Arnott's publications and personal texts identify a number of key figures in Umbundu society, the family she features most prominently is that of Mueno, headman (*sekulu*) or elder of the Cisanje settlement near Kamundongo. Indigenous families like his struggled to accommodate shifting political realities of colonial rule—sometimes seeking protection of the mission, sometimes opposing Europeans' interventions into their traditional customs and practices. Mueno, for example, permitted missionaries to hold classes in Cisanje, though he resisted becoming a Christian himself. He seems to have recognized the value of literacy and to have embraced the tacit alliance with the mission that a school represented.[63]

Arnott's response to the community's grieving practices after Mueno's death highlights one of the ongoing tensions in relationships between missionaries and the local culture. Arnott reported being relieved when Mueno was buried, complaining in her diary (November

18 and 22, 1906) about the noise of the "drumming & dancing to apease [sic] the spirits" that took place at lengthy ritual ceremonies. Of course, she did not acknowledge the significance of these traditional religious practices. From the perspective of Arnott and her colleagues, reducing the influence of the indigenous healer and priest (*ocimbanda*) who conducted burials and other rites was integral to attracting and reforming converts. Known in missionary writings as the "witch-doctor," his presumed ability to communicate with the spirits through his "divining basket" as well as his knowledge of native plants, roots, and herbs gave him great authority in the community. While traditional healers could be quite skilled, missionaries generally regarded their potions as ineffective or dangerous. Further, healing or religious rituals might involve use of tobacco or beer brewed from native plants, both abominations to Arnott and her colleagues. Despite the missionaries' entreaties, some Umbundu men and women who had ostensibly become Christians nonetheless feared disregarding the healer's advice. Many others, like Mueno, saw no reason to follow new Christian ways that would necessitate abandoning the counsel of a traditional priest who had inherited generations of knowledge.[64]

Another point of contention between ABCFM workers and Umbundu peoples was polygyny.[65] In one of Arnott's personal accounts, a situation involving one of Mueno's wives underscores the vulnerability of a woman who might be one of several in a household. "Since Mueno's death a man has come to claim one of his wives [sic] & all his children as his slaves, saying when the woman was a girl she was taken from him & he has never received anything for her," Arnott wrote in the collection of unpublished journal notes that she titled "Happenings in Africa." In Umbundu society, polygyny was common, though the missionaries did not distinguish between women who were actually wives, for whom a man had paid bridewealth, and concubines. Concubines could be acquired as a result of debt settlements, and while theoretically they were pawns that would eventually be returned when the debt was paid, they were often sold as slaves in the meantime.[66]

Although missionaries found polygyny abhorrent, the Umbundu social system presented several rationales for the practice. Marriage represented the union of two extended families; for a male to take more than one wife could be advantageous in establishing political and social connections, thus increasing status and economic power. Further, since women spent a great deal of time with their parents after the birth of a child, men might seek another wife or concubine to take care of household tasks. Women were not necessarily opposed to the practice either; their workload, especially in preparing food for a household that might include many family members and guests, was sometimes so heavy that they welcomed an additional wife or concubine to help out. In fact, being one of several wives of an important leader might offer more protection than being the single wife of a poor man who might end up having to pawn her or her children for his debts. However, giving up all wives except one was necessary if missionaries were to accept a local man as a Christian; this requirement could present someone like Mueno, as well as his wives, with such personal, social and economic difficulties that it surely deterred conversion.[67]

If polygyny was an instance in which Arnott and her colleagues reflected their Western prejudice, they played a more positive role in opposing the use of women as pawns or slaves. Once again, Mueno's family serves as an illustration. Since we do not know the identity of the man who tried to seize Mueno's wife and children, several possible scenarios emerge. The interloper could have been one of the wife's relatives, for the descendants of a common great-grandmother (*oluina*) retained considerable control over women born into the kin group as well as over their children, with power exercised especially through the mother's elder brother. He could pawn her children or even sell them to pay his own debts. Another possibility is that the wife's father could have given her in exchange for a debt while she was a child. In either case, after Mueno's death, she was vulnerable to claims from another male.[68]

"I feel we cannot lose them this way," Arnott confided in her notebook, worried over the fate in store for the woman and children. Arnott would have had particular cause for alarm if the woman had once been a slave rather than a pawn for debt. Umbundu slaves were generally of other ethnicities, purchased through trade or captured in raids, and were typically treated more harshly than pawns and other dependents. Ordinary Umbundu people—and even slaves themselves—might own slaves. Free Umbundu women often depended upon slave labor to spare them the most onerous work. Enslaved women performed menial tasks, could be traded, and, not surprisingly, were vulnerable to sexual exploitation. Children of a slave woman were considered slaves as well.[69]

While Arnott herself was opposed to domestic slavery in principle, the official mission stance during her service was somewhat ambivalent. Christianized Ovimbundu sometimes held slaves or pawns, especially those they had inherited. In traditional Umbundu society, this situation implied responsibility toward the person in bondage; to free such an individual might leave him or her destitute. From the missionaries' standpoint, this issue was one to address gradually, as a number of men and women connected with the mission stations had such dependents in their households.[70]

Arnott frequently became involved with women who fled to the missions for protection because they were enslaved or feared they might be. "Saving" such women, in the literal as well as the religious sense, became one of Arnott's main goals in her mission work.[71] The system of slavery and contract labor was especially harsh for women who had been wrenched from their traditional local and family ties; lacking the protection afforded by male relatives, they were more easily available for sexual or labor use. As traditional Umbundu trade patterns and social networks disintegrated, women were increasingly likely to end up as workers on Portuguese plantations or as contract laborers on the cocoa plantations.[72] Even young girls who lived on the Kamundongo station were sometimes in danger, as indicated by the experience of Mueno's daughter, Cipuku, who had come to live at the station and attend school. On more than one occasion, Cipuku found strangers near the girls' house—men who she and the other girls believed had "been sent out to catch people to deliver up as slaves." As a result, Arnott reported, "women are afraid to go to their fields."[73]

Rescuing young girls from potential enslavement was one way in which Arnott hoped to improve women's lives; saving young women from forced marriages was another of her focal points. Cipuku and her sisters exemplify Arnott's approach. In an article published in *Mission Studies*, Arnott explained that, before his death, Mueno had opposed Cipuku's desire to live at Kamundongo. Angered and perhaps humiliated, Mueno promised her to a man who Arnott claimed had "very bad habits," including keeping Mueno supplied with rum. Cipuku, then about thirteen years old, sought and received the missionaries' assistance in ending the arrangement. Cipuku's mother later attempted to marry off her two younger daughters against their wishes, sending her son to try to retrieve one of them from the mission. An important element of Arnott's account of the incident is that the missionaries not only rescued the girls but also reimbursed the mother for her lost dowry money. Though to Arnott the mother's motives were reprehensible, we should recognize the economic loss of three daughters whose prospective husbands would have paid bridewealth for them.[74]

Arnott's reaction to the marriage arrangements reveals not only tension over these customs but also her horror at the girls' young ages. When Cipuku married Sakalumbu, a Christian teacher, about two years after she came to the mission, Arnott, though happy for her, was still worried about her youth. Cipuku, then around fifteen, "had only been developed nine months" at the time of her marriage, Arnott wrote. As Cipuku left Kamundongo to join her husband in Owayanda, a Protestant outstation settlement nearby, Arnott confided to her diary that she missed Cipuku "very much," and the two women maintained their close relationship. Arnott was thus anguished when, about a year later, Cipuku almost died in childbirth. The difficult delivery, and the death of her infant daughter a short time later, Arnott blamed on Cipuku's age. "She is suffering all this I believe because she was too young when married," Arnott confided in her notebook.[75] Such incidents led Arnott to become committed to changing the social practices around what she considered premature marriage of young girls—one reason behind her campaign to establish a boarding school.

Meanwhile, Cipuku's mother blamed her daughter's near-fatal experience on Cipuku's refusal to seek remedies from the native healer. The mother, no doubt anguished herself, went to Cipuku just after the baby's birth and tried to persuade her to visit a traditional healer, but Cipuku refused. While the mother was a "real heathen," according to Arnott, Sakalumbu surprised the American missionary in his loving care of Cipuku: "Sakalumbu never left her but would hold her so lovingly when the convulsions came on. I never expected to see such love among the natives," Arnott wrote, simultaneously revealing her bias as an observer of local culture and her ability, at least on some fronts, to adjust her perspective.[76]

Though Arnott criticized traditional Umbundu marriage customs, she admired women's skill in agriculture. In the early twentieth century, the task of cultivating, harvesting, and processing food was almost exclusively the work of Umbundu women. Crop production, though sometimes exhausting, gave them a measure of economic power as they had the right to dispose of food they grew, deciding how much to consume and how much to store or trade. Married women like Cipuku tilled their own fields according to traditional practices based in considerable knowledge of crop management. Women prepared their all-important corn fields in September, before the rainy season. Planting beans with corn to enhance crop fertility and squash with large leaves to shade the soil, they carefully contoured rows to preserve moisture. While the corn was young, women often took their children and lived in a small house near the cornfield for several weeks as older children helped keep birds away from the crop. Once the corn was picked, it was stored and dried in this same structure.[77]

After drying the corn, women held a corn-shelling bee (*onjuluka*). Cipuku invited Arnott and Sarah Stimpson to attend such an event, which Arnott recorded in detail in her notebook. Cipuku had carefully picked her corn three months before and put it away to dry in her "little house in her field." Her husband, Sakalumbu, "had cut some long straight sticks for her & several girls took one forming a circle in the midst of the corn, & began pounding with the end of the stick as they pound their meal," Arnott wrote. Singing as they worked, other women added corn to be beaten. Inspecting the cobs for remaining kernels provided an occasion for laughing and talking. After cleaning the corn, the women, with help from Sakalumbu and his friends, carried the corn to Cipuku's house and enjoyed food and drink. While Arnott developed an appreciative and informed view of such communal activities, she lamented that women's work in cultivation, in pounding corn into meal, and in food preparation left them little time to attend school.[78]

Arnott worried even more about young girls who sometimes traveled with trading caravans, carrying goods, gathering firewood and cooking. The plight of such young females especially moved Arnott, who wrote that it was "pitiful to see them walk all the way with those loads." While some female carriers were slaves, for free women, caravan work could present economic opportunity and possibly less-demanding labor than cultivation and food-related tasks. The absence of young women on caravans sometimes left their mothers without sufficient labor for their fields, a situation that could create a need for female slave workers.[79]

Young, unmarried women were most likely to travel with caravans; married women's child-rearing activities would have usually required them to remain settled while their husbands traveled. Umbundu women had significant responsibilities for child care and for acculturating children, who were integrated into the life of the community from birth. Cipuku and Sakalumbu, who had been "heart broken" at their daughter's death, surely rejoiced when they had a son, for Umbundu society prized children. Girls learned skills from early childhood to prepare for their roles as mothers. An Umbundu mother commonly took her infants to the fields by securing them to her back with a length of cloth, and even very young children helped with tasks such as gathering wood or fetching water. Children essentially learned by example and through participating in rituals, adult conversation, and traditional music. According to missionary Mary Floyd Cushman, children joined in "evening village gatherings" at the community meeting house, "listening to the talk of the older men and absorbing the history, tradition, laws and customs of the Umbundu people." This knowledge was frequently conveyed through fables containing maxims.[80]

Given the Umbundu culture's emphasis on learning social practices in experiential context, missionary teachers like Arnott faced many challenges in trying to deliver an appealing education program that would also be consistent with their evangelical vision. The goals, content, and method of her pedagogy were not completely in tune with local customs, especially in the early days of her posting. Initially, Arnott's main aim was to teach her students to read print texts of the Bible through written materials since she was not yet fluent in Umbundu. Nonetheless, with her training in kindergarten curriculum, Arnott was prepared from the outset to build on the program for local children's learning established by one of the early ABCFM missionaries in Angola, Annie M. Fay, whose teaching was based on songs, games, and pictures and was thus relatively compatible with Umbundu practices for children to learn experientially.[81] Furthermore, as she acquired the local language and grew to appreciate many Umbundu customs, Arnott's teaching methods expanded, and she synthesized her training in childhood education back home in the U.S. with her developing understanding of local differences. Accordingly, in a 1908 letter published in *Mission Studies*, Arnott described smaller children as sitting in front of the school's "big fireplace," looking at "picture books," and playing with blocks and a sand table while she used her developing fluency in Umbundu to teach older children to "read, write and do numbers." Arnott also coordinated several schools in outlying settlements, where she sometimes lived for several weeks at a time as she trained young Umbundu men to teach reading and writing themselves. In turn, these men guided and counseled junior teachers. It was in one such community that Sakalumbu became the lead teacher, a position of respect and authority to which he acceded upon the death of his mentor, Cituvika.[82]

From Arnott's perspective, educating young women to be proper "helpmates to their future husbands" in teaching and ministerial work was one of her most important tasks in Angola.[83] While Arnott did not support adoption of a completely nonagricultural domestic model for women, she hoped that their lives might become less physically demanding, leaving time to assist husbands in teaching or ministerial work. Cipuku represented a model of what Arnott hoped Angolan women might become. She had learned teaching skills through assisting Arnott in outstation work and was thus prepared to assist Sakalumbu in his school; the couple was, Arnott reported, "loved and respected by the people." The girls' boarding school that Arnott worked to establish would, she hoped, provide more formal preparation for other young women to become similarly successful.[84]

In assessing Arnott's attitudes toward the Umbundu women and men with whom she worked, we cannot fully resolve the contradictions in her stance. Resisting polygyny and indigenous rituals and customs such as use of alcohol and tobacco, she appears to suit the description of a missionary colonialist who sought to change Umbundu habits to conform to her Christian ideal. On the other hand, her obvious affection for Cipuku, Sakalumbu and other students somewhat modifies the picture, especially coupled with her admiration for women's skills. Seeking to free young women from premature marriages, caravan work and the heaviest of field work, she not surprisingly advocated some features of a Western domestic model. She envisioned a network of Christian settlements in which literacy in Umbundu was the norm. She came to believe strongly in the local people's ability to serve as teachers and leaders themselves. To her, preparing future educators and ministers was the most important work of the missions: "it pays to give one's life to the training of native teachers," she explained. "They are the ones who must reach the Angola population."[85]

Notes

1. As noted in the Introduction, Ovimbundu is the name of the people among whom Arnott worked in Angola, while Umbundu refers to the language or culture of the people and is also the descriptive adjective for them.

Childs, *Umbundu Kinship & Character*, xi. Frank Collins, a linguist at the University of Toronto who grew up in Angola as the child of missionaries, further explains: "'Ovimbundu' means 'the Umbundu,' or 'the Umbundu people.' The language is 'Umbundu,' and the people are 'Umbundu.' I love the fact that 'Umbundu' means 'the language of the people.' The word is cognate to 'Omunu' (person) and 'Omanu' people. These words are (with phonetic variations) common to all 'bantu' languages—'abantu' in Zulu, Xhosa, etc. meaning 'people,' 'muntu'= person" (Frank Collins, e-mail message to Ann Pullen, February 17, 2005). Even though the phrase "the Ovimbundu" is thus actually redundant, we use that construction for clarity.

2. Nellie J. Arnott to Miss [Sarah] Pollock, December 12, 1899 (copy); Sarah Pollock to C.H. Daniels, February 5, 1900; Charles H. Daniels, February 3, 1900, "Record of Candidates . . . Miss Nellie J. Arnott," ABCFM Archives.

3. John Von Rohr, *The Shaping of American Congregationalism, 1620– 1957* (Cleveland: Pilgrim Press, 1992), 355–56; Nellie J. Arnott to C.H. Daniels, March 14, 1900, labeled "Doctrinal Questions"; A[lverus] N. Hitchcock to C.H. Daniels, February 21, 1900, " Record of Candidates . . . Miss Nellie J. Arnott," ABCFM Archives; Dorsett, *A Passion for Souls*, 307–08 and 408–09. William R. Hutchison points out that even among conservative evangelicals, premillennialism was a "minority faith" (*Errand to the World*, 112). Moody Bible Institute was one of some fifty training schools sending out mission workers committed to this belief. According to historian Brian Stanley, premillennialists thought that the mission of the church was "not to transform human society into the kingdom of God, but to rescue the individual from an increasingly evil world, and hasten the return of Christ by a policy of rapid evangelistic expansion." Postmillennialists, on the other hand, thought that through medical and educational work, missionaries could help to "bring the Kingdom of God to fulfillment in human history"; hence these endeavors were critical adjuncts to preaching the gospel. *The Bible and the Flag: Protestant Missions and British Imperialism in the Nineteenth and Twentieth Centuries* (Leicester: APOLLOS, 1990), 74–77.

4. The ABCFM was governed by its Prudential (Executive) Committee, which had around a dozen members at the time Arnott went to Angola. The Board itself had over two hundred members, with the President of the Board serving as an ex-officio member of the Prudential Committee. In the early twentieth century the staff in Boston responsible for correspondence and publications included two Corresponding Secretaries, an Assistant Secretary, and an Editorial Secretary. Other officers of the Board included a Vice-President, Recording Secretary, Treasurer, and Auditor. The WBM in Boston and the WBMI in Chicago were established in 1868 as auxiliaries to the ABCFM. William E. Strong, *The Story of the American Board: An*

Account of the First Hundred Years of the American Board of Commissioners for Foreign Missions (Boston: Pilgrim Press, 1910) provides a history of the ABCFM; Strong lists officers by name and years of service in Appendix II.

5. Rufus Anderson, Secretary of the ABCFM from 1822 to 1866, supported "three-self" mission theory: that is, that the best route to conversions in non-evangelized areas of the world was to found self-supporting, self-governing and self-propagating churches in those areas. Dana L. Robert, *American Women in Mission: A Social History of Their Thought and Practice* (Macon: Mercer Univ. Press, 1998), 89.

6. Lawrence Henderson, *Church in Angola*, 52–53; Fola Soremekun, "Religion and Politics in Angola: the American Board Missions and the Portuguese Government, 1880–1922," *Cahiers d'études africaines* 11, no. 3 (1971): 342. Soremekun writes that the ABCFM tried to avoid proselytizing in Catholic-controlled areas; the government in Lisbon had indicated, however, that it had little effective control in the Angola highlands (341–343). In its own publications, the ABCFM used the name Portuguese West Africa Mission although the geographic area was Angola.

7. Von Rohr, *American Congregationalism*, 308, 373–74. William R. Hutchison, *Errand to the World,* 91–124, describes conflict within the ABCFM and other Protestant organizations over the "evangelizing" and "civilizing" functions of missions. Hutchison points out that those committed to evangelization and those in the Social Gospel camp found much common ground in the early twentieth century in the belief that medical and educational activities prepared the way for evangelization. World War I "shattered hopes and complacencies on which the missionary movement had been founded, bringing to the surface tensions that had been building for decades, more or less unacknowledged," over the weight missions assigned to social service and "true evangelization" (125).

8. For example, in 1909 while Arnott spent several weeks in the village of Olutu, near Kamundongo, she reported in her diary (Feb. 7, 1909) that Sakamana "was here by seven to go over his sermon," and on February 14, she "[w]ent over Sakamana's sermon with him." Female missionaries in frontier settings such as Angola were more likely to engage in activities (like teaching or mentoring indigenous young men) that challenged traditional gender roles than women in well-established missions, who often were more circumscribed by gender conventions. See Wendy Urban-Mead, "An Unwomanly Woman and Her Sons in Christ: Faith, Empire and Gender in Colonial Rhodesia, 1899-1906," in Reeves-Ellington, Sklar and Shemo, *Competing Kingdoms*, 100-02.

9. Patricia R. Hill, *The World Their Household*, 3; Dana L. Robert, introduction to *Gospel Bearers, Gender Barriers: Missionary Women in the Twentieth Century* (Maryknoll, N.Y.: Orbis Books, 2002), 5–7. On social/cultural

organizations, see Ann Firor Scott, *Natural Allies: Women's Associations in American History* (Urbana: Univ. of Illinois Press, 1991).

10. Elizabeth Ellen Rohan, "Imagined Communions: One Woman's Spiritual Journey" (PhD diss., Univ. of Illinois, 2002), 13. Chapter 4 of the dissertation analyzes Miller's work as a "translator" of African culture to women at home (187-96). Rhonda Semple likewise argues that "women's work in missions should properly include the myriad of women at home who . . . raised funds for home and foreign missions." Letters from missionaries in the field helped to make missions "real" to their counterparts at home (*Missionary Women*, 18, 195).

11. Dana L. Robert, in *American Women in Mission* (256), dates the high point of the movement in 1910-11, with the Woman's Missionary Jubilee being celebrated in cities and towns all across America, and with its major publication appearing—Helen Montgomery's *Western Women in Eastern Lands: An Outline Study of Fifty Years of Women's Work in Foreign Missions* (New York: Macmillan Co., 1910).

12. Hill, *The World Their Household*, 3. On the role of education, see, for example, Laura A. Haygood, "Relation of Female Education to Home Mission Work," in *Life and Letters of Laura Askew Haygood*, ed. Oswald Eugene Brown and Anna Muse Brown, 89-95 (Nashville: Smith and Lamar, M. E. Church, South, 1904).

13. In *Missionary Women*, Chapter 6, Rhonda Semple traces corresponding developments for female British missionaries.

14. Nellie J. Arnott to Miss [Sarah] Pollock, December 12, 1899; A.N. Hitchcock to Rev. C.H. Daniels, February 21, 1900, "Record of Candidates . . . Miss Nellie J. Arnott," ABCFM Archives. Arnott's teaching of young children at Beach Institute in Savannah would indeed have served her well in Angola. This AMA school included secondary as well as primary grades and was dedicated to the education of future African-American teachers, ministers and community leaders; such education became the focus of much of Arnott's foreign mission work. See Joe M. Richardson, *Christian Reconstruction: The American Missionary Association and Southern Blacks, 1861–1890* (Athens: Univ. of Georgia Press, 1986), 115–16, 152, 259.

15. Semple, *Missionary Women*, points to a similar concern among British mission organizations that female recruits demonstrate suitable educational requirements, not just good family connections and "ladylike" behavior (191–92). The selection process for women missionaries could be highly competitive in Arnott's day, as Rosemary Seton has reported in a British context. Between 1875 and 1907, Seton notes that the London Missionary Society reviewed applications from some 400 women and rejected 186 of

those. Rosemary Seton, "'Open Doors for Female Labourers,'" in Bickers and Seton, *Missionary Encounters*, 56; 60–61.

16. Francis E. Clark, "A Quarter-Century of Christian Endeavor," *Outlook* 82 (January 13, 1906): 80; Ian Tyrrell, *Woman's World, Woman's Empire: The Woman's Christian Temperance Union in International Perspective, 1880–1930* (Chapel Hill: Univ. of North Carolina Press, 1991), 12, 152–54. See also Tyrrell's "Woman, Missions, and Empire: New Approaches to American Cultural Expansion," in Reeves-Ellington, Sklar and Shemo, *Competing Kingdoms*, for a discussion of the innovative ways in which transnational organizations such as the WCTU and Christian Endeavor encouraged "specific foms of Protestant Christian moral expansionism" throughout the world (47-49).

17. We thank Susan K. Harris for sharing analyses of American responses to imperialism during this era, especially in "Mark Twain's America: Race, Religion, and American Identity in the Annexation Debates of 1899," manuscript in progress, Univ. of Kansas, 2008. See also Harris's "Mark Twain and America's Christian Mission Abroad," in *A Companion to Mark Twain*, ed. Louis J. Budd and Peter Messant, 38–52 (New York: Wiley-Blackwell, 2006) and her "Women, Anti-imperialism and America's Christian Mission Abroad: The Impact of the Philippine-American War," in *Becoming Visible: Women's Presence in Late Nineteenth-Century America*, ed. Janet Floyd, Alison Easton, R.J. Ellis and Lindsey Traub (Amsterdam: Rodopi, 2010), 307-26.

18. Eric T. L. Love, *Race Over Empire: Racism and U.S. Imperialism, 1865–1900* (Chapel Hill: Univ. of North Carolina Press, 2004), 146, 154. Paul Kramer observes that Anglo-Saxonism, having begun "as a British defense of the superiority of the Anglican Church," was "closely allied to Protestantism" and "often said to share its virtues." See "Empires, Exceptions, and Anglo-Saxons: Race and Rule between the British and United States Empires, 1880–1910," *Journal of American History* 88 (March 2002): 1318.

19. D.W. Bebbington points to similar attitudes in Britain, where evangelicals who were "haunted by the specter of Roman Catholicism" displayed "[e]normous sympathy" with the U.S. in its war with Spain. "Atonement, Sin, and Empire, 1880–1914" in Porter, *Imperial Horizons of British Protestant Missions*, 27.

20. Von Rohr, *Shaping of American Congregationalism*, 347. Eric Love (in Chapter 1 of *Race Over Empire*) demonstrates that anti-imperialists also used a race-based rationale in arguing against annexation of Hawaii or the Philippines on the grounds that their peoples could never be assimilated into the white majority; he outlines the debate over Hawaii and the Philippines in Chapters 4 and 5.

21. Missionary interests in Africa were frequently at odds with the concerns of colonial governments; for example, British missionaries in the Congo led the campaign against slavery and those in Cape Colony were often in conflict with other European settlers. See Kevin Grant, *A Civilized Savagery: Britain and the New Slaveries in Africa, 1884–1926* (New York: Routledge, 2005), Chapter 2, for a history of the Congo Reform Campaign; on Cape Colony, see Richard Elphick, "Evangelical Missions," in Robert, *Converting Colonialism*, 112–33. Brian Stanley's work demonstrates that it is difficult to make generalizations about the support of British missionaries for British colonial government in southern Africa; the record is quite ambiguous (*The Bible and the Flag*, 120–31).

22. Arnott, "News from Kamundongo," *Mission Studies*, April 1908, 107. Catherine Hall warns of the importance of distinguishing between the language of paternalistic discourse, with its "notions of black sisters and brothers," and that of "'scientific racists,' with their emphasis on fixed, immutable racial differences" in *Civilizing Subjects: Colony and Metropole in the English Imagination, 1830–1867* (Chicago: Univ. of Chicago Press, 2001), 13. Arnott's missionary colleague Thomas W. Woodside, in a July 1908 *Missionary Herald* article ("Is the African Worth While?") provides a vehement argument against "race superiority" in which "we put the Anglo-Saxon in the front rank." "While we do recognize the superiority of the white man today," he asked, "may it not be an open question how much is due to race and how much to environment, not only the environment of the man himself, but that of his father and his grandfathers?" (320).

23. John MacKenzie says missionaries sought to reconstruct the "unbridled circularity of nature" evident in traditional African buildings into settlements characterized by straight lines based on rational geometric principles. "Modern, empirical science was what distinguished their [missionaries'] society from that of the Africans" ("Missionaries, Science, and the Environment in Nineteenth-Century Africa," in Porter, *Imperial Horizons of British Protestant Missions*, 116, 129).

24. Arnott, "Kamundongo II," *Mission Studies*, May 1906, 134–36; Mary Floyd Cushman, *Missionary Doctor: The Story of Twenty Years in Africa* (New York: Harper & Brothers, 1944), 66–67, 104. Cushman's chapters entitled "An Umbundu Village" and "The New Life" provide contrasts between traditional and Christian communities. Her service as a Congregational missionary in Angola began in 1922.

25. John L. Comaroff, "Images of Empire, Contests of Conscience: Models of Colonial Domination in South Africa," in *Tensions of Empire: Colonial Cultures in a Bourgeois World*, ed. Frederick Cooper and Ann Laura Stoler (Berkeley: Univ. of California Press, 1997), 181–82.

26. Lamin Sanneh, *Encountering the West: Christianity and the Global Cultural Process: The African Dimension* (Maryknoll, NY: Orbis Books, 1993), 17, 77. J. D. Y. Peel makes a similar point in connection with the Yoruba. While the goal of missionary education and translation was simply to "enable Yoruba Christians to read the Bible in their mother tongue," Peel argues that "nationalist initiatives . . . derived their primary impetus" from such efforts. *Religious Encounter and the Making of the Yoruba* (Bloomington: Univ. of Indiana Press, 2003), 128.

27. Andrew Porter, "'Cultural Imperialism,'" 379; Ryan Dunch, "Beyond Cultural Imperialism: Cultural Theory, Christian Missions, and Global Modernity," *History and Theory* 41 (October 2002): 310. Catherine Hall argues in *Civilizing Subjects* that we must examine how the vision of missionaries (in her case, English nonconformists in Jamaica) differed from that of other colonizers, such as planters and colonial officials; she proposes asking: what was the "nature of the transformation" missionaries sought—and what actually happened? (13).

28. Nellie J. Arnott to "Dear Friends," March 22, 1911, C.N. (Chauncey Northrop) Pond (1841–1920) Papers, 1852–1920, OCA 30/42, Series I: Correspondence of Foreign Missionaries, Collected and Received by Chauncey N. Pond, Oberlin College Archives (hereafter cited as C.N. Pond Papers, Oberlin College Archives); Sanneh, *Encountering the West*, 17, 239–40. John T. Tucker, in *Angola: The Land of the Blacksmith Prince* (New York: World Dominion, 1933), provides a list of works written in or translated into Umbundu (147–48). William Sanders, Wesley M. Stover and John Tucker were the most prolific translators of religious materials; female missionaries Margaret Melville, Emma Cecilia Redick, Sarah Stimpson, Elisabeth Ennis and Janette Miller contributed texts for primary students.

29. Porter points to the "irrepressible tendency for colonial peoples to construct the West for themselves"; if missionaries "appeared to stand in the way of local interests," then it was the missions which often changed in response ("'Cultural Imperialism,'" 386–87). Ann Laura Stoler and Frederick Cooper ("Between Metropole and Colony: Rethinking a Research Agenda," in Cooper and Stoler, *Tensions of Empire*, 7) note the importance of understanding that the "otherness of colonized persons was neither inherent nor stable: his or her difference had to be defined and maintained"; "otherness" varied as colonized people themselves sought to accommodate to changing political dynamics. See also Dunch, "Beyond Cultural Imperialism," 305, and Sanneh, *Encountering the West*, 71.

30. Stoler and Cooper argue for the need to recognize tensions between administrators, settlers and other colonizers as well as tensions between colonizers and indigenous peoples. In Angola, tensions between Portuguese and

North American missionaries added to an already volatile mix ("Between Metropole and Colony," 7–8).

31. Henderson in *Church in Angola* (53–55 and 79) gives information about the founding of the various stations. William Sanders, "Reminiscences," ABCFM Archives, ABC 76:2, Personal Papers, 26–50, describes the early days of the Bailundu station, sometimes spelled "Bailundo." Bié is the modern spelling of Kamundongo's region; Arnott usually spells the area as "Bihe." Arnott refers to the Chilesso station as "Ocileso."

32. Henderson, *Church in Angola*, 56; Fola Soremekun, "A History of the American Board Missions in Angola" (PhD diss., Northwestern Univ., 1965), 100–01. Walter T. Currie's papers are in the United Church of Canada/Victoria University Archives in Toronto. Archives of the United Church of Canada include materials related to Canadian missions in Angola as well as missionaries' correspondence. According to David B. Marshall, Canadian missions "tended to minimize the importance of doctrine and saving souls while emphasizing Christianity's role in promoting moral reform and social justice," including improvements in the status of women. *Secularizing the Faith: Canadian Protestant Clergy and the Crisis of Belief, 1850–1940* (Toronto: Univ. of Toronto Press, 1992), 103. Arnott seemingly would have agreed with this assessment; she confided to her diary while visiting at the Cisamba station (October 29, 1905), for example, that "[o]ne certainly feels a lack of spiritual things here."

33. Both of these missions were in Bié; Arnott identifies them as Uchilonda and Ohualondo. Henderson, *Church in Angola*, 59–60, provides brief information on the Plymouth Brethren, an English evangelical group founded in the early 1800s by John Nelson Darby. Brethren editors William T. Stunt, et al. wrote their account of work in Angola in *Turning the World Upside Down: A Century of Missionary Endeavor* (Eastbourne, Sussex: Upperton, 1972), 363–429. The Brethren missions were faith-based, interested in evangelizing rather than in education or social services. Arnott admired their earnestness, spirituality and "real desire to know & do the will of the Lord" (Diary, September 17 -18, 1905).

34. Methodist Bishop William Taylor founded this station, along with churches in Mozambique and several other African countries. Frequently at odds with the Methodist mission board, he backed self-supporting and self-governing churches. David Bundy, "William Taylor," in *Biographical Dictionary of Christian Mission*, ed. Gerald Anderson (Cambridge: William B. Eerdmans, 1998), 660.

35. Henderson in *The Church in Angola* describes the early Catholic missions in the highlands (61–63). One other Protestant mission group, the Philafrican Liberators' League, operated in the Umbundu-speaking area of Angola in the early 1900s, but apparently had little direct involvement

with the ABCFM missions during Arnott's term of service. With the help of American supporters, linguist Héli Chatelain (who had initially served with Methodist Bishop Taylor) founded this mission near Kalukembe in 1897. Chatelain later moved the base of his group to Switzerland and renamed it "Mission Philafricaine en Angola" (*Church in Angola*, 60). David Birmingham gives a history of Chatelain's mission in *Empire in Africa: Angola and its Neighbors* (Athens: Ohio Univ. Press, 2006), 41-61.

36. Linda Heywood discusses these issues in *Contested Power in Angola, 1840s to the Present* (Rochester: Univ. of Rochester Press, 2000), 24–28, as does Fola Soremekun, "The Bailundu Revolt, 1902," *African Social Research* 16 (December 1973): 450–53.

37. Heywood, *Contested Power*, 40, 46. Wild rubber accounted for 86% of all exports from Angola in 1903. Linda M. Heywood, "The Growth and Decline of African Agriculture in Central Angola, 1890–1950," *Journal of Southern African Studies* 13 (April 1987): 357. The development of Umbundu trade is discussed in Fola Soremekun, "Trade and Dependency in Central Angola: The Ovimbundu in the Nineteenth Century," in *The Roots of Rural Poverty in Central and Southern Africa*, ed. Robin Palmer and Neil Parsons, 82-95 (Berkeley: Univ. of California Press, 1977).

38. Heywood, *Contested Power*, 26–27; Soremekun, "Bailundu Revolt," 454–55; Douglas Wheeler and C. Diane Christensen, "To Rise with One Mind: The Bailundo War of 1902," in *Social Change in Angola*, ed. Franz-Wilhelm Heimer (Munich: Weltforum Verlag, 1973), 58. Deborah Gaitskell analyzes reasons which led men and women to seek mission protection, arguing that among the Nguni in South Africa men were more likely to be seeking economic improvement; women, on the other hand, might be escaping an accusation of witchcraft, an unwanted marriage, a malicious co-wife, etc. "Devout Domesticity? A Century of African Women's Christianity in South Africa," in *Women and Gender in Southern Africa to 1945*, ed. Cherryl Walker (Cape Town: D. Philip, 1990), 253.

39. Wheeler and Christensen, "To Rise with One Mind," 66–70, 79; Soremekun, "Bailundu Revolt," 467–68 and 470–71; Heywood, *Contested Power*, 28–30. John T. Tucker discusses the false accusations against missionaries Wesley Stover and Walter Currie in *Currie of Chissamba (Herald of the Dawn)* (Toronto: United Church of Canada, 1945), 76-79. Soremekun notes the lack of Umbundu sources and thus the absence of "words of the Africans themselves saying . . . why they felt they had no recourse but to take up arms," adding that Umbundu leaders in 1902 were "the victims and also the vanquished" (467).

40. Soremekun explains these events and the background of Portuguese-ABCFM strife in "Religion and Politics in Angola," 355–58.

41. Soremekun, "Religion and Politics in Angola," 358. Soremekun has suggested that the ending of the Bailundu Revolt and the beginning of railroad construction in 1904 brought profound, but unforeseen changes to the highlands. By that date, he says, "Umbunduland was being changed forever" ("Bailundu Revolt," 469–70). Wheeler and Christensen similarly argue that the Bailundu Revolt "sealed the fate of traditional ways" of the Umbundu and was a "watershed" in the Portuguese government's "restrictions on the foreign mission's activities" ("To Rise with One Mind," 78–79). See also Birmingham, *Empire in Africa*, 40.

42. Heywood, *Contested Power*, 39; Arnott, Circular Letter, June 6, 1905, NJADP. While recognizing the exploitative nature of the contract labor system, we should note that Umbundu peoples themselves permitted a form of slavery, chiefly for debt repayment, and consequently at times participated in the contract labor trade or bartered their own slaves to Portuguese agents of coastal trading companies, often in exchange for rum. See Linda Heywood, "Slavery and Forced Labor in the Changing Political Economy of Central Angola, 1850–1949," in *The End of Slavery in Africa*, ed. Suzanne Miers and Richard Roberts (Madison: Univ. of Wisconsin Press, 1988), 418, 420–22.

43. Hochschild, *King Leopold's Ghost*, 241–42; Grant, *Civilized Savagery*, 64. Missionaries of the Baptist Missionary Society and the Congo Balolo Mission were among the leaders in exposing conditions in the Congo Free State. Grant argues that mission leaders, worried that they would be expelled from their stations, did not begin public protest until state practices began to interfere with their access to local African communities and to thwart their expansion. However, as conflict with the state escalated, missionaries John and Alice Harris, in Britain on furlough late in 1905, engaged in an enormously successful lecture tour featuring a series of "atrocity photographs" to garner support for the work of the Congo Reform Association (45–47, 59–60, 66–70). Twain's *King Leopold's Soliloquy* included a selection of these photographs.

44. The reprint edition is Henry W. Nevinson, *A Modern Slavery*, with an introduction by Basil Davidson (London: Harper and Brothers, 1963). See especially 64–70 and 90–91. On the slave issue and Nevinson's journey, see Lowell J. Satre, *Chocolate on Trial: Slavery, Politics, and the Ethics of Business* (Athens: Ohio Univ. Press, 2005), 1–12.

45. The expedition report is in William A. Cadbury, *Labour in Portuguese West Africa*, 2nd ed. (London: Routledge, 1910; New York: Negro Universities Press, 1969). Cadbury was careful not to boycott São Tomé chocolate until he had secured an alternate source, according to Grant in *A Civilized Savagery*, 133–34. Grant describes in detail Cadbury's connections with Edmund Morel and the Congo Reform Association, noting that

neither Cadbury nor his close friend Morel believed that labor conditions on Saõ Tomé and Príncipe were as atrocious as those in the Congo. Satre likewise describes Cadbury's genuine concern over slavery in Portuguese Africa although he finds Cadbury slow to condemn the contract labor system (*Chocolate on Trial*, 145–48).

46. Charles A. Swan, *The Slavery of To-Day or The Present Position of the Open Sore of Africa* (Glasgow: Pickering & Inglis: [1909]). Cadbury thought that Swan's information would supplement his own, since Swan spoke Umbundu and could travel to the interior to investigate conditions. See Satre, *Chocolate on Trial*, 111, 144.

47. Soremekun, "Religion and Politics in Angola," 358; Nevinson, *Modern Slavery*, 81. Nevinson observes that the Portuguese could have done far more harm to the missions than they did. See also Soremekun, "Religion and Politics in Angola," 358. Arnott's diary entries and especially her public writings tended to gloss over the potential danger the missionaries faced. Her seeming calm was in part due to her deep religious conviction; for example, she wrote in her diary on August 18, 1905: "We know not what moment another fire will break out or how long we will have a roof over our heads. Our eyes are unto God. We are in His keeping." Missionaries in the Congo likewise faced harassment from local traders and officials, especially after they began to complain about the brutality of "native policy" (Grant, *Civilized Savagery*, 59).

48. Soremekun, "Religion and Politics in Angola," 358; Heywood, *Contested Power in Angola*, 37–40. Soremekun points out that for Umbundu traders, the "significance of trade . . . appears to have been centered more on the very acts of bargaining and travelling than on the profit that trade brought," because trade activities "reinforced the functions of the body politic" of each Umbundu kingdom ("Trade and Dependency," 92 and 90–93).

49. Heywood, *Contested Power in Angola*, 7–9, 35–36; Soremekun, "History of the American Board Missions," 7–8. See also Gladwyn Murray Childs, *Umbundu Kinship & Character*, 20–24. The singular of *olosoma* is *osoma;* the missionaries used the word *soma* and the Portuguese, *soba*.

50. Along the same line, J. D. Y. Peel explains how Yoruba leaders furthered their own best interest in negotiating between Protestant missionaries, Muslim authorities and hostile local rulers. "They want us without our religion," as one missionary explained; political and economic considerations were primary (*Religious Encounter*, 126–27).

51. Linda Heywood discusses the gradual, though incomplete, erosion of traditional lineages among Umbundu Christians along with the growth of a new identity based on religion and language (*Contested Power*, 52–56). Heywood and John Thornton examine tax collection and other economic

factors affecting the highlands up to the 1920s; at that time the highlands furnished most of the colony's tax revenue. "Demography, Production and Labor: Central Angola, 1890–1950" in *African Population and Capitalism: Historical Perspectives,* ed. Dennis D. Cordell and Joel W. Gregory (Boulder, CO: Westview, 1987), 241–49. See also Nevinson, *Modern Slavery,* 81–83.

52. On the Stover case, see Soremekun, "Religion and Politics in Angola," 359–60; "Dr. Stover at Bailundu," *Missionary Herald,* September 1910, 379. William H. Sanders, in his "Reminiscences," argues that Stover warned the local Portuguese captain about the brewing revolt, but Stover was "pooh-poohed and disregarded" (120). David Birmigham describes similar difficulties between Héli Chatelain and Portuguese authorities in *Empire in Africa,* 58-60. Sanders describes the imprisonment of Kanjundu (which he spells Canjundo) on 123–24 of his "Reminiscences." John T. Tucker writes of Kanjundu's struggles and death in *Drums in the Darkness* (New York: George H. Doran, 1927), 108–13, and in *A Tucker Treasury,* 67–68,164–65. Arnott's account, "Chief Kanjundu's Death," appeared in *Mission Studies* in April 1914 and is reprinted in Chapter 6. See also Heywood, *Contested Power,* 56–57.

53. A republic was proclaimed in Portugal in 1910, but there was little substantive change in Portuguese administrative practices in Angola until after World War I. In the 1920s, Decree 77, specifying that Portuguese would be the language of schools rather than Umbundu (and that all teachers must pass an examination in Portuguese) profoundly affected the Protestant missions and essentially brought them under Portuguese control. Soremekun, "Religion and Politics in Angola," 363–66; 373–75; Heywood, *Contested Power,* 58–59.

54. Fola Soremekun's article "Religion and Politics in Angola" explains developments in the 1920s, during which goals of Congregational missionaries and Portuguese authorities coalesced around changing Umbundu itinerant traders to settled agriculturalists, a cooperation which came "at the expense" of the Umbundu peoples (376). Heywood and Thornton in "Demography, Production and Labor" examine ways in which governmental policies begun in the 1920s had destroyed the prosperity of the highlands by 1950 (249–54). As accounts of succeeding years indicate, the complex cross-cultural relationships in the region during Arnott's time there have continued to shape the political life in Angola to the present day. See Linda Heywood, *Contested Power,* Chapters 3–7, on this topic; see also Heywood's "Towards an Understanding of Modern Political Ideology in Africa: The Case of the Ovimbundu of Angola," *Journal of Modern African Studies* 26 (March 1998): 139–67.

55. Contrasting the situation of Arnott's team with that of missionaries in Hawaii through various stages of the nineteenth century is instructive, since there the mission organization—the ABCFM—was the same, but the

political context strikingly different. In Hawaii, as Patricia Grimshaw has noted, many of the first generation of missionaries focused on converting the locals while adhering to ABCFM guidance about spiritual commitment as paramount. Later, however, as American political and economic power coalesced after 1850 and as missionaries began to devote considerable energy to securing economic well-being for their children, many members of the missionary community became intensely embedded in the secular imperial agenda, including acquiring extensive land holdings, seeking governmental positions, and building lucrative businesses. Although some members of the original mission community, such as the widow Maria Chamberlain, complained to ABCFM officials about the loss of spiritual commitment in the face of increasing worldliness and although the Board itself did urge the missionary band to reconfirm its primary aims, some critics, then and now, have pointed to the ABCFM's failure to provide strong leadership for genuinely charitable values versus a tendency to give implicit approval of economic moves that were, in fact, saving the Board money by reducing the dependence of missionaries and the next generations on funds from the U.S. See especially the introduction and the "Family Fortunes" chapter in Grimshaw's *Paths of Duty: American Missionary Wives in Nineteenth-Century Hawaii* (Honolulu: Univ. of Hawaii Press, 1989), xi-xxiii and 179–96.

56. John L. and Jean Comaroff, *Of Revelation and Revolution, Vol. II: The Dialectics of Modernity on a South African Frontier* (Chicago: Univ. of Chicago Press, 1997), 35. Terence Ranger notes that in evaluating cultural exchanges, one cannot assume that white presence meant white cultural domination, as the Comaroffs argue; rather, especially in areas with inconsistent colonial authority, "Africans and Europeans [had] some sort of equality of interaction." See "Europeans in Black Africa," 262.

57. Historians such as Soremekun, Wheeler and Christensen lament the shortage of oral sources for building a history of Angola. Soremekun, "The Bailundu Revolt," 447; Wheeler and Christensen, "To Rise With One Mind," 80. As long ago as 1971, Soremekun ("Religion and Politics in Angola," 357) lamented that political conditions in Angola made it impossible to do first-hand research in the interior; travel to the highlands remains difficult today.

58. Trinh T. Minh-ha, *Woman, Native, Other: Writing Postcoloniality and Feminism* (Bloomington: Indiana Univ. Press, 1989), 58, 59. Arnott's diaries reveal instances when she faced resistance from girls at Kamundongo station; for example, on January 6, 1907, she noted that she "got mad & lost [her] temper" at their behavior. "I pray for them to try to love them into doing right," she continued, "but they try me to death." Arnott attributed these problems to her ongoing struggle to communicate fluently in Umbundu. Fortunately, we are beginning to acquire more accounts of Angolan women's

responses to missionary culture, though in a time period later than that of Arnott's service. See discussion of works by Eva de Carvalho Chipenda and Maria Chela Chikueka in Chapter 3.

59. J.D.Y. Peel, "Problems and Opportunities in an Anthropologist's Use of a Mission Archive," in Bickers and Seton, *Missionary Encounters*, 71. In this same volume, see also Brian Stanley, "Some Problems in Writing a Missionary Society History Today: The Example of the Baptist Missionary Society," 38–49.

60. Luisa Mastrobuono, "Ovimbundu Women and Coercive Labour Systems, 1850–1940: From Still Life to Moving Picture" (M.A. thesis, University of Toronto, 1992), 11. Mastrobuono comments (9–10) that most older anthropological sources provide a static, rather than dynamic, view of Umbundu women's roles, for example in Childs's *Umbundu Kinship & Character* or Wilfrid D. Hambly's *The Ovimbundu of Angola* (Chicago: Field Museum of Natural History, 1934). For accounts that can provide a "moving, living history" of Umbundu women's lives, Mastrobuono argues that the writings of female missionaries, along with those of a few travelers (like Nevinson) and translations of folk tales and proverbs, are the best detailed sources available (10–12).

61. Arnott wrote about her journey to the 1907 meeting in "A Trip to the Woman's Conference in the West Central Africa Mission," *Life and Light*, January 1908, 43-45. Arnott noted in her diary that she had received "a real spiritual blessing" from the conference and trusted that "the results may be marked in our future work" (July 29, 1907). Tucker's analysis of the Women's Conferences and their significance is in *Drums in the Darkness*, 148–149. Mrs. T.W. (Emma) Woodside's report is in "A Summer Conference of Ovimbundu Women," *Life and Light*, June 1913, 255–59. In addition to the annual conferences, Arnott's diaries indicate that she (or another female missionary) often coordinated local women's meetings on Sunday afternoons (for example, July 10, 17, 24 and 31, 1910). Deborah Gaitskell's research on missions in South Africa points to the popularity there of African women's Christian organizations *(manyanos)* which discussed themes of home and motherhood as well as religious topics. "Power in Prayer and Service: Women's Christian Organizations," in *Christianity in South Africa: A Political, Social, and Cultural History*, ed. Richard Elphick and Rodney Davenport (Berkeley: Univ. of California Press, 1997), 253–56.

62. Indigenous women might use Christian ideology regarding family and marriage to further their own goals, as Deborah Gaitskell found in studying the resistance of African women in Orange Free State to 1913 legislation requiring passes to demonstrate that they were employed by whites. The ideology of domesticity was not necessarily "alien to the needs of black Christians" according to Gaitskell; in fact, having a defined domestic role

could help to bolster "the right of African women to independence from labour control." "Housewives, Maids or Mothers: Some Contradictions of Domesticity for Christian Women in Johannesburg, 1903–39," in "The History of the Family in Africa," special issue, *Journal of African History*, 24, no. 2 (1983): 255.

63. Arnott, Diary, November 18, 1906. Her diary for that year mentions several visits to the school at Cisanje; e.g., on August 7, 1906. Though Arnott does not comment on Mueno's reasons for not embracing Christianity, probably he did not wish to give up his multiple wives or his rum-drinking. Mueno might have thought affiliation with a mission school could provide some protection against the Portuguese. In Nigeria, for example, J. D. Y. Peel found that in the early years of mission activity, the most important reason that Yoruba rulers sought association with a mission or a missionary was "that he would bring protection" (*Religious Encounter and the Making of the Yoruba*, 128).

64. Cushman, *Missionary Doctor*, 56–64; Tucker, *Tucker Treasury*, 121–24. Cushman, from her perspective as a physician, much admired the skill of Umbundu healers in using "native herbs and drugs," though she could not condone what she considered "occult practices" (56). David Chidester in *Savage Systems: Colonialism and Comparative Religions in Southern Africa* (Charlottesville: Univ. Press of Virginia) emphasizes that missionaries and colonial officials in Africa, in relegating indigenous religion to "superstition" or to "ignorance and fear," helped to support the perspective that Africans had no civilization and thus needed European intervention (234–36).

65. As Obioma Nnaemeka has pointed out, western writers rarely acknowledge the potential benefits of polygyny, choosing instead to stress its drawbacks. "Polygyny has been condemned in the West as one of the worst symbols of African women's oppression without any assessment of the advantages the practice accords women: sharing child care, emotional and economic support, sisterhood, companionship, and so on." Obioma Nnaemeka, "Bringing African Women into the Classroom: Rethinking Pedagogy and Epistemology," in *African Gender Studies: A Reader*, ed. Oyèrónké Oyěwùmí (New York: Palgrave, 2005), 62. Fiona Bowie likewise points to the "benefits offered by institutionalized polygyny" in indigenous societies in Cameroon. "The Elusive Christian Family: Missionary Attempts to Define Women's Roles; Case Studies from Cameroon" in *Women and Missions: Past and Present; Anthropological and Historical Perceptions*, ed. Fiona Bowie, Deborah Kirkwood and Shirley Ardener (Providence, RI: Berg Publishers, 1993), 146. Adrian Hastings, in the same volume, argues, however, that polygyny could "for junior wives, be very enslaving" ("Were Women a Special Case?" 116). Arnott and other missionaries used the term "polygamy" to describe marriage customs among the Ovimbundu; "polygyny" is the more accurate term, since Umbundu men, but not women, might have plural spouses or mates.

66. Nellie Arnott, "Happenings in Africa, not recorded in letters or diary" [personal journal], August 2, 1907, NJADP; Linda Heywood, "Slavery and Forced Labor," 418. While the missionaries often referred to men as having several "wives," a common custom was to have one "wife," along with one or more slave (or pawn) concubines. This system was more prevalent in border areas where female slaves were relatively inexpensive compared to paying bridewealth (*ilombo*) for a free wife. See Luisa Mastrobuono, "Ovimbundu Women," 20, 34.

67. Sanders, "Reminiscences," 93; Mastrobuono, "Ovimbundu Women," 30–31; John T. Tucker, *Drums in the Darkness*, 137–39. When Kanjundu became a Christian and gave up his "many wives," he suffered considerable monetary loss, as he provided "each of his plural wives a dowry" (Tucker, *Drums*, 105). Fiona Bowie emphasizes that women could face considerable loss in such a situation as well; she found in Cameroon that wives who were "'drive[n] away'" might have no means of support and no status in society; they might also lose their children ("The Elusive Christian Family," 153). E.A. Ayandele describes polygyny as "a product of the economic, social and political circumstances" of indigenous societies in Nigeria; in his view, it "could upset the society" if missionaries insisted that "polygamists who wanted full membership and privileges of the Church must first disown all wives but one." *The Missionary Impact on Modern Nigeria*, 330, 335–37.

68. Heywood, "Slavery and Forced Labor," 418; Mastrobuono, "Ovimbundu Women," 21–22; Tucker, *Drums in the Darkness*, 139–40. Both Mastrobuono and Tucker point out that the *oluina* might also provide protection for a woman against her husband in certain circumstances, especially if he mistreated her. See also Hambly, *Ovimbundu of Angola*, 200 and 205.

69. Arnott, "Happenings in Africa," August 2, 1907; Mastrobuono, "Ovimbundu Women," 32–39. Domestic slavery was common in other areas of Africa; on slavery among the Yoruba, for example, see Toyin Falola, "Missionaries and Domestic Slavery in Yorubaland in the Nineteenth Century," *Journal of Religious History* 14 (1986): 182–83.

70. Linda Heywood argues that missionaries were "relatively powerless to change established practices" relating to domestic slavery. When the government of the Portuguese Republic banned slavery in its colonies in 1910, ABCFM missionaries in Angola decided that owning slaves was "incompatible with church membership." A few converts freed their slaves (one *sekulu* freed more than 100). But most slave-owners, converts or not, found it impossible to do so because consent of the many relatives who shared an interest in a slave was difficult to procure. In addition, slaves who had been held for years might have no families to return to, but Umbundu practices forbade their incorporation into the former master's kin group. Heywood concluded that the decree of 1910 had "no real effect in changing the status of slaves

under local law" ("Slavery and Forced Labor," 424). Toyin Falola similarly recounts a number of reasons for the failure of the (Anglican) Church Missionary Society's crusade against domestic slavery among the Yoruba, including the difficulty of persuading "most of the converts that domestic slavery was a social evil" (188), the difficulty in distinguishing slaves from pawns and the ambiguous stance that other mission groups in the area took on the issue ("Missionaries and Domestic Slavery," 188–91).

71. Line Nyhagen Predelli and Jon Miller point out that missionaries in their Christian zeal to reform women's lives profoundly affected the status of indigenous women, making it necessary to look at the intended and unintended implications of missionary activity. See "Piety and Patriarchy: Contested Regimes in Nineteenth-Century Evangelical Missions," in Huber and Lutkehaus, *Gendered Missions*, 72. The "rescue" of women thought to be downtrodden was a central theme in American women's home and foreign mission service. For example, see Hunter, *The Gospel of Gentility*, 177-82, and Peggy Pascoe, *Relations of Rescue: The Search for Female Moral Authority in the American West, 1874–1939* (New York: Oxford Univ. Press, 1993), 95-102. Emily S. Rosenberg argues that "U.S. missionaries in China, India, and Africa (as well as among American Indians at home) often made the case for Westernization and Americanization by highlighting signs of women's subordinated status, such as foot binding, suttee, and load carrying." See "Rescuing Women and Children," *Journal of American History* 89 (September 2002): 457–58.

72. Heywood, "Slavery and Forced Labor," 418, 424; Mastrobuono, "Ovimbundu Women," 49–50, 63–64. Charles Swan, the Brethren missionary who investigated labor abuses in 1909, provides numerous graphic accounts of the mistreatment of women who were slaves or contract laborers in *The Slavery of To-Day*.

73. Arnott, "A Visit to an African Village (Continued)," *Mission Studies*, June 1913, 185–86; "Happenings in Africa," May 12, 1908, NJADP. While those who fled to missions might be marginal women such as escaped slaves, Arnott's writings demonstrate that in an unsettled area like the Angola highlands, even Umbundu women from prominent families were vulnerable to being seized by the Portuguese. Justin Willis describes a similar situation in "The Nature of a Mission Community: The Universities' Mission to Central Africa in Bonde." Without any powerful central authority in the region, many local people, not just the "outcast and vulnerable" were at high risk of being kidnapped or captured (in Bickers and Seton, *Missionary Encounters*, 129–31).

74. Arnott, "A Visit to an African Village (Continued)," 185–86. Mastrobuono argues in "Ovimbundu Women" that while a woman's father or maternal uncle might select her future husband, her willing consent was customary (18); the amount of bridewealth varied, depending on the woman's

status and kinship ties (13). The maternal uncle might contract marriages for his nieces when they were young and receive a portion of the bridewealth at that time. (Tucker, *Drums in the Darkness*, 140). Tucker argued that mission interference in such a custom "inherent in tribal life" was "inadvisable," as long as the young woman herself consented to the marriage (140–41). Accounts of Arnott (and other female missionaries in Angola) likely overstated the prevalence of forced marriages when writing for a home audience naturally drawn to rescue narratives. Fiona Bowie similarly found in Cameroon that the bridewealth system involved a "wide network of kin," all having some financial stake in the bride's marriage; sometimes payments began at birth, so that a woman "could not be extricated from these obligations without considerable difficulty" ("The Elusive Christian Family," 152).

75. Arnott, "A Visit to an African Village (Continued)," 185–86; "Happenings in Africa," June 1, 1909, and Diary, July 13, 1908, NJADP; "A Missionary Symposium: Miss Nellie J. Arnott, Benguella, Africa," *Life and Light for Woman*, April 1911, 190.

76. Arnott, "Happenings in Africa," June 1, 1909, NJADP. Although her notebook story of Cipuku's suffering is lengthy, Arnott's public writings contain no mention of the situation surrounding Cipuku's difficulties in childbirth. Rather, her *Mission Studies* account of Cipuku, not published until 1913, presents only the "saving" of Cipuku and her sisters from traditional marriages that they opposed. Arnott perhaps thought that her readers would find information about the infant's struggles unduly intimate or that such an account would detract from the uplifting rescue narrative. Arnott might also have hesitated to convey her own personal distress.

77. Arnott, "Happenings in Africa," August 26, 1908. NJADP; Cushman, *Missionary Doctor*, 72–75; Mastrobuono, "Ovimbundu Women," 27. Cushman commented that "American experts are just catching up with the methods the Umbundu women have practiced for centuries" (74).

78. Arnott's account of the corn-shelling bee is in "Happenings in Africa," August 26, 1908, NJADP. John T. Tucker also praises women's efficient communal agricultural work (*Drums in the Darkness*, 147–48). Wilfrid Hambly, in *Ovimbundu of Angola*, includes a description of time-consuming traditional methods of pounding corn into meal and preparing it for consumption (146–47).

79. Circular letter of Arnott, August 10, 1905, NJADP; Mastrobuono, "Ovimbudu Women," 43–48. In traditional society, Umbundu men were traders and hunters. Especially in trading, women played a role as well, selling surplus food for cloth, salt and other necessities (Mastrobuono, 29).

80. Arnott, "Happenings in Africa," July 11, 1909, and "A Visit to an African Village (Continued)," 185–86; Cushman, *Missionary Doctor*, 81;

Childs, *Umbundu Kinship & Character*, 135–36. Missionary Merlin Ennis translated many of the traditional fables in *Umbundu: Folk-Tales from Angola* (Boston: Beacon, 1962).

81. John Erni Remick, in "American Influence on the Education of the Ovimbundu (the Benguela and Bie Highlands) of Angola, Africa, from 1880–1914" (PhD diss., Miami Univ., Ohio, 1976), analyzes Annie Fay's work (65–73). In 1903 Fay produced a booklet of 105 songs in Umbundu for kindergarten children, some original, some written to "native music." Several pages from her book, including one of her handwritten songs, with words and music, are reproduced in the dissertation. Fay also advocated innovative strategies such as teaching numerical skills through basket weaving, a traditional Umbundu craft.

82. "A Letter from Miss Nellie J. Arnott, *Mission Studies*, October, 1908, 316. While Arnott taught students in Africa, children back home in the U.S. studied her school. An article entitled "Miss Arnott's School," *Mission Studies*, November 1909, 344–45, in the "Children's Work" section of the journal, featured study questions for young readers in the U.S. The 1909 "Plan of Work for Mission Bands [elementary age children] of the W.B. M.I." established "Africa: Miss Arnott's School" as the unit for November. See the monthly topics for 1909 in *Mission Studies*, February 1909, 42. Other units for Mission Band study included mission schools in Turkey, India, China, Japan, and Mexico. On Sakalumbu, see Arnott's "A Missionary Symposium," 190.

83. Arnott "To the Friends of Mrs. Jane C. Means," *Ideal Scrapbook*, box 2, NJADP. Arnott hand-dated the letter 1912–1913.

84. Arnott, "Happenings in Africa," September 6, 1908, and "A Visit to an African Village (Continued)," 185–86. The model of training young Christian women to be helpmeets to their husbands was one followed in other African school settings although in some instances missionaries sought to train young women for domestic service for whites. Arnott herself believed emphatically in education that would produce self-reliant young women to work alongside their husbands in Christian communities. See Dana L. Robert, "The 'Christian Home' as a Cornerstone of Anglo-American Missionary Thought and Practice," in Robert, *Converting Colonialism*, 153–57. Modupe Labode has criticized this model as applied by Anglican missionaries in South Africa, asserting that it implied that traditional African homes were "defective" and young women thus had to be "taught how to live." "From Heathen Kraal to Christian Home: Anglican Missionary Education and African Christian Girls, 1850–1900," in Bowie, Kirkwood and Ardener, *Women and Missions*, 128–29.

85. Nellie J. Arnott, "Circular Letter–A.B.C.F.M, Benguella, Africa, August 5, 1910," typescript in *The Ideal Scrapbook*, Box 2, NJADP.

3 Writing on Multiple Journeys

Public Writing and Arnott's Literacy Network

Nellie Arnott was a highly prolific writer, composing in a wide range of public genres. While in Africa and for decades afterward, she had numerous correspondents connected to the mission movement, and she expected they would share her letters with others. She submitted regular reports to mission organizations. She published articles for specialty periodicals. And, for many years, she kept scrapbooks based on her foreign mission experience—visually rich archives for herself and for future generations. The large quantity and range of Arnott's writing for diverse audiences demonstrate that she was quite comfortable viewing her writing as communally oriented and that she envisioned the connections her writing made with readers as a foundation of the foreign mission movement.[1]

Whether reporting from overseas or as a home-based supporter, missionary authors often signaled their belief that their reading-and-writing network was crucial to the movement's success. Arnott herself explicitly affirmed this point, frequently invoking the ways in which those stationed abroad depended on counterparts in the U.S. to provide both financial and spiritual support. One telling example of Arnott's own views about this literacy-oriented community appeared in both *Life and Light for Woman* and *Mission Studies* in early 1908. This particular narrative described a formal gathering of women held near her station for both missionaries and Angolan Christians. To present a gendered solidarity that cut across other differences, Arnott's article constructed the women's conference as a celebration of shared Christian commitment, uniting missionaries from England and the U.S. with African counterparts who had successfully been prepared to assist in evangelical work. After describing recent achievements in the mission enterprise in Angola, Arnott built to a climax by underscoring the important role that readers at home were also playing to sustain those serving overseas: "My heart often fills with joy for the privilege of being here myself, and knowing you are helping in this blessed work by your prayers and gifts."[2] As she crafted messages like this one, Arnott positioned her authorship within a well-established community of women using collaborative literacy practices to affiliate with the mission movement. Arnott's mission publications were multidimensional, blending pragmatic goals such as fundraising with related ideological aims such as fostering solidarity among supporters based on shared religious beliefs. Her content varied in line with her multiple audiences, ranging from the sisterly colleagues who contributed directly to her upkeep in the mission field to the officials who set priorities for organizational-level policy, from the Sunday school children she hoped would study her narratives about teaching young Angolans to the managers of the publications where such an account might appear. Sometimes she wrote for one of those very specific audiences; other times she crafted her texts for a blended readership. Always she described her travel to and within Africa, as well as her daily experiences there, in ways that would appeal to those at home—audiences whose Protestant middle-class American values she understood well.

Interestingly, one helpful key to understanding Arnott's public writings today is the set of small leather diaries she maintained while in Angola and for many months after her return to the U.S.[3] The diaries illuminate her daily life, sometimes revealing that the messages she sent home in public texts painted a different, more positive picture of her experience than her private writing. In contrast to her goals for formal reports and magazine articles, Nellie Arnott used her diaries for her own personal purposes. Even when overwhelmed by her many missionary duties, she found time to jot a few lines cataloging her activities or listing some Bible verses. Arnott's daily observations generally match what Jennifer Sinor has characterized as "ordinary writing," versus a contrasting body of personal texts Sinor identifies as more self-consciously "aesthetic"—like the diaries of Mary Boykin Chestnut, Charlotte Forten Grimké, Virginia Woolf, or Anaïs Nin.[4] Arnott's diaries, like the brief notes kept by Sinor's great-great-great-aunt Annie Ray in the Midwestern U.S. during the late 1880s, fill small, contained spaces with everyday records. In describing intense spiritual challenges, Arnott's diary writing was often more reflective than Ray's, and Arnott's travels to, from, and within Africa generated some compelling bursts of narration that would sometimes reappear in a published piece months later. But the activity listings in typical entries during her mission service were more in line with Sinor's "ordinary" category, mainly cataloging unfiltered experiences. Thus, most of Arnott's diary entries clearly differ from her public writing, which is more crafted in organization, content, and tone. Overall, the diaries convey a sense of work as-yet-unfinished. They chronicle her never-ending round of activity at the mission and her ongoing efforts to mesh that labor with an elusive spiritual vision. Private and unpolished, the diaries are more artifact than artifice. Nonetheless, we can draw on their content to contextualize her published texts, reading her daily notes and musings to deepen our understanding of the lived experiences that fed into her writing for others back in the U.S.

While Arnott's diaries addressed very personal needs, her public writing fulfilled a core institutional responsibility: maintaining U.S.-based supporters' engagement in the mission enterprise. Arnott's public writing fed into a blend of mixed-gender and women's texts produced by and for the ABCFM and affiliated Protestant groups from the U.S., England, and Canada. Her most broadly circulating texts—her largest body of writing outside her diaries—appeared in specialty magazines, including *Mission Studies, Life and Light,* and the *Missionary Herald.* Another body of public writing arose from the requirement to submit official reports to the ABCFM and the WBMI. Although such pieces reached a smaller group of readers than the periodical stories, these narratives were nonetheless quite "public" in that they circulated among multiple administrators, potentially influencing the whole organization.

Arnott's official mission reports actually aimed at two distinct audiences: female supporters of the mission movement and male managers of the enterprise. The distinction between these supporters and managers was significant. While women donated funds and built a shared literacy network for missions, men set the major policies and held ultimate authority.[5] Therefore, when writing to the male-led ABCFM headquarters in Boston, Arnott and her women colleagues in Africa took a different stance than when composing texts for venues like the WBMI annual report for women enthusiasts. In the first case, Arnott needed to present herself as capable and the work as progressing well; in the second, she emphasized challenges that money and prayers from women at home could address.[6]

One audience very specific to Arnott was the Substitute Circle. As outlined in Chapter 1, she had a longstanding relationship with a group of missionary supporters who raised funds for her passage to Africa and who followed her work for years through her writing. Her "circular letters" for this community of readers often included other friends and family members in the distribution list, so these texts struck a personal tone. However, this correspondence could also serve as drafts for more formal reports or submissions to periodicals. Therefore, the circular letters were both public in reaching a larger audience than we would normally associate with personal letters and in regularly being adapted for later publication.

Whatever venue Arnott was writing for—magazine pieces, institutional reports, or letters for her "circle"—she capitalized on readily available genre patterns, some specific to the mission movement and others drawn from the larger culture of women's writing in her day. More specifically, in composing her texts as a foreign missionary, Arnott took advantage of the popularity and the norms of women's travel writing. She also tailored features of travel writing for her movement's institutional agenda as missionary authors had been doing for decades. Accordingly, she wrote about several types of journeys simultaneously: literal travels to the location of her service (like her initial passage to Africa or her frequent treks to outstations), journey-like stages in her learning to be a successful foreign missionary, and the passage to Christianized, Americanized culture that she envisioned for the Umbundu people.

Below, we locate Arnott's public writing within the broader literacy networks of the American women's Protestant missionary movement and offer historicized close readings of representative pieces.[7] We identify recurring rhetorical trends in Arnott's oeuvre, setting her texts in dialogue with others of her day that operated in what Mary Louise Pratt has called "contact zones," spaces of cross-cultural interaction shaped by striking social differences.[8] We situate Arnott's authorship in a specific chronological and geographical context with very particular shifting contingencies. Overall, we will argue that her public writings responded to strong genre expectations yet carved out a distinctive position among an array of authors writing for and about ABCFM enterprises in West Africa.

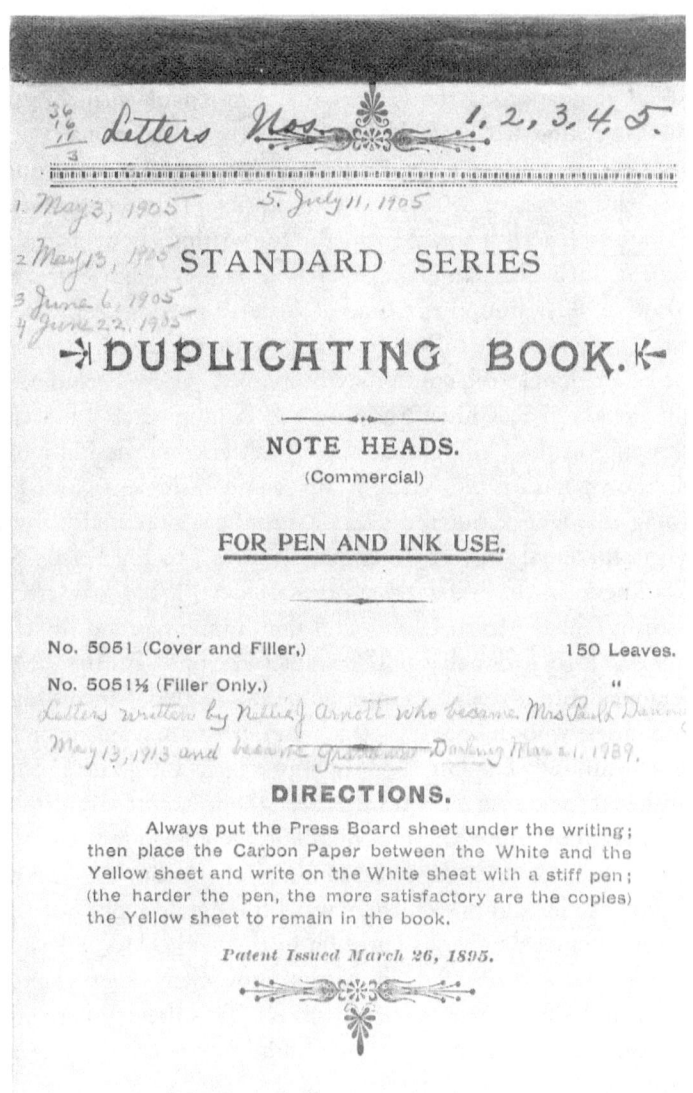

Figure 7: Arnott's circular letter notebook for 1905. Courtesy of The Bancroft Library, University of California, Berkeley.

Women's Mission-Oriented Travel Writing

Nellie Arnott's publications on African mission service appeared during an era when travel writing had enormous appeal for American middle-class women. With increased opportunities for education and professional work, many more women were traveling overseas than in previous generations. Arnott's assignment to Angola also corresponded with a period when the U.S.'s role on the international stage was expanding, as evident in political developments like the acquisition of the Philippines and Caribbean territories. This move to claim a U.S. empire fed an increased appetite for writing about places where American influence was being exercised in new ways. For example, the early 1900s, around the time of Arnott's posting overseas, saw a burst of articles in the influential *Atlantic Monthly*, with titles such as "The Educational Problem in the Philippines," "Race Prejudice in the Philippines," "The United States in the Philippines," "Our Spanish Inheritance in the Philippines," and "A Letter from the Philippines."[9] Well-known authors like Mark Twain (Samuel Clemens) joined in the ongoing dialogue about the U.S.'s assuming a potentially troubling new international role. For example, Twain's "To the Person Sitting in Darkness" in the *North American Review* critiqued Western imperialism in Cuba, Africa, China, and the Philippines and linked mission work to questionable political interventions. Twain's 1901 text generated vigorous responses from numerous readers—including some missionaries, who dubbed his attack on Christian evangelism abroad patently unfair.[10] The larger debate represented by Twain's piece and published responses to it continued throughout Arnott's time in Africa.

Among the white Protestant middle-class women for whom Nellie Arnott wrote, whatever their position might be on the U.S.'s becoming an imperial political power, there was little doubt about the rightful place of American religious outreach in the world. Home-based supporters of the women's foreign mission movement eagerly consumed texts by and about their overseas workers. This literacy network bolstered the missionary endeavor itself both by generating funds and by supporting the audience's tendency to see their movement as contributing to national and transnational goals. Arnott crafted her public writing to take advantage of this *ethos*. Composing for colleagues already committed to foreign missions, Nellie Arnott presented herself as a motherly servant reshaping the "heathen" culture of Africa into an Americanized Christianity. Over time, she gained increasing skill in this mission discourse.

From the outset, her reports and magazine articles reflected a sound understanding of her audience and purpose. She had been consuming this literature herself for years, and she had ongoing access to models even while stationed overseas. (One recurring element in her diaries is lists of readings both completed and anticipated.) So, to hone her rhetorical techniques, Arnott had a rich tradition to draw upon—ranging from broad-based travel narratives aimed at general audiences to the niche sub-genre of ABCFM foreign missionaries' writing, which cultivated Protestant American women's intense interest in faraway places as fields for spiritual work.

By the early twentieth century, travel writing was well established as a popular genre among middle-class U.S. readers with many nineteenth-century accounts by European Americans having shaped conventions for describing foreign lands and peoples. For example, texts typically focused on ways in which the foreign place contrasted with one's home and framed that difference at least in part around themes of national identity. An American travel writer might speculate on what family and friends were doing at home on a holiday while the author was in a place where the event (e.g., Christmas Day, Thanksgiving) was not officially celebrated. Whether based on a grand tour of Europe or on exploration of more remote locales, travel accounts presented other places through a lens of U.S. cultural values. So, for instance, an author might complain about the stuffy manners of the British (payback to English writers like Charles Dickens and Frances Trollope for casting America as uncouth) or note the grandeur of art and architecture reflecting a richer cultural history than in the U.S. If visiting what today could be called a developing country, the author might complain about the dirtiness and unhealthy environment of a local street scene and then turn, just a paragraph later, to praising a landscape's unique appeal.[11] These motifs of difference accrued cultural power for writer and reader alike both by claiming new knowledge of the world being gained through travel and by making that vision available to the audience at home.

Africa held a special fascination for many Euro-American readers in the late nineteenth and early twentieth centuries. Accounts by well-known explorers and by imperialism's managers and critics drew a highly engaged readership. Henry Morton Stanley had stoked his personal fame with accounts such as *Through the Dark Continent: Or, The Sources of the Nile, around the Great Lakes of Equatorial Africa, and down the Livingstone River to the Atlantic Ocean*. By the time Nellie Arnott reached Angola, Joseph Conrad's *Heart of Darkness* had been in print for several years. Thus, a discourse depicting Africa as remote yet fascinating, dangerous yet enthralling, was already circulating in the larger culture.[12]

Missionary travel writing about Africa had a special appeal for Arnott's social group. The renowned David Livingstone had drawn many English and American readers to the subject with publications like the multivolume *Missionary Travels and Researches in South Africa*, appearing originally in 1857. Livingstone himself was a touchstone.[13] Reissuings and extensions of his earliest writings (such as *The Life and African Explorations of David Livingstone*, published in the U.S. in 1874) fed a persistent mythology. Allusions to his work abound in mission literature well on into the twentieth century. As early as 1858, a review in *Harper's* positioned Livingstone as more of a secular, progressive leader than a dedicated missionary society functionary, and Livingstone himself had increasingly distanced his own view of mission service from that of the London Missionary Society. Yet, later movement authors continued to tout him as a role model both for his religious service and for his abilities as an interpreter of African culture. A major dimension of Livingstone's appeal, for those closely affiliated with the mission movement as well as for general, more secularly oriented readers, was the heroic persona of an explorer taming the vast landscape of Africa. Indeed, though the title of Livingstone's first book highlights his "Missionary" identity in its initial adjective, the "Travels and Researches," rather than preaching and teaching, claim most of the textual space.[14] Given this role model, we should not be surprised to see echoes of secular heroism in some stories about male missionaries who served in Arnott's cohort—traces of Livingstone-the-manly-explorer taking precedence over Livingstone-the-minister in accounts of ABCFM male ministers' hunting expeditions or their sage and forceful management of both native and Portuguese leaders.[15]

More than to Livingstone, Nellie Arnott was drawn to Frederick Stanley Arnot (no relation), another manly missionary who began writing on Africa in the 1880s. She had the good fortune to meet Arnot during her journey to Angola, and she viewed him primarily as a spiritual leader. Significantly, though, whereas she focused on his religious energy in writing about him, Arnot himself had embraced recognition as an explorer as well as a minister, as seen in an 1889 address to the Royal Geographical Society on his travels from Natal to Bié and Benguela.[16] The narrative content and diction of Arnot's published talk exemplified a lingering tendency among male missionary travel authors to blend their religious mandate with adventures à la Livingstone. Arnot described himself as inspired, while still "quite a child" in 1864, by hearing Livingstone speak "in a school in Hamilton."[17] He reinforced his affiliation with the Livingstone model by stressing links between work "to establish a station in a healthy part of the interior" and forays around the African region where Nellie Arnott would later serve. Arnot's audience certainly affirmed this framework. The first respondent, a "Rev. Horace Waller," declared that "Mr. Arnot had followed in the footsteps of Livingstone" by successfully charting important new areas of Africa. In further dialogue after the address itself, other audience members repeatedly linked Arnot's report with Livingstone's explorations, noting how both men embodied "British pluck" in the face of daunting physical challenges.[18]

Texts like David Livingstone's and F. S. Arnot's provide an important context for reading the public writing of Nellie Arnott. Protestant women's publications on foreign mission service would both align with the heritage of admired male authors like Livingstone and show how women's overseas work contrasted with men's, a crucial move for delineating a special role in the enterprise. Indeed, by the time Arnott was writing for periodicals like *Mission Studies* and *Life and Light*, subgenre patterns linked to gender differences were as strong as those associated with the shared, cross-gender aims of the mission movement.

These rhetorical distinctions were consistent with contrasts between men's and women's travel writing in a broader genre framework. As Mary Suzanne Schriber has noted, beginning in the nineteenth century, "women took hold of the conventions of the [travel literature] genre as developed by men, historically the world's travelers and travel writers by privilege of their gender, and turned them to their own purposes."[19] Claiming travel literature as a women's genre not only involved transporting features from other literary forms already established as appropriately feminine (such as sentimental and didactic stories) but also included strategies such as satirically resisting stereotypes of lady travelers and reconfiguring features of men's travel texts.

Taking on what had been a male genre could be challenging. As Kristi Siegel has explained, there was a delicate balance between generating "material that was reasonably exciting" and needing "to remain a lady." Accordingly, Siegel suggests women authors "strained the conventions of femininity, but did not break them."[20] Mary Gaunt exemplifies this negotiation process in *Alone in West Africa*, based on a 1911 journey. Gaunt's narrative about visiting Liberia blends a sentimentalized critique of U.S. slavery with a historical synopsis of America's founding of its African colony (which the author associates with the movement to "return" blacks to Africa). Her account of conversations with her ship's captain (who discouraged her from going ashore at the capital, Monrovia) and with the consul (who provided the most genteel tour of the city possible) demonstrate the position a woman writing on Africa in Arnott's day had to assume, navigating between intrepid traveler and well-bred lady.[21]

Based on a survey of numerous women's texts on Africa composed between the time of the first missionaries and the era of independence for former colonies, Patricia W. Romero posits several notable differences between men's and women's reports on African travel: "For women travelers accent [is] on detail; intensity of individual experiences; empathy for some people; criticisms of others." Romero argues that "Men travelers in Africa doted on describing their heroic exploits (sometimes with exaggeration) as well as the mountains, lakes, and savannah," whereas a woman writer's account would focus on specific flora and fauna when treating the natural setting and on ongoing interpersonal relationships more than on impressive exploits.[22] Where

Figure 8: Arnott (left, in a tepoia) and Mrs. [Elisabeth] Ennis in a bush-cart. Courtesy of The Bancroft Library, University of California, Berkeley.

men travel writers would depict problems as solved and obstacles as conquered, women were more open to fluidity and uncertainty. These general differences between men's and women's travel writing were certainly borne out in missionary texts from Arnott's day and in her own writing.

An equally important lens for evaluating Arnott's work sets up contrasts in another direction—between writing by mission women who lived overseas for an extended period and publications by women operating from a more secular and less embedded perspective. Cheryl McEwan has pointed to salient differences between writing on Africa by Mary Kingsley (*Travels in West Africa*, 1897) and Constance Larymore (*A Resident's Wife in Nigeria*, 1908) on the one hand and by the Scottish missionary Mary Slessor on the other. (Slessor served in the Calabar region of Nigeria from 1876 to 1915 and wrote for journals such as *Missionary Record* and *Women's Missionary Magazine*.) McEwan cites Kingsley and Larymore as examples of British women travel authors' frequent tendency to cast Africans as anonymous, negative stereotypes rather than as individuals. These depictions were consistent, McEwan suggests, with an authorial stance framed as observing instead of affiliating—i.e., written as "detached" and "objective" instead of empathetic. In contrast, McEwan argues, Mary Slessor, who "came to identify Calabar as 'home,'" viewed West African women as allies with individual identities and positioned herself as respecting African customs even while striving to bring her neighbors into Christian allegiance.[23] In highlighting Slessor's stance, McEwan resists simplistic conflations of missionaries' work with imperial agendas. By extension, this analysis demonstrates that we need to read each missionary woman author not only as influenced by discursive conventions and beliefs associated with her organization's goals but also as an individual rhetor capable of carving out a distinctive standpoint. Nellie Arnott never went so far as Mary Slessor in affiliating with local African culture or in resisting guidance from her sponsoring organization. (Slessor moved far into the interior of Nigeria, away from the mission administration's reach, and even achieved economic independence by building a trading system). But as we shall see later in this chapter, Arnott did develop a perspective more progressive than some earlier-generation women affiliated with her station. In addition, Arnott eventually used her writing about Africa to seek expanded authority for ABCFM women's missionary work and enhanced opportunities for the Umbundu people themselves.

Nellie Arnott as a Character in Mission Literature

The discourse community to which Arnott belonged cut across geographic and temporal boundaries by bringing together thousands of readers. The texts they exchanged provided ongoing guidance for movement members at home and abroad. If shared literacy practices shaped the movement, though, the movement also shaped its published texts. These white middle-class women shared a spiritual vision based on transnational religious work, an ideology that left its mark on their texts' content, structure, diction, tone, and even strategies for visual design. To illuminate this connection, we will preface our analysis of writing *by* Nellie Arnott with discussion of missionary magazine publications *about* her. Genre-based features of Arnott as a literary figure would carry over into her own compositions as she depicted herself in ways consistent with the character readers had come to know in stories about her. Though certainly far less renowned than Livingstone, Arnott and other women serving at ABCFM stations were very well known to their own readership. Establishing dedicated servants like Arnott as familiar friends with whom the audience could identify supported the movement's goals while also influencing its literature.

Like other authors crafting accounts of women's work at foreign stations, ABCFM writers associated mission service with an idealized Christian motherhood.[24] We can see this characterization process beginning very early in the development of mission literature about Arnott cast as a motherly Christian traveler enlightening and domesticating her work site.[25] A 1905 *Missionary Herald* piece announced:

> The first new missionary sent out by the Board in 1905 is Miss Nellie J. Arnott, who sailed from Boston April 25, in company with Rev. and Mrs. William H. Sanders, who were returning to the West Central African Mission. Miss Arnott was born in Minneapolis, but her parents have since resided in Iowa. Her studies were pursued in Nashua, Io., and in the Bible Institute at Chicago. She has taught in connection with the schools of the American Missionary Association for five years—two years at Savannah, Ga., and three years at Meridian, Miss. In one of these schools, she was an associate of Miss Stimpson, now of Kamundongo, West Africa, and the two have long desired

to work together under the American Board. This reinforcement for the West Central African Mission has been greatly needed, and Miss Arnott carries out a long cherished wish to enter upon mission work in Africa.[26]

Even in this brief profile, the *Missionary Herald*'s seemingly straightforward report emphasizes aspects of Arnott's biography that

Figure 9: Arnott's official ABCFM photograph. Courtesy of The Bancroft Library, University of California, Berkeley.

would have resonated with ideals of American motherhood as they were then being adapted for single women in foreign mission service. Arnott appears as a woman well educated, already experienced in mission teaching, and now ready for a new pedagogical assignment consistent with feminized Christian values. The report includes a catalog of Arnott's past schooling at Moody Bible Institute and her teaching for the AMA, whose educational programs would have been highly regarded by the *Herald*'s readers. The sketch points to her prior AMA-based ties to Sarah Stimpson, who would have already been well known among the periodical's readership. School teaching itself would have been a highly coded reference. As the first profession open to women in the nineteenth century, teaching was, by the turn into the 1900s, thoroughly feminized; the percentage of positions had shifted to well over two thirds female, and the discourse that had helped make that shift possible also continually reinscribed connections between teaching and motherly, benevolent work. By describing Arnott's journey to the West Central African Mission as the fulfillment of "a long cherished wish," the article also associates her personal story with a plotline familiar to the periodical's readers, who could have easily matched this goal with the photograph of "Miss Nellie J. Arnott" reproduced just above this text—a portrait emphasizing her proper womanliness in attire, hairstyle, and pose ("Recruit" 267).

Depictions of Arnott as a capable yet highly feminized mission worker continued in the reports published about her throughout her stay in Angola. Sometimes addressing readers directly as "you," a narrative about Arnott was also, implicitly, about the shared values being developed among the mothers, teachers, and children studying the exemplary life of this faraway missionary. "At Kamundongo," a 1908 *Mission Studies* piece, designates her as "your own missionary in Africa, Miss Nellie Arnott," stressing bonds between her service and her supporters at home. Emphasizing the crucial role that missionary women were playing in carrying American civilization to peoples otherwise lost to Christian values, this sketch noted: "She has been there three years and has learned the strange language and can speak to the people and teach the boys and girls. Of course you know that before the missionaries go to them[,] the people of Africa have no books, no letters and no schools."[27]

Typical of stories on women missionaries at work, this update on Arnott's activities seems straightforward on the surface but actually navigates a number of complex issues of gender and cross-cultural relationships. A number of genre patterns in these mission magazine stories were adapted from nineteenth-century American domestic literacy narratives, which depicted women's motherly teaching in home-based and home-oriented settings as crucial cultural work.[28] In that vein, finessing ongoing questions about prioritizing the evangelical and service dimensions of missionary action, this text's implicit contrast between "the people of Africa" before and after ABCFM engagement there temporarily suspends questions about how the activities of women teaching at mission stations could best complement the gendered ministerial activities of male missionaries. Foregrounding "books" and "schools" for the moment, the account celebrates appropriately feminized pedagogical work in this foreign mission setting. The story's portrayal of Arnott as now ably running a large school, partly because she can rely on local helpers, skirts a related, complicated element in her situational context. Her aides are "some Christian young men . . . who have themselves been taught in such schools." By invoking rhetorical patterns long established in domestic literacy narratives about school teaching—particularly that genre's idealized visions of motherly teachers guiding male learners—this report adroitly copes with (and even capitalizes on) the otherwise troubling scenario of a single American woman interacting closely with African males. Rather than portraying the young men of Kamundongo as savage brutes or pitiful victims (two of the stereotypes circulating in many of the travel narratives on Africa at this time), this story trumpets how, "having learned to read and write and live better lives themselves, they are glad to teach their own people."[29] Behind the portrait of these now-capable local African teachers, of course, is the enlightened teaching of motherly Nellie Arnott, who has transformed these young men so that they can lead others to a Christian path.

Teaching in Africa may seem to be a radical departure from ideals of true womanhood. But mission magazines positioned such work within the context of the domestic pedagogical tradition whereby mothers influenced the larger society through educating their children and motherly schoolteachers exercised comparable power through guiding their students. By Arnott's day, domestic literacy narratives' plots and characterizations had long been appearing in travel writing depicting women's foreign mission work as consistent with conservative views of American women's proper social role.[30] Writers limned schools run by women missionaries as transplanting American social practices and religious vision along with literacy skills. For example, this "At Kamundongo" article points out, "The schools begin in the fall and close in the spring at about the same time yours do," and the students study "the Bible and Pilgrim's Progress" once they have progressed beyond "the blackboard" and primers. Practicing their "writing and arithmetic" while memorizing "many psalms and hymns," the story explains, these students are experiencing the same basic curriculum as white middle-class American children.

Meanwhile, the narrative does acknowledge how challenging it was for Arnott to learn "the strange language"—a process viewed by the ABCFM as necessary for effective teaching. Here too, the apparently straightforward reporting skims over what was actually a complex matter: in choosing to teach in the Angolans' native language (as outlined in Chapter 2), ABCFM mission educators like Arnott and her colleagues allied themselves with their students as opposed to the Portuguese, who were seeking political control of the region and who would eventually enforce the use of their European language in colonized education settings. For Arnott's readers, though, this alliance is framed in domestic rather than political terms.

Counterbalancing the rhetorical spin associating Arnott's mission work with American domestic(ated) teaching, an equally persistent trend in this writing emphasized difference and distance while weaving in vicarious journeys for readers. So, for example, the 1908 magazine piece referenced above described the "heavy rains in Africa" that sometimes made it "impossible" to hold school sessions. Similarly, a pronunciation and location guide at the end of the core article marked the exotic nature of the setting. In an appendix, a curriculum for studying Arnott's mission station recommended acquiring a good map "from Rand McNally & Co. 160 Adams St., Chicago, for 25 cts. each" and yoking this study to "school geographies" (L.L., "At Kamundongo," 252). In inviting children to study Arnott's story, *Mission Studies* envisioned both those young readers and the U.S.-based, maternal adult "you" addressed as their teacher as taking an imaginative journey of their own by way of this curriculum.

Significantly, of course, traveling to Africa by reading about it is far less daunting an enterprise than actually going there. In this regard, we might consider an analogy between Arnott's riding in a tepoia (or hammock-like carrier) and a reader's being "carried" through this text to get a view of the Angolan highlands. Somebody else is doing the hard work, and the passenger is getting only a limited view. At the same time, however, the directions provided for this imaginary trek do at least encourage readers (in this case, white American middle-class teachers and their students) to place themselves in a new and different environment and to project themselves toward becoming real travelers:

> Invite the children to go on a long trip with you. . . . , and as a large part of the trip will be by water those who have sailor suits might wear them. . . . Tell the children you are going to take them on a trip to see their missionary in Africa, Miss Nellie J. Arnott, of Kamundongo. Ask if they can remember any Bible characters who journeyed to Africa (Abraham, Joseph, his brethren, etc.) and for the Scripture lessons read Matt. 2:1–15.
>
> Now let them start on their own journey—to New York by rail, then by boat to Lisbon, changing there to a Portuguese steamer bound for Benguella, 860 miles south of the Equator on the west coast of Africa. . . .
>
> If you can get hold of any pictures illustrating life in West Central Africa so much the better. ("At Kamundongo," 252)

Miss May J. Johnston presented a parallel story for the Young People's Department of *Mission Studies* in October 1908, several months after "At Kamundongo" had appeared in the same publication. Johnston's piece offered a blend of affiliating and distancing strategies. In Johnston's "A Trip to Kamundongo and Ochileso," we see an extended travel metaphor developed to draw young readers into study of African mission work with Johnston casting herself as fellow traveler. Here, the imaginary, shared journey is framed initially as a pleasant excursion with picturesque sights worthy of being chronicled in a tourist guidebook. "A trip to Africa? Yes, indeed, we'll go," the article declares. "We young people are ready to go anywhere, anytime. Moreover Africa promises to be a fashionable ex-official resort" (307). Johnston describes the first stage of the journey—its multiple sea voyages—in language reminiscent of tourist memoirs: "Our first campagnon de voyage is old Father Neptune, who for a month entertains us as we sail to Liverpool, Lisbon, and finally Benguella. . . ." (307). But she hints at a theme of difference that will emerge more forcefully later in the text when she adds a qualifier to describe Benguella as "on the coast of the Dark Continent, 12°, which is eight hundred miles south of the equator." With its views of "ravines" full of wild animals and "a robber tribe of men," the ride by "hammock-like tepoia" from "the malarial coast" also invokes distance and difference. Once readers arrive at the ABCFM station, Johnston shifts her rhetoric to suggest how this site offers a promising ground for missionary work. She characterizes the area as "situated in a beautiful well-watered region" and worthy of inclusion in a "Baedeker" (a familiar brand of tourist guide in this era). At the same time, by saying that "our Baedeker" is actually "as yet unwritten," she conjures up the place as still remote and underdeveloped.

In Johnston's text, the village of Kamundongo and surrounding areas embody cross-cultural interaction. While a strong narrative line emphasizes the positive impact of the missionaries' work, an equally persistent subtext acknowledges ways in which the values of the local community continue to shape daily life. Tracing this tension throughout Johnston's narrative, we recognize the complex framework into which Arnott would need to position her own writings. For example, Johnston declares that the people of Kamundongo "[f]ormerly" lived "in one-room huts, mudded and thatched, with one door and no window," but that they now have "a village of straight, clean streets, and neat, wattled houses with grass roofs and an adjoining garden" thanks to the guidance of the missionary team.[31] The local people are "great travelers," participating in caravans that help bring Christianity to a people Johnston characterizes as from "the Bantu family of the brown race," an "erect, well formed" group "with regular features, kindly disposed and intelligent." However, even in this Christianized village, troubling signs of the pre-mission past persist as unconverted villagers remain caught up in "fetishism, superstition and witchcraft": "men and women are tortured, poisoned, tried by fire and killed in the belief they have caused another's death by sorcery." In contrasting the still-unconverted dimensions of the community with the order evident in the "missionary compounds" (including "a church, school house, cloth house, press house, missionary and girls' home"), Johnston underlines both material features (such as sun-dried bricks and shiny windows) and social practices reflecting Christianity's power. In school, she explains, the young children here are learning from their capable teacher, Miss Arnott, with the curriculum including "sewing, weaving, clay work, songs and games, just as . . . in America" (308). At the same time, however, Johnston reports that although Mrs. Sanders tries to teach the adults basic medical care, "The ignorance and need of the people" are "appalling" (308).

As in Arnott's own publications, Johnston seeks a tricky balance in her characterizations. Johnston praises the progress already made in evangelizing the local people, but she also points insistently at work still to be done. Given the mandate mission movement publications faced for raising funds, this approach is certainly strategic. Readers wanted to know that contributions (financial, personal, and otherwise) already made were having the desired effect. However, they also needed to be reminded how crucial their future donations could be to the cause. Over time, Arnott's own writing would gradually place a greater focus on the capabilities of the local people than on the deficiencies of pre-Christian society in the places where she worked. This discursive gap, as outlined in our introduction, would not only mark some distance between her writing and that prepared by home-based interpreters of her mission service but also a contrast between her early and later writing on Africa.

Meanwhile, additional articles in *Mission Studies* would extend the portrait of Arnott while continuing to emphasize her identity as a motherly traveler, carrying Christianity to even more places, formerly isolated but now possible to serve through her presence. Like the articles reviewed above, these texts wavered back and forth between celebrating successes already achieved and delineating unfinished work. In September of 1909, for instance, a brief piece on "Miss Arnott's Schools" described her increasing efforts to train "native young men, who work earnestly and faithfully" teaching at remote outstations but who were clearly dependent on Nellie Arnott's willingness to travel from location to location, providing guidance and "sometimes staying six weeks at an out-station far from any other white person" so as to extend her mission station's impact. "Are we not thankful to help such a missionary?" this article asked just below a reprint of Arnott's mission service photograph. In an unsigned story for the Children's Work section of *Mission Studies* appearing later that fall, Arnott herself again claimed center stage. Adapting techniques already identified in Johnston's essay of the previous year, this narrative explicitly called on "children" to revisit the long "journey" of "our missionary, Miss Nellie Arnott," from the U.S. to Africa, this time in even more detail. While stressing that Kamundongo "is so far" away and "so hard to reach" that readers would "never go there" in person, the unnamed author still declared that "the little children in the central western part of Africa" were actually learning "many of the things you are learning" thanks to their missionary teacher.[32] Echoing several other reports on the widening circle of Arnott's influence, this article reminded readers:

> Those that live in the villages far away cannot come to Miss Arnott's school, so she has been teaching some of the big boys so that they may teach the little ones to read and write. Then they go to one of these little villages and try to have a school just as much like Miss Arnott's as they can. But, alas! They do not know how as well as she does.
>
> I think if we ask her she will take us with her to one of these little schools that was begun last November. She has a very large native house for a school room built of sticks and mudded inside, with a thatched roof. . . .
>
> There are several such schools in the villages near Kamundongo and Miss Arnott goes from village to village to visit these schools. Sometimes she stays three or four weeks in a village, when it is a long way from Kamundongo, and then she lives in a native hut, too. (345)

Envisioning Arnott as a benevolent itinerant teacher and Africa as her needy student, such texts invited readers to share in her journeys—both the literal trips to outstations around Kamundongo and her progressive journey of professional and spiritual development. To create an admirable figure with whom the periodical's audience could easily identify, stories about Arnott reinforced familiar features of the motherly missionary character. As a reader of these texts herself, Arnott would draw on their models in her own writing, and her editors back in the U.S. would encourage this interactive process in the ways they managed her texts.

Arnott's Contributions to WBMI Reports

Over the years of her service in Angola, we regularly see Nellie Arnott's own words woven into annual reports of the Woman's Board of

Missions of the Interior (WBMI), the mission support organization founded in 1868 and headquartered in Chicago. As a women's arm of the ABCFM, the WBMI cosponsored Arnott's mission service. Thus, the documents of this highly gendered organization provide a valuable window into her position within a larger social enterprise highly dependent on its publications network. The reports also reflect how the collaborative process that continually reinforced traits of women's mission literature was as dependent on U.S.-based editors as on authors stationed overseas.

Beginning in the 1905 year-end report, in its brief mention of Nellie Arnott's arrival at the West Africa station of Kamundongo, the WBMI signaled the degree to which her writing home to supporters was an expected element in her job as a woman missionary. Reminding readers that Sarah Stimpson had been faithfully working as the sole teacher at the Kamundongo station, the report dubbed the arrival of Arnott with Reverend and Mrs. Sanders an exciting moment: "How happy she [Stimpson] must have been to see our dear Miss Arnott." Then, in appending the promise that WBMI supporters would "soon be hearing" from Arnott about her work, the editor alerted the organization's members that a new voice would now be sending dispatches from Africa.[33]

The editors of these official documents were accomplished writers in their own right. They were skilled at synthesizing reports from scores of correspondents stationed all over the globe into an overarching narrative aimed at guaranteeing involvement by American women at home. Of course, for these official accounts to be created and circulated, individual missionaries like Arnott and her colleagues in West Africa had to send in their own submissions, and that writing needed to fit the expectations of the community of readers the editors cultivated. Accordingly, in the 1906 report, editor Mrs. Joseph B. Leake drew on materials from Miss Emma Redick and Mrs. M. M. Webster, as well as from Nellie Arnott, to offer readers an appealing picture of the work in Angola. Describing a new school's impressive structure, the section on Kamundongo (based on materials from Arnott) explained that building this essential facility "cost about $300." Chronicling expanded outstation activities made possible by Arnott's having joined the team there, the report also emphasized that a young male "native teacher" was applying approaches learned from the recent arrival and her colleagues. These lessons were implicitly bound to familiar American ideology for feminized teaching's outward-reaching influence by casting the new Umbundu teacher as "go[ing] to read and explain a Bible lesson and [to] have songs and prayers" with potential converts. Reiterating the benefit of adding another missionary to the team, the report cited impressive attendance figures at services and portrayed Nellie Arnott as making progress in her language study since she "must be able to do more than to sing with them, the desire of her heart having been to be able to talk with them and lead them heavenward."[34]

By 1907, the annual report indicated Arnott was still finding language learning challenging, but she described herself as "'well and happy.'" The report also integrated into its larger narrative on Africa her account of teaching local children the story of Christmas and the Christ-child partly by using "pictures" that would help them "get hold of the real Christmas thought." Drawing directly from one of Arnott's own submissions, the editor shared an appealing portrayal of the holiday celebration: "'On Christmas Day I had all the children on the Station here for a feast. Seventy-two children sat down at tables in the yard.'"[35]

Again assigned the byline for the "Africa" section of the report in 1908, Mrs. Joseph B. Leake brought together a range of material from Arnott and other West Africa colleagues. This time, alongside the number of students in weekday school and in catechism classes, the overview gave data on hymnals printed by the station press—another sign of progress. But Arnott's voice was invoked to stress how much work remained to be done. Leake noted that "Miss Arnott, in writing of the sore need of re-enforcement in the Africa mission, quotes, 'Long delays on God's part involve no forgetfulness of His promises. When the destined moment comes, no good thing will fail, of all that He hath spoken.'"[36] Since God would never forsake His missionaries, this Biblical reference implies, shortcomings in achieving the work must be due to recalcitrance among mission supporters in the U.S., who still had time to remedy the situation.

In these WBMI annual reports, where excerpts from individual missionaries' submissions became part of a larger textual pastiche, we gain a strong sense of how rhetorical conventions helped unite the organization's widely dispersed writers and readers. Content and diction from authors in other WBMI-supported locales echoed contributions from Arnott and her Angola-based colleagues. Reappearing regularly over many years, the names of specific editors and writers became familiar to every reader even as the textual features the authors used accentuated gendered affiliation over individualized identity.

One important dimension of this community-building resided in the print medium itself. With business-like design, attentive editing, and regularized presentation sequences for their recurring topics, the WBMI annual reports affirmed the maturity of the organization. Like the printed annual reports prepared for many middle-class American women's clubs during this same era, the formal publications of groups like the WBMI promoted solidarity by embodying language skill, seriousness, and effective management principles in the medium then most effective for promoting long-distance affiliation associated, more recently, with media such as radio, television, and the internet. Using their literacy to fortify their network, women like Arnott simultaneously strengthened their sense of gendered social efficacy.[37]

Gender, Colonial Discourse, and Mission Magazines

Like the multi-vocal WBMI annual reports, the periodicals where Arnott published her own single-author stories played a key role in the foreign mission network's public relations agenda. Both *Life and Light* (headquartered in Boston and aimed at women readers in New England and the northeast) and *Mission Studies* (based in Chicago and addressing women in the midwestern states), her two major publishing venues, focused on women missionaries.[38] Whereas WBMI annual reports briefly summarized the key events in many regions over a full year, women's mission magazines offered longer narrative accounts inviting readers to journey, imaginatively, to a particular mission site. These stories placed a high premium on personalizing particular missionaries, rendering the location of their service in compelling terms and making the case for that station's current needs. In addition, while the annual reports of the WBMI took on the official tone and features also typical of *Missionary Herald* (an ABCFM publication aiming for mixed-gender readership), the narratives in publications like *Mission Studies* made their gender affiliation paramount.

"Our Literature," an article in the September 1910 issue of *Mission Studies*, makes the distinction between women's and mixed-gender publications quite explicit:

The Woman's Board of Missions of the Interior publishes a monthly periodical called MISSION STUDIES. . . . The purpose of MISSION STUDIES is to acquaint the women of our Congregational churches with the work which is being carried on among the women and children of Christless lands and their need. The magazine contains short, crisp articles, showing the conditions abroad and their rapid change; letters from missionaries showing progress in their respective fields; information about the Home Department of the Board; and attractive pictures of foreign life. Those who contribute to Foreign Missions should read it to see where their money goes.[39] Those who do not contribute can scarcely resist its mute appeal as they learn of the condition of other women and children whom Christ loves but who have no knowledge of that Love.[40]

Highlighting the WBMI's commitment to reaching the "Christless," this description of *Mission Studies* presents one important rationale that women's groups often gave for maintaining an identity distinct from the larger shared goal of men and women working together in mission service. Specifically, "the women and children" in mission fields had particular needs that women were best suited to address; meanwhile, women at home could contribute in gendered ways too, such as teaching children about the enterprise. Women's engagement in the mission movement was to be a collaborative endeavor supported by women's publishing.

In declaring that *Mission Studies* would report specifically about "the work" being done by women missionaries, "Our Literature" identified one dimension of the periodical's focus. Another important element, announced in the same sentence, was the "need" being addressed by the movement—that is, the rationale driving the work. The theme of "need" actually ran throughout writing for women's mission publications, ranging from the letters field workers sent to would-be donors, to short leaflets describing the desperate situation of "the heathen," to extended periodical accounts from particular locales. This theme provided one strategy for adapting travel writing's and sentimentalism's literary conventions to an evangelical goal by linking *need* to *difference* and soliciting affective responses from readers. For Arnott and other writers involved in her literacy community, *need* actually applied both to the white middle-class American women involved in the movement and to the people foreign missionaries aimed to serve. Texts Arnott created for mission magazines and her letters to supporters addressed the needs of white middle-class Protestant women in the U.S. by underscoring the benefits they could accrue from spiritual service. Rhetorical patterns in narratives for these audiences established equivalencies between missionaries abroad and supporters at home.[41]

One equivalency argument focused on women donors. Arnott often used this technique at the beginning or end of an article, depicting the funds that supporters should send as absolutely essential. Linking the need that the foreign mission site had for financial support with the ability of women at home to provide aid, such passages suggested that home-based women's donations were as important to the enterprise's success as the activities of women in the field, like Arnott, Sarah Stimpson, and Emma Redick. So, Arnott frequently infused her writing with observations about what the mission could accomplish if given additional personnel and funds. She wrote in "News from Kamundongo" for *Mission Studies* in April 1908, for example, that she had many plans for improving schools and housing for her female students, but "these require time and money, neither of which we have at present." She noted, "[I]f you could only look into one of the heathen villages and see the women and children living in all their dirt and trusting in all their spirits and superstitions, without schools or any kind of knowledge of the Savior who died for them, I'm sure your hearts would be stirred to help them" (106–07).

When we recognize how familiar and appealing this equivalency principle would have been for Protestant women in the U.S., we can appreciate the sophistication of such narrative patterns as inviting readers to go along on an imaginative journey from America to a station or from the main site of mission activity to an outstation. These descriptions helped readers picture the location of a missionary's work, and they also tied into the equivalency principle's system of shared identification and gendered Christian service. Strengthening the financial and spiritual power of the women's foreign mission network, these motifs also established genre conventions that, in turn, reinforced movement ideology.

This ongoing community-building enterprise was closely connected to the "imagined communities" of national identity that Benedict

Anderson has explained were crystallizing beginning in the nineteenth century, with mechanisms like print culture playing a pivotal role. As women read (and/or wrote for) such publications as *Mission Studies* or *Life and Light* and connected with each other through the medium of print, they overcame separations of geography and time to achieve mutual identification based in gendered, collaborative benevolence.[42] In this case, print texts sought to capitalize on U.S.-based women's affiliation with an increasingly forceful vision of the nation as extending influence on a far-reaching international scale and to reinforce their commitment to a transnational agenda of Christian service with highly gendered dimensions.

Significantly, however, the imagined community of women in mission (both women missionaries and women supporters) was also dependent on another dimension in their rhetoric: limning the local people around the foreign mission station as needing the movement's cultural intervention in the first place. Here, in the published texts by mission authors like Nellie Arnott, we see related discursive conventions that synthesize techniques from imperial-era travel writing and sentimental literature, envisioning social outreach by women as a "traveling" extension of their domestic teaching role (as in the domestic literacy narratives referenced above) but with complex linkages to Euro-American colonial discourse also coming into play.

One stock-in-trade plot element was the conversion story demonstrating that the native's need to be saved had been met by the missionary enabled by her home-based supporters. Perhaps Arnott's most compelling example was her account of Chief Kanjundu, who "brought his fetishes to be burned, put away all of his wives but one, and became a Christian," after which he "built a church and school house in his village" and even learned to read. Enduring false imprisonment at the hands of the Portuguese, he was eventually acquitted and, upon returning home, "gave all his slaves their liberty, although since being a Christian he had treated them as children rather than slaves."[43]

Variations on the conversion storyline include the saved native redeeming others—and being able to do so because of learning from the woman missionary and her network—along with accounts describing the site of missionary intervention as achieving a new, Christian identity uplifted from its previous precarious existence. In Arnott's writing, we see an example of the first plotline in the story of the young boy Fumika in *Mission Studies* in May 1910. Fumika's parents "told him sickness and trouble would come to him" if he attended the mission school. Yet, according to Arnott, he persisted in his education. He eventually became an outstation teacher and converted several family members to Christianity. An example of the second motif occurs in Arnott's account of the Umbundu girl Cipuku. When Cipuku's father chose an unacceptable husband for her, she escaped to the mission and eventually married a Christian. Based on Cipuku's success, her sisters also overcame harassment and an attempted kidnapping by a brother by fleeing to the mission. Arnott depicts the Kamundongo station itself as a haven for imperiled young women, who, she suggests, needed a boarding school to ensure full safety—vital protection only her readers had the power to give.[44]

Stories like these brought together the home-based woman supporter of the movement, the missionary living abroad, and the site of intervention (physical locale and/or people). Using an explicit or implicit "endeavor-in-jeopardy" scenario, a mission movement author like Arnott would first convey a challenging problem and then communicate how the help of women living in the U.S. could address it. This network of home-based supporter, mission site, and missionary was also, by extension, reconfiguring conceptions of travel to erase the reader's need for actual in-person journeys overseas. Missionaries, mission supporters, and the objects of their evangelical benevolence all came together in a shared spiritual space created in writing.

Around this nexus of need, links between foreign mission publications like Arnott's and the broadly circulating colonial discourse of her era are crucial to acknowledge. Even though she and her colleagues viewed their work in community-building terms, and despite her particular station's ongoing conflicts with the Portuguese attempting to control the Angolan highlands, such tropes invoke core features of colonial rhetoric, thereby reinforcing hierarchies associated with the more political versions of cross-cultural intervention. In particular, postcolonial critics have decried the longstanding impact of such texts on the very people a missionary sought to "save." To construct the object of social intervention as helpless—indeed, doomed—without the righteous intervention envisioned in mission discourse is to establish a framework for future thinking, doing, and interacting that constrains those on both sides of the equation. African authors such as Ngũgĩ wa Thiong'o, who has thoughtfully drawn on histories of African mission pedagogy in his work, are prominent voices around these points.[45] In situating Arnott's magazine writing within a rhetorical context of colonial discourse, we join other scholars who have called for analyses of colonialism as a cultural (i.e., broader than a political) phenomenon in which discourse plays a central part. As outlined in our introduction and in Chapter 2, reading Arnott's writings as representations of experience for a particular audience rather than as transparent records offers an approach for addressing what we have called the discursive gap between actual everyday life and movement-shaped narratives.

Along those lines, when positioning decades' worth of American women's foreign mission texts within the broader category of travel writing, Mary Suzanne Schriber discerns a recurring insistence on cultural hierarchy: "Missionary accounts," she finds, "are exercises in colonizing and 'othering,' authorized by belief in the absolute truth of Christianity and the superiority of the United States, understood as the apex of civilization, Protestant and Anglo-Saxon."[46] Similarly, Nicholas Thomas, surveying an array of materials (such as photos as well as print texts) from both the Pacific and African theaters, has tracked recurring rhetorical patterns in British mission literature associated with a pervasive colonial culture, including dramatizations of "savagery or heathenism," "the before-after narrative," "infantilization of the indigenous people," and a related "discourse of racial types."[47] So, too, David Spurr has suggested that studies of colonial discourse should broaden the frame of analysis, "explod[ing] . . . categories of genre in the effort to seize hold of a more global system of representation." For Spurr, a central question to ask about colonial discourse is "how writing works, in whatever form, to produce knowledge about other cultures," with a broad array of texts included under the rubric of writing (Spurr, *The Rhetoric of Empire*, 10–11). Such calls to expand and complicate our interpretation of colonial discourse are particularly relevant for studying a missionary author like Nellie Arnott. Considering "discourse" as our purview, we should contextualize Arnott's print texts within a more extensive compositional framework, including not only her own diaries and scrapbooks but also such material culture "writing" as her helping redesign village sites into neat, orderly patterns that would undo the local (mis)arrangements missionaries equated with uncivilized behavior. (See, in this regard, the description of reformed native space in Miss May J. Johnston's "A Trip to Kamundongo and Ochileso," referenced earlier in this chapter. See also Chapter 2's discussion of layouts for traditional Umbundu villages versus Christianized ones.)

Taken altogether, Nellie Arnott's texts reflect a hierarchical stance consistent with colonialism's *ethos*—though not as consistently as the sweeping characterizations of mission writing by Schriber and Thomas would suggest. Intriguingly, in her private diary writing and correspondence, we can trace a decided shift over time in her depictions of the Umbundu people with whom she worked—including a deep affection for particular individuals and an associated valuing, however limited, of the local culture as expressed in everyday practices.[48] Letters former students sent to Arnott many years after her return to the U.S. verify that the bonds of affection evident in her own writing were hardly one-sided.[49] However, even after many years in Angola and even though she had developed such treasured personal relationships, Arnott continued to invoke such terms as "heathen" when referencing Africans she did not know personally; furthermore, her appreciation of some social practices (such as Umbundu women's interactions with their young children) did not dissuade her from determined critiques of polygyny, alcohol consumption, and food preparation techniques she considered unclean. In addition, Arnott's stories for public consumption by missionary supporters at home in the U.S. continued to utilize techniques such as the "before-and-after" conversion storyline Thomas describes as emphasizing the depravity of a convert's "before" stage.

COMPARATIVE READING OF ARNOTT'S WRITING

One helpful approach for assessing relationships between Arnott's oeuvre and the complicated larger category of colonial discourse is to read her publications for women's mission supporters comparatively. Texts by other women serving at her station are particularly useful points of reference, encouraging us to see Arnott as operating in an approximate middle ground on a continuum ranging from a decidedly colonialist stance (including diction consistent with racial essentialism and racial Darwinism) to a perspective more affirming of local culture and even approaching cultural relativism. Bertha Stover's "Women of West Central Africa" exemplifies one side of that continuum while Elisabeth Ennis's "Umbundu Baby and Its Mother" illustrates a viewpoint nearer the other side. Perhaps unsurprisingly, these two women also embody generational differences that may help explain their contrasting standpoints, with the elder Stover coming from a period before shifts in thinking within the larger context of the WBMI and ABCFM organizations had come to the forefront along with new educational backgrounds among many women missionaries.[50]

Stover and Ennis both overlapped with Arnott in their Angolan service. Stover came to Africa before Arnott as a spousal adjunct, typical of early generations of women foreign missionaries, whereas Ennis (though also a mission wife) arrived later, bringing her own academic preparation for her posting and, with that educational background, a more progressive discourse. Mrs. Stover's long career as a foreign missionary embodied the traditional helpmate model as she supported her husband's preaching with woman's-work-style teaching. As Elisabeth Ennis would observe in her own published history of the ABCFM in Africa, Stover ran "a large Bible class for women" and managed "evangelistic work" aimed exclusively at women in outlying areas.[51] Like other ABCFM women serving overseas, whether married or single, Stover wrote for mission supporters at home in the U.S., and her "Women of West Central Africa" pamphlet epitomized the extreme hierarchical language readers of her generation would have expected in reports of the movement's activities in sites like Angola.

Although Stover began her narrative with rather neutral descriptions of the founding of "The West Central African Mission" in 1881 and the location of the work "in the countries of Bailundu and Bihé," she quickly moved in her second paragraph to characterizations consistent with Schriber's and Thomas's linkages between mission texts and colonial rhetoric: "Here, amidst the squalor of an African village, surrounded by her children, chickens and pigs, we will find the typical Umbundu woman." A little further into her report, Stover forcefully stressed the distance between her American middle-class readers' commitment to an idealized model of (nuclear) familial domesticity and Angolan women's more community-oriented views: "No word for Home exists in the Umbundu language. They always say 'my village,' never 'my home.' These villages are composed of several men with their various wives, children, concubines, and slaves. . . ." With "polygamy . . . the rule," Stover declared, there was "no end of strife and unhappiness." Overall, Stover stressed, before Christian intervention, there was only "utter blankness, desolation, and hopelessness of these lives without the Gospel of Christ!" Accordingly, much of her pamphlet celebrated the "divine ray even in [a local woman's] dark mind," which had been awakened through the Christian mission endeavor in which Stover and her readers were participating. Squalor had been replaced with "whitewashed" walls. "Christian motherhood" was embodied in a new vision: a "neatly dressed, placid-faced woman sitting there" with "no palm oil on her hair," as "she spells out the words of her Sabbath-school lesson, and the little children playing on the floor are singing 'I am so glad that Jesus loves me.'" From Stover's perspective, "Christian homes" were now "lead[ing] into light these who for ages have been groping in darkness."[52]

Elisabeth Ennis, though working in the same Angolan area as Stover and also serving in the capacity of mission wife, brought a different perspective to her assignment and to writing about it. Ennis, who did not come with her husband, Merlin, to Angola until 1907, had studied at Lawrence University, the University of Oregon, and Wellesley College. While her mission movement publications drew on features that had been associated with the literature for many decades, her writing also marked ways in which the rhetoric was evolving to accommodate new perspectives, including a more academic, if not a totally affirming, stance toward local social practices.

Ennis's "The Umbundu Baby and Its Mother" offers a case in point. Even in her opening sentence, she signals one significant shift in perspective, alerting readers that African women should not be carelessly overgeneralized: "Much that may be said of the Umbundu woman is no doubt true of the average African woman, yet tribes quite near each other present many differences and what I shall say here refers only to the women of the Ovimbundu tribe in the uplands of Angola." Highlighting variations across tribal communities, Ennis here adopts a stance avoiding the kind of stereotyping often criticized in colonial discourse. Ennis employs a strategy of affiliation rather than the traditional approach in colonial rhetoric: highlighting difference. Rather than painting Umbundu women as radically different from their American counterparts, she invokes gender solidarity via a women's rights vocabulary consistent with her generation's progressive agenda within the U.S.: "The 'female of the species' is difficult of description, be she militant, domestic or professional, and the Umbundu woman is no exception. I have sometimes thought her the original suffragette." Ennis goes on to admit to "contradictions" within the "character" of Umbundu women, leading them to range between being "spirited and docile, hard-working and easy-going, willing to learn and slow to practice." However, Ennis explains, on balance, Umbundu women exercise great cultural influence her readers should admire: "It is usual for us to look upon the 'heathen' woman as down-trodden, the natural man as the natural woman's oppressor, but I have come to feel the idea quite an erroneous one. True she tills the soil and wins her daily 'mush' by the sweat of her brow, but possessing the key to the granary she possesses the key to the situation, and the Umbundu woman is not the only one who complains over tasks she would not have taken away from her for the world."[53]

For readers schooled in the traditional patterns of women's mission literature, Ennis's pamphlet represents a striking, even if relatively subtle, departure from the rhetoric of earlier-generation authors. Directly rejecting the term "'heathen'" via the use of scare quotes, she likewise terms stereotypes of "down-trodden" women and oppressive native men as "erroneous." Instead, Ennis explains, Umbundu women, though carrying out very different kinds of labor than their American counterparts, hold significant social influence by "possessing the key to the granary," that is, by having control of the vital food resource for the community. In these passages, Ennis clearly alludes to the many previous portrayals of African women in mission literature as oppressed since they were (supposedly) forced to assume responsibility for field work that Americans would deem more appropriately assigned to men. Here, Ennis's cross-cultural vision accommodates the Umbundu woman's duties more positively—even observing that "her conservatism" in this regard (i.e., not adopting Euro-American divisions for gendered labor) is a choice enabling her to serve as "the guardian of the tradition of mothers, the keeper of the sacred fire of tribal life" (2). Viewing "tribal life" as "sacred" is, of course, a telling move on Ennis's part since it signals her openness to synthesizing values and practices honored by the local culture into any Christianizing endeavor. Indeed, though Ennis terms the social vision of Umbundu women "narrow" and asserts that "she is down-trodden in the bonds of her own superstition," this missionary author of a later generation than Bertha Stover constructs conversion goals for the particular Umbundu tribal woman as aiming to "broaden her vision," not to overturn her cultural heritage entirely (3).[54]

Ennis's writing, in contrast to Stover's, anticipates shifts in the culture of the women's mission movement that would reach fuller, more explicit expression in the 1920s. The WBMI, in particular, would become more and more sensitive to potential connections between imperialism and evangelism, according to the organization's historian, Grace T. Davis. Writing about the WBMI's own language practices, Davis would assert that the "very vocabulary" of the annual reports had appropriately changed over the years: "The word 'foreign' may go, and the word 'missionary' may finally go. Certainly we cannot retain it unless we can remove from it any ancient flavor of condescension which it appears to have acquired in many minds." Attributing an increasingly collegial stance to the women's foreign mission enterprise, Davis affirmed a "sense of the value of working together" and noted that "Such words as cooperation, interdenominationalism, internationalism, unification, occur with increasing frequency," as, she claimed, "the word 'heathen' has disappeared," and instead "'Together-'ness is everywhere."[55]

Even in the 1920s, Davis's assessment may have been more aspirational than descriptive. Certainly, in the time frame of Arnott's public mission writings for the venues where her work appeared, a wider range of stances was the norm. Reading authors like Bertha Stover and Elisabeth Ennis—both colleagues in Arnott's area of service—helps delineate that range. The differences in their perspectives remind us that missionary publications in that period were flexible enough to embrace noteworthy internal contradictions and that a gradual movement toward more progressive viewpoints was not fully or even uniformly achieved.[56]

Inconsistencies in Arnott's writing for women in the U.S. are, therefore, consistent with the larger body of evolving mission publications to which she contributed. Though in some cases Arnott moved beyond the language of Bertha Stover's model, she never adopted a perspective akin to Ennis's—at least not in her public writing. Like many missionary teachers—including those working within U.S. geographic borders to "uplift" post-Reconstruction African Americans, to manage Chinese and marginalized European immigrant workers, or to "assimilate" Native Americans during this same era—Nellie Arnott struggled to understand and represent her relationship with the people she viewed herself as serving. Encouraged throughout her life to celebrate Protestant Christianity's superiority and denied the advanced education of college women like Elisabeth Ennis, Arnott would have been unlikely to arrive at a position of cultural relativism—however much she might have come to care for individuals where she was stationed.[57] Trained to write for an audience of readers anticipating constructions of Africa and Africans in line with traditional mission movement ideology, she would have been hard put to reject the literary conventions already established in her regular publication venues. Within this persistent institutional context, therefore, even the partial and unstable changes in stance emerging in some of her public writing over time mark discursive gaps. Overall, therefore, we must accept the fact that Arnott's public texts for women readers, as "colonial discourse," cannot be easily compartmentalized since her writing spanned a number of years, appeared in a wide range of forms, and necessarily addressed audience expectations so influential that we cannot simply equate what she says in a given text with what she feels/believes at the time.

Neither, however, should we assume that her public language masked "true" feelings hiding behind others' conventions. Significantly, the ongoing instability in perspective evident in her published texts is often echoed in her private writing, suggesting that we cannot attribute these lingering inconsistencies to intense audience and genre awareness. For example, in a diary entry on March 29, 1912, as she began the trek from the interior that would carry her home on furlough, Arnott described young Angolan women who came to visit her camp in highly positive terms as "nice looking bright girls," a far cry from the characterizations she had penned in diary pieces composed upon her arrival in Angola years earlier. She hoped her conversation would somehow "linger in their hearts" after this brief encounter. But that same day's entry also chronicled her evening's efforts to read the Bible to the local village "boys" and bearers from a caravan that her traveling group had encountered. They were, she observed, in a familiar yet nonetheless striking phrase, "heathen of the heathen."

WRITING FOR MALE ADMINISTRATORS

As we have pointed out, the complex position of being an American Protestant missionary in a Portuguese Catholic colony should discourage any straightforward equation of Arnott's work in Angola with the European power's imperial agenda there, however much her writing aligned itself with colonial discourse models. Another factor making such a characterization problematic is the gender dynamic at the heart of mission service in Arnott's time period. Although women had made substantial progress in claiming leadership within the foreign mission movement, men still held the positions of greatest authority. This distinction was clear in day-to-day interactions at mission stations, and it was forcefully embodied within mission rhetoric. When writing to women supporters at home and to each other, women missionaries adopted a collaborative voice. When writing to male mission officials, deference was the expected stance. A few women tried a more assertive standpoint, at least on occasion, but this approach carried risks, especially given the public nature of mission organizations' correspondence. As in other dimensions of her oeuvre, here, too, Arnott's case resonates with larger cultural trends.

When Nellie Arnott composed letters to male officials of the ABCFM both during her stay in Africa and after her return to the U.S., she knew that these texts served a very public function shaped by gender. While she could count on home-based women supporters of the foreign mission movement for moral if not always financial support, the relationship she and women colleagues in Angola had with the men who led their sponsoring organization was far more complex. Issues of authority and access, traceable to the historical position of women in foreign mission service, are evident in the writing Arnott sent home to male leaders.

In the early days of the American foreign mission movement, only men were eligible for appointment to service overseas. Saintly women pioneers like Mrs. Harriet Newell and the various wives of Reverend Adoniram Judson had elicited admiration as role models dedicated to their husbands' service. Gradually, the distinctive gender-based contributions that wives of missionaries could make earned more recognition. Some wives began to carve out informal duties as teachers, complementing their husbands' work as preachers, and missionary societies slowly came to grips with the reality that, in many foreign settings, wives could gain far better access to women and children as objects of evangelism than could their minister husbands. Bertha Stover's career, referenced above, exemplifies this trend. Still, women working at foreign missions were often unpaid adjuncts for their husbands rather than leaders in their own right.[58]

After the Civil War, the access that American women had to foreign mission service improved, partly in response to the demographics of a depleted population of males and also due to women's beginning to claim some entrée into postsecondary education and the professions. At foreign stations, women's success as teachers, health care providers, and social workers among women and children gained increasing respect from male officials—though that appreciation was sometimes grudgingly given. Even after they began to earn their own appointments as workers in foreign fields, women like Nellie Arnott and her colleague Sarah Stimpson still faced constraints in their relations with their male superiors, both day-to-day at their overseas postings and in long-distance exchanges with U.S.-based leaders. Women's abilities were not fully trusted, and their roles were still circumscribed by ideological structures such as the cult of domesticity and, in some cases, by male church leaders' discomfort with female advancement in the institution.[59]

Arnott grappled with this situation throughout her stay in Africa and during her first months back in the U.S. on furlough when she was campaigning to raise funds for a girls' school in Angola. Reading her correspondence with male administrators alongside her other public texts—such as the circular letters and magazine stories she wrote for other women—we can discern one reason why the interactions between female missionaries and people living around a station often took on a different character than relations between male missionaries and the locals there. How could a female missionary like Arnott—despite the white, Protestant American dimensions of her identity—take on a straightforwardly hierarchical stance toward the Africans with whom she worked when she was being reminded, on a daily basis, of her inferior position in the mission movement hierarchy based on her gender?[60]

Noteworthy signs of this gender hierarchy in action—and Arnott's efforts to navigate this terrain—are her letters to Judson Smith, James L. Barton, and Enoch F. Bell, some of which are printed in this volume. Smith (whose family had hosted Arnott just before her departure to Africa), Barton (the Secretary of the ABCFM), and Bell (the Assistant Secretary) worked in Boston at the organization's headquarters, directing policy all over the globe. By virtue of the positions they held, Arnott realized that her correspondence with these men would be shared with other readers. Indeed, in some of her Barton- and Bell-addressed letters, Arnott seems to be reaching out to the entire hierarchy of her sponsoring mission organization. Taking on a goal of institutional-level persuasion, this correspondence occupies a liminal space on the private/public continuum of Arnott's written archive.

To illustrate how Arnott's writing engaged with the challenge of gender relations, we have included in this edition correspondence from several different periods in her mission career. One telling text is a 1905 letter to Smith when she was very new to her foreign mission work and was just beginning to use her writing to male administrators to advocate for resources. An example from the midpoint of her overseas work is a 1909 letter written while she was still in Africa and crafted to convince the organization that she and Sarah Stimpson should be allowed to work on their own at a Gamba outstation.

In these first two example letters, we see her most deferential tone. Indeed, to grasp the full import of her gentle suggestions to the Boston-based administrators in these early letters, we need to juxtapose this exchange with a message sent from Sarah Stimpson to a female ally in the U.S. around the same time as Arnott's 1909 message. In Stimpson's letter, evidently cultivating a female back channel of communication, we find much more overt protests against the male missionaries in the region for attempting to limit the activities of Arnott and Stimpson around Gamba—a context that Arnott skirts far more delicately in her own missives to such leaders. In a complaint implicitly linked to the ongoing suffrage campaign in the U.S., Stimpson describes male leaders in Africa as having exerted unethical pressure via a staged "vote" at a meeting where the women were not allowed to participate.[61] Pointing out that in Gamba at that time "over 400 people" were "left alone without a missionary" despite their wish for their children "to be taught the true way," Stimpson protests that "Miss Arnott & I had expected to come here after the first of June to stay during the dry season, but a little before that some opposition" emerged among male mission leaders in the region. Quoting some of the objections raised, Stimpson simultaneously pokes fun at them: "That it 'was not safe'—'that single ladies ought not to travel alone in this country'—'that they ought not to be at the outstation alone.' If we had to wait to be escorted, we'd never go anywhere."[62]

This discursive gap between Arnott's and Stimpson's letters about the Gamba controversy is defined in large part by a difference in tone. Whereas Arnott positions herself as a suppliant addressing male superiors, Stimpson affiliates, through satire bordering on sarcasm, with female allies. But Arnott's voice changes over time in her official correspondence. Chapter 6 reproduces a series of letters she sent to Barton and Bell during the first months of her furlough when she had acquired a stronger professional identity.

In contrast to her tentative stance during much of her overseas assignment and more in line with Stimpson's 1909 text, by the time Arnott has returned to the U.S. on furlough later in her career, she was much more assertive. She advocated for her own agenda for the West Africa mission and claimed experience-based knowledge. Whether sent from a stop on her cross-continental journey to her family's home or from California after she arrived there, these final letters from Arnott to ABCFM male officials still reflect the gender politics inherent in the American foreign mission movement. Highly dependent on the contributions of middle-class Christian women all over the U.S., the ABCFM was eager to capitalize on Arnott's potential ability to attract donors. The letters show that managing the campaign for funds for her special project (a school for girls) was requiring Arnott to navigate the hierarchy of male power quite carefully. We can also see signs that she had matured as a writer and a political player within the mission movement. However limited the likelihood that she could direct the future course of the ABCFM program in West Africa, Arnott was determined to try. One of her major tools was the language of travel writing as she repeatedly invoked her experience in Angola to claim authority. She had lived a long time in Africa, her texts reminded recipients. Accordingly, her letters extended beyond such agendas as pushing forward her school campaign (a goal in line with her feminized missionary identity as a teacher) to her determined defense of colleagues (the Cammacks) who had fallen from favor within the organization.

Another discursive tool available to Arnott at this point also derived from travel writing's conventions. She repeatedly invoked her current status as a transcontinental traveler doing what missionaries on furlough were expected to do: journeying from support group to support group to strengthen the organization's infrastructure by disseminating stories about Christianity taking root in a faraway place. Her descriptions of this public relations campaign were modest and respectful, but they nonetheless stressed her ability to do work her male superiors could not do—to speak from the experience of having served recently in Africa herself.

In the end, to convey surprising news, Arnott used yet another familiar argument associated with women in mission—their ability to serve the movement from an American domestic setting—in a letter announcing that she was marrying California businessman Paul Darling and that she therefore would not be returning to Africa as scheduled. To describe how she planned to continue as an active agent for missions despite her marriage, Arnott called upon the same rhetoric she had used in her magazine stories and reports to the ABCFM and WBMI. As a home-based supporter, she asserted, she could still contribute to women's work for women.

Arnott's self-characterizations here certainly meshed with the very rhetoric she had used when cultivating the support of U.S. women for her overseas service. Significantly, however, by leaving behind her role as a single woman missionary posted overseas, she was reinforcing anxieties that male movement leaders had expressed for years about the long-term reliability of unmarried women for work in the field. In that vein, Rhonda Semple has noted that British mission societies' screening committees and management groups continually worried over the potential problem of losing a single woman missionary to marriage. The London Missionary Society (LMS) actually required candidates to sign a pledge promising to remain single for at least five years from the start of their service or to reimburse some of their salary to the LMS.[63]

Do the tensions around the mission movement's gendered power relations, which are so conspicuously embedded within Arnott's correspondence, provide one explanation behind her decision to wed Paul Darling rather than to return to Africa? Perhaps. In any case, these semipublic letters offer an effective example of how a woman missionary could try to use her writing as a potential avenue for influence—not only on her women supporters at home but also on the male leaders who had the greatest control over the enterprise.

Mementos, Mixed Messages, and African Voices

After her marriage, Nellie Arnott published several magazine articles with her new "Darling" surname in the byline.[64] She continued fundraising for the girls' boarding school. She stayed actively involved in the movement as she had promised Bell and Barton. However, her role soon shifted. No longer able to report on direct experiences in the field, she became one of the committed supporters like those she had written to throughout her time in Africa. That this new identity might have been less than satisfying is suggested by her attempts to convince her husband to join her in Africa as a mission couple. (Well aware that Paul Darling had no ministerial ambitions, she urged him to consider a business position, such as managing the Angola mission press.) When it became clear that her spouse would not agree, she began to re-envision her own experience overseas as a retrospective rather than a forward-looking story.

The change in Arnott's mission movement engagement took her to a different genre for her writing—composing scrapbooks. No longer assigned the task of fundraising and network-building through her writing, she could draw from the full trajectory of her mission experience reframed through memory. Arnott assembled at least three scrapbooks. Each one took on a somewhat different character, with one organized to revisit her African journey from start to finish, one serving mainly as a repository of mission publications (including some of her own) relevant to her assigned region, and one crafted as a picture-book of mission-oriented images seemingly aimed at young readers. As a form associated with domestic collecting and reminiscence, Arnott's scrapbooks can be viewed as a private memoir. However, she apparently also intended them as a pedagogical tool for future generations—especially for her two grandchildren. Margin notes captioning photos and explanatory glosses for mission magazine articles pasted in the text—as in "grandma's station" jotted under one image from Kamundongo—show that she planned for Truman and Mary Darling to study her story.

Although a detailed analysis of Arnott's scrapbooks is certainly beyond the scope of this current project, they should be taken into account as part of her travel writing oeuvre. For one thing, Arnott's scrapbooks make extensive use of textual resources closely associated with travel memoirs. For instance, photographs, postcards, and maps adorn her pages. She also assembled official documents (such as pamphlets about the West Africa mission during and after her stay there) and copies of texts signaling her continued affiliation with the movement after returning to the U.S. (such as a talk given to a support group and a bulletin listing her as an officer in a home mission organization). As her final word on her mission career, the scrapbooks tell a personal story linked to a larger social history.

In the scrapbooks, as in the rest of Arnott's large and multifaceted body of missionary texts, we find a consistent inconsistency, especially in her representations of Africans as recipients of missionaries' benevolence.[65] On one page, we see a pair of images with the familiar pre-/post-conversion hierarchy invoked from mission rhetoric through juxtaposed, captioned photographs: "A pagan mother and child—Around her neck many fetishes," versus "A Christian mother and child—Around her heart no fears."[66] In contrast, on a nearby page, we find a mission magazine article touting the success of local Umbundu teachers who have fully taken over the school Arnott had formerly managed, and, in the margin, we find an affirming note: "my students."[67]

Striking (and, of course, troubling) as these contradictory images are today, they would not have been as unusual to find so close together in the myriad discursive spaces missionaries used in Arnott's day. As John W. De Gruchy has observed, missionaries of that era were often struggling to synthesize the conflicting messages of the Bible and the (purportedly) scientific rhetoric on racial differences that were circulating at that time. On the one hand, for English and North American missionaries like Arnott, who had intellectual and emotional ties to the abolitionist movement's values and to the language of the Bible, an egalitarian stance could sometimes be achievable in belief and social practices. On the other hand, missionaries of this time period were constantly exposed to "'findings' of science on matters of race [which] reinforced the racism of the colonists" in many of their foreign field sites, so that some missionaries wound up affiliating more with white European settlers there (and their negative attitudes toward local peoples) than with "their own converts."[68] In this historical context, Arnott's wavering stance toward those with whom she had worked in Angola may be understandable even though disappointing in personal terms. Perhaps the longer she remained at home in the U.S., the more difficult it would have become to hold on to the affiliative stance she had developed and often communicated in her writing during the later stages of her actual stay in Africa.

Along those lines, Corinne Fowler's analyses of more recent and more secular journeys than Arnott's provide some useful observations. Fowler has identified some women travel authors who cultivate an "antitouristic" stance achieved through such efforts toward "cultural embeddedness" as learning the local language, adopting a local name, and dressing like a native. For Fowler, such moves can be associated with a "traveler" rather than a more "voyeuristic tourist" who is not "genuinely interested in the lives" of those about whom she writes.[69] To some extent, Arnott fits Fowler's pattern, having struggled for years to learn (and use effectively) the Umbundu language, having acquired an affectionate Umbundu nickname ("teacher Nellie") among the Angolans that some continued to use when writing her after her return to the U.S., and having brought back to California such items as a native baby-carrier that she employed for her own son and grandchildren. In Arnott's scrapbooks, we see numerous, diverse signs of this embedded traveler identity being communicated. With margin notes (e.g., "my students") proclaiming her close relationships with various figures in mission texts, for example, Arnott claims authority as a reporter while simultaneously asserting her commitment to the places and people being commemorated in her new writing space.

How, given Arnott's inconsistency of stance, can we construct a coherent narrative of her experience, much less of the movement in which she participated, from the diverse array of mementos assembled in her three scrapbooks? Through institutional records, we have been able to place most of the missionaries who appear in Arnott's scrapbook within a historical framework not only embracing but also extending beyond her own time in mission service overseas. Still, Arnott's representations of Africans in her scrapbooks are more challenging to interpret both as individual artifacts and as a more comprehensive account.

For instance, how should we read a postcard, a Christmas greeting from the Means school, evidently mailed to Arnott (now Mrs. Paul Darling) in the 1930s? The photograph shows a line of young girls in uniform. With a printed message labeling the scene "Happy Girlhood," the postcard commemorates the work of the boarding school Arnott had helped to establish.[70] Is her choice to display this postcard an affirmation of her confidence in the learning and future capacity for leadership that these students can achieve, consistent with libratory literacy ideals? Or should we instead focus on the ways in which the visually embodied curriculum—as represented in the highly Westernized dress of the students' uniforms—enacts an ongoing exercise in cross-cultural power, leading us to critique Mrs. Darling's sustained role in the enterprise?[71] Of course, both readings are available in such a text. On the one hand, we should take into account the forceful critiques that point to converts attending such schools as coming disproportionately from outcast groups rather than from the local mainstream and to ways that the European values and social practices inculcated were at odds with important native traditions. In this sense, a picture of young African women marching along in European dress can be seen as restraining rather than liberating. On the other hand, some of the same researchers who have identified the limitations mission schools placed on students have also highlighted ways in which these institutions, in some individual cases, could provide a means of escape from cruel parents or an unwanted marriage. In evaluating the curriculum itself, there are similar contradictory forces to take into account. Were lessons in sewing, cooking, and household skills such as doing laundry effective avenues to an enhanced social role or merely preparation for domestic service in white settlers' homes and a model of domesticity not suitable to the African setting? And, in the long run, did teachings suggesting women could embrace social and political leadership advance or undermine the postcolonial societies that would eventually replace the sites of much mission teaching in Africa? The Inanda Seminary, which Nellie Arnott had visited on her way back to the U.S. and which she had hoped to cast as a model for a seminary in Angola, could be the object of just such a range of queries.[72]

Looking at the scrapbooks' many representations of Africans as a body of artifacts is even more challenging. Arnott does include affirming and individualized captions for some of the images she assembled—whether from mission magazine stories, postcards, or photos. For example, one figure appearing in several places is Jonas Soma, whose journey to the Tuskegee Institute in the U.S. and completion of his studies there Arnott clearly celebrates. Similarly, Cipuku, familiar from several of Arnott's writings, is identified by name and valued as a former student. In many cases, however, the subjects remain unnamed and undifferentiated. Whatever her intentions, one story emerging from these texts depicting Africans in diverse ways is actually about Arnott herself. In that vein, Douglas Wheeler and Diane Christensen have argued that mission accounts "reveal more about missionary attitudes than about African views" (Wheeler and Christensen, "To Rise With One Mind," 80). In this case, the contradictory mix of artifacts shows that Arnott, like many missionary writers of her era, did not ever develop a coherent, unified perspective.

So how should we characterize her work as teacher and writer in the end? One important strategy for addressing this question is to turn to African women's own texts. This goal is challenging. Since Western representations of cross-cultural exchange like Arnott's have created an incomplete and distorted picture of African women and since relatively few African women have had access to traditional publishing venues, to recover relevant African voices from her era is no simple task.[73] A detailed analysis of the interplay between such texts and Arnott's public writing is necessarily beyond the purview of this initial foray into her work. However, two authors with particularly salient responses to mission enterprises like Arnott's should be at the center of future scholarship.[74] One, Eva de Carvalho Chipenda, born in the 1930s, studied in Methodist mission schools in Angola and eventually became the wife of influential African pastor Jose Chipenda. Another, Maria Chela Chikueka, attended 1940s' Congregational schools in the same area where Arnott had taught decades earlier.

Chipenda's *The Visitor: An African Woman's Story of Travel and Discovery* turns the white traveler/black native relationship on its head by writing about her experiences in such varied locales as Brazil, North America, and Europe. She blends critique of her Methodist mission schooling experiences with recognition of the access to social influence she acquired through that education. Specifically, Chipenda says her understanding of mission teaching's limitations was heightened when she was chosen for advanced study in Brazil,

> It was . . . an eye-opening experience to discover that the lessons the missionaries taught us in Angola were not necessarily applied elsewhere. The missionaries had intended to build a system in which Christians lived separately from non-Christians. They advocated the idea of not mixing with 'pagans.' Christianity in Angola was based on too many don't's: don't drink, don't dance, don't watch football on Sundays, don't go to the movies. . . . So it was a surprise to visit other countries and discover that not everyone acted in the way the missionaries advocated. I was unable to distinguish Christians from non-Christians. They looked alike and in many ways behaved alike. (23-24)

Although Chipenda saves many of her most pointed critiques of Western intervention in Angola for the Portuguese rulers of her youth, her reflections on missionary teaching's constraints do offer a telling response to mission-oriented rhetoric like Arnott's, both in the earlier public writings and in the scrapbooks.[75] For instance, Chipenda's surprise at being "unable to distinguish Christians from non-Christians" while studying in Brazil offers a strong counterpoint to the before/after conversion images still appearing in Arnott's scrapbooks and in much mission discourse in Chipenda's day.

According to Muriel "Ki" Henderson, an ABCFM missionary wife and activist who served in Angola as a contemporary of Chipenda's, the critique of mission education put forward in *The Visitor: An African Woman's Story of Travel and Discovery* surprised—and even hurt— some of the missionaries who had known Eva since they had viewed their own labors in Africa as unselfish service and had assumed it was welcomed as such. Henderson herself, however, despite clearly being proud of her husband Lawrence's ministry and her contributions to it, has characterized Chipenda's story as honest and insightful. "She was truthful," Henderson declared.[76]

A much more positive portrait of missionaries' interactions with Angolans over time emerges in two texts by Maria Chela Chikueka, who studied in ABCFM classrooms in the region where Arnott had served and who eventually became a minister, teacher, and writer herself.[77] In *Angola Torchbearers*, Chikueka traces the history of Congregational missionaries' work in the highlands and presents an account of native Christian leaders (a number of whom were originally trained by Arnott and her colleagues). *The Trail of My Life Journey* presents Chikueka's autobiography, including her forced exile from her beloved Angola. Edited and published soon after her unexpected death by heart attack in early 1999, Chikueka's personal story offers a fascinating and fitting companion to Arnott's. Echoing language in the biographical letters Arnott left for her grandchildren, Chikueka's accounts of enthusiastically dedicating herself to Christian pedagogy provide an important reminder that we must balance critiques of missionaries' constraining influence on African peoples with an awareness that many Angolan leaders, men and women, have drawn on the learning the mission movement provided for strength, skill, and dedication. In that regard, Chikueka argues that, since the colonial government had no schools for Angolans when she was growing up, mission education was "a blessing . . . opening many doors which otherwise would have been closed."[78]

That the different visions of mission-sponsored learning in these two authors' works both resonate with elements of Arnott's writing again shows that her own stance—like her experience of Africa—was highly inconsistent, encompassing a broad range of attitudes. In light of those contradictions, we must avoid any temptation to cast Arnott herself as a trustworthy, straightforward reporter on Angolan culture or even on her own interactions with Umbundu people in her day. We should nonetheless recognize the value of her writing as an example of cross-cultural authorship's inherent complexities and of the powerful influence the foreign mission enterprise exercised over so many American women's lives.

Notes

1. Focusing on European missionaries, David Arnold and Robert A. Bickers have emphasized that mission writing was often the major source of information about foreign places for the public at large. Arnold and Bickers explain that what this writing offers us today is more a record of the *perceptions* that movement participants circulated about the societies where they served, than a reliable portrait. Furthermore, editors played a role in filtering what reached the public, especially given that "marketing" the movement was a core goal of these texts. "Introduction," in Bickers and Seton, *Missionary Encounters*, 1, 3–4, 9.

2. Miss Nellie J. Arnott, "A Trip to an African Woman's Conference," *Mission Studies*, January 1908, 23; Nellie Jane Arnott, "A Trip to the Woman's Conference in the West Central Africa Mission," *Life and Light for Woman*, January 1908, 45. See Chapter 5 for a full text of the report. Such references to readers as supporting the enterprise regularly appeared in writing by many women missionaries. (See Robbins, "*Woman's Work*," 259–63.)

3. For one year of her Angolan assignment, 1911, we have found no diary. (The Bancroft library, which holds the bulk of her papers, has no record of a diary having been donated for that year.) Also, although Arnott did maintain her diary during the first year of her marriage, her family has not found others. The day-to-day experiences of a California wife and mother may have seemed less worthy of sustained record-keeping, or she may have chosen not to save diaries from that later period. The last diary held by the Bancroft library stops somewhat abruptly in 1914, a year after Arnott's marriage.

4. Traits Sinor associates with diaries that are more literary than ordinary include a strong plot, recurring literary devices, and polished diction. Jennifer Sinor, *The Extraordinary Work of Ordinary Writing: Annie Ray's Diary* (Iowa City: Univ. of Iowa Press, 2002), 12.

5. Rhonda Semple's study of gender-based differences in the work of British Protestant men and women missionaries shows that women's roles became increasingly important to the movement in the early twentieth century but that a woman missionary was still "subordinate to that of her male

colleagues" (*Missionary Women*, 1). Among American missionary organizations, a similar pattern persisted. On the male/female hierarchy in English foreign missionary culture, see Patricia Romero, who posits that "The missionary societies were long run by men. When women were permitted to go to the mission stations, they reported directly to male supervisors who, in turn, reported back to the church organizations at home." Introduction to *Women's Voices on Africa: A Century of Travel Writing*, ed. Patricia W. Romero (Princeton: Markus Wiener Publishing, 1992), 12. Scholars have traced a trajectory of American women in foreign mission work progressing from serving only as helpmates to male preachers, to missionary couples partnering in the enterprise, to single professional women serving as missionaries. But male authority persisted in U.S. Protestant culture, even after the Civil War. James M. Hoppin, a theology professor at Yale, wrote a book for ministers aiming "to brake the accelerating locomotion of leadership among ministers' wives." See Leonard I. Sweet, *The Minister's Wife: Her Role in Nineteenth-Century American Evangelicalism* (Philadelphia: Temple Univ. Press, 1982), 236.

6. Based on her study of missionaries working in the southwestern U.S., Susan M. Yohn found what she terms "an odd schizophrenia" in their writing: "they wrote with a rhetorical flourish about the ideals of the enterprise in the reports intended for public consumption in the pages of mission journals such as *Home Mission Monthly* or in fund-raising letters to mission societies. Their letters to administrators of the WEC [Women's Executive Committee], however, show little concern with ideology; they are primarily concerned with administrative neglect." Susan M. Yohn, *A Contest of Faiths: Missionary Women and Pluralism in the American Southwest* (Ithaca: Cornell Univ. Press, 1995), 107. While Yohn's description of differences in that body of mission discourse has some parallels in Nellie Arnott's writing, we see more rhetorical self-awareness in Arnott's texts.

7. This approach aligns our work with scholarship advocated by Catherine Hall, whereby "Historians and cultural critics concerned with understanding colonialism as a culture have made discursive analysis a central tool," to emphasize that "Differences, whether of race, ethnicity or gender, are always socially constituted, and they always have a dimension of power." Catherine Hall, introduction to *Cultures of Empire: Colonizers in Britain and the empire in the nineteenth and twentieth centuries—A Reader*, ed. Catherine Hall (Manchester: Manchester Univ. Press, 2000), 12, 16.

8. Mary Louise Pratt, *Imperial Eyes: Travel Writing and Transculturation* (New York: Routledge, 1992) stresses that transcultural exchange within such contact zones is fluid and relational: "A 'contact' perspective emphasizes how subjects are constituted in and by their relations to each other. It treats the relations among colonizers and colonized, or travelers and 'travelees,' not in terms of separateness or apartheid, but in terms of copresence, in-

teractions, interlocking understandings and practices, often within radically asymmetrical relations to power" (7).

9. Fred W. Atkinson, "The Educational Problem in the Philippines," *The Atlantic Monthly* 89 (March 1902): 360–65; James A. Le Roy, "Race Prejudice in the Philippines," *The Atlantic Monthly* 90 (July 1902): 100–17; Arthur Stanley Riggs, "A Letter from the Philippines," *The Atlantic Monthly* 92 (August 1903): 256–66; Alleyne Ireland, "The United States in the Philippines," *The Atlantic Monthly* 94 (November 1904): 575–94; James A. Le Roy, "Our Spanish Inheritance in the Philippines," *The Atlantic Monthly* 95 (March 1905): 340–46. In a history of the *Atlantic*'s first half-century, Ellery Sedgwick has noted: "Although the *Atlantic* had a smaller circulation than the others [*Century, Harpers'* and *Scribner's*—other major, "quality" magazines growing up second half of the nineteenth century], it often carried greater intellectual prestige and represented an influential, relatively highbrow portion of that culture. The *Atlantic* . . . contained in varying proportions not only literature but also commentary on politics, science, economics, art, and current social issues" (2–3). Referencing Bliss Perry, editor of the magazine in the years before and after the Spanish-American War, Sedgwick reports that Perry's tenure maintained the *Atlantic*'s longstanding "emphasis on social issues, politics, and economics," and that, in particular, "His coverage of the aftermath of the Spanish-American War represented the whole spectrum of opinion, but the majority, including his own editorials, resolutely opposed colonialism as a violation of American principles" (310–11). The Atlantic Monthly *1857–1909: Yankee Humanism at High Tide and Ebb* (Amherst: Univ. of Massachusetts Press, 1994).

10. We thank Susan K. Harris for sharing her manuscript, "Mark Twain's America." As William R. Hutchison has pointed out, the turn-of-the-century heyday of Protestant foreign missions coincided with an era when many Americans wished for the U.S. to exercise sustained imperial power, but missionaries and their supporters did not generally envision a seamless connection between the two enterprises. Hutchison argues: "While missionary attitudes toward imperialism ran the gamut from wholesale enthusiasm to condemnation, and varied with particular locales and embodiments, the most common response voiced two assertions: that imperialism was an inexorable force, and that this force must somehow be tamed. . . . American missionary thinkers, by and large, wished to displace the evil or dubious forms of expansionism—those involving exploitation or colonization—in favor of the 'fine spiritual imperialism' that their own movement aimed to represent" (*Errand to the World*, 92). Hutchison uses the term "colonization" more narrowly than the way we have defined the term in our introduction.

11. An example of this mix appears in an unsigned 1910 essay in *Mission Studies*. The U.S.-based author references Nellie Arnott's challenging

journey to her mission station but extols the impressive landscape; the article also praises a new railroad into the highlands but laments that it can take the hardworking missionaries only "part of the way" to their destination. Even within some individual sentences, we can track this continual shift back and forth, as in these examples: "Swinging in a hammock [tepoia] is very pleasant for a time, but when one has swung there for hour after hour it grows tiresome, and your good missionary is often glad to get out and rest herself by walking" and "There are many picturesque things about such a journey—listening to the songs of the carriers as they jog along, and to their peculiar signal whistles; watching for the approach of another caravan and exchanging news items; selecting and making the camp for the night or fording a stream, while perhaps the terrifying cries of wild animals may be heard in the forest." See "The Way Our Missionaries Travel," *Mission Studies*, April 1910, 119. Such accounts' emphasis on the unusual (even the exotic) features encountered on a journey contributed to what Kristin Fitzpatrick has dubbed the "project of difference" often associated with travel writing as a genre. See "American National Identity Abroad: The Travels of Nancy Prince," in *Gender, Genre, and Identity in Women's Travel Writing*, ed. Kristi Siegel (New York: Peter Lang, 2004), 264

12. An illustration of how women missionary writers in Arnott's own ABCFM group circulated this complex view of Africa emerges in a story on witchcraft that Mrs. Merlin Ennis submitted for the Children's Work section of *Mission Studies*. Mrs. Ennis's account vividly describes a "mysterious" ceremony she observed in a neighboring village, when a "divination" aimed at helping several patients included wild dancing, chicken-tossing, and chanting. Though she found the proceedings "wearisome," Mrs. Ennis also admitted to being fascinated—so much so that she "resolved to witness" a follow-up ceremony the next day. Mrs. Merlin [Elisabeth R.] Ennis, "African Witchcraft," *Mission Studies*, October 1910, 317–19. A copy of this article is in one of Arnott's scrapbooks; on it she noted, "I was with them & saw this. N.J.A." She added the date Jan. 1910. (*Ideal Scrapbook*, box 2, NJADP).

13. For thoughtful discussion of Livingstone's career as explorer and writer, including significant contrasts between his heritage and that of Henry Morton Stanley, see Tim Youngs, "Africa/The Congo: the politics of darkness," in *The Cambridge Companion to Travel Writing*, ed. Peter Hulme and Tim Youngs (Cambridge: Cambridge Univ. Press, 2007), 160–64.

14. David Livingstone, *Missionary Travels and Researches in South Africa: Including a Sketch of Sixteen Years' Residence in the Interior of Africa*. 2 vols (New York: Narrative Press, 2001; reprint, London: 1857); Dr. David Livingstone, *The Life and African Explorations of David Livingstone* (New York: Copper Square, 2002; reprint, St. Louis, 1874); Andrew C. Ross, *David Livingstone: Mission and Empire* (New York: Hambledon and London, 2002).

Ross interestingly classifies Livingstone as both "patron saint of imperialism and the ideal Protestant missionary" (240). Whether or not one views Livingstone as an imperialist, Ross's treatment of the famous author's progressive movement away from the program of the London Missionary Society that originally sponsored Livingstone's work in Africa is compelling. Ross argues that, already in the 1850s, caught up in the appeal of exploration, "it was clear that [Livingstone] knew that he was not going to go back to settled mission station type service" (93). Ross also documents Livingstone's increasing interest in alternative models for mission work, emphasizing sustained community-building with local populations over individual conversion efforts (122). Even in the initial responses to his first book, commentators had begun circulating characterizations of Livingstone that cast him more as explorer-hero than as missionary. The 1858 *Harper's New Monthly Magazine* review of *Missionary Travels and Researches in South Africa* and *Travels and Discoveries in North and Central Africa* is a case in point. Although the reviewer suggests that Livingstone "regards his discoveries from a religious stand-point," the review itself focuses on his explorations ("the results of years of travel and research" which "entirely revolutionalize all our theories as to the geographical and physical character of Central Africa"—368). Further, *Harper's* approvingly asserts that "Livingstone's missionary scheme is accommodated to the actual state of things," i.e., that he adopts a worldly attitude toward his work (394–95). For this reviewer as for others of this era, it was Livingstone's "travels" more than his missionary identity which made him "no ordinary man" (369).

15. Here is an exemplary excerpt from an undated magazine clipping in Arnott's scrapbook collection: "Dr. Hollenbeck, of Angola, appears to be the particular hero of the month, in that he secured two hippos in connection with an expedition to the Kuanza River, dispatching each animal with a single shot. There was great joy throughout the countryside. Not less than a thousand natives gathered to share in the feast. The Doctor dried large quantities of the meat, and took back a plenteous supply to the schoolboys at Kamundongo." Scrapbook Volume 1, NJADP, 3. In line with the tendency to focus on Livingstone's manly exploits, Andrew Ross has pointed to representations of the missionary-explorer in the early twentieth century. Ross underscores biographical details indicating that Livingstone himself was a conversionist with an egalitarian perspective rather than a promoter of the hierarchical "trusteeship" view of Africans. Nonetheless, Ross's survey of biographies demonstrates that Livingstone was most often portrayed, via omissions of information and overt characterizations, as "the pioneer of European imperialism" (103). Andrew Ross, "Christian Missions and Mid-Nineteenth-Century Change," in Porter, *Imperial Horizons of British Protestant Missions*, 85–105.

16. John M. MacKenzie describes Arnot's writing as representative of a trend among missionary authors to focus on the landscape and its beauty, often via an Eden motif. "Missionaries, Science, and the Environment in Nineteenth-Century Africa," in Porter, *Imperial Horizons of British Protestant Missions*, 112.

17. According to J. Keir Howard, the Livingstone and Arnot families were friendly neighbors. "Livingstone was his [Arnot's] hero and he would spend much time at the Livingstone home looking at the explorer's various maps and artifacts in the attic and, as a boy, he determined to go to Central Africa and follow in his hero's footsteps." See Dr. J. Keir Howard, "Arnot, Frederick Stanley," *Dictionary of African Christian Biography*, http://www.dacb.org/stories/demrepcongo/arnot_stanley.html.

18. F. S. Arnot, "Journey From Natal to Bihé and Benguella," *Proceedings of the Royal Geographical Society and Monthly Record of Geography* 2 (February 1889): 65, 78–80. See Chapter 4 for Arnott's report on meeting this well-known missionary, whose work with the Plymouth Brethren she greatly admired. Arnot's explorations took him into remote regions. In 1884, he trekked through central west Africa from Natal, crossing both the Zambezi and Congo rivers and eventually arriving at Benguella, on the west coast. After his initial explorations, Arnot responded to an invitation from the powerful chief Msidi, then ruling over a large area that included the Katanga province of Congo (what Arnot called Garenganze), to come to that area. Arnot's relationship with Msidi was complex, leading some to question the Scot's failure to assist Msidi later when the chieftain was assassinated by agents of King Leopold of Belgium. Defenders of Arnot point out that he was in Angola at the time of Msidi's death, working at another mission station, and too ill to travel. In any case, Arnot had established a successful mission in the Katanga region and had tried to maintain an officially neutral stance typical of the Plymouth Brethren while also advising Msidi on how to manage relations with the European political leaders so intent on plundering Africa's resources. See Howard, "Arnot, Frederick Stanley," *Dictionary of African Christian Biography*.

19. Mary Suzanne Schriber, *Writing Home: American Women Abroad, 1830–1920* (Charlottesville: Univ. Press of Virginia, 1997). Notes Schriber: "At a time when women were assiduously moving into public spaces both geographic and literary, travel writing was another space in the public domain for the voices of women" (7).

20. Kristi Siegel, "Intersections: Women's Travel and Theory," in *Gender, Genre, and Identity in Women's Travel Writing*, 2–3. Schriber strikes a similar note, explaining: "In the later nineteenth century, when the female traveler who ventured into international spaces was often a type of the New Woman, women's travel was a magnet for diverse and complicated reactions.

On the one hand, through clever marketing that played on stereotypes of Woman, the public in the last quarter of the century was drawn into the exploits of journalists like Nellie Bly and Elizabeth Bisland—lauded, lionized, and applauded for circumnavigating the globe in record time. On the other hand, some segments of the public continued through the turn of the century to be uneasy about what they perceived to be excessive numbers of female travelers" (*Writing Home*, 7). Susan Bassnett strikes a helpful balance between identifying trends in women's travel writing and pointing to the wide diversity evident in various women's travel accounts. See "Travel Writing and Gender" in Hulme and Youngs, *Cambridge Companion to Travel Writing*, 225–41.

21. Gaunt, an Australian, had been widowed early in life and made the best of that situation by traveling to remote locales and writing about her experiences in a distinctively female voice. Mary Gaunt, *Alone in West Africa* (London: T. W. Lowrie, 1912).

22. Romero suggests that the "personal nature of their experiences distinguishes the women" and their texts from their male counterparts. Introduction, *Women's Voices on Africa*, 10.

23. Cheryl McEwan, "Encounters with West African Women: Textual Representations of Difference by White Women Abroad," in *Writing Women and Space: Colonial and Postcolonial Geographies*, eds. Alison Blunt and Gillian Rose (New York: Guilford Press, 1994), 74–75, 77. The "heroes of the faith" series has published one enthusiastic account of Slessor's ministry. See Sam Wellman, *Mary Slessor: Queen of Calabar* (Uhrichsville, Ohio: Barbour Books, 1998).

24. On links between motherhood and mission service, see Hill, *The World Their Household*, 24–27, 61.

25. Publications where Arnott appeared as a subject of missionary writing and as an author included the formal annual reports of the WBMI, *Life and Light*, *Mission Studies* and the *Missionary Herald*. For the specific group of women readers engaged in the foreign mission movement of her day, Arnott would have been something of a celebrity. Coming to this realization only through the gradual process of tracking down her publications in many archives reaffirmed to us that the recovery of major missionary women's writing remains unfinished.

26. "Recruit for Africa," *Missionary Herald*, June 1905, 267. *Missionary Herald* was a publication aiming for a mixed-gender audience of mission supporters at home in the U.S.

27. L. L. [initials only], "At Kamundongo," *Mission Studies*, August 1908, 251, 252. Often reports about the work overseas were unsigned, particularly when the author was synthesizing input from multiple correspondents.

28. See Sarah Robbins's "Missionary Motherhood" chapter in *Managing Literacy, Mothering America*. Domestic literacy narratives were a broad genre with several sub-genres tied to women's benevolent work outside the home.

29. L. L., "At Kamundongo," 251, 252. Here the text affiliates the ABCFM with an egalitarian view of African Christians as quite capable of leading religious work in their own societies, thereby resisting the "trusteeship" model. Dana L. Robert characterizes the late nineteenth and early twentieth centuries as a period when some British missionaries were "pragmatic and responsive to the immediate needs of the particular context," but other individual missionaries and organizations were increasingly influenced by racial hierarchy and imperialism, so that they increasingly embraced a "trustee" model for interactions with Africans, including Christians. Introduction to *Converting Colonialism*, 14–15.

30. See Sarah Robbins's analysis of characterizations for Laura Haygood, who served in China during the same generation as Arnott's overseas posting (*Managing Literacy, Mothering America*, 205–10). Deborah Gaitskell has commented on the evident contradictions between this ideology and the actual work by women in the mission field. For example, she notes that "urban missionary wives themselves did not lead a purely domestic life, in two ways. Though not in paid employment, they were frequently out at meetings, like their husbands; they also employed domestic servants to help 'keep the home,' a further ideological twist." Thus, Gaitskell explains, efforts by American Board missionaries like Mrs. Clara Bridgman in Johannesburg to promote a Euro-American version of housewifery among converts was at odds with the proselytizers' own lived experiences. "Housewives, Maids or Mothers: Some Contradictions of Domesticity for Christian Women in Johannesburg, 1903–39," *Journal of African History* 24 (1983): 241.

31. Based on missions sponsored by the Society for the Propagation of the Gospel in Foreign Parts, an Anglican organization, Modupe Labode posits that the push to substitute square houses for round huts and related physical changes in Christianized settings marked "nothing less than restructuring of African society" as a mission movement goal. "From Heathen Kraal to Christian Home," in Bowie, Kirkwood, and Ardener, *Women and Missions*, 126.

32. "Miss Arnott's Schools," *Mission Studies*, 282; "Children's Work: Miss Arnott's School," *Mission Studies*, November 1909, 344. The titles of these articles point to the periodical's efforts to make Arnott herself familiar to readers as a character in the ongoing, larger narrative about mission work.

33. Mrs. Joseph B. Leake, "West Central Africa," *37th Annual Report of the Woman's Board of Missions of the Interior* (Chicago: WBMI, 1905), 31. Annual reports used many of the same rhetorical techniques as the mission

magazine narratives but positioned accounts of overseas work in a broad institutional context.

34. Mrs. Joseph B. Leake, "Africa," *38th Annual Report of the Woman's Board of Missions of the Interior* (Chicago: WBMI, 1906), 29. U.S.-based writers like Mrs. Leake gained expertise by reporting on the same regions over several years.

35. "West Central Africa," *39th Annual Report of the Woman's Board of Missions of the Interior* (Chicago: WBMI, 1907), 48. References to holidays that readers in the U.S. could identify with often appeared in reports from foreign mission stations, along with details marking the difference between celebrating at home and working abroad.

36. Mrs. Joseph B. Leake, "Africa," *40th Annual Report of the Woman's Board of Missions of the Interior* (Chicago: WBMI, 1908), 47. Leake's invocation of Arnott's own words blends confidence in God's capacity with an implied critique of home-based women's failure to fully carry out His will so far.

37. For discussion of the impact of print culture on the clubwomen's movement around this time and, in particular, of the role played by publications such as annual reports, see Anne Ruggles Gere and Sarah R. Robbins, "Gendered Literacy in Black and White: Turn-of-the-Century African-American and European-American Club Women's Printed Texts," *Signs* 21 (Spring 1996): 643–78.

38. The latter magazine showcased Arnott's articles more frequently, probably because of her sponsorship being situated in the midwestern organization and because of her longtime ties to the region. At least one of Arnott's American magazine pieces was apparently reprinted in *Canadian Congregationalist*. John T. Tucker quotes from it and credits Arnott in his *Drums in the Darkness*, 143, citing the *Canadian Congregationalist* of November 23, 1911.

39. This description's reference to "Those who contribute" and to "where their money goes" blurs the line between fundraising for the magazine and fundraising for mission service. Periodicals like *Mission Studies* and *Woman's Work for Woman* (whose audience was Presbyterian women) certainly helped publicize the labors of women missionaries stationed overseas to stoke supporters' enthusiasm and elicit funds. However, at times the necessity of attracting subscribers for the magazines themselves could distract readers from the goals of the larger movement. Along those lines, the "Current Topics" piece opening one issue of *Mission Studies* in 1911 focused *only* on a call to increase subscriptions. See "Current Topics," *Mission Studies*, August 1911, 1.

40. "Our Literature," *Mission Studies*, September 1910, 310. We thank Elizabeth (Liz) Rohan for sharing this article.

41. In correspondence about our work, Semple helpfully suggested that we consider how this relationship might be viewed as a kind of "Christian feminism." "Parlor Press Reader's Report," June 2008, 3. From Semple's cue, we might consider if the mission movement had transnational dimensions comparable to suffrage activities, yet shaped more by shared religious than political commitment. See, too, Sarah Robbins, "*Woman's Work for Woman*," 258–63.

42. Benedict Anderson, *Imagined Communities: Reflections on the Origin and Spread of Nationalism*. Revised edition (London, Verso, 1991), 43. For a discussion of Anderson's concepts as they apply to American women's writing, see Robbins, *Managing Literacy, Mothering America*, 26. In her dissertation on Janette Miller, Elizabeth (Liz) Rohan also discusses the role of an "imagining of communions" among women of the mission movement, with this group identification process "facilitated by true womanhood ideals, based on Christian beliefs," as well as "the exchange of texts." Rohan, "Imagined Communions" (Ph.D. diss) Chapter 4, 1–2.

43. Nellie Arnott Darling, "Chief Kanjundu's Death," *Mission Studies*, April 1914, 118–19. Here Arnott touches on a delicate subject—the fact that some African Christians owned slaves themselves—but she also asserts that Kanjundu had finally come to understand that his own liberty was no more precious than theirs. Nicholas Thomas has offered a related description of what he calls "the before and after story" as a "central feature of mission discourse." Noting that this recurring plot "is not just a matter of religious change but of wider social transformation," Thomas also points to descriptions of pre-Christianization practices as playing a key role in these narratives and cites cannibalism and widow-killing stories set in Fiji or India as examples which, we think, have their parallels in accounts of witchcraft and polygyny in stories about Africa penned by Arnott and her colleagues. Thomas's analysis of how missionaries' narratives often struggle with the contradiction between an impulse to infantilize indigenous people (in both verbal and visual texts) and a competing discourse of shared humanity through Christ's eyes is relevant as well. Nicholas Thomas, "Colonial Conversions: Difference, Hierarchy, and History in Early Twentieth-century Evangelical Propaganda," in Hall, *Cultures of Empire*, 302–03, 306.

44. Nellie J. Arnott, "Kamundongo and Vicinity," *Mission Studies*, May 1910, 144–45. See also "A Visit to an African Village (Continued)," *Mission Studies*, June 1913, 185–86. The latter article was published after Arnott's return to the U.S and her marriage to Paul Darling, a shift in identity noted by the byline's now listing her as Nellie Arnott Darling. For more on Arnott's relationship with Cipuku, see Chapter 2.

45. See especially Ngũgĩ wa Thiong'o, *Decolonising the Mind* and Ngũgĩ wa Thiong'o, *The River Between*. Focusing especially on Africa, but

theorizing expansively, Albert Memmi has argued that "Colonization distorts relationships, destroys or petrifies institutions, and corrupts men, both colonizers and colonized." Envisioning a hopeful alternative, he adds: "To live, the colonized needs to do away with colonization. To become a man, he must do away with the colonized being that he has become. If the European must annihilate the colonizer within himself, the colonized must rise above his colonized being." *The Colonizer and the Colonized*, 151. See also Frantz Fanon, *Black Skin, White Masks* (London: Pluto Press, 1952) and Fanon, *The Wretched of the Earth*.

46. To illustrate her point, Schriber draws on writing by Agnes McAllister, who worked as a Methodist missionary on the Kroo Coast of West Africa and who published a book about her experience (*A Lone Woman in Africa*) in 1896. Schriber notes that McAllister "places Liberia outside of civilization," equating Christianity and civilization, while associating the familiar trope of "'the darkness of the heathen mind'" with the pre-intervention status of the people she was hoping to save. Schriber, *Writing Home*, 134–35.

47. Nicholas Thomas, *Colonialism's Culture*, 127, 131, 132–33. Thomas asserts: "In one sense it is apparent that evangelical missions in both Africa and the Pacific had entirely different objectives to, say, Stanley's expedition or the Fijian administration, but it is also true more specifically that missionary work employed and enacted notions of infantilization and quasi-familial hierarchy in a far more thorough way than any other colonial project. . . ." (135–36).

48. Desiree Lewis has described traits of an informed "cultural studies" being promoted by African women scholars, and Arnott's writing includes a number of the features Lewis extols. "African feminist scholarship" Lewis explains, "has encouraged attention to the everyday, the ordinary and the seemingly insignificant." Lewis also points to how such studies avoid viewing women's culture as "static and unchanging." In contrast, Lewis critiques writings which "present African women as frozen in time and place," having "rituals and customs but lacking any real history," and she notes that such a stance is often associated with "an effort to demonstrate (and inscribe) the radical difference of African from western societies," including "conjur[ing] up a sense of all-pervasive 'strangeness.'" While Arnott's writing about African women does embody such negative features at times, Lewis's critique would apply more clearly to Bertha Stover's stance, outlined below, than to Arnott's writings. Desiree Lewis, "African Gender Research and Postcoloniality," in *African Gender Studies*, ed. Oyèrónké Oyěwùmí, 382–83.

49. For example, João Batista wrote to "My dear Teacher Mrs. N.A. Darling," February 17, 1936, that "[t]here is never a day that I forget to think of you, my teachers, [like] Miss Stimpson. . . . And you, also, though many

years have passed, I have never forgotten you" (Box 2, "Loose Letters, 1910–1943," NJADP).

50. Soremekun, in "History of the American Board Mission in Angola," provides some evidence of a parallel generational difference in the attitudes toward Umbundu Christians expressed by Merlin Ennis (Elisabeth's minister spouse) and Reverend William Sanders. Soremekun notes that Sanders decried "the mental limitation of these people," who should not be entrusted with their own churches because they were "not prepared to stand alone and should not be expected to any more than children from eight to fifteen years old." Ennis, in contrast, argued that "Anyone who has kept tabs on the workings of the native church for the last ten years knows that they are competent" to lead their own congregations (157–58 and 283–85). The contrasting views and backgrounds of Bertha Stover and Elisabeth Ennis fit the distinction that Jane Hunter draws between nineteeth-century female missionaries, who saw themselves primarily as helpmeets to their husbands and who often held conservative views on racial issues, and twentieth-century "New Women" missionaries, who were often college-educated, were confident that they "had something of their own to offer" (27) in the mission field and were sometimes opposed to prevailing views on race. "Women's Missions in History," in Reeves-Ellington, Sklar and Shemo, *Competing Kingdoms*, 22-31.

51. Elisabeth Logan Ennis, *The Hope of Glory: An Account of the Work of the West Central Africa Mission of the American Board for the Year 1916–1917* (Kamundongo: Sarah H. Bates Memorial Press, 1917), 25.

52. Mrs. Bertha D. Stover, *Women of West Central Africa* (Chicago: Woman's Board of Missions of the Interior, 19—[undated]), 2, 3, 9, 8. An editor's note on this pamphlet observes that this "new edition" of Mrs. Stover's text celebrates recent additions to the West African mission, including "Miss Nellie J. Arnott at Kamundongo, who arrived in 1905 and entered upon her work with joy," as well as "Mrs. Marion M. Webster of Bailundu" and "Miss Emma C. Redick at the new Ochileso station" (9). These comments date this edition as after Arnott's 1905 arrival but also suggest the first circulation might have been before the end of the nineteenth century.

53. Elisabeth Ennis, *The Umbundu Baby and Its Mother* (Boston: Woman's Board of Missions, 19—[undated]), 1–2. While the writing by Ennis that we review here was, like Arnott's, for women mission movement supporters, by the late stages of her career, she produced at least one publication for an academic audience: "Women's Names Among the Ovimbundu of Angola," *African Studies* 4, no. 1 (March 1945): 1–8.

54. Although we have not attempted the kind of extensive review of Ennis's writings as we have taken on for Arnott, we can affirm that the relatively accepting stance she adopts in *The Umbundu Baby and Its Mother* is echoed in her longer text, *The Hope of Glory*, referenced above. For instance,

she provides highly positive, individualized portraits of two young men (Ferramenta and Kunjuka) who progressed from studying at a station school to preaching and teaching (18); she offers an appealing account of "a wise man, a magician" named Kunanga, who gave up his work as a "witch-doctor" to study a mission curriculum, eventually becoming "a church member and a trusted elder of the village" and finally "open[ing] a school in a[nother] village" with his "wife . . . a worthy helpmate" (18–19). Like Ennis's portrayals of Umbundu women in her earlier pamphlet, these depictions emphasize the new leadership of converted local men without invoking the negative stereotypes typical of pre-conversion characterizations in many earlier missionary accounts.

55. Grace T. Davis, *Neighbors in Christ*, 200, 205. Davis also wrote that the WBMI could not ignore mission churches' demands for freedom. "More and more the control of affairs must drop from our hands into those of their own leaders" (204). Dana Robert argues that after World War I, an ideology of "World Friendship" replaced the former ideals of Woman's Work for Woman. "World Friendship assumed that Western culture no longer had a monopoly on virtue," according to Robert, "and that women around the world stood poised to lead their own people not to Western, Christian civilization, but to their own forms of Christian life" (*American Women in Mission*, 273).

56. Related critiques recognize imperialist assumptions in Euro-American feminists' views of non-Western women as needing to be saved. As Laura Briggs, Gladys McCormick, and J. T. Way note, global feminism has not been achieved, when we can still point to such phenomena as "human rights discourse construct[ing] a female object of imperial intervention, as in the U.S. project of 'rescuing' Afghan women from the Taliban (by bombing them)" (635). Even among feminists themselves, there have been "struggles, in academic scholarship and international conferences" over issues related to colonialism. Indeed, they note, in the 1980s, when "Robin Morgan proposed that there was a 'global feminism,'" Pratibha Parmar and Valerie Amos "rejoined that its proper name was 'imperial feminism'" (631). See "Transnationalism: A Category of Analysis," *American Quarterly* 60, no. 3 (September 2008): 625–48.

57. In emphasizing the fluidity of Arnott's perspective, we affirm Alison Blunt's emphasis on the capacity of travel to change the traveler's perspective through shifts in time and space. As Blunt notes, and as Arnott experienced, travel "involves the familiarization or domestication of the unfamiliar at the same time as the defamiliarization of the familiar or domestic." In that sense, travel can be "liberating," Blunt points out, by encouraging the traveler to question "ideas formulated at home." See *Travel, Gender and Imperialism: Mary Kingsley and West Africa* (New York: Guilford Press, 1994), 17. Build-

ing upon Blunt's analysis, we should recognize how travel may undo or at least dislodge the perspective with which someone begins a journey, leading to shifts in discursive standpoint as well. At the same time, however, as our reading of Arnott's oeuvre demonstrates, even as one journeys, there may be cultural materials and practices from home that still exercise a powerful influence, leading to a push-pull around one's standpoint, potentially inhibiting the kind of "liberating" process Blunt identifies within travel. In Arnott's case, her affiliation with both the mission movement itself and with the women's literacy network for which she wrote would have exercised such a restraining influence.

58. Decades after Arnott's service in Africa, mission wives often continued to be relegated to a second-class status. In that vein, Muriel "Ki" Henderson has pointed out that her years of ABCFM work supporting her husband's ministry, in the same region where Arnott had labored, did not merit a missionary pension, leaving a burden on her children after Reverend Henderson died. Ann Pullen and Sarah Robbins, interview with Ki Henderson, Chapel Hill, North Carolina, August 31, 2005. On the importance of Harriet Newell as an "iconic figure" whose "story came to symbolize for many women evangelicals the central role" that they as individuals (rather than spouses) might be "called to play in world history," see Mary Kupiec Cayton, "Canonizing Harriet Newell: Women, the Evangelical Press, and the Foreign Mission Movement in New England, 1800-1840," in Reeves-Ellington, Sklar and Shemo, *Competing Kingdoms*, 69-70.

59. Leonard I. Sweet argues that, between the 1880s and the beginning of the twentieth century, just as women were claiming political power within the U.S. by finally achieving voting rights, many male religious leaders were feeling increasingly uncomfortable with women's enhanced leadership in church affairs. Sweet sees these decades as marking an "aggressive re-entry of men into American religious life" and associated efforts to render women "less visible and public," such as limiting their "right to speak in church." *The Minister's Wife*, 234–35. Deborah Gaitskell, writing on missionary women in southern Africa, has outlined conflicts between single women missionaries and their male superiors, sometimes grounded in the men's unwillingness to honor the expertise of the women. Gaitskell identifies the American widow-missionaries Katherine Lloyd and Mary Edwards as facing this challenge in Natal. "Rethinking Gender Roles: The Field Experience of Women Missionaries in South Africa," in Porter, *The Imperial Horizons of British Protestant Missions*, 145–46. Also, Rhonda Semple has observed in the context of British mission history, that although women's numbers in overseas mission work "grew exponentially" between 1865 and 1910, men "continued to dominate mission administration" (Semple, *Missionary Women*, 3).

60. Sweet has explained that, in the nineteenth and early twentieth centuries, "When women were permitted to go to mission stations, they reported directly to male supervisors who, in turn, reported back to the church organization at home" (Sweet, *The Minister's Wife*, 12).

61. Stimpson eventually became such a thorn in the side of mission officials that there was discussion about withdrawing her from service. See, for example, Nellie J. Arnott to Miss [Kate] Lamson, Sept. 25, 1912. ABCFM Papers, 15.5: Southern Africa, Women's Board, Vol. 2, Rhodesia, West Central Africa, Zulu, 1900–1914, Documents and Letters, A-Z, reel 215, Pitts Theological Library, Emory University. Along related lines, as Elizabeth Rohan's dissertation has recorded, Janette Miller, whose African assignment overlapped with the end of Arnott's Angolan service, eventually left the ABCFM, choosing instead to labor on her own in the region more as social worker than missionary. Taken together, Stimpson's and Miller's experiences suggest that however much the ABCFM sought single women missionaries in this era, relationships with the male hierarchy of the institution were challenging. It is noteworthy in this context that, after her marriage, anecdotal evidence suggests that Arnott proposed adopting at least one child from the region where she had worked in Africa, but her husband rejected the idea.

62. Sarah Stimpson to Miss [Kate] Lamson, Aug. 3, 1909, ABCFM Papers, 15.5: Southern Africa, Women's Board, Vol. 2, Rhodesia, West Central Africa, Zulu, 1900–1914, Documents and Letters, A-Z, reel 215, Pitts Theological Library, Emory University. Characterizing the Umbundu peoples living in Gamba as trustworthy colleagues who would help ensure the women missionaries' safety, Stimpson forcefully critiques the male authority figures—both on site and in the U.S.—who initially prevented her and Arnott from making the move. Although a formal vote held at the annual meeting in Kamundongo had rejected their proposal, Stimpson reports that she and Arnott decided to go ahead with their plans, and she contrasts the support they gained from Reverend Sanders for this endeavor with the machinations of other mission men then serving in the region.

63. Semple contrasts this wish to maintain single missionary women's unmarried status with the perennial push for male missionaries to marry. Whereas men were encouraged to take a wife both as a helpmate and as a safeguard against sexual dangers in the field, single women were assumed to be immune to sexual temptation there and were urged to maintain their unmarried status so they could devote all their energies to the work. See *Missionary Women*, 54–55. Semple also cites "financial considerations" and "administrative difficulties caused by the loss of women's services" if they did marry as motivations for the mission organizations to encourage single women missionaries to remain unmarried (201). See also Rosemary Seton, "'Open Doors for Female Labourers,'" 66.

64. Our choice of "Arnott" in this section is made with full awareness that her "Mrs. Darling" identity was surely shaping these scrapbooks, perhaps even more than "Arnott" did. Given this project's focus on ways in which this missionary movement author publicly represented her foreign service, which occurred before her marriage, we continue in this closing section to use the name under which she worked while in Africa.

65. The seeming contradictions in Arnott's stance, here and in her earlier texts, echo patterns which Susan M. Yohn has identified among missionary women who worked with Hispanos (Yohn's term) in the American Southwest. For instance, Yohn notes that Mollie Clements, who taught in both New Mexico and Colorado for over thirty years beginning in 1891, at times brought together contradictory views within the same individual text. "She could, in one sentence, call Hispanos 'sickly and immoral' but then in another assert that they were 'bright, uncomplaining, and naturally sympathetic'" (Yohn, *Contest of Faiths*, 145).

66. Scrapbook Volume 1, NJADP, 8. Such re-inscriptions of hierarchy echo discourse not only in the mission literature Arnott had written for periodicals but also in other women's travel writing of her day. Ruth Y. Jenkins highlights how some British women authors constructed their own identities by generating discourse about Other women encountered during travel. In these portrayals, Jenkins argues, Victorian women travelers often aligned their gaze with an imperialist, race-based perspective more than with an affiliative stance based in gender. In that vein, Nellie Arnott's scrapbooks sometimes draw stark distinctions that separate her own sense of self from the Africans with whom she worked. Ruth Y. Jenkins, "The Gaze of the Victorian Woman Traveler," in Siegel, *Gender, Genre and Identity in Women's Travel Writing*, 15–30. John MacKenzie comments that missionary societies commonly distributed postcards to encourage support of their work; such cards invariably highlighted "the heroism of missionary endeavour and the 'permissiveness' and 'superstitions' of the peoples of the missionary fields" (*Propaganda and Empire*, 23).

67. Comparable references are scattered throughout the scrapbooks, suggesting that Arnott made special efforts to document the successes of past students. For example, above the title of a pamphlet celebrating the work of the African pastor Enoque Gomes Sacamana and his wife Lucia ("An African Pastor and His Wife Go to Their New Field"), Arnott has added this pencil note: "Lucia and Nele were 2 of the nine girls in the Kamundongo Girls Boarding school started by Nellie in 1910. Eno[qu]e my helper at Olutu." "The Ideal Scrapbook," NJADP.

68. De Gruchy relates this "social tension" to a "confusion of identities" among missionaries themselves. John W. De Gruchy, "'Who Did They Think They Were?': Some Reflections from a Theologian on Grand Narra-

tives and Identity in the History of Missions," in Porter, *Imperial Horizons of British Protestant Missions*, 219.

69. Corinne Fowler, "The Problem of Narrative Authority," *Gender, Genre, and Identity in Women's Travel Writing*, ed. Kristi Siegel, 210. Fowler's analysis has a parallel in work Roberta Wollons has done on ABCFM missionaries serving in Turkey. See "Travelling for God and Adventure: Women Missionaries in the Late 19th Century," *Asian Journal of Social Science* 31, no. 1 (2003): 55–71. Wollons's study determines that interactions between missionaries and indigenous people led to "mutual accommodation. Culturally hybridized mission schools came to reflect the power of local politics and local people to transform the foreign missionary agenda. In the process, 'successful' American missionaries became bilingual, deeply bicultural, and accommodated themselves to multiple views of religious practice and womanhood" (55–56). Two of Wollons's subjects, Mary and her sister Charlotte Ely, were single women college graduates who helped found schools for girls, eventually leading to "unanticipated conversion from evangelists to educators, and from educators to political partisans" (56).

70. "Happy Girlhood" postcard, Scrapbook Volume 2, NJADP, 65. Arnott added the 1937 date in pencil.

71. Tucker, in *Drums in the Darkness*, comments on the uniforms of the Means students as symbols of acculturation, especially given that, in Umbundu society, men had traditionally made the clothing, with the needle being "part of the man's equipment": "Dresses made by the girls with their own hands for graduation at Means signify a new day for African womanhood" (147). The frequent images of converted African women laboring at their sewing machines in vocational education programs are also relevant.

72. While thorough treatment of the conflicting evaluations of mission-sponsored schools for girls and women is beyond the scope of our current work, we recommend these sources: Adrian Hastings, "Were Women a Special Case," 104–125; Modupe Labode, "From Heathen Kraal to Christian Home: Anglican Missionary Education and African Christian Girls, 1850–1900," 126–44; and Tabitha Kanogo, "Mission Impact on Women in Colonial Kenya," 165–186—all in Bowie, Kirkwood, and Ardener, *Women and Missions*. See also Dana L. Robert, "The 'Christian Home,'" in Robert, *Converting Colonialism*, especially 155–58; Heather Hughes, "'A Lighthouse for African Womanhood': Inanda Seminary, 1869–1945," in Walker, *Women and Gender*, 197–220. Hughes's discussion of Inanda Seminary is noteworthy in light of Arnott's envisioning that site as a model for the school she wanted to found. On the somewhat contradictory legacy of Inanda, see Lynette Hlongwane, "The Role of Inanda Seminary in the Education of African Girls in South Africa: A Report of Graduates' Views" (Ed.D diss., Columbia Univ., 1998).

73. Marnia Lazreg points out that, as we move African women's own stories to the forefront of cultural analysis, we must remember that there have been multiple factors promoting silence as well as speech. Lazreg insists that "Silence as the absence of public voice is not synonymous with absence of talk or action." Referencing Algerian women, in particular, she identifies "circumstantial," "structural" and "strategic" causes of silence, with the first relating to social circumstances discouraging public speech, the second referencing constraining forces such as the requirement to use a European colonial language in public discourse, and the third being a "voluntary act" linked to "self-preservation." See "Decolonizing Feminism" in Oyĕwùmí, *African Gender Studies*, 77. Besides helping to explain the dearth of public texts available from Angolan women of Arnott's time period, Lazreg provides useful tools to help us read the silences—as well as the overt statements—in writing like Chipenda's and Chikueka's.

74. Though the perspectives on missionary work offered by Chipenda and Chikueka are quite different, both serve as examples of an important dimension of colonial studies that Frederick Cooper has called for—identifying and engaging with "the ongoing encounters through which colonial rule was tested, limited, and sometimes reshaped by those who sought niches within systems of colonial power as well as those who fought it." Frederick Cooper, *Colonialism in Question*, 235. In both Chipenda's and Chikueka's stories, we see distinctions between their views of the political imperialism of the Portuguese and the sustained cross-cultural engagement they experienced through mission-sponsored education. For both women (and in spite of the contrasting stances they adopt when depicting their schooling experiences), their interactions with missionaries helped provide what Cooper has called "handles by which the [colonial] system itself could be moved" (242).

75. Chipenda complains, "The Portuguese colonizers wanted us to become Portuguese to look like them, to take on the Portuguese life-style. For many urban Angolans especially, this meant living a double life: the Portuguese way and the African way" (9). Though she draws clear distinctions between the overt rule of the Portuguese and the social position of the missionaries, Chipenda also depicts the mission culture as exploitative. For instance, she complains that "Black pastors were paid very low salaries," criticizes missionaries' efforts to separate Christian from non-Christian Angolans, and suggests that black spiritual leaders like her brother could be easily recruited and cynically used by mission leaders (4). Chipenda recounts details of her brother Julio's work as an ordained "Methodist pastor," beginning at only seventeen years of age, when he was already "the perfect man to be planted among his people and convert them to Christianity" through labor both rewarding and challenging (4–5). Chipenda notes that when her brother and other family members were posted to an isolated station, they "were often sick, but the missionaries gave very little support of any kind"

initially (5). However, she declares, "a new post in Mazozo" was an improvement, and her parents clearly felt that living there with her brother offered some advantages for Eva, so that they arranged for her to spend part of each year aiding her brother's ministry away from her home village, where, sadly, she began to feel like "a visitor." Indeed, Chipenda explains, hers became a "dual life" with both "positive and negative sides," since living part-time with her brother "meant the chance of growing in a better environment, an environment that would lead me to better opportunities and advantages for my future, such as a good education" (7–8). Significantly, Chipenda also offers plenty of criticism of Angolans' own social practices that constrained children and women (13).

76. Muriel "Ki" Henderson and daughter Nancy Henderson-James, interview, August 31, 2005. Henderson's descriptions of her work with the ABCFM as a mission spouse emphasized associations between gender differences and power differences among those in Angola during her day—almost a full generation later than Arnott.

77. Worth noting in this context is the fact—stressed by Ki Henderson's daughter Nancy—that Eva Chipenda was of the Kimbundu and not the Umbundu group and that her education was provided not by ABCFM-run Congregational schools but by a different group of missionaries. Interview, August 31, 2005.

78. Maria Chela Chikueka, *The Trail of My Life Journey* (Toronto: Chela Book Group, 1999), 27–28. Chikueka also recounts how her parents, Protestant church members, "used to tell us children the way to be liberated from the oppression of colonialism was to go to school"—i.e., to the schools provided by missionaries like the ABCFM team. "The Portuguese did not like this and we often heard them say that the Protestant missions were spoiling their labourers" (7). See also Maria Chela Chikueka, *Angola Torchbearers* (Toronto: Chela Book Group, 1999). One of our most helpful sources on the experience of mission-sponsored education was our colleague from Kennesaw State, Dr. Sam Abaidoo, who described his own experiences in Ghana, including underscoring the degree to which most first-generation postcolonial leaders had been educated at some point in Christian schools. Currently a professor of sociology, Dr. Abaidoo described his own past work as including involvement with the Baptist Mission Board and in that regard emphasized that missions were not always "hand in glove with the colonial government," but rather had "many facets to their work." Although some retrospective rhetoric has cast the mission schools in Ghana in a highly negative light, suggesting they were linked closely to colonialism's aims, Abaidoo stressed to us that these same schools were also well regarded for their rigorous curriculum and attention to positive discipline, which led many to credit the institutions with contributing to the "acceleration of the process

of decolonization." As an indicator of a potentially productive view of the schools today, Dr. Abaidoo noted that a number of the mission schools are still operating in Ghana, though with such symbolically meaningful changes in the recent past as replacing the bells that formerly marked change of class time with drums and substituting elements in the curriculum that conveyed "symbolic representations" of British rule (e.g., songs and literature) with more locally significant content. Sam Abaidoo, interview with Ann Pullen and Sarah Robbins, June 25, 2008. The positive view of the role of missions is also reflected by current discussion within government circles to return some supervisory roles over ex-mission schools to mission organizations. In the context of Dr. Abaidoo's comment on the shift from bells to drums, see John M. MacKenzie who relates the purposeful management of space in missionary settings to a comparable effort to regulate time. Among British-sponsored sites in Africa, he observes, "Missions were run with the discipline of the factories at home," as days were "carefully broken up into blocks of time, demarcated by the ringing of bells." See "Missionaries, Science, and the Environment in Nineteenth-Century Africa," 122.

Part II The Public Writings of Nellie J. Arnott (Darling)

NOTES ON EDITORIAL METHOD

To prepare our edition of Nellie Arnott's public missionary writing, we have followed principles of textual scholarship articulated by the Modern Language Association (MLA) and the American Association for State and Local History (AASLH). More specifically, our editorial techniques come from studying the MLA's *Scholarly Editing: A Guide to Research* and the AASLH's *Editing Historical Documents: A Handbook of Practice.*

We have chosen a transcription approach in line with what the AASLH's handbook terms conservative style (Stevens and Burg, *Editing Historical Documents,* 72–77). Generally, therefore, our edition provides printed versions of Arnott's public writing in a form as close as is practical to the way it reached her original readers—whether published in mission periodicals or circulated in handwritten form. Our rationale for choosing a conservative approach, making relatively few adjustments to her texts, has been to convey a strong sense of her distinctive writing style. Thus, for our edited versions of Arnott's ABCFM-related correspondence and her circular letters, we keep grammar and usage patterns as they appeared in the original, including phrasing that would be considered an error in formal standard English. For instance, just as many speakers and writers do today when addressing a familiar audience, Arnott sometimes violated usage rules around subject-verb and pronoun-reference agreement; we have retained her patterns in such cases. However, where a usage choice Arnott made could render her meaning confusing for our readers, we have corrected her wording and placed the amended terms in brackets. Similarly, Arnott's diction might occasionally be unclear by virtue of her using a term unfamiliar to today's readers; in such cases, we have added a brief rewording or an explanation in brackets.

This overarching aim of making her texts accessible to our readers has also led us to some minor adjustments in her punctuation. In her circular letters especially, Arnott's punctuation patterns tended to violate such standards as using a comma between parts of a long compound sentence or setting off an introductory clause with a comma—rules that were more regularly adhered to in her in published work. Similarly, Arnott sometimes signaled the start of a new sentence with a capital letter but failed to mark the close of the previous sentence with a period. In such cases where her punctuation choices or omissions break up the flow of reading, we have emended the text, adding necessary periods without any notation but commas and semicolons with brackets to mark our adjustments.

Other nonstandard practices in Arnott's correspondence have not necessitated changes for clarity of reading; therefore, we have left those patterns intact to preserve her personal style. For instance, Arnott's liberal use of dashes and symbols (particularly her frequent use of "&") as well as her penchant for underlining appear in this edition as they do in her original circular letters and reports to the ABCFM or WBMI. Arnott also employed irregular capitalization patterns, including incorporating uppercase letters to highlight key terms (e.g., Mission and Missionary). We have generally retained those choices from her original texts—except in cases where we could identify a dominant recurring pattern (e.g., Station versus outstation).

While honoring Arnott's personal style around points of usage and punctuation, we have silently addressed inconsistencies in her spelling. Arnott's correspondence and her edited publications are relatively free of spelling errors. However, in handwritten pieces, she occasionally reversed individual letters, and she frequently misspelled a few words (such as "across," which she often wrote as "accross," and the verb "passed," which she often wrote as "past"). We have corrected those spelling errors throughout, perhaps sacrificing a direct marker of how producing her texts in haste likely led to such slips but, we trust, aiding our own audience's ease of reading. (Our readers can still note other signs of a writer producing material without much time to revise or reflect, such as Arnott's frequent use of abbreviations, which we maintain as in her original.)

Unlike our approach to the spelling inconsistencies outlined above, our "correcting" for proper nouns (especially place names) has been quite limited; we wanted to recognize some variations in spelling that were accepted in Arnott's own day. These variants were, in fact, affirmed as acceptable by her initial editors' decision to maintain her spelling in their publications. In such cases we have followed their lead while acknowledging the distinctions in our endnotes, as needed. On a related point, Arnott's editors occasionally locate her submissions as coming from "Benguella" even when she actually wrote from Kamundongo, Gamba, or some other specific location. We have maintained the geographic markers appended to such publications as they appeared in the originals. (See Chapter 5 for several examples.)

In preparing explanatory endnotes, we have tried to supply our readers with information establishing the cultural context of Arnott's original writing experience and the knowledge base of her first readers. Consistent with the MLA's *Scholarly Editing: A Guide to Research*, we believe that "scholarly editors" are "historians of the text" who "attempt to reconstruct a form of the text that, without their intervention, would be otherwise inaccessible." Thus, as C. D. Greetham recommends, we have seen ourselves as carrying out not only an "archaeology" but also a "sociology and the psychology" enterprise around Arnott's writing, including "attempting [as much as possible] to gain access to the consciousness (and even the unconscious) of the author and the subsequent bearers of the text's message." Accordingly, we have tried to communicate what Greetham calls the "personal vision" of the author, Nellie Arnott, including, when appropriate, informed critique of that vision, thereby taking on "the role of interpreter, of standing between the author, the document, and the past, on the one hand, and the reader, the edition, and the present, on the other" (Greetham, 4, 6).

In Arnott's case, what Greetham would view as the "subsequent bearers of the text's message" would include her original editors, who played a major part in carrying her stories to a broader group of readers than she reached through her mission reports and circular letters. To preserve that mediating role, our transcriptions maintain her periodical texts in the form in which they first appeared except when slight adjustments for clarity were required, as outlined above. An appendix illustrates ways in which editors shaped Arnott's magazine pieces.

We hope our approach will provide readers with a clear view of Arnott's and her first editors' strategies for telling the story of her mission service to readers at home—as well as some sense of her own distinctive personality and her time in Africa. Our primary focus is more on the former—recapturing rhetorical choices—than the latter—recording a life. On the one hand, to provide our readers with the most informed access to Arnott's public writing possible, we have drawn on sources about her personal life and the larger historical moment to contextualize her writing. On the other hand, this project is not a definitive biography of Arnott. Instead, we have focused on her own representations of one particular stage in her life—her mission service in Angola—as she depicted that experience for specific public audiences. By designating that topic as our focus, we have made decisions, in our role as editors, to exclude substantial materials from Arnott's entire body of writing and from details of her personal life, particularly in the years after she married and settled in California.

In stressing the incomplete nature of the portrait we have provided, we are affiliating with other scholars who have underscored epistemological issues associated with studies of women's lives, as outlined in *The Challenge of Feminist Biography* by Sara Alpern, Joyce Antler, Elisabeth Israels Perry, and Ingrid Winther Scobie. Alpern, Antler, Perry, and Scobie point out that feminist scholars sometimes have difficulty determining which elements of a subject's personal life are relevant to a history being shaped for public use. For feminists, this question is probably unavoidable since we recognize the close connections between the personal and the political, the private and the public, in any woman's life. In Nellie Arnott Darling's case, her choice to leave behind diaries and a scrapbook collection as well as more public records of her service in Africa immediately opens up questions about how her private writing can supplement our understanding of her public texts and about the extent to which her personal life both shaped and responded to her public role. We have indeed drawn on the archive of her personal compositions to help illuminate dimensions of the social writing Arnott produced for institution-specific audiences engaged in the mission movement of her day. But we have not foregrounded the material from that rich body of personal writing in this edition. Thus, one point to emphasize in terms of our editorial method is that it is not all-inclusive for Arnott as an author; it "selects out" significant written records that could be the focus for later projects, including her diaries and scrapbooks. Overall, in making the core decision of what our current subject would be, we have chosen Arnott's public representations of her mission experience and not her experience itself, or her personal reflections on it, for this project. That is, as our book's title and subtitle indicate, our editorial method is designed to recover and interpret the various public narratives she produced to link mission movement readers at home in America to her work in Africa.

4 Traveling to Portuguese West Africa

Arnott's initial body of public writing took the form of letters to friends, family members, and supporters of her work in Africa. Some of these readers merited special attention because they supplied the funds for her journey and for her salary. During her passage across the Atlantic and through subsequent stages of her trip to the ABCFM West Africa station, Arnott had long blocks of time to write, so her letters are full of enthusiastic detail. Besides describing various stops in Europe and along the African shore, she also shared reflections on her experiences—sometimes with hints of the misgivings she was describing with more openness in her diary, but mainly (for these public texts) with emphasis on her spiritual commitment.

Due to her earlier AMA assignments within the U.S., Arnott was already an experienced traveler when she embarked for Africa. But she had never encountered as many striking sights as awaited her now or people so different from those she had known: Catholic Portuguese officials in their home country and in Africa, settlers in the port towns, the West Africans who would literally carry the missionaries inland to the highlands, and the local residents of the Umbundu lands. Arnott used her writing during her journey to Africa's interior to report on these experiences for readers at home and to begin the complex process of creating a new identity for herself in a challenging environment. One aspect of that effort involved situating what she was observing in relation to past travels and life within the U.S. Therefore, Arnott often referenced ways in which such sights as street design and shops in Lisbon or landscapes between the African coast and the highlands differed from locations in her home country.

CIRCULAR LETTER #1

S. S. Saxonia, May 3, 1905

My dear friends:

As some of you know I left beautiful Cal[ifornia] and my dear parents and sister Apr. 10th. After a disappointing trip in some ways, because of a mistake made at Los Angeles, I finally arrived in Chicago Sat. morning Apr 15th.[1] I had stayed over night at Los Angeles with a friend there & had a short visit at Kansas City with a cousin. I came by the S. P. & Rock Island to Chicago. Had pleasant traveling companions on the way & received blessing from conversations with those who were Christians & trust God in turn made me a blessing [to them].

In Chicago I only had a few hours, so just called on the Ladies of the Woman's Board for a little while.[2]

I went on to Youngstown, O[hio] that day, getting in there at midnight. Charlie (my brother) met me and we spent a happy Sabbath day together. It was very pleasant to meet my many friends there & to look into their faces once more. In the p.m. on Sun. I spoke at the new Y.W.C.A. there & I felt we had a blessed meeting. May God follow it with His Spirit, is my prayer.

Mon. morning I left Youngstown and went as far as Clifton Springs, N. Y. where I stayed over Tues. with Dr. & Mrs. Sanders & my friends there.[3] It was a very restful & pleasant day. A day of Christian fellowship with those who love the Lord. Tues. evening I left[,] going on to Boston & arriving there Wed. a.m. Rev. E. E. Strong, one of the Secretaries of our American Board, took me to his home at Auburndale to remain while there.[4] And now I wish I could tell you of this sweet Christian home. Dr. Strong is getting old & feeble & we can't hope to keep him long, but while we have him we have his prayers & the influence of a holy life which is certainly a rare one in this world. His loving wife & faithful daughter, Annie, are saints too. Then living with them is his sister Mrs. Means, whose husband, before his death, led in the opening of this Mission to which I am going.[5] The "Stronghold" [family,] as it is called[,] have a special love and care for our West Central Africa Mission & we are rich missionaries who have such friends.

Each morning I went into Boston with Dr. Strong and spent the rest of that week in shopping & in overseeing my packing in the packing room. The Congregational House is a fine building with every dept of Cong[regational] work under one roof. On Fri. I spoke for a few moments at the Woman's Board meeting & met many of the ladies there.[6]

Fri. Dr. Judson Smith invited me to his home for dinner & to spend the night.[7] Again I felt thankful for the opportunity to meet in the home [of] another member of our Board. They are all such consecrated men that they make you want to be & do your best.

A dear friend, Miss Grace Lynch, came from Scranton, Pa. to spend the last few days with me so on Sat. she too was invited into the "Stronghold" to be with me until I sailed.[8] This was certainly one of God's sweet surprises for me to have such a dear friend with me over that blessed Easter Sun. in such happy surroundings. God is good!

Sun. we attend[ed] church in Auburndale in the morning, but remained in the rest of the day as I needed the rest & quiet. It was a beautiful, beautiful Easter Day & my heart is still filled with the blessings it brought.

On Mon. Miss Lynch took me with her on a trip to Plymouth & we both stood on the Rock of 1620. It is a beautiful old-fashioned place by the sea & is full of interest.[9]

Tues. bright & early we were up preparing for our departure from that home. We met the friends Mr. and Mrs. [William] Sanders, with whom I am sailing & after attending to the last things & having dinner we went to our Steamer. Mr. Sanders' brothers, Dr. J. A. Sanders of Clifton & Dean Sanders of Yale, were with us to give us a good sendoff.[10] Also several young women, who are members of the Substitute Circle, of which I will tell you later, were there to bid us farewell. After a little time of pleasant conversation & the saying the last good byes we moved forth from our dear native land. We waved until we lost sight of all & then lifted our hearts to God to give us all the grace we needed in parting with those most dear. Mr. & Mrs. Sanders are leaving two dear little boys, one 8 the other 11. Just offer a prayer for these dear parents.[11]

Our voyage has been very pleasant thus far. We could not ask for better weather or a smoother sea. We sailed the 25th of Apr. & today the 3rd of May we are nearing Queenstown & will be in Liverpool some time tomorrow. For 3 days I was quite sea-sick but since Sat. have quite enjoyed it. I have a state-room alone & one with an outside window for which I am very thankful. We spend our time sitting on deck, dressed in our warmest clothing. There we read & think, taking walks now & then, but always answering the dinner bell whenever it rings.[12]

Now, I must tell you about the Substitute Circle & then close & continue this in my next edition. The "S.C." was started by a few young women livng in Auburndale, Mass. As some of you know [missionaries at] the place [i.e., the assignment in Kamundongo that] I am going out to fill [have] been calling for a worker [for] nearly seven years. Miss Stimpson, who has been alone all this time in the school & children's work at Kamundongo, has worked bravely on & uncomplainingly day after day, yet needing a helper so much. Because of this great need & there being no one to go[,] these young women became interested & formed a circle of prayer, praying that God would prepare a worker & if it pleased Him to let them raise the money for sending her & for her support. This was formed in June 1903 & I became a member of it. Later when God gave me health & [made] my way clear[,][13] I offered myself to our Board & became the "S.C." missionary. God has led them & blessed them & in answer to prayer they have raised the $600 necessary for outfit & travelling expenses and have the money in hand to meet half of the 1st year[']s salary. There are now about 50 members & these are scattered all over the world & although I have met only a few of them, I feel that I know them as I know few friends. There is a Round Robin letter sent around once a year & through this we are becoming well acquainted. I can't tell you what it means to me to have such a band remembering me in prayer day by day. These [friends] have a special interest in me which it isn't possible for the women of the W. B. M. I. to have. I can't help but say again, "God is good." If any one who reads this is led of God to become a member of this circle or is led at any time to find out more about it, you can write to Miss Blanche Noyes, Auburndale, Mass. She is our Secretary & Treasurer.

The last night in the home-land was spent with the members of this Circle in Dr. Strong's parlor. We sang & talked and prayed together & to me came a blessing which I know will remain forever. They are all earnest consecrated young women & the work I am going to is as truly their work as mine. They are helping together in prayer & I thank God for them.

And now dear friends, I want to thank you one & all for the steamer letters & for the gifts & pictures received.[14] May God bless each one of you & don't forget to pray for me & for Africa's dear little ones.

With love & prayer to one & all.
Very Sincerely,
Nellie J. Arnott

Circular Letter #2

May 13, 1905
S.S. Panama, Pacific Line. In port at La Pallice-Rochelle, France

My last letter to you[,]¹⁵ I closed as we were nearing Queenstown on May 3rd. That evening I remained up until midnight in order to see Queenstown & to watch the Tender come out & take the passengers ashore. Queenstown looked beautiful with its many lights. The next day was eventful. It was interesting to watch the land & see the different light-houses as we drew near to Liverpool. We finally reached dock about six Thurs. evening, being over nine days since leaving Boston. The Captain had gone out of his course somewhat in order to avoid the Icebergs. I was sorry not to have seen some.[16]

Mr. Mercer, our shipping agent in Liverpool[,] was at the dock to meet us. He is an earnest Christian man and interested in all that concerns us and our Mission. So it was a great relief to us to commit everything into his care. We went to the Lawrence Temperance Hotel & there found Mr. Bagster, who has been the business agent for our Mission in Eng[land] since the Mission was opened.[17] He had come from his home near London to be with us a little while. His brother went out with Mr. Sanders when the mission was first opened, but was called to the Heavenly Home after a year & a half service & the first to lay down his life in our Mission. Mr. Bagster has always remained a faithful friend to all of the missionaries of our Mission. We had a good visit with him that evening & he returned home the next morning.

Friday May 15—Mrs. Sanders and I spent the day in shopping. That evening Mr. & Mrs. Sanders took a boat for Ireland where they spent the next few days visiting her brother & sister.

Saturday morning I left Liverpool & took the train for London. The trains are quite different, being divided into compartments which accommodate about eight persons, & each compartment opens out on the platform. There was a nice dinner on the train & they served a very nice dinner at much less costs than our American dinners. The freight cars or "goods cars" as they call them are smaller & look strange as the car looks as though it was set on top of the wheels. The engines, too[,] are quite different.

The road took us through a beautiful country. The fields were divided by green hedges & the farm houses & yards were well kept. Sheep & cattle seemed to be plentiful & they looked beautiful in the green pastures & beside the still waters. The streams & ponds were inviting & gave freshness & beauty to the meadows & hills. The houses were mostly of stone & brick & many of the places had small orchards which were in bloom. All the way it was a delight to the eye.

On arriving in London I went to Mrs. Corey's. She keeps a private boardinghouse in American style. That is, she gives you a room & serves three meals a day. In most of the other boardinghouses & hotels one meal—<u>dinner</u>—is served & you order what you want for breakfast & supper & they will buy it & cook it for you. Some places you even buy your food & they will cook it & serve it for you. Mrs. Corey is an earnest Christian woman & has entertained most of our missionaries when in London. She makes your plans for you & if you follow them as I did you will be able to see a good deal in a few days. At once on arriving she sent me off on a Bus ride. The London Bus is drawn by two big horses & will accommodate about 24 passengers. Twelve inside & twelve on top. I went up on top & took a seat near the driver & as we drove along I asked him questions. We drove along Piccadilly, past Hyde Park corner, Albert Memorial, Albert Hall, along by Hyde Park & Kensington Gardens. The driver was full of interest all the way.

Sun. May 7 was my last Sabbath in an English congregation & it was a most blessed day. For morning service I attended the City Temple with Mrs. Corey and family. Rev. J. R. Campbell is the pastor & he preached a very good sermon. This church is the oldest & largest Congregational Church in London. He has been pastor of his church about two years,—follow[ing] Dr. Joseph Parker. This large church was <u>filled</u>, even the pulpit platform being seated with men. The communion service followed the preaching & it was a very blessed service for me, one long to be remembered.

Sun. evening I went to Westminster Chapel to hear G. Campbell Morgan.[18] As I stepped into this large church[,] it seemed like being in the Chicago Ave. Church, Chicago. And seeing Dr. Morgan's familiar face made me feel at home. He had been preaching several sermons & holding services preparatory to the organization of a missionary auxiliar[y] in his church. This evening sermon was the climax. It was wonderful & if I had not been on my way to the Mission field, I would certainly have had to offer myself that night. If I can get hold of a few copies of that sermon[,] I mean to send them around to my friends & I hope any who receive one will pass it on to others. At the close of the service he said there would be a Missionary prayer-meeting & at this meeting he called for the consecration of his young people to the cause of foreign missions. Four young women & one young man rose & then he offered such a wonderful prayer for them. As I was so near the platform I stepped forward & spoke to him & he remembered meeting me in Chicago. He took my hand & said, "God bless you. I'm so glad you have been here in this service." This large church too was packed & you could see from their faces how his people love him. So closed my Sabbath in London & it was a blessed one. I thank God for it.

Mon. morning I went at once to Westminster Abbey[;] this wonderful cathedral with its great memories & its long series of memorials of famous men, is too wonderful for me to describe. The external effect is grand & they say internally there is nothing finer in England. The cloisters date from the 13th to the 15th century. One may read about it but can realize little of its majesty & grandeur until they have seen it.

The same day I also was in The National Gallery & Tate Gallery selecting in each a few of the most famous pictures I wished to see. Beautiful pictures are an inspiration to me & I wished I might spend several days in looking at just a few of those I liked best.

Tuesday, my dear friend, Miss Hawksley whose home is in London came to spend the rest of the time with me.[19] We first visited St. Paul's Cathedral. Its great dome is magnificent. We went to the top & had a splendid view of the river & city. The interior has been newly decorated & I must say there was too much gilding to please my eye, although the mosaics in the highest dome are beautiful. The Whispering Gallery in the dome was very curious. It is reached by a flight of 260 steps & a whisper uttered by the wall on one side is distinctly heard if the ear is by the wall on the other side at a distance of 108 ft. in a direct line. We saw where the Duke of Wellington, General Gordon & Lord Leighton & many others were buried.

From here we went to the Tower & we could not help but step softly as we entered the grounds, for the remembrance of England's early history brought a quiet heart. One wish[es] they might visit these places when studying English history. I felt as though I would like to take my course in English history over again, as I called to mind such names as Anne Boleyn, Thomas Cromwell, Lady Jane Gray & others. The collection of ancient armour in the White Tower was full of interest to me. I think I shall always read Eph[esians] 6th chapter with a new interest.[20]

After taking a walk around Buckingham Palace, the residence of the King, & a walk in Hyde Park we went to Brixton to attend the evening meeting of Torrey-Alexander meetings. It was so good to me to take the hands of old friends & to be in one of their meetings once more. Mrs. Torrey had just returned from Germany that day so being able to see her was a happy surprise. Mr. Torrey preached & conducted the service as he always does & at the close some fifty or more came to the front & confessed their sins & accepted Jesus as Savior.[21] After service he took us to his study & we had a short visit with him & Mrs. Torrey. His "God bless you" to me as I go on my way means much to me. Our ride home that evening gave me a splendid view of Westminster bridge, the river & House of Parliament. It was beautiful everywhere. Above the moon was shining & below the lights reflecting in the river & my heart was glad.

On Wednesday I just went to the British Museum long enough to look at some of the old manuscripts of the Bible, also at a few of the Egyptian & Assyrian antiquities, some of which made the Bible history more real to me. This closed my visit in London & to me it has meant much in many ways. I returned to Liverpool Wed. afternoon & my friend went with me to remain until after our steamer sailed on Thurs. Mr. & Mrs. Sanders had returned from Ireland & had all things ready for our onward journey. We sailed Thurs. morning May 11 about noon & I said good-bye to my last friend, & turned my face toward Africa to love & bring her children to Jesus.

We have had a very quiet voyage from Liverpool to Lisbon. We were on one of the through steamers going to South America. It stopped at three or four ports but we only went ashore once & that was at La Pallice-Rochelle, France, where I began this letter. We were there for the day so we took a small steam car and went five miles to Rochelle, a quaint old city. The streets including side walks were only 20 feet wide & the side walks were covered with stone arch-ways, very good to keep off the sun & rain. The women looked neat & well dressed & all boys & many of the working men wore long sleeved black aprons over their waists & trousers. They looked strange but these kept them clean. There were two grand old churches or cathedrals, an arched gateway leading into the city, & two old towers on each side of a well built canal, all of which were interesting. It is certainly an old ancient city & I found much to interest me. I sent some of you post-cards from there.

We arrived here & are stopping at the Hotel Durand for a few days. We sail from here Mon. May 22nd. But of Lisbon and of our stay I will write in my next letter. I think this is long enough.

I think of all of you very often & remember you at the throne of grace. It is so blessed that we can meet each other there if not otherwise. I feel sure you are all praying for me. I have been kept from serious sea-sickness & am very well. Our voyage & all connected with our journey & the transferring of goods etc. has all gone along so smoothly. God has heard & is answering prayer for us. As we three meet each morning in our state-room or in our hotel room to read together His Word & to pray[,] our dear friends in the Home land are always remembered.

We received letters here from America which were so full of love & good news. Also some from Africa which were full of thanksgiving for our coming to them. The work there is encouraging, 33 united with the church in Jan. & they have a communicants class [i.e., people studying for church membership] of nearly 100.

Dear ones & friends[,] pray for us & for Africa's children. May God be with you all.

Phil. 1: 3–11.[22]

With loving greetings to all[.]
Sincerely,
Nellie J. Arnott
May 18, 1905.
Lisbon.
Address. American Mission
Benguella[23]
Via Lisbon. W.C. Africa

Circular Letter #3

S.S. Ambaca June 6, 1905
In port at St. Thomas Island

I closed my last letter to you while in Lisbon but wrote you nothing of our stay there.

As one leaves the ocean and enters the river and harbor of Lisbon, one is impressed with the beauty of that old city. It is built on hills, so one can see rows of buildings beyond & above those in the foreground. In front of where our steamer was anchored there is a large open square with a large monument, of some Portuguese general mounted on a horse, in the center of it. Just beyond it is a large arch leading to one of the principal streets of the city.

On landing, I was at once impressed with the modern aspect of the city in many way[s]. The last few years they have begun using the electric cars. Most of them [are] marked as being made in St. Louis. They still use some strange looking horse cars largely. One evening we took an electric car ride through their most beautiful avenue & around the city. This avenue is very wide with squares, monuments, fountains & plots of gardens in the center of it extending the whole length of it. Nearly all the pavements are made of small pieces of white & black stone & most of these are laid in beautiful designs, the designs being formed of the black stone. Most of their open squares are also paved, for they have no turf. One of these squares is called "Rolly Motion Square" in English, as the design is such to give the appearance, as you walk across it, of walking over rolling pavement. One is inclined to step up on the rolls. One feels as he looks at these pavements & squares all over the city, that there has been an effort to make their city beautiful, & that they have not done things in such haste as we Americans do.

Their houses seem to be made largely of broken stone & mortar & then plastered or tiled on the outside. As the outside colors are delicate shades[,] the city presents a very white appearance. Many of the houses that are tiled are beautiful, in their design. As I said[,] the city is built on hills so that many of the houses facing one street will be four stor[ies] high & as they face the other they are only two stor[ies], and perhaps the cross street connecting these streets will consist of a wide row of stairs. On one street there is a large elevator that will take people up to the different streets above, so as to save their climbing the steep hilly streets or the step streets [i.e., streets taking the form of stair-steps].

There are also a large number of public & many private gardens all over the city. Vines & flowers overhang many of the walls in profusion.

All the shops are very unlike our American stores. They are very small. In the dairy shop the cows are tied right in the shop & as the milk is called for by customers the cows are milked. For the dairy wagon you will see a man driving a couple of cows through the streets, stopping in front of the houses of his customers & milking the amount they desire. One advantage over our America[n] way, there is no opportunity to dilute the milk.

The garden market is also brought to the door on the back of a little donkey. He will have a very large basket tied on each side & these will be loaded with vegetables. Often the loads are so large & heavy that the donkey can hardly be seen & one feels sorry for it. The fish & chickens are sold by women going through the streets with large baskets on their heads. In all parts of the city you can hear them soon after daylight begin yelling & they keep it up all day. These women dress in a very strange way. They are in bare feet & the skirt is short & very full, arranged at the waist over large rolls. Sometimes these rolls are also on the outside & the ends tied at one side. Those who sell chickens have a net arranged over their baskets, for the chickens are alive & need to be kept in.

Our American Minister at Lisbon is Col[onel] Cha[rle]s Page Bryan. He lives on this beautiful avenue I mentioned. Mr. Sanders had some business dealing with him & when he learned Mrs. Sanders & myself were in the city also, he invited us to take lunch with him one day. He showed us over his house, which is most beautiful. The stairway is beautiful. It is considered the finest in Europe. He is very pleasant to meet & I enjoyed the lunch but the best part of the visit was to sit in his library & see American papers, magazines, pictures etc. and our own dear flag. I forgot for a little while that I was in a foreign city.

One afternoon we visited Belem, about [a] one[-]hour street car ride from the city. Here there is an old mammoth cathedral with two high towers at each end of it. But in the center the walls have fallen away caused from poor foundation. The view of this cathedral from the harbor is very effective.

There are two English speaking churches in Lisbon, the Episcopal and Presbyterian. On Sunday we attended the Presbyterian church and heard a very good sermon by the pastor, Mr. Lithgow. After service we had a little visit with him. He said they had a membership of about fifty and the church carried on two Missions in the city among the Portuguese. That is[,] they are under the direction of the church, but the pastor & teachers are themselves Portuguese. As you know, Portugal is a Catholic country, but as in many foreign countries, Catholicism is in a very degraded condition compared with it in our country. So I was very glad to know that there was some mission work being done among them. It was certainly saddening to me to go through the streets & look into the faces of men & women, who expressed no spiritual light on their faces & of whom we can truly say, they have no Bible & know not the power of the indwelling Christ.

Mr. Sanders has Portuguese acquaintances living in Lisbon and while there we were invited to take dinner in their home. They seemed very much pleased at our accepting their invitation. Mr. Silva has business in Benguella & used to live there, but now is very wealthy & makes his home in Lisbon, but still has business in Benguella. His wife is a mulatto & he has four daughters and a son. The oldest daughter is married & lives near her father in a beautiful house. Two daughters are now young ladies & have had a very good education. They speak English & French and one of them paints and embroiders very well. The youngest daughter is only twelve & for her they have an English governess. The son is an invalid.

Their home is about five miles out of Lisbon, reached by the electric cars. Their grounds are very extensive [&] surrounded by a high stone wall. The entrance gate & drive way is beautiful, with its great trees & flowers on either side. Roses & flowers of all kinds are in profusion & great grape arbors extended both ways across their grounds. There are gardens of all kinds of vegetables & chicken, rabbits, pigeons, cats, dogs, & many other pets, of both animals & fowl. We took a walk all over the place & through the gardens & enjoyed it, too.

Their house is very large but furnished quite different than an American home. They have all the modern conveniences, & one of the parlors was quite home-like. The view from the parlors looked out over a beautiful country of hills. The dinner was thoroughly Portuguese but I liked many of their dishes. Mrs. Silva speaks the Umbundu language so Mrs. Sanders visited with her. Mr. Sanders visited with the men in his Portuguese & the young women visited with me in English. I had an opportunity in a quiet way to talk with these young women concerning the Bible & Jesus. They seemed very much interested to hear about Christian & missionary work & expressed a real soul-hunger. They asked many questions & expressed a desire to have their own lives count for something. I have come to have a real love for them & long to help them. I have been praying much for them & I want you to pray for them too, from time to time. I have a New Test[ament] for each of them which I had hoped to give them the morning we left Lisbon, but on account of the storm they did not come to the wharf. I am writing to them & if their father has no objections, I hope to send them to them. They said they would read them and seemed pleased to have a copy of the Book I love so much. So now all we can do is to pray for them & if we do this believingly, we may expect God's Spirit to reveal to them our Savior.

We left Lisbon Mon. morning May 22nd, sailing on a Portuguese steamer, "The Ambaca." The steamer was anchored out in the middle of the river, so we had to take a small sail boat from the wharf out to it. The tide was in & as it was windy & raining[,] we found this little trip very disagreeable. As we went up the steps on the steamer, the great waves dashed up getting us very wet. As we went out to sea[,] we found it very rough & for two days the waves dashed up to the deck making it impossible for us to have our port-holes open. With the bad air & this roughness I will confess to you that I was very, very sea-sick for a few days & have been more or less sea-sick all the time thus far. The accommodations are very different on this steamer than on the other two. We left Boston on a 14 thousand ton steamer; we left Liverpool on a 7 thousand ton steamer & this is about 3 thousand ton & we will land at Benguella on a tug.

We have been in port one day at St. Iago while they took on coal. We were in port all day Mon. at St. Prince Island & at present we are in port at St. Thomas Island.[24] These islands are owned by the Portuguese & consist of plantations of coco. They are beautiful islands, the verdure extending to the water's edge.[25] They say this Island is very rich & one would think so, to see the amount of cargo that is being unloaded here. Some 8 thousand volumes are being left by this steamer. We will be here four or five days.

I am becoming accustomed at seeing the people with whom I expect to work, these days. They are Africans, who are doing the work of unloading. Many of the natives on this Island have been brought from the interior of Africa & while the Portuguese call them "contracted laborers," yet they are really held as slaves. Mrs. Sanders says, they look and dress as the Biheans, that is, those who come out on the boats & are helping in unloading the cargo. Of course, we have not been ashore & do not see those who work the plantations.

We still have about eight days sailing on this steamer. We will be in port off & on all the rest of the way.[26] We hope to arrive in Benguella by the 18th or 19th.

I have tried to write these letters in such a way, so as to interest the boys & girls who are in many of the homes into which they will be sent. To them I send special love & want them to know they are remembered by me.[27] I want them to remember me & to pray for the children of Africa.

With best wishes and Christian love to all and thanking you for your remembrance of me, I am

Very Sincerely Your friend,
Nellie J. Arnott
American Mission
Benguella,
Via Lisbon. W.C. Africa
Mailed at St. Thomas Island.
June 7th, 1905

Circular Letter #4

Benguella, Africa. June 22, 1905[28]

The boys and girls in America are saying today, "This is the longest day in the year," but I am saying, "June 22 is the shortest day in the year." We are both right and I wonder how many can tell why June 22 is the longest day in the year in America and the shortest day in the year in Benguella, Africa.[29]

I mailed my last letter to you while we were in port at St. Thomas Island. We left there Friday June 9th at about four o'clock in the afternoon & were to cross the equator about seven that evening. But at seven the steamer suddenly stopped. Something about the engine had broken so we were there in mid ocean until long in the night waiting until the engine was mended.

There is quite a difference in the appearance of the northern & southern Atlantic. The North Atlantic is always more or less rough, usually white-caps all the time, but the South Atlantic has a glassy appearance, while there are often large swelling rolls, yet they are smooth on the surface much of the time.

Sunday, June 11, I had my first view of Africa. The coast is low and unattractive in appearance. Some places there are hills but they are bare & sandy. On this day, we were in port at Cabinda all day.[30] Here the steamer took on a crew of Cabinda natives to go with them and help in unloading cargo at the different ports. The Ambaca goes as far south as Tiger Bay then returns. It will be here the 25th of this month and will stop at all the ports on its return trip taking on cargo & mail. It takes these Cabinda natives as far as St. Thomas Island where they help in taking on a large load of coco[;] here they are left until the next steamer comes[,] which takes them on & carries them back to Cabinda. Some will remain at their home for a rest, others go on another trip.

June 12th we were in port at St. Antonio all day. This is at the mouth of the Congo River. For some distance before entering the river one can see its muddy waters out in the ocean. The Congo is very wide and has a swift current. We went up the river some distance before reaching the port. At all these ports[,] the Steamer is anchored some distance from land & the cargo is loaded from tugs & taken ashore. The steamer has a small steam launch which helps in this work by attaching the tugs to it [the launch] by a long rope & taking them to shore. While here the Captain invited Mr. & Mrs. Sanders & myself to go ashore with him in the launch so we did. St. Antonio is just a small place consisting of a post office, store, Governor's house, Steamboat headquarters & a few other buildings aside from the native houses. There are ten white men & one white woman living there, the rest being natives. It is a hot and sandy place, but as the rainy season has just closed[,] the plants & fruits were beautiful and abundant. We were given a very nice pine-apple, which we had for lunch the next day.

June 13th we were at Ambrisette & Ambriz. These ports are near together so we made them both in one day. They require that the steamer be in port at least six hours of daylight and then as much longer as is necessary.

June 14th we arrived at Loanda and were at this place four days while the steamer took off cargo & took on coal.[31] As at other places, we were anchored far out from the shore, so the coal was brought out on tugs & carried on in baskets. To have 650 tons brought on in this way caused a great deal of coal dust greatly to the discomfort of the passengers. This Steamer makes a month's voyage &[,] besides the coal they left Lisbon with[,] they took on about 800 tons on the voyage, while some of the North Atlantic steamers, the rapid ones, [use] about 600 tons in one day. The Ambaca only made about 12 knots an hour. At Loanda Mr. Taylor the English missionary, who had been in our company from Lisbon, left us. From Loanda he took the train which runs 200 miles inland to Lucalla.[32] It takes two days to make this trip on an African Railroad. They go 100 miles each day & tie up for the night. I saw the engine & cars & I fear our American boys would hardly have recognized them as a train. The story was told me of one of the interior native boys, who had seen the engine & train but had never seen a steam-launch. He came down to Loanda & from the house where he stopped he had a good view of the ocean, & when he saw the small steam launch running rapidly on the water he cried out, "I didn't know that the train ran on the water." Another Bihé boy was taken to London a few years ago by a Mr. Swan, one of the English missionaries.[33] He had never seen a train of cars & after landing Mr. Swan took him on the train with him. When it started[,] he became very much excited & leaned out of one window[,] then the other[,] & finally said, "Where is the horse[?] I want to see it."

At Loanda [illegible, crossed-out word] capital of Angola. The Governor & the English Consul live there. The Portuguese Government keeps several War Boats in the harbor at Loanda all the time and one afternoon our Captain invited Mrs. Sanders & myself to go out with him in the Steam launch & view these. They looked fine. There was one Hospital Boat among them. We landed on Loanda Island which is the Naval headquarters. We took a long walk & watched the marines from the Min[istry] of War drill. There was also a ship repair float in the harbor, which we visited. They were repairing one of the Congo River Steamers—Putting a new bottom in it.

Loanda has a population of about 600 white & 20,000 black people. It is built on the side of the hills & presents very much the same appearance from the harbor as Lisbon. That is, the buildings are of the same material & there are a large number of trees & public gardens & open squares. The Streets are very wide. Of course, there are no Street cars & very little traffic except by native carriers. One evening we went ashore with the Captain & promenaded while the band played. The band consisted wholly of negroes. Another evening we walked all over the city. It was bright moon light, so we were able to get a very good idea of it. They have a very large & modern hospital there.

You will understand the character of many of the white people living in Angola when I tell you that our steamer brought 10 prisoners from Portugal. According to their sentence they are imprisoned or do government work or are allowed to live independently except as they are watched by officials. Many after they serve their turn of sentence are freed & become traders throughout this province. These were landed at Loanda under the guard of several soldiers.

We spent one very happy day at Loanda in visiting the Methodist Episcopal Mission.[34] They own a very nice place there[;] the grounds are large & the buildings convenient. It is situated on a hill that overlooks the ocean. The missionaries are Mr. and Mrs. Shields, Mrs. Shuitt, whose husband died in Africa a few years ago, Miss Turner, Miss Mason & a mulatto worker, and I don't think I ever met a group of more earnest, happy, joyous Christians in my life than they were. They had been transformed so that their very faces shone. No sacrifice had been too great for them. In most mission fields it is possible for parents to keep their children until they are about ten[,] but at Loanda little white children do not live. Mrs. Shields has four little ones in England.[35] About two years ago during the sickness of two of the little ones, her only hope was to start with them for Eng[land]. In the first two weeks on the steamer she didn't know what moment one or both might be taken, but through the goodness of God they recovered after being brought very near death. In a most remarkable way in Eng[land] a home was opened to these little ones. While there the fourth little one came to gladden a mother's heart & yes, to sadden it too for when this baby was only six weeks old she left it with the other three & returned to her husband & work at Loanda. She has full charge of an important school at Loanda & as it was not possible to have any one take her place at that time[,] she felt her duty was to return, seeing God had provided a home as perfect as possible for her children, apart from her own. I'm sure you will be glad to know, as I was that Mr. & Mrs. Shields are to have a furlough this fall & so will be with their children for a time. They have been in this mission a long time & have passed through many trying experiences aside from making this great sacrifice of separation from children. I felt I understood the glow on their faces somewhat, for they have lived so close to God & have drawn on His grace & help so constantly that they reveal His likeness through these mortal bodies. Will you not pray for these missionaries, as I have been led to do[?]. II Cor. 3:18.[36]

We had another happy surprise while at Loanda. Mr. F. S. Arnot, who was the first to go to Africa under the English "Brethren" Mission, about 1881, & who has traveled over Africa largely & has written a book "Garanganza," arrived at Loanda from the interior.[37] He had been called to London to consider accepting the position as one of the two directors of the Müller Orphan Homes. While Africa will miss him, if he decides to accept, yet on account of his health being so poor in Africa we feel that this is an opening for longer service for him. I am sure many of you will be interested in reading his book & will add it to your Missionary Library. We had a good visit with him & to me, it was a great pleasure to meet the missionary of whom I had read & heard so much.

Sunday June 18th we were in port at Novo Redondo all day, but being Sunday we remained on ship-board & read all day. The next day we spent at Lobito Bay. That is a beautiful bay & the only place where the steamer can go up to dock. A company of Englishmen have been given the contract to build a railroad extending inland from this point.[38] They are building a strong pier & most of the material for the R.R. will be unloaded there. At Lobito we took a long walk on the sea shore & gathered some very pretty shells. As it is only 2 ½ hours from Lobito to Benguella we came on Mon. evening June 19th & the ocean that evening was the most beautiful sight, I think I ever saw. During this run we remained on deck & just watched the beautiful sea. The sea was flecked with phosphorescent light. As the flying fish & ducks would touch the surface of the water they would leave a light & the propeller caused a stream of light to follow the boat. Until we anchored, the sea was beautiful. Being late we remained on board over night & landed in Benguella June 20, being almost two months since we left Boston.

I must now tell you about the news we received from our Station & then close as this will be too long if I tell you all I should like to in this [letter]. At Loanda, we received letters from Miss [Sarah] Stimpson who is at Kamundongo—the station to which we go. Some of you will remember of my telling you of the fires there during the dry season. At that time it was thought the buildings were set on fire by enemies & now again this dry season the fires have begun again. Several of the native houses had been burned & Lumbo, whose house was burned last season & he had built a new one, had his new one burned. Two of the girls['] houses in Miss Stimpson's compound had been burned. When the letter was closed[,][39] the fires had been spread out over a month's time & they had watched nights & yet had been unable to catch anyone. It is generally believed that the buildings are set on fire by the slaves of the Portuguese.[40] That as soon [as] they see any prosperity in the Station then there is the effort to hinder the work if possible. But God uses such things to work out His best purposes. Miss Stimpson writes that the natives are keeping in good spirits & are making earnest prayers. They are being tried by fire in a very literal sense & we believe they will be stronger Christians because of these trials. But you must all pray for them & so help them by prayer. In April, 32 joined the church. Thus making 65 since Jan. 1st.

With love and best wishes to all, I am
Faithfully yours in His Service,
Nellie J. Arnott
American Mission
Benguella
Via Lisbon. W.C. Africa
Mailed July 14, 1905

Circular Letter #5[41]

Benguella, W. C. Africa, July 11, 1905

We landed in Benguella June 20th and have been detained here longer than we expected on account of the Steamer we came on from Lisbon, being unable to bring all of our goods. So we have had to wait here for the next Steamer which arrived here Sunday, being nearly a week late. They have been unloading the last two days & we hope to get everything through the custom-house during the next two days. If so we will start on our journey up country the last of the week. We feel that we have much to be grateful for in the safe arrival of our goods, as this Steamer "The Benguella" had a fire in the hold for three days on the way down. Some 14000 volumes of cargo were burned, but ours are unhurt.

Benguella is a town of about 2000 inhabitants, 600 of them being white. It is spread out over a large area, with many large open spaces. There are a very few straight streets, but what there are[, are] very wide. It looks as though each one had chosen his place to build without any regard to streets. There are no side-walks but all walk in the middle of the street. There is very little traffic outside of carriers. The Governor of Benguella district lives here & his jurisdiction extends over Bihé, the district in which we live. Of course, he has a nice place & then the Manager of the Telegraph, Mr. Kitchen[,] has a very nice place. He is English & we have enjoy[ed] taking tea with him several afternoons since being here. There are two hotels, several shops & a few other buildings. There is also a good jail, hospital, custom house & a good market place.

We visited the market this morning. It is a large square fenced in with a high iron fence. There are two long sheds[,] one on either side extending across it. Under these sheds the natives sit with their provisions. They just spread out a piece of cloth & on this is fish, meats, manioc [i.e., cassava or yucca plant], beans, eggs[,] etc. Women with their babies sit around selling what they can from their baskets. It is all so dirty that one feels as though they never could eat some things again. Some have bundles of sticks, others baskets of char-coal. As we were leaving[,] several came in with a basket on their heads in which was one very large fish just brought from the ocean. Here they would cut them up & sell them piece by piece.

Some of the women in this district wear a very large collar. Two of the women in the market had these on & Mr. Sanders asked one of them if I might lift her collar. I did so & it weighs fully ten pounds. Mr. Sanders says some of them are larger & weigh even more. It is about five inches in diameter & is made of strings & strings of small beads that have been matted together with palm-oil, dirt, etc. and then all bound together with bands of brass or iron so that it is solid like a stone. It cannot be taken off but they wear it night and day. At night the wearer pushes it up as far as she can on her neck and uses it as a pillow.[42]

Across the corner from where we are boarding is a large public garden. It is fenced in with an iron fence and in the center is a fountain from which the women get water in large cans. These they carry on their heads to the remotest parts of the garden & water the plants & trees. Every morning we can see them sweeping the paths with brush & making a great dust. They do not need any signs [such as] "Keep off the grass," as there is no grass in all Benguella. The plants & trees in the garden are very pretty. At present the oleanders are in bloom & a few very pretty roses as well as other varieties of flowers. I am sure the boys & girls would think some of the trees here very strange, for they not only send roots down into the ground but many of them send long roots out on their branches.

Today[,] July 14th, Mrs. Sanders & I took a walk & in one of the streets we found a washing of cloths spread out on the ground to dry. Nearby was a pig wandering around. It is very seldom one sees a clothsline here and much of the washing is done in the ocean.

We have been told that the Ambaca, the steamer we came on, on its return took 150 "contracted laborers" to St. Thomas Island to work on the coco plantations.⁴³ I am very sorry we missed seeing them embark. As I told you in a previous letter, these "contracted laborers" are really slaves. They have been bought or captured in the far interior of Africa & are tied or chained together & brought to the coast & here sold to some plantation owner. Under the Portuguese law[,] each one is asked if he will go to St. Thomas & work for seven years. He puts a cross for his name & is given a number which is tied about his neck. They are also given clothing or rather clothes, tobacco & most any little thing to make them happy as they start off. Many of them have little idea as to what they are going to. Within a few years as a result of the climate, hard labor & treatment[,] most of them sicken & die. If any live the seven years[,] the contract is renewed, their being too ignorant to know when the time is up or what the renewal means. So those who go never return & they transport them in gangs of 150 and more constantly, as so many are dying all of the time. To me, this seems like a terrible form of slavery. Mr. Cadbury, who buys much of the coco from St. Thomas Island, is sending an inspector out to investigate the cultivation of the coco & he says, if he finds that it is being cultivated by slaves he will not buy it.⁴⁴ The great pity is that most inspectors are unable to see things as they really are, but his report is to be published in one of Harper's publications & I hope all will watch for them & read them.⁴⁵ I think the boys & girls will be interested in reading about the cultivation of the coco.

August 10, 1905[,] Kamundongo [continuation of the same letter]

It took so long to get our goods from the custom-house at Benguella that we did not succeed in getting away from there until July 17ᵗʰ.

We had expected about 125 carriers to come for us but only 35 came. It is very hard to get carriers in this district because so many have gone to the interior to get rubber.⁴⁶ The 35 were only enough to take us & our camping supplies & a few loads that are much needed. I was interested in watching Mr. Sanders give out the loads the morning we left Benguella. Among them were our two steamer trunks that are carried as double loads. The carriers do not like to carry double loads, & knowing this, Mr. Sanders brought them out first. The carriers were all standing around him in the court & these two loads were on the ground. One after another would lift & then they would talk to each other & to Mr. Sanders about them. But he remained patient &

would joke [with] them some. Finally two offered to take one of them, but [for] the other he had to call the names of two & ask them to take it. While they will complain & talk much before taking such loads, after they once take them never a word of complaint is heard. The rest being single loads were quickly taken. The double loads weigh about 100 pounds & the single loads about 64 pounds. The carriers take them & tie long sticks[,] one on either side. These help them in loading them to their shoulder or head & thus they carry all of our supplies the 300 miles inland. Each load costs us about $5 to be brought from Benguella to Kamundongo.

For our camping on the way[,] we each had a bed load, then we had four loads of food supplies, including pots & dishes. Each tent made two loads and our chairs a load. Then six men carried each tepoia, that is, two carried at a time for three hours or less & then change to another two. Besides our loads some of the carriers had loads of salt or cloth & for these they had with them some relative to carry. Then there were several children in the caravan who carried the meal & pots for the carriers. These children were about 12, 13 & 14 years of age & some of them were girls. It was pitiful to see them walk all the way with those loads. This is the way they get their training for carrying.[47] For their food & the cooking of it, they group together. Relatives & friends form what they call an "iko." If there is a girl in the group she gets the water & gathers the wood & cooks the mush for her group. All along the road are camping places, usually near the streams. At these places are huts made of branches or grass where the caravans stop. These are very dirty places, you can imagine & it is rather fortunate that at least once a year these places are all burned off. For this whole country is burned off every dry season. It is done in order to destroy the wild animals, reptiles & insects that would multiply to too great numbers if it was not done. This had already been done in large measure & so the country was black, but some places they were just burning & the boys would run with us past these places, the fire coming right up to the path. Nights we sometimes saw the fires on the hills in the distance & they were very pretty.

I can't say that I enjoyed traveling in the tepoia. It seems like a very lazy mode of travel, but nevertheless I found I was very tired each day at the end of our six hours journey.

The tepoia has an upper part that is about 2 feet by 6 feet & is covered with a heavy white canvas that hangs down on each side about six inches so shading the eyes. This top is fastened to a long palm-pole that extends beyond it four or five feet [from each] end. A short distance beyond the top & to this pole are fastened two iron hooks at each end. From these is hung a strong net or hammock. There is a pad fastened on each end of the pole & the carriers let these rest on their shoulders or head when they carry. When one gets in[,] they stoop & you throw yourself in & with a pillow at your head you start out very comfortable. But sometimes they run & then you get a good shaking up. Then every hill you come to you must get out & walk up. I enjoyed this when there were not too many. At most of the streams we would get out & cross them on a few sticks, that answered for a bridge. Some days it was constant getting out and in.

Mr. Sanders bought a donkey in Lisbon and he rode it some of the time, but much of the way he had great trouble with it in getting it over the rocky mountain passes & over the muddy streams. So he had to walk much of the way.

The tepoia men are the last to leave camp in the morning but usually arrive a full hour before the load men in the afternoon. As the tepoia passed the load-men, they were made to step out of the path as the tepoia has the right of way. It was often hard to see this done, although my carriers were often very considerate.

Our first day's travel was from Benguella to Catumbella, a distance of 15 miles.[48] There we stopped with a Dutch family. He acted, at one time, as the agent for our Mission at the coast. There we were fortunate in meeting Rev. W. S. Curry and wife from the Cisamba Station and Mrs. [Marion] Webster from Bailundu Station.[49] They had just arrived from the interior & were on their way home for furlough. That afternoon and evening we all had a nice visit together. I hope some who read this letter may have opportunity to meet these missionaries while they are in America.

Mrs. Curry told me something of the trip they took two years ago, going far into the interior. She said for five months they traveled and did not see a white person or a missionary. The opportunities there are in Africa for teaching the Word, while so many in America are being over-fed. Oh, that God would put it into the hearts of many more to come to this dark land. Here in our own Station we need a physician very badly and Miss [Emma] Redick at Ocileso needs some young woman to be associated with her in the school work there. Will you not pray especially that these two workers may be sent out this next year[?]

I still have many things I want to tell you about our journey inland, but as this letter is long enough, I will leave them until the next mail. I am now at Kamundongo and am spending about five hours each day in language study. I need your prayers very much these days, and I do feel that I already have them. I can hardly wait for the time when I can understand the natives and when I can talk to them easily.

Will you not begin praying for Kapitango[?] He is the chief of Kamundongo village, which is only a few moments['] walk from our Station. He has heard the Words all these years, but has never been very friendly. But lately he has favored a school being started in the village and seems to be near the kingdom. If he would take a stand he would have a great influence not only in his own village but in many others where he is known.

"Pray without ceasing." 1 Thess. 5:17.

Sincerely yours,
Nellie J. Arnott
American Mission Benguella, W. C. Africa (Via Lisbon)
Mailed from Kamundongo Aug. 21–05[50]

Inland in a Tepoia

From *Life and Light for Woman*, March 1906

Kamundongo, Africa, August 26, 1905.

Before telling you of our welcome here and of the happenings since our arrival I want to tell you something more of our journey inland. We left Catumbella Tuesday, July 18, and we arrived here just three weeks later. As the first two days' journey from Catumbella are over a desert country[,] we did not leave until one o'clock, and traveled until dark, carrying with us what water we could in bottles. Wednesday morning we arose by four, and started out with the first ray of light, and traveled until about ten, when we reached a river. Here we stopped while the carriers cooked mush and ate and drank and washed. Many of them had not eaten since leaving Catumbella, and had had no water. Their custom is not to eat in the morning, but wait until they get in camp each day. This desert is a continuation of stony hills and mountains. We had to walk a great part of the way these days through narrow mountain passes, and up and down steep hills. In the hot sun this became very tiresome to me, and seeing the carriers with their heavy loads made my heart ache. While sitting on the bank of the river waiting for the carriers[,] I counted nine large, black monkeys in the trees across the stream. It is very pretty at this place. The stream flows through a rocky bed with green trees on either side, and rocky mountains in the distance.

We journeyed on a couple of hours, and then camped near the river Wednesday night, and remained in camp until about ten Thursday morning, as again we had to travel two days before reaching water. The path was harder and worse in every way than the first two days. We had to walk or rather climb nearly all the way. Some places the path was very narrow between rocks or on the edge of a precipice. It is a wonder to me how the carriers get our loads and furniture through these places.[51] Friday of that week we camped in the Cisanji country. Here our carriers bought food, or rather exchanged the rations they received at the coast, of cloth, salt, and hoes, for meal, potatoes, beans, and native beer. The women from the villages near[by] came to the camp with these provisions, carrying them in baskets on their heads, and with their babies tied on their backs.[52] I sat all the afternoon and watched them exchange, and I began to realize as never before what that word "heathen" means. The women had their hair braided and soaked with palm oil, and their faces and bodies were marked. One very young girl had her baby on her back. How my heart went out to these women; I just wanted to stay there and work. They have never been touched with the gospel. I felt very much depressed these first days as I came in contact with our carriers and with the people here and there on the road. And I have prayed since as never before that God would send out some of the young people in America into this field of heathen darkness. No sacrifice is too great to make for Him, if He calls you here.

Saturday we passed a military post, and a large Portuguese plantation of sugar-cane, coffee, and sweet potatoes. The latter they use for making rum which they sell to the natives. Rum is even a greater curse in this country, it seems to me, than at home.[53] We were sorry that it was necessary to travel the next day, being Sunday, but on account of the carriers not having sufficient food we had to push on where food could be bought. Every evening the carriers would gather around one of their fires and have prayers together. It almost made me homesick when I would hear their voices ring out on some of our familiar hymns.[54]

Sunday evening they had a prayer meeting, and the next Sunday when we remained in camp all day Mr. Sanders held a service, and about thirty came from the villages near[by]. After the first week we reached the made road and followed it most of the way. This we liked much better than the narrow paths. There was not as much shade, but we were saved from having the bushes and branches scratching us on either side. These roads are little used, and there [is] no low undergrowth of bushes. After the first week we left most of the mountains, but remained among the hills until we reached Bailundu the end of the second week. After the country is burned off[,] the leaves and flowers come out in such beautiful colors. At home the children gather colored leaves when the leaves are falling in the fall, but here the trees put on their brightest dresses of greens and reds and browns when they leave out in August. The variety of colors made some of the hillsides very beautiful. And the flowers! They were so pretty all the way, and such a variety. Many of them [are] very different from any I had ever seen. One day I gathered fifty different varieties in just a short distance.

One of my tepoia carriers, Balaca, had a sister in the caravan as meal carrier, and after a few days out they asked if she might sleep in my tent. So every night she would bring her cloth and lie down on a bed of leaves and sleep. How I wished I could talk to her, but all I could say was their word of greeting and a few disconnected words. She is one of Miss Stimpson's girls. Miss Stimpson has about thirty girls who sleep in our compound. She has four houses for them. But I must not stop here to tell you about these girls.

July 26th we camped in the Civula country. The people in the surrounding villages hold themselves as Mr. Sanders' friends, so we were camped only a short time when one chief came with a present of a goat, and later another chief from another village came with a goat and a large basket of meal. Mr. Sanders received these gifts and passed them over to our carriers who were delighted to have meat for their supper that night. While these things were brought as gifts, yet they expect Mr. Sanders to send them a present in return. So the first time any of our carriers go through their villages he will send them a present of cloth which will equal the value of the goats.[55] This way of giving presents reminds one of much of the Christmas giving in America. While in camp here many of the women and children from the villages came to look at the white women. They would stand outside of our tents and watch every movement, and make remarks regarding our appearance and dress. The people in these villages also have been given the Bread of Life. This tribe and the Cisanji tribe is small, so the missionaries have passed them by and come to the Biheans, which is a large tribe, and who travel to nearly all parts of Africa.

August 1st: Shortly after leaving camp we reached the Kevi River. It was the only large stream we crossed. Mrs. Sanders and myself and the carriers and tepoias were first towed over in a large boat. You can imagine it had to make a good many trips to take over all of our loads and carriers. All the other streams we crossed by crude bridges of sticks, or the carriers carried us across where there were no bridges. About two hours after leaving the Kevi River we entered Bailundu, one of our mission stations.[56] Here we remained over one day so as to have a visit with the missionaries there. At Bailundu is Mr. [Wesley] Stover, one of the early missionaries. His wife is in Chicago at present. Also Mr. and Mrs. [William] Fay and their two youngest children. They have three in America being educated. Also Mr. and Mrs. [Henri] Neipp, who have been out a year under our Board, although they have been missionaries in Africa before. Miss [Elizabeth] Campbell belongs there, although for the past year she has been here with Miss Stimpson. She has just returned. I enjoyed our visit there very much, but was not there long enough to see any of the work. They told us that every part of the work there was encouraging, and the missionaries seemed happy and grateful to be there.

We were six days coming from Bailundu here, and from there I did not have a tent, as the tent carriers were Bailundu men, and did not want to come on, so my tepoia men made me a sort of a hut to sleep in each night. They just surrounded a space with branches, but put nothing overhead, so it was like sleeping in the open. I really enjoyed this, as it was moonlight and all beautiful above. It was rather cold, so the girls would have a fire in the center of the hut each night. The first of August we saw quite heavy frosts along the stream. We made this journey during the coldest part of the year, and many nights I felt the cold very much. There was hardly a day while on the road but that we met two or more caravans going toward the coast. Some of them were carrying rubber from the far interior, others going to the coast for loads. The largest one we met was a caravan of over one hundred. There were in it a large number of loads of rubber, besides eleven elephants' tusks, each a load for one man. One of the men tried to steal a dried fish from one of the meal carriers in our caravan, which made some trouble. Mrs. Sanders happened to be near, so was able to settle the trouble.

In this caravan were a large number of women with light loads, and some of them had babies on their backs. Mr. Sanders said, "Without doubt, most of these would be shipped slaves when they reached the coast." He knows the Portuguese to whom this caravan belonged, and he is a successful trader. We were told that there are two men (Portuguese) here in Bihé who are licensed to buy slaves.[57]

The last night on the road we camped about twelve miles out from Kamundongo. Here we heard from a near village of the death of the best man in our station. He had been the leader among the Christians here, and really acted as pastor of the church. Everybody loved him and looked up to him for advice. He was a teacher also in one of the villages near[by]. Mr. and Mrs. Sanders felt very badly to hear of his death, and felt that their best worker had gone.

August 8th we arose early and were soon nearing our home. We were met out a long distance by one man, who made known our approach by firing a gun several times. Then next we were met by all the children, each carrying a banana leaf and singing. They also had two flags, the Portuguese and the United States. And then we were met by the men and women of our own station and the surrounding villages. Every man had his gun, which he fired every few moments, and the women made a curious noise with their mouths. They ran alongside our tepoias screaming, yelling and shouting, and shooting their guns for a long distance before we reached Mr. Sanders' house.[58] I am sure I was never in such a noise in all my life, not even on Fourth of July at home. I must say all this seemed very heathenish to me, but it is their way of rejoicing and showing they were glad we had come; but it was certainly a noisy welcome.

After reaching Mr. Sanders' yard we got out of our tepoias, and Mr. [Merlin] Ennis, Miss Stimpson and Miss Campbell greeted us; then we entered the house and took chairs, and the natives came in to greet us. When one comes from a long distance they say their word of greeting three times; that is, each one stooped or sat on the floor in front of us and said Kalunga, and then we replied Kalunga, and so on for three times. It seemed to me I sat there a very long time and just said Kalunga over and over. After this was over we had dinner together and visited. There is one thing we feel very strongly, and that is that we have a most cordial welcome from both missionaries and natives.[59]

KAMUNDONGO, WEST CENTRAL AFRICA

From *Mission Studies*, April 1906[60]

Kamundongo, Africa, Sept. 11, 1905.

The Station consists of the Mission buildings and about seventy-five native houses. The Mission buildings are an old church building, Mr. Sanders' house, Mr. Ennis' house, a store building, a large medicine house, and the house Miss Stimpson and myself occupy. The church building is unsafe and looks ready to fall down, and the school building was burned a year ago; so on our arrival Mr. Sanders felt that we must have a new building. He called all the men on the Station together the second evening after we arrived and talked over with them the possibilities of putting up a building before the rains should set in. They decided it could be done, so Mr. Ennis took charge of the men and the next Monday they began our new school building. The outside walls are made of sun-dried bricks and the roof will be thatched with long grass. It has one door and three windows on either side and two windows at each end. At present there will be just one room, but next year, after we get a church building, we hope to have it divided into rooms giving us one large center room for the Kindergarten and two class rooms at each end. This year we must do the best we can with the one large room.

We trust that this building will not be burned. Since I wrote you last we have had another fire. A native house was set on fire about midnight and as the wind was very strong another house was set from it. We hardly think our enemies will dare to set fire to any Mission property, and we hope all fires will soon cease. The rains are about beginning, so there will not be quite so much danger the next few months.

I wish you might see all our beautiful orange trees. Mr. Sanders planted the seed years ago and now we have about thirty trees that are bearing well. They have been loaded ever since we have been here and Mr. Sanders sends loads of them to the Stations that do not have them. At Bailundu they also have plenty of oranges. We also have plenty of bananas, guavas, strawberries and all garden vegetables. The gardens can be planted so we can have fresh vegetables the year around.

Since we have been here we have had plenty of fresh meat, as August, September, and October are the months for hunts. The men in the village have had one or two hunts each week and usually kill one or more "ombambi," which is a small antelope, or an "onusi," a large antelope. Mr. Ennis often goes with them on these hunts, and the other day he shot both an onusi and an ombambi. They have two kinds of hunts—the drive hunt, when men go to the head of two streams and form a line across the country between the streams and then walk down, driving the animals before them to the place where the streams come together or empty into another stream. At this point[,] a few of the best hunters are in waiting and shoot the animals as they appear and try to escape by crossing the stream. The other is a fire hunt. I told you in a previous letter how they burn off the country each year. They usually leave places where they do not burn and into these the animals flee. Then some day when they wish a hunt the men will surround one of these unburned places and set fire to the long grass. As the fire gets near the center the animals try to escape and are shot by the hunters.[61] So during these months we have plenty of fresh meat, and one of the ladies in the Mission has discovered how to can the extra meat on hand and it has proven to be much better than the American canned meats.

On our arrival Miss Stimpson was in the midst of having her house rethatched. Last rainy season the roof leaked very badly, so it was necessary to have new grass put on. They take all the old grass off and then tie little bundles of new grass to the sticks. These are tied so closely together and on top of one another until the whole roof is well covered and it has been so well done that we found it did not leak anywhere during the first hard rain. Of course after the thatching was done we had to clean house, as the taking off and the putting on of the new grass caused dirt to sift down constantly. I used to dislike house cleaning in America, but it is certainly much worse here. First we took up our mats, then let down our ceilings. Our walls are as high as our rooms, and over the top of these are stretched white cotton cloth for ceilings. So much grass had fallen on these that they had to be taken down and cleaned. After they were put up[,] the ceilings and walls were whitewashed. There is a place near the brook where the boys dig up the white earth, thin it with water, strain the sand out and make us all the whitewash we need. As our floors are earth, these are wet down and swept off each day while the mats are up. The mats are made of heavy reeds woven together with bark string and make very nice coverings for our floors. These with a few rugs here and there give very good protection. One does not mind spilling water on the floor, as the more often our floors are wet down[,] the less apt we are to have jiggers. This little insect has been a great annoyance to me. They are smaller, but look very much like a flea, and they work their way under the skin around the toenails. If they are not found within a few hours they begin to form a little sack. Often they are not discovered until this begins to inflame, and then you can remove the little white sack whole. If it is broken it is apt to make a bad sore. Among the natives one will often see parts of the toe gone and deformed feet because of continued jigger sores.

Figure 10: Four Photographs from Ocileso. Courtesy of The Bancroft Library, University of California, Berkeley.

Letter to ABCFM Official Reverend Judson Smith[62]

Ocileso, Africa
Oct. 4, 1905
Judson Smith, D.D.
14 Beacon St.
Boston, Mass.

My Dear Dr. Smith—You may wonder at my being away from Kamundongo so soon after my arrival on the field. But on reaching Kamundongo[,] we found Miss Stimpson very tired and nervous and all felt she should have a complete change. As it did not seem best for her to come here alone, they delegated me to accompany her.

I am devoting a large part of each day to language study and Miss Stimpson is giving me a daily drill.

Miss Stimpson is improving under the baths and with the outings that are possible here. This is a beautiful place and I believe will prove to be a great blessing to all of the stations as a resting place for the missionaries, as well as grow into a successful work among the natives.[63]

Miss Redick does need some one to help her very much. Already the school is too large for one teacher. Mr. & Mrs. Woodside hope to help her some but their work in school can not be permanent & they are more or less interrupted all of the time. The work here is growing rapidly and there are such large opportunities on every side. The villages are almost untouched, as yet. This is a splendid field and it is a great pity that some young woman isn't enjoying the blessed privilege of service here.

I have been sorry that I didn't tell you, while in Boston, of a Miss Olive Norris I knew in Oberlin. She graduated last June from the College and although she is a Presbyterian[,] she [was] very much interested through her stay in Oberlin in our Mission. The other day Miss Redick received a letter from her concerning the Volunteer Band at Oberlin & in it she mentioned the possibility of going out as a missionary.[64] Knowing her interest in our Mission & her readiness to come here, I just felt perhaps she might be secured for this Station. I'm very sure she will make a good missionary. She used to speak of the difficulty of getting a language, but I'm sure that is because she underrates her own ability. With the mental training she has had, she could get the language better than I ever can, and I hope to get it so I can do a real work at Kamundongo.

Miss Norris' present address is Spencer New York. The work is so great here that I hope she or some one else may be found soon. If Miss Redick goes home in two years[,] some one should be here soon so as to be prepared to take up the work here while she is away. If she could go home next year it would be far better, for she has fever rather often and all think that after she has had a year in America that she will be better on her return.

It is hard too to be so far from a physician. It seems to me it is a mistake to have Dr. Wellman so far away until after the arrival of another physician in Bihé. Last week Miss Redick was sick a few days and it did not seem to be her usual attack of fever. We did all we knew for her but one evening while suffering a good deal she said, "I do wish Dr. Wellman was nearer." Her remark just set me to thinking how helpless we are with him so far away. So we will all be very glad when a physician is found for Bihé.

Because of the continued fires at Kamundongo, Mr. Ennis will likely remain there for the present. We are very glad for he is much needed & all like him. He is a good worker in many ways and I know if he remains there Mr. Sanders will be able to help him much in the language, as he is such a good teacher.

As I have been able to see the work this far, I think the work at Kamundongo is much larger than at the other Stations. The Station is large & this makes the school large, besides the villages are near enough so the people come from them to services and school. Then there are a large number of outstation schools where there are large opportunities for work.

Before Mr. Sanders knew Mr. Ennis was to leave, he had expected to spend a large part of his time in working in these outstations, but if he is left alone, it will not be possible. Mr. Sanders is so nice with the natives and they all love him and are ready to follow him. I just pray that I may be such a missionary as Mr. & Mrs. Sanders are. I thank God for placing me with them and that our work is at Kamundongo.

Miss Stimpson has been here just seven years and she is very much in need of her furlough but does not want to take it. We hope to be able to persuade her to go to America next year. She has done a good and faithful work.

Mr. and Mrs. Niepp are also here for a short rest & in order to have their teeth fixed, so we are having quite a reunion. They are very nice. I like the spirit they manifest in all things very much.

I often remember with pleasure my little visit in your home. Remember me to Mrs. Smith and your daughters.

Very Sincerely Yours,
Nellie J. Arnott

Kamundongo No. II.

From *Mission Studies*, May 1906

We have [a] very good water supply. At the brook near[by] there is a very large rock and from this runs out a small stream of clear cold water all the time. Then from another stream above our Station have been dug irrigation ditches to our gardens and other points where water is desired. This enables us to have gardens both in the rainy and dry season.

One out-station has been opened since our arrival. The village is near; Kaputango, the old chief, has heard the Word for years, and Mr. Sanders has often talked with him and prayed for him all these years, but he would not become a Christian himself, nor allow a school in his village, nor allow the children at his village to come to the school at the Station.[65] But the last few months he has been changing and invited one of our men to have a school at his village, so we all went up one afternoon and had a formal opening of the school. The teacher goes up every morning and calls all together who will come and is now teaching them the one hundred syllables which make up their language. These are printed on a piece of cloth which is hung up in the center of the village and around this the men, women and children gather and repeat them over after the teacher until they know them all. As fast as these are learned they get a primer and read from that, and then they begin reading the different books of the Bible. I am sure some boys and girls in America would be very glad if they did not have to learn to spell. It is not necessary in this language[,] for as soon as one can pronounce a word he can write it.

Kapitango attends the Sunday services and seems to be very happy to have Mr. Sanders back and he says he is going to be a Christian. It means he must give up all but one of his many wives, he must stop drinking beer and give up all his charms and fetishes.[66] He is a man of large influence and has been a great hindrance to the work here, but now we are hopeful and are praying earnestly for him. Will you not pray for him too? The teacher also goes to the village each afternoon and has reading and explaining of the Bible and songs and prayers with them.

In every village is an onjango, which is the native sitting room. It is in a central place and here the men sit and eat their meals. The afternoon we went to Kapitango's village[,] we sat on little stools in the shade of the onjango. The chief sat next to Mr. Sanders on a stool, but the rest sat on the ground. Some of our Station people went up so there was quite a large gathering, but in the midst of Mr. Sanders' remarks (which I could not understand of course), the funny side came to me. There we sat in the dirt among half clothed men and women and naked children with pigs, chickens and goats running here and there among them. Two kids became separated from their mother and such crying and bleating. Mr. Sanders could hardly be heard. While he could hardly think because of these disturbances, yet the people are so used to them that they listened and did not seem to mind them.

Every evening prayers are held with all on the Station. They gather in the church and since Mr. Sanders has returned he has been leading them. He reads a portion of scripture and explains it and then they have a couple of prayers offered by the native Christians, and sing a couple of songs. Our first Sunday was full of interest to me. The church was filled, there being present about five hundred people. Their faces were happy and they were glad to have Mr. Sanders preach to them again. It was a sad service too, for just about two weeks before our arrival the best Christian man on the Station died. He had been the leader and Mr. Sanders was sad over his loss. There were three hundred and forty-five at Sunday school. The classes sat on the ground in groups here and there and Miss Stimpson had the little ones in her yard. This does very well during the dry season, but when the rain comes it is necessary to be under cover.

It will be hard to have Sunday school as it should be, as long as we only have the one building. Sunday afternoon Mrs. Sanders has the meeting for women and during this hour I am entertaining the little children. At present I can only sing with them and show them pictures and say a few words.

Notes

1. Arnott gives no indication elsewhere in her writings as to what this "mistake" in Los Angeles may have been; perhaps it related to her train schedule.

2. The WBMI, affiliated with the ABCFM in Boston, supported mission work and publications, including *Mission Studies*, which was aimed at women in the midwestern U.S. The WBMI paid most of Arnott's salary while she was in Angola.

3. Dr. Joseph Sanders was the brother of Rev. William H. Sanders, who accompanied Arnott to Angola. Dr. Sanders had been one of Arnott's physicians when she had surgery at the sanitarium in Clifton Springs in 1903.

4. Arnott is referencing the ABCFM. Rev. Elnathan E. Strong was the Editorial Secretary of the Board.

5. The leaders Arnott alludes to here are John O. Means and his wife, Jane. Reverend Means, who died in 1883, had supported a mission in Angola since his youth, when he visited Príncipe and saw conditions among the enslaved Africans. The ABCFM, of which he was a member, appointed him to investigate possible sites for a new African mission, and he recommended the highlands of Angola (Soremekun, "History of the American Board Missions," 47). His wife, Jane, was a strong supporter of women's missions; the Means School in Angola was eventually named for her at Nellie Arnott's request.

6. The Woman's Board of Missions (WBM) of the ABCFM in Boston sponsored mission work and publications aimed primarily at women in the northeastern U.S.

7. Dr. Judson Smith was the Foreign Secretary of the ABCFM and particularly encouraged a larger role for women missionaries. He died in 1906. His papers are at the Billy Graham Center, Wheaton College; biographical information is at http://www.wheaton.edu/bgc/archives/GUIDES/173.htm#3.

8. Lynch, a friend of Arnott's from Moody Bible Institute, became a missionary in China, where she died of typhoid less than a year after her arrival. Arnott writes about Lynch's service in China and death in a February 13, 1908, diary entry.

9. Arnott's invocation of Plymouth Rock is noteworthy given nineteenth- and early twentieth-century Protestant missionaries' tendency to link their work with building the nation.

10. William Sanders's brother, Frank Knight Sanders, was then Dean of the Divinity School at Yale University. His papers are in the Divinity Library at Yale, with a guide (by Martha Lund Smalley) containing biographical information at http://drs.library.yale.edu:8083/fedora/get/divinity:122/PDF.

11. The Sanders children were Marshall (then 11) and Danforth (then 8). In Arnott's day, American missionaries often sent their children to the U.S. for schooling. Both Muriel (Ki) Henderson and Nancy Henderson James, the missionary wife of Lawrence Henderson and his daughter, shared vivid memories of "missionary kids" enduring long international journeys to attend school away from their families' African postings—even during the second half of the twentieth century. Interview, August 31, 2005.

12. In contrast to her rather positive view of the voyage in her circular letter, Arnott's diary describes seeking solace in her faith as she was seasick, homesick and ambivalent over her decision to leave Paul Darling. For example, she wrote on May 5, 1905: "Already my heart is hungry for the presence of some one who really loves me & especially for my own dear Paul. I realize more & more how human I am & how much I need to draw near to God & let Him be to me all this heart craves for. "

13. Original reads "my way clear made clear."

14. Arnott has written a list at the end of this first circular letter, with directions for the dissemination of thirty-four copies, with most copies designated for individuals (such as family members and friends) but some for groups (such as "Oberlin people," friends from the kindergarten-teaching program she had attended; "Nashua," her hometown in Iowa; and "Youngstown," Ohio, where a number of her relatives lived). She includes similar lists on later letters and, given her use of carbon paper in the copybook where she composed the pieces and her directions to recipients to make additional copies for other readers, it is clear that these letters had a much larger readership than we might anticipate for personal correspondence.

15. A note at the end of this letter lists many of the same anticipated readers Arnott designated for her first one, but she adds directions for copies to be made for additional correspondents, building her list to at least forty-nine.

16. Arnott's journey occurred several years before the sinking of the Titanic, so her wish to see some icebergs in the north Atlantic would not have invoked the same response from correspondents as readers would likely have today.

17. Like many missionaries, Arnott was an avid promoter of temperance. Temperance hotels drew their clientele from enthusiasts of the movement, which had supporters from all social classes in England. Walter Weldon Bagster was one of the original three ABCFM missionaries in Angola. He died there in 1882.

18. Morgan was a renowned British preacher who drew thousands of the faithful to his stirring sermons. Among his well-known books were *The Crises of the Christ* and *The Westminster Pulpit*. Morgan was a friend of Dwight L. Moody, who invited him to preach in the U.S. several times (Dorsett, *A Passion for Souls*, 159, 351, 361).

19. Alice Hawksley, who met Arnott at Moody Bible Institute, became a lifelong friend. Mary Caris, one of Arnott's grandchildren, would later remember having met Miss Hawksley when Hawksley visited the U.S.

20. Arnott refers to Ephesians 6:11–17, in which Paul instructs the Ephesians to "Put on the whole armor of God, that ye may be able to stand

against the wiles of the devil" (v11). In the passage, Paul describes various parts of a suit of armor: the "breastplate of righteousness" (v14), the "shield of faith" (v16), the "helmet of salvation" and the "sword of the Spirit" (v17). Since Arnott used the King James Version, we do as well in our citations.

21. Reuben A. Torrey was Superintendent of Moody Bible Institute; see Dorsett, *A Passion for Souls*, 307–11.

22. This passage, which Arnott invokes to thank her friends for their support, begins with the verse, "I thank my God upon every remembrance of you."

23. The modern spelling is "Benguela."

24. Arnott gives the English names of the Portuguese islands of Príncipe and São Tomé. British journalist Henry W. Nevinson visited the islands in 1904–05, just ahead of Arnott, to investigate the contract labor system. (See Chapter 2.)

25. Arnott interrupts the text of her letter here with a sheet where she lists some of her anticipated recipients. Then on the next page, she resumes her copy of the letter.

26. Another page of names and addresses is inserted here before the next sheet continues with the text of the letter. For this circular letter #3, Arnott again adds some new readers beyond her first and second lists and in several cases she provides specific street addresses as well as names. Her American addressees include supporters from the south (Mississippi and Tennessee), midwest (Illinois, Missouri, Ohio, Michigan, Minnesota, Nebraska), northeast (Connecticut, Massachusetts, New York) and even the far west (Oregon).

27. Arnott would also direct a number of her magazine pieces specifically to children. Like many colleagues in the mission movement, she aimed to prepare a new generation to support foreign missions. This agenda affiliated her career with her own upbringing in a community where organizations such as the Christian Endeavor society promoted engagement in mission work by Protestant churches' youngest members.

28. This letter has the same recipient list as the third one in the copybook. As with most others from this period (the first one being the lone exception), there is no formal salutation.

29. As Arnott mentioned in Circular Letter #3, she expected that her adult correspondents would be sharing her letters with "boys and girls." Here, as in much of her writing, she casts herself as teacher for such young readers by posing a geography-based question based on seasonal differences north and south of the equator.

30. Cabinda is a Portuguese territory north of the Congo River.

31. Arnott's spelling is "Loanda," rather than the modern spelling "Luanda."

32. Cuthbert Taylor was a Plymouth Brethren missionary from England. The first railroad in Angola was completed from Luanda to Lucala (which Arnott spells "Lucalla") in 1899 and to Malanje in 1909, after which building ceased due to financial difficulties (Henderson, *Church in Angola*, 81).

33. Charles A. Swan was a Plymouth Brethren missionary in Angola and author of an exposé of the contract labor system in Angola entitled *The Slavery of To-Day*.

34. The Luanda mission station was begun in 1885. The Methodist missionaries worked among the Kimbundu peoples of northern Angola, staffing the mission in Luanda and two in the interior of northern Angola (Henderson, *The Church in Angola*, 46, 79). The Kimbundu are a different ethnolinguistic group from the Ovimbundu; in the modern civil war in Angola the two groups were, in general, on opposing sides of the conflict. See Heywood, *Contested Power in Angola*, 151–61.

35. Louise Raven Shields attended public school in Chicago, where she taught for six years before going to Angola. She was "personally responsible for much of the educational developments of the MEC missions thereafter" and was especially interested in giving her students practical, industrial training like the program at Tuskegee. See Michael Anthony Samuels, *Education in Angola, 1878–1914: A History of Culture Transfer and Administration* (New York: Teachers College, 1970), 89 and 146, fn. 58.

36. Arnott's portrait of the Methodist missionaries echoes II Cor. 3:18: "But we all, with open face beholding as in a glass the glory of the Lord, are changed into the same image from glory to glory, even as by the Spirit of the Lord."

37. Frederick Stanley Arnot was a Scottish missionary who doubled as an intrepid explorer. See Chapter 3 for discussion of Arnot's presentation to the Royal Geographic Society, linked to the masculine model of Dr. Livingstone. Arnott misspelled the name of Arnot's book, *Garenganze: Or, Seven Years' Pioneer Mission Work in Central Africa* (London: James E. Hawkins, 1889). F.S. Arnot would later found *Across the Seas*, a missionary magazine for young people.

38. The contract for the Benguela Railroad was awarded by the Portuguese government to an English company associated with Robert Williams, an associate of Cecil Rhodes. Williams had obtained a concession from King Leopold of Belgium to explore Katanga in the Congo. Upon the discovery of extensive deposits of copper, the English needed the railroad to connect Katanga and Benguela; the Portuguese needed the railroad to facilitate ef-

fective political control over the interior highlands (Henderson, *The Church in Angola*, 81–82.).

39. With the sentence beginning "When the letter was closed," Arnott likely means to suggest that, at the time when she was completing her current circular letter (#4), the situation at the inland station had been going on for over a month, without successful resolution (i.e., without her colleagues being able to catch those setting the fires). Another possible interpretation may be that the phrase references the point when Sarah Stimpson completed her letter.

40. Nevinson notes, "Lately [in 1904] the American mission village at Kamundongo has been set on fire at night three or four times, and about half of it burned down. But this appears to be the work of one particular Portuguese trader, who has a spite against the mission and sends his slaves from time to time to destroy it" (*A Modern Slavery*, 81). The fires continued during Arnott's first years at the station. See Soremekun, "Religion and Politics in Angola," 358.

41. This letter's first section, based on Arnott's entry of July 11, appears in *Mission Studies*' February 1906 issue under the title "Benguella." The magazine version reflects only minor adjustments made to this piece (e.g., changing her use of "&" to "and" and making a few adjectives more specific). However, since we have not located any published version of the second part of this circular letter, we include the letter in its entirety here and provide a copy of the related *Mission Studies* article in the appendix to give one example of the editing process at work.

42. Missionary Bertha Stover gave a similar description: "Among the Mundombe and Chisanze [Cisanji] tribes we see women with immense coils about their necks. A string of beads is placed on the neck of a baby; to this is added, year after year, more beads, cowry shells, tacks, etc., all being matted together with palm oil, red clay, mingled with charcoal, and the accumulated filth of years, till its weight often exceeds twenty pounds." See *Women of West Central Africa*, 6. In *Ovimbundu of Angola* Hambly describes large, decorative collars worn by women from ethnic groups in the southern part of Angola. Those of the Luvando women he characterizes as being made of a "tough, elastic cane-like substance," so extensive that the woman's neck was completely covered, "thickly smeared with grease and red powder from *tukula* wood," and ornamented in various ways (description on 131; illustration in plates 58- 59).

43. Charles Swan traveled from Angola to the islands on the *Ambaca* in 1909 and also reports on the presence of contract laborers. On board, the Portuguese seemed unbothered by Swan's presence, as he talked with the workers in Umbundu and made photographs. See Charles Swan, *Slavery of*

Today, 154–56 and 160, for a description and photographs of female *serviçães* and their children on the *Ambaca*.

44. William A. Cadbury was a leader of the English cocoa manufacturing firm Cadbury Brothers. Cadbury asked his friend Joseph Burtt to go to the African Portuguese colonies to investigate the contract labor system, and Burtt reached São Tomé on June 13, 1905. Burtt spent five months on the islands and on the mainland of Angola; he prepared a thorough report, which is Appendix A in William A. Cadbury, *Labour in Portuguese West Africa*, 103–31. On Cadbury's role in the contract labor investigation and Burtt's report, see Satre, *Chocolate on Trial*, 13–32 and 73–99.

45. Arnott apparently confused Burtt's report with Nevinson's, as it was Nevinson's work which was published in *Harper's Monthly Magazine* ("The New Slave Trade," August 1905 through February 1906), before being collected in book form as *A Modern Slavery*. Satre discusses Nevinson's report in *Chocolate on Trial*, 1–12.

46. Trade in wild rubber, procured from regions as far off as the Congo, was very lucrative between 1902 and 1910, as prices rose and demand increased in the world market. Linda Heywood estimates that in 1910 as many as 100,000 Umbundu men and women were involved in trading through roles such as caravan porters (*Contested Power*, 46).

47. Women served a valuable place in the caravan because of their cooking skills and their strength; younger girls carried bags of meal while women might carry a regular load of 50–60 pounds. See Mastrobuono, "Ovimbundu Women," 44; Hambly, *Ovimbundu of Angola*, 212.

48. Catumbella was at the end of the path by which slaves had for generations been brought to the coast from the Congo basin, according to Henry Nevinson (*A Modern Slavery*, 24).

49. Though she spells their name "Curry" and gives an incorrect middle initial for Walter Currie, Arnott is clearly referring to Canadian Congregational missionary Walter T. Currie and his wife Amy Johnston Currie.

50. The recipient list for this letter repeats Arnott's catalogue for letter #3, except that she adds "Mrs. Pond—Oberlin" (whom she had come to know while enrolled in the kindergarten program there) and "Miss Hawksley," whom she had visited in England. One copy of another circular letter sent to Mrs. Pond later on in Arnott's mission career is held by the Oberlin College Archives and reproduced in Chapter 6.

51. On her journey, Arnott and her party had to climb from sea level up to the plateau of the highlands at an elevation of some 5400 feet. The area Arnott comments upon here was particularly steep. Nevinson described it as a "long, dry cañon, where the carriers have to climb like goats from rock

to rock along the steep mountain-side, with fifty or sixty pounds on their heads" (*A Modern Slavery*, 95).

52. This camp was at the intersection of several paths from the interior, converging on the route through the mountains which Arnott had just left. According to Nevinson, the "number of rest-huts" gave the camp the appearance of a "large native village." He noted: "Natives here come down from the nearest villages and sell sweet-potatoes and maize to the carriers in exchange for salt and chips of tobacco or sips of rum, so that at this season, when the carriers every night number a thousand or more, there is something like a fair" (*A Modern Slavery*, 94).

53. Arnott's diaries reflect related concerns about various family members' inclinations to drink alcohol and about how much that practice was inconsistent with her vision of sober Christianity.

54. Arnott refers to prayers and hymns of the Christian carriers, who proselytized in the camps. Some caravans were organized by missionaries such as Walter Currie and composed solely of Christian carriers (Soremekun, "Religion and Politics in Angola," 354).

55. Missionary John Tucker described similar gift-giving when he arrived in Angola in 1913 (*A Tucker Treasury*, 63). Imported cloth was the principal currency in the highlands (Heywood, "Slavery and Forced Labor," 417).

56. Bailundu was the first ABCFM mission station in Angola, founded by Reverend Sanders, Walter Bagster and Samuel Miller. Arriving in 1881, this group was received cordially by the ruler of the Bailundu kingdom, but within a few years the chief was duped by a hostile Portuguese trader into expelling them. After the intervention of Plymouth Brethren missionary Frederick Arnot, who was knowledgeable about native customs and fluent in Umbundu, the ABCFM leaders were allowed to return (Sanders, "Reminiscences," 35–38; Henderson, *Church in Angola*, 53–55, 59). By the time Nellie Arnott arrived, the local chiefdom had fallen in the wake of the Bailundu Revolt, and the old *ombala* (capital village) was deserted. The mission station, a short distance away, was a large and thriving station, but Nevinson worried that "the Portuguese have crept up to it with their rum and plantations and slavery" (*A Modern Slavery*, 90–91).

57. Nevinson's *A Modern Slavery* discusses operations of the "two or three" Portuguese "trading-houses" through which the buying of slaves was conducted in the area around Belmonte, the fort near Kamundongo (48–49).

58. John Tucker reported a similar welcome at Cisamba station in 1913: "The u-lu-lu-ling of the women was impressive. Songs were sung. Palm branches [were] held aloft by the children, salvos of guns fired and greetings showered upon us" (*A Tucker Treasury*, 63).

59. Here and in her articles about Kamundongo, Arnott gives an enthusiastic account of her new work. In her diary entries during the same time period, however, she expressed anxiety when contemplating her seven-year term of service: "The uneventful days have already begun. My heart almost stops when I think of the number [of days] that are before me," she wrote on August 11, 1905.

60. One of Arnott's scrapbooks contains another printing of this article, in pamphlet form, perhaps aimed at broader circulation than *Mission Studies*. The pamphlet version includes a photograph of Arnott, with a handwritten margin note labeled as follows: "1905–1912, Grandma Darling to Mary and Truman." Here, as elsewhere in her personal papers, we see signs of her re-presenting her missionary experience for another generation—her grandchildren.

61. In *Missionary Doctor*, Mary Floyd Cushman provides details about the fire hunts, with men spaced "in sight of one another" around a ring of grass ("perhaps one or two square miles" in size), to which they set fire (114–16).

62. Nellie J. Arnott to Dr. Judson Smith, October 4, 1905, ABCFM Papers, 15.1, Unit 2, Vol. 15: West Central Africa, 1900–1909, Documents and Letters, A-E, reel 164, Pitts Theological Library, Emory University. Arnott felt personally attached to the Smith family, having spent some time with them just before her passage to Africa. Upon Smith's death, she apparently found it more difficult to write to his replacement in the ABCFM offices in Boston, Reverend James Barton. In a February 1909 letter to Barton, she apologized for being remiss in her correspondence. Referencing a critique that Barton seems to have sent, she explains: "I too have regretted that the exchange of letters between the Foreign Department of the American Board and myself has not been more frequent since my coming to the field. I suppose I am somewhat at fault as I have not written since Dr. Smith's death. My correspondence had always been with him." Nellie J. Arnott to James L. Barton, February 25, 1909, ABCFM Papers, Vol. 15, reel 164.

63. The mission station at Ocileso (often spelled Chilesso), established in 1900, was in an area of hot mineral springs, the "baths" to which Arnott refers. Mary Floyd Cushman describes them as "ranging from 110 degrees Fahrenheit, up" and being "laden with soda, borax, sulphur, and salt." The "salt-spring water," Cushman explains, flowed into the nearby river, forming "beautiful falls, which cascade from a series of crescent-shaped ledges that build higher each year" (*Missionary Doctor*, 14–15).

64. Arnott's handwriting is difficult to decipher in the microfilm copy of the letter to which we had access. We believe our transcription to be accurate.

65. Arnott (or the editor at *Mission Studies*) spells the chief's name with a "u" (Kaputango) the first time and then shifts to an "i" (Kapitango) later in her article.

66. In the original, this word is spelled "fetiches." Soremekun dubs fetishes "symbols of history and tradition." Giving them up often meant burning them, which angered non-Christians, but, to the missionaries, represented a genuine commitment to Christianity. Soremekun notes that while the missionaries might "rejoice" at fetish-burning, "thousands of works of art were thus destroyed" ("History of the American Board Missions," 120–21).

5 Woman's Work at a Highlands Mission Station

In the first stage of her assignment, Arnott devoted most of her time to acculturation—learning the language and building strong working relationships with Umbundu students and her mission colleagues. Once Sarah Stimpson left for a long-delayed furlough in the U.S., Arnott took on more leadership and gradually grew more self-confident. After Stimpson returned to Angola, the missionary team at Kamundongo—Arnott, Stimpson, and Reverend and Mrs. Sanders—accelerated efforts to serve several outstations in settlements of Umbundu Christians clustered around the Kamundongo mission. While some of these schools were within walking distance, a visit to others required a journey of a day or more. Taking on a role that must have seemed truly foreign to her readers in the U.S., Arnott was the lone missionary at a remote outstation for a period of six weeks, during which she not only taught women and children but also tutored male Umbundu preachers and teachers. While describing progress at Owayanda, Olutu, Cisanje and Gamba outstations, Arnott's publications during this middle phase of her African service often use these accounts to lobby for more personnel. Like other themes, this one involved a balancing act between celebrating success and pointing to the ways that enhanced resources for the mission could promote greater achievements there.

A Trip to the Woman's Conference in the West Central Africa Mission[1]

From *Life and Light for Woman*, January 1908

BENGUELLA, AFRICA, AUGUST 21, 1907.

The Monday morning before the Conference I left here with six *tepoia* men and two load men; also thirteen of our women church members, representing the Station and out-Stations, went with me. With the exception of three[,] the women had their babies on their backs, and each carried her basket on her head, containing a little food for the road, a clean cloth and shirt, and her books.²

For a time we traveled together, but the *tepoias* soon left all of the women except two behind. We arrived in camp about two o'clock, and leaving the carriers to gather wood and prepare camp, I went a short distance in the woods, and had a quiet afternoon for reading and thought.³

When I returned to camp about supper time[,] I found my cot bed up under a big tree, which they had surrounded with branches and bushes, leaving it open above. It is called in Umbundu a *saika*.⁴ They had a good fire, so in a short time I was enjoying a cup of tea and a supper of cold chicken and potatoes, which had been baked in the coals.

The women, whom we had left behind, made a mistake in taking another path, and so slept at a nearby village. We were sorry to be separated from them, but it was so cold that it was really better for them with their babies to be in a village.

After supper all gathered around the fire, and we had prayers, after which we sang until we were tired.⁵ Then soon all settled down for the night. The two women each made a bed of leaves on the ground in my *saika* near the fire. Although they kept a big fire all night, still they found it rather cold. I slept very comfortably.

With the first streak of morning light all were astir, and we were soon on the path again. Just before arriving at Ocilonda we overtook our lost women, and so we all entered Ocilonda together. We stopped there for a rest, and I called on Mrs. [Frank] Figg and Mrs. E[dward] Sanders. Then we went on to Chualonda, which is only two hours distance.⁶ We arrived shortly after noon, and found that missionaries and women from some of the other Stations had already arrived. All afternoon they continued to arrive from the different places, and we were kept busy and happy in meeting each other, and in greeting the women.

Chualonda is one of the Stations of the English Mission, and located there are Mr. and Mrs. Murrian, with their family of ten children, and Mr. and Mrs. Phillips, who have two little boys.⁷ Mr. and Mrs. Murrian and Mr. and Mrs. Phillips are colored people from Demerara.⁸ Mr. Phillips teaches the children of the two families, so they are receiving quite a good common school education here, but they are

Figure 11: Missionary delegates at Ohualondo Conference, 1907. Courtesy of The Bancroft Library, University of California, Berkeley.

ambitious children, and really should be sent to America for education, as they complete their studies with Mr. Phillips. Jack, the oldest boy, has already completed his studies with him, and is now doing carpenter work for some Portuguese. I saw some of the doors he is making, and they look well. He is saving every cent, he says, to take him to America. He is also spending his odd moments in studying medicine, under the direction of his father. Ever since knowing Jack I have longed to see him placed in one of our American Missionary Association schools.[9] He could work his way through could he once get there. I have often wished some of our large givers for the promotion of education at home, could reach their hand across the sea to this lovely family in Africa, and help educate them.

Mr. and Mrs. Murrian are fine missionaries, and are doing a noble self-sacrificing work for the people of Africa. Their children are well trained; and Jack says, when he gets a good education he wants to go to the Interior and spend his life there. I hope some, who read this, will be led to pray for these children, that the way may open for their education.

Miss Phillipson, an English young woman, is also located at Chualonda. These three households very pleasantly entertained seventeen missionaries during the conference. I was with Mr. and Mrs. Murrian and family. The closing evening we all took supper together at Mrs. Murrian's. Twenty adults and fourteen children sat down together. You may be sure we had a happy time.[10]

The conference closed Thursday evening, and Friday morning all turned their faces homeward. On the return trip I had the pleasure of Mrs. Wellman, little Alice [Wellman] and Mrs. Ennis' company, as they came home with me. Friday we took dinner with the ladies at Ocilonda, and then traveled until late in the afternoon, camping that night at the same place I did going. We arrived here at Kamundongo about noon on Saturday and Mrs. Sanders had a good dinner awaiting us. Mrs. Wellman and Mrs. Ennis remained with us four days and then went to Chisamba for a visit there.

In a letter I wrote last year I told you about Buta, one of our church members whose wife had died, and who had gone to his relations' village to teach them the way of Life. This village[,] being about ten miles from Ocilonda, has become one of its out-stations. Buta has done all the work there without the help of white missionaries and he now has a good daily attendance at his school and there are a number of believers. Every Sunday he and a few followers attend the services at Ocilonda. This season they are putting up a house for school and meetings. The week before conference Mr. and Mrs. Figg visited this village, and they told me Buta's work gave every reason for rejoicing and gratitude. While there Mr. Figg married him to one of the women who has become a believer. Now that he has a home again he has taken his little girl to be with him.

After Mr. Sanders left for the coast I shut up my house and moved in with Mrs. Sanders. It makes it very lonely when Mr. Sanders is away. He will likely be away in all about ten weeks.

Two weeks ago a woman with her two-year-old child came in one morning from our out-station an hour away. She is the wife of one of our church members, and she herself is in the catechumen's class. When a child[,] she was bought in the Interior and brought to Bihe. Her owners live near her husband, and, as far as I know, have made no claims on her since she was married. Her husband is planning to move to Camba this season,[11] and when her owners heard they were to leave these parts[,] they laid hold on her and her child and took them to their own house. They were preparing meal[s] to go to the Interior, and told her they were going to take her and her child with them and sell them for oxen and rubber. The day she came here her owners had gone to a funeral, so she ran away. She is now staying in the girls' compound. Her husband brings her corn and food from her field. She is safe here as they do not dare to take her from the Station.[12]

It is only because of the grace and goodness of God that we were not born in this dark land. It should make us feel very thankful to God for the blessings that surround our lives in America when we realize the conditions in which these people are born. Still they are dear to God and for them Jesus died. My heart often fills with joy for the privilege of being here myself, and of knowing you are helping in this blessed work by your prayers and gifts.

News from Kamundongo

From *Mission Studies*, April 1908

I have been in Africa nearly two years, and while they tell me the first two years are the hardest in a missionary's life, still I have found a measure of blessing.

The inability to understand and speak the language well has been the only thing that has caused discouragement.[13]

There are only four missionaries for this Station, Mr. and Mrs. Sanders, Miss Stimpson and myself. I was only here seven months when Miss Stimpson left for her furlough, and she is still in America. We have not heard whether she is to return this season or not. So for over a year there have only been three of us here at Kamundongo.

I live in the house for teachers, but since Miss Stimpson left I have taken my meals with Mr. and Mrs. Sanders, who live nearby.

One end of the compound is walled off for the girls. At present we have three small houses with two rooms each. In one, Nanjumbe, who is a widow, lives with her five children. Another is used for kitchens, two girls in each. These four girls live here all the time. The third is used for sleeping rooms for all the girls on the Station. There are about twenty girls here most of the time and they are all more or less under my care. Nanjumbe, who is an earnest Christian, is a great help to me. Three of the girls are members of the church. Many of my evenings are given to them. Sometimes they sew[;] other evenings we have meetings or study the Sunday school lessons or sing. Moonlight evenings they enjoy playing their games outside. There are many plans we would like to see carried out for the girls, but they require time and money, neither of which we have at present.

From the last of September until the first of June most of my time and strength is given to the schools, the children's school in the morning and the school for girls and women in the later part of the afternoon. Since Miss Stimpson left, Mrs. Sanders has had charge of the boys' school. I am very thankful I have the children's school, as work with them is very interesting and promising, and as I gain a better use of the language[,] there are many ways in which I hope to improve these schools.[14]

During last vacation I spent many afternoons in visiting and helping in two nearby out-station schools, and I hope to be able to do the same this vacation. Much of the vacation time must be given to study, to writing letters long neglected, to sewing and doing the many things one is unable to do during the school year. These things keep one so busy that the days pass too quickly.

The work of the Mission Press is at this Station under the charge of Mrs. Sanders. The past year one thousand copies each of Genesis (first edition) and of a school primer have been printed, and two thousand copies of the hymn book. Four of the boys set up the type and do the printing on a small hand machine, but Mrs. Sanders has no end of work in keeping watch over them, in reading proof and in covering the books when printed.[15]

The attendance upon the Sunday services has been very good when we consider how the population has been, and is, moving away. Our church, which seats over three hundred, is usually comfortably filled. Sixteen have been received during the year, giving a present membership of one hundred and seventy-six.

It would be very nice could there be three lady teachers for each Station, but as it has been[,] there have been few years when more than two are at a Station. Then when there are two, one has to be loaned to some Station that is without [adequate personnel]. If there were three, then while one is home on furlough there would still be two, who are always needed for the Station schools, and years when three are here[,] one could devote her time to out-station schools.

. These out-stations present a most encouraging outlook. If one could remain in each out-station for a few months at a time each year, directing the teachers, helping in getting better methods established, and seeking out the most hopeful for the Station schools, what a stream of blessing would be started for Africa's future.

So you see that young women are very much needed, and I believe, were there young women offering themselves to God for this needy land, that the means for sending them would be supplied.[16]

If you could only look into one of the heathen villages and see the women and children living in all their dirt and trusting in all their spirits and superstitions, without schools or any kind of knowledge of the Savior who died for them, I'm sure your hearts would be stirred to help them. You would want to have a part in giving the Bread of Life to these people, who are just as dear to the Father as any one of us.

Mrs. Neipp of Ocileso has been with us and our hearts have been gladdened as she has told of the spiritual blessings that have come to them the past months, and as we read of the outpouring of the Holy Spirit in different parts of the earth we long for the same blessing among us here.

After Mr. Sanders left for the coast, I shut up my house and moved in with Mrs. Sanders. It makes it very lonely when Mr. Sanders is away. He will likely be away in all about ten weeks.

It is only because of the grace and goodness of God that we were not born in this dark land. It should make us feel very thankful to God for the blessings that surround our lives in America when we realize the conditions in which these people are born. Still they are dear to God and for them Jesus died. My heart often fills with joy for the privilege of being here myself and of knowing you are helping in this blessed work by your prayers and gifts.[17]

A Letter from Miss Nellie J. Arnott

Excerpt from "Lesson: Our New Missionary"
in Children's Work Section

From *Mission Studies*, October 1908

Kamundongo, Africa
January 27, 1908

TO THE CHILDREN OF THE INTERIOR:[18]

As I am unable to have school this morning with my children here in Africa, I will spend the time in writing to you.

I wonder whether you would like it if there was no school the days it rained. Here in Africa when it rains[,] we do not have school. Sometimes, when it clears up later in the forenoon, we ring the bell and the children soon come together.

These little boys and girls do not have coats and mackintoshes [i.e., raincoats] to put on to keep out the rain. Most of them have only the one dress and cloth at a time, so if this gets wet they must sit by the fire while it dries. For this reason it is best for them not to be called out in the rain to attend school.

We are having quite a happy time in school this year, although there are only about thirty children here. The rest of our children have gone to Gamba, a new district, to which we all hope to go next year. We have such a nice school house here and in the largest room is a big fireplace. Many mornings are cool and cloudy, so we have a fire, in front of which the little children enjoy sitting, while they play with their blocks and look at picture books. They also like to play at the sand table. They make houses, roads and gardens with walls around them. These smaller children are left very much to themselves in their play, with only a small boy to oversee them. I spend my time with the older children teaching them to read, write and do numbers. Several of them are just finishing their first primer and will soon be able to read the Bible. As some of them come from homes whose parents are unable to read, we are glad their children will be able to read to them. Sometimes the little babies are brought to school, too. They are fastened on their sisters' backs with a cloth and there they laugh and coo or sleep, while the sister does her writing and reading.

I wish you might have made us a visit on Christmas day. The day before we had a pig killed and the cook boy cut it all up and cooked it in the boiler. He put in seasoning which he said made it taste very nice. Christmas morning we rang the bell and soon all the children came. There were about fifty, counting the babies. We brought over the school tables and put them here in my yard. They were not set with white cloths and pretty dishes, but we did put flowers on them.

The children all sat down, and we sang a couple of Christmas songs, and Mr. Sanders asked the blessing. Then the larger girls brought on plates [of] mush, which is made from corn[meal]. This mush is made very stiff and is [illegible] seasoned with salt. Then each ch[ild] was given a dish of the meat and a [illegible] of well-cooked beans. They do not use spoons, knives or forks, but with their fingers they take a piece of mush, dip it in the meat or beans and then eat it.[19] They ate all they could and carried home what they could not eat for their supper. As each one left he was given a cup of peanuts and a piece of sugar cane. With happy faces and a hearty "Tua pandula," which means, "We thank you," they went to their homes, where they played the rest of the day. A little mission band in Ohio had sent Mrs. Sanders a box of beads, so each girl was given a string, with which they were pleased.[20]

Will all the mission bands pray for the children in Africa that they may grow up to love and serve Jesus?

With hearty greetings to all,
NELLIE J. ARNOTT.[21]

AFRICA

From *Life and Light for Woman*, February 1909

Miss Nellie J. Arnott writes from Kamundongo, Africa, September 3, 1908:—

You will be glad to know that I am no longer alone. Miss Stimpson and I are settled at housekeeping again, so the house is not so big and lonely.[22]

We are having our vacation, but still I have been just as busy as I can be. We didn't get back from the conference and Gamba trip until the third of July. Then there were the unpacking and settling of Miss Stimpson's loads and some repairing and house cleaning to do.

I have been going to Cisanje afternoons the last three weeks, helping with the school there. It is just a nice walk and does me good to get away. I would rather do it than sew or anything else. I am in hopes, now that as I shall be relieved of part of the Station schools, to be able to visit these nearby out-station schools often. It makes a difference in the attendance and the work done if one of us can go often.[23]

Since Miss Stimpson has been back she takes the Station children for their Sunday afternoon meeting, and I have been going to our nearest village for a meeting with the children there. Sometimes one of the Christian girls goes with me and helps[;] thus she is getting in training. Last Sunday I was unable to go, so she went alone.

Mr. Sanders is just returning from a trip to Gamba. We expect him here tomorrow. A letter came from him yesterday, in which he said he received five into the church and held a communion service with them. It all puts such longings in our hearts to be with them.

West Central Africa Mission: Fresh Interest

From *Missionary Herald*, June 1909

Miss Nellie J. Arnott, writing from Benguella under date of February 25,[24] gives the following particulars as to "new interest that has lately been manifested in these regions":

"Some villages where the people have refused all advances to them in the past have begun attending the Sunday services. There have been larger audiences lately at Kamundongo than any I have seen. Miss Stimpson has started a school in one of these near villages, and has had a very good attendance."

"At Kowayanda outstation there is a gradual growth.[25] I have spent two weeks in that school this year, and find Cituvika, the teacher, a most faithful worker. Nearly all of the old attendants upon his school have gone to Gamba, so he is working largely with new material."

"The school here at Olutu is under the care of Sakamana and Fumika, who are unpaid teachers. Many of the people who once lived here have gone to Gamba, leaving the church members here small in number. Mr. Sanders has advised those who are now here to remain and help in building up a work here. He has been down and laid out streets for them, and they are rebuilding their village, making it more modern. They are also building a new schoolhouse, much larger than the old one.

"There are over two hundred enrolled in the schools here. These teachers, with the help of some others, conduct the three schools and evening prayers daily, also a Sunday service and Sunday school. Last Sunday there was an attendance of 275, the week before 360. Sunday afternoons the church members go in groups of three or four and hold services in the surrounding villages. But there are not enough who are able to read to visit all of the villages that are asking for such services.

One of the greatest needs is that of native teachers and evangelists. There are a few who are capable, but have not the right spirit. We very much need the outpouring of the Holy Spirit upon our mission."

Migration to Gamba

With reference to the removal of many of the people from Kamundongo to Gamba, Miss Arnott writes:—

"We cannot blame the people for moving, for the fields are worn out and unproductive. The few who remain make up the Station schools. The Gamba schools will be at least three times as large, so you can see that Gamba offers attractions to us as teachers. Many of the people there are Christians, and their children are the first generation we have of Christian parentage. I feel strongly that those boys and girls should be given the best school possible. We have not native teachers to carry on the kind of schools they need, so it seems to me that white teachers should be placed among them. From among them we look for our future teachers and evangelists, so they should be given a good preparation for that work."

LETTER FROM MISS ARNOTT

From *Life and Light for Woman*, September 1909

AMERICAN MISSION, BENGUELLA, AFRICA, 1909

I have come for a six weeks' stay at one of our out-station schools, a day's journey from Kamondongo.[26] I shall return next week and shall be glad to see white faces again and receive the affection that is awaiting me. While I am here, Mr. Sanders is at Gamba, so Mrs. Sanders and Miss Stimpson are alone at Kamondongo.

This year Miss Stimpson has charge of the two afternoon schools and I of the children. I took in a young man to train at the beginning of the year, and he has proved so efficient that I have been able to leave him in charge while I am visiting and helping in these out-station schools. I have spent two weeks at Owayanda and was here nearly three weeks last of November and the first of December. This time I'm making a six weeks' stay and it is not too long to accomplish all I long to do.

The work here is under the care of Sakamana and Funika,[27] and others who are able, help them some. They are unpaid teachers and are doing faithful work. The three schools have an enrollment of over two hundred, and they conduct these and evening prayers daily, besides holding a Sunday service and Sunday school, all of which are well attended.

I very much enjoy this out-station work and wish I could devote more time to it. I think, could we spend a few weeks, three or four times a year, in each out-station this way, that the results would be much greater.

Kamondongo, March 5th.—I went to children's school this morning and find that the native teacher did very well indeed. Wish we had a dozen such faithful ones and with the same earnest spirit.

Mr. Sanders received fourteen into the church while at Gamba. The work in all of the Stations of our own mission and of the English mission seems to be increasing of late. There is a new interest in all of the villages, many asking for teachers where we are unable to supply them. Not for schools, but for someone to come to them and read the words. We are earnestly praying that God will put it into the hearts of many more of the natives to give themselves to this work.

Letter to ABCFM Official Reverend James Barton: #1

Report of three months
At Gamba

Benguella, Africa[28]
Oct. 5, 1909
Rev. James L. Barton, D.D.[29]
Boston, Mass.

My dear Dr. Barton:—Your kind and welcome letter was received in our last mail and I am answering it at once, as I have had it in mind to write to you from this place.

Miss Stimpson and I came to Gamba the middle of July and have been here nearly three months. We leave next Monday, returning to Kamundongo by way of Ocileso, where we will make a short visit.

As you know[,] this is the place to which most of our people have moved and where we desired to move the Station, but were refused by the Portuguese government.[30] There are about five hundred people here and among them a hundred and thirty church members.

Within an hour's distance are a number of villages, several of which Miss Stimpson and I have visited afternoons. The people in them are quite ready to listen and have come to the Sunday services.

We came here in order to start the schools and to get the teachers better fitted to carry them on when we leave. But it will take [a] much longer time than we can stay to prepare any of them to carry on the schools satisfactorily. They do quite well as helpers with one of us to superintend them, but the schools are too large for them to carry on, as they should be, alone. None of them seem fitted to carry on the children's schools. I have had one hundred and fifty in two sessions each morning, and in this school they need a white teacher to take charge, even more than in the afternoon schools. But we are doing the best we can in preparing them for the work that they must do alone, for the present.

It seems such a pity that missionaries cannot be placed here. All these children need the best training that can be given them, to prepare them for the work in the future. From these, the first children of Christian parents, we should expect our home missionaries for the Umbundu people. But they need a Christian training which they will not receive from native teachers.

The older Christians conduct the evening prayers and Sunday services. They do very well, but oh, I have realized how much they need Mr. Sanders['] exposition of the scriptures and his good Sunday morning sermons.

The spirit among them is very good. Lumbo is the leader and they all have respect for all he says and does. He has a catechumen[']s class of fifty-five members. Last Sunday afternoon he called a meeting of the church members and they considered twelve persons they think ready to unite with the church.

Since being here we have had visitors over three Sundays. One Sunday Dr. Hollenbeck was with us and the following Sunday both he and Mr. Neipp were here. Mr. Neipp conducted a communion service. Two weeks ago Mr. Lane, one of the English missionaries, was with us over Sunday.[31] He preached three times and we all greatly enjoyed his visit. We are in hopes Mr. Sanders will be able to come over soon after our return.

I suppose Mr. Sanders has written you of the great loss the Kamundongo church has met in the death of Cituvika. His Christian life and faithfulness was an example to us all. It is hard indeed to part with one so dear to us and see such a large place in the work left vacant. We pray and hope to see others soon raised up to take up such work as he did. One of the young men, who grew up in Cituvika's school at Okambueyo, has been chosen to take this school in Cituvika's place. His name is Sakalumbu and it was he who helped us so faithfully in the Kamundongo schools last year.

With the exception of colds[,] Miss Stimpson and I have kept quite well since being here. We have enjoyed being with the people, and they have shown their appreciation for all we have tried to do. We are very sorry indeed that we must leave them. The handful left at Kamundongo will seem smaller than ever to us. I am hoping and praying that something may be done for this place. If we cannot move, I hope some missionaries may be placed here. I do not think that all these people should be left as sheep without a shepherd. Mr. Lane said when here,

"They are not yet ready to be left alone. They need to be farther taught in the Word.["] And we realize it more every day we are here.

Miss Stimpson and I have been doing what we can in giving those who are teachers Bible lessons, but they need such teaching all the time.

Miss Stimpson joins me in sending best wishes to you and to those in the Rooms.

Cordially yours,
Nellie J. Arnott
Susua, Gamba

A GLIMPSE AT AN AFRICAN SCHOOL

From *Life and Light for Woman*, March 1910

Miss Nellie J. Arnott, of Kamundongo, West Central Africa, June 7, 1909:—

The children's school opened the fifth of October and continued, with the exception of two weeks' vacation at Christmas time, until the fourteenth of May.

The total enrollment was forty-five, with an average attendance of thirty-six, a small gain over last year. In looking over the record of the past three years, I find there is a marked improvement in the average attendance[,] which is encouraging.[32]

A young man has been in the school through the year as [a] helper. From the beginning he has been faithful and sought to teach as directed. During the weeks I spent at the out-stations he took charge of the school.[33]

Twenty-four of the number enrolled were taught reading, writing and numbers. Three of these had begun the primers last year, and after completing them, read *The Stories of Jesus*. Ten finished reading from the blackboard during the year, and are now reading the primer. Eleven were beginners this year and are still reading from the blackboard. The children were taught Bible-stories and are able to repeat six different Psalms.[34]

During the year[,] two weeks were spent in Owayanda out-station school, eight weeks in Olutu out-station school, and the Cisanje out-station school was attended for twelve weeks, three afternoons each week. The aim in this work has been to show the native teachers better ways of teaching and to encourage them in the work. Sunday afternoons, when the weather has permitted, a meeting has been held at one of the near-by villages for children and any others who came.

Total enrolled for the year, 45 Average attendance, 36

KAMUNDONGO AND VICINITY

From *Mission Studies*, May 1910

AMERICAN MISSION, BENGUELLA, AFRICA.

I spent another week at our out-station at Owayanda. I was encouraged to see the progress made by many of the children and the faithfulness of Cituvika, the teacher. In these three schools he has an enrollment of about 90. Every evening they gather around the open fire while Cituvika reads and explains the Scriptures.[35]

I went again to Lutu and remained six weeks.[36] In addition to helping in the schools, as I described in my last letter, I had all the older ones in an evening class twice a week for some lessons in Acts and talks along the line of personal work. Sunday afternoons I went to the villages with some of the men, who hold meetings. At some villages the people would gather around and listen attentively[;] at others they would be too much afraid; the women would stand afar off and tremble if I went near them.[37]

Then also I entered a new line of work. Mr. Sanders had the previous week gone down and laid out streets for them, as they wished to build new houses and have a straight village. I had been there only a few days when asked to help stake out a house straight with the street.

The natives can do nothing of this kind. That was the beginning, and while I was there I staked out 35 houses and three more streets and blocks. I found it quite a job, as I did not know how very well, and had only pieces of rope, string and bark string tied together to measure with. But I think when the houses are built there will be a large improvement over the old village.[38] They are also building a new school house, much larger than the old one.

We are thankful there is one fitted to take Sakamana's place. Fumika is one of the fruits of Cituvika's work. He and his parents lived at Kambueyo when Cituvika began school there. He was then only a young boy and he soon learned to read and became a Christian. His parents did not like it at all, so decided to move to a distant village so Fumika could not be under the influence of the school.

He did not want to leave school, though, so he told them he would not go with them. They threatened him in many ways and told him sickness and trouble would come to him. Being unable to persuade him, his father said he would sell him. Cituvika told him to go to Mr. Sanders and tell him all about it. Mr. Sanders advised him to go and help his parents move and then return to school.

When his parents saw that he was going with them they were glad, thinking that they had conquered. After their arrival at their new home he remained with them only one day, and then he took his Matthew and cloth and ran away back to Kambueyo.[39] His parents were very angry, and sent a threatening message after him. He was soon able to help Cituvika in the school.

One time after a trip to the Coast with Mr. Sanders[,] he took some of the cloth he had earned and took it as a present to his parents.[40] Their anger lessened somewhat, and later he went to live in that village as a teacher. He remained there some time and then moved to Olutu. His parents and other relatives went also, and now three of them are Christians and his father attends the Sunday services at Olutu regularly.

At one time when he first visited his father[,] he found him sick and in various troubles. Fumika himself had been perfectly well and had met with success on every hand. He said his father remembered his threats and said, "God sent me what I said would come to you." This persecution has made Fumika a strong and earnest Christian, well fitted to take charge of the work at Olutu. His wife has only recently united with the church. I want you all to pray that many of the people in the surrounding villages may become believers.

Miss Stimpson and I are now at Gamba. We left Kamundongo on a Monday and arrived here the following Friday. We enjoyed the trip, although it was very cold nights and mornings. With plenty of grass for mattresses and our blankets, we were able to keep warm, in spite of [being in] the open. Here, at Gamba, Mr. Sanders has had a house built for the use of the missionaries. It has a sitting room, bed-room and dining room, and a small building near for a kitchen.

This is the cold season, and as there is no place for a fire in the house, we are uncomfortable with the cold nights and mornings. During the middle of the day we can keep warm in the sun. Next month will bring us warmer weather. Our houses at Kamundongo have white cloth ceilings, but here there are none. It is open to the peak of the thatch roof, which I like, though we feel more wind. The floors are matted, and Lumbo has made two very good tables and a cupboard. These things, aside from the two cot-beds, three chairs, a small table and our trunks and boxes, make up our furnishings.

One of the men has built an adobe oven in the kitchen which works very well, so we can have fresh bread. Then, as we need them, we have a load of oranges from Kamundongo, so with what tinned food we brought and what we can buy here, we get along very well in the food line.

The people here have built a large house of sticks and mud for a school house and church. The morning after we arrived[,] we opened the schools. I was met by 160 children and decided at once that they could be better taught by having two sessions, so I have 50 of the larger ones come from 8–9:30 and the rest from 9:30–11. In the first all are taught reading, writing and numbers; in the second, only about 35 are taught reading and writing. The rest are children of kindergarten age.

Afternoons[,] Miss Stimpson has the Men and Boys' School, and following it, the school for the women and girls. As she has 150 women[,] I go over and help her by taking a class of beginners in reading. We are hoping during our stay here to get the native teachers better fitted to carry on these schools by themselves.

There are about 500 people here, and they all come from Kamundongo and its out-stations. Nearly 130 of them are our church members, and there are 40 in the catechism class. Prayers are held every evening, led by one of the older members, who also conducts Sunday services, including a Sunday school. They have done very well without any resident missionary. Responsibility has seemed to develop them. Still, we wish we could remain here. However, as long as the government will not let us move[,] we must be content with these occasional visits.[41]

Mr. Sanders has been here twice each year for a few weeks' stay, and now that Dr. Hollenbeck is with us, we may hope that more frequent visits can be made at all our out-stations.

Circular Letter #6

A.B.C.F.M., Benguella, Africa. August 5, 1910.

Dear Friends:

My last letter to you started on its way in March, so it is time another began the long journey to you.[42] I never send these general letters as often as I should wish, but my hands and heart are always so full that the days pass quickly.[43] I was in Ciyaka when I sent my last letter to you. The first of May the Mission Annual Meeting was held there, with Mr. Woodside, Dr. Cammack, Dr. Hollenbeck, Mr. and Mrs. Ennis, and myself being present. The meeting was not as large as last year, but I enjoyed it just the same. Much to my surprise, Dr. Hollenbeck brought carriers for me so I could return to Kamundongo[;] thus after the meeting was over, I left Ciyaka, traveling as far as Bailundu with Mr. Woodside. We had a good trip. The evenings[,] we were able to have meetings in the villages. I visited a week at Bailundu, staying with the Bells meanwhile. Mr. Stover had arrived at Ochileso quite sick, so Mrs. Stover had gone to stay with him till he could go home. (In June he went on to Bailundu, so he is now finally settled at home). Dr. Hollenbeck was also called to Ochileso to attend Mr. Stover. He has a new bicycle, so he made quick time, only two days from Bailundu to Ochileso and one on the return trip. The natives were greatly surprised since they always take three or four days for the journey.

From Bailundu, Dr. Hollenbeck accompanied me home. It was so good to be with my own Station friends once more and at home. Mr. and Mrs. Sanders look tired, so we are glad that the new rules of the Board permit them to take their furlough next year. We shall miss them. I wonder what we will do while they are away. They are always a great help and blessing to us. We were only together a couple of weeks when Dr. Hollenbeck was asked by Cisamba Station to go to the Coast to meet Miss Bell[,] who was returning alone. He went as far as Ciyaka, where he remained while Mr. Ennis went on to the Coast. Dr. Hollenbeck got back to Kamundongo about the 1st of July after going to Cisamba with Miss Bell.

I had only been at Kamundongo a month when Miss Stimpson and I left to come here to Gamba for a stay of some such as we made last year. We came by way of Ochileso where we had a nice visit over Sunday. We missed Mr. and Mrs. Neipp who had left for their furlough. At Ochileso, Miss Redick joined us and has spent the month of July with us here.

But I must tell you about our trip from Ochileso to Gamba. Last year Mr. Neipp in some of his travels found some beautiful falls. Since then, Mr. and Mrs. Woodside have seen them and advised us to take a couple of days and visit them also. We did so and certainly felt repaid. We three, Miss Stimpson, Miss Redick, and I left Ochileso on a Tuesday morning. Miss Redick used Mr. Woodside's one-wheeled cart instead of a tepoia.[44] Only two boys are needed for it and they like it much better than a tepoia, but I do not care for it for ladies' use. I rode in it some of the time, giving Miss Redick a rest in my tepoia. It goes quite well on good roads, but in the narrow paths it is rough. Besides as with a tepoia, one must walk up all the hills. I think I shall prefer the tepoia until the railroad comes or until the roads are made easy for carts and wheels.[45] We slept in the woods Tuesday night and on Wednesday morning I reached Onoma, an out-station of Ochileso, where we left part of our carriers. Then we left the main path and took what the boys call an animal path through the woods. The grass and bushes were high and the walking hard. Cart and tepoia were of little use. The path followed the descent on the side of the stream over the rocks, through thickets and then across on trees and rocks to the middle of the stream where there is an island with a few trees. After getting wet we dispensed with our shoes and stockings[,] and with the help of the two boys who remained our faithful guardians, we succeeded in getting over. From there we had a fine view of the falls from below. After our return to the bank we followed the stream and found that it narrowed into a rocky gorge and then made a very steep descent. We could only see this fall from above, but the view was fine. As far as we could see, it continues in this narrow rocky bed. It is all white and foamy. We followed the Kune River going up and down the hills and along the sides of the mountains, and over the little streams that flow into the Kune. The river is quite wide in some places and full of rapids. The woods were fine with no sign of man since we left Onoma, though there were evidences of wild animals in several places. After over three hours of travel we arrived in hearing distance of the big Falls. As we drew near, I was reminded of Niagara. We saw these from above also. The stream spreads and then makes a deep descent over great rocks. The water is white foam and shows rain-bow colors here and there in the sunlight. Grass and mosses [are] growing on some of the rocks that are not wholly covered by the water. Miss Redick and I wished we could follow it further, but to do so we had to cross a deep ravine that looked impassable. At sunset we went to the camp the boys had made and had our supper of broiled venison and baked potatoes. The boys took all precautions against wild animals but none disturbed us. In the morning we took one last look at the Falls and returned to Onoma. We spent that day and night there.[46]

This out-station was started about a year ago by Cingangu, a Christian from Ocilonda, one of the English Mission Stations. As Onoma is near Ochileso, he took his letter to the Ochileso Church, thus bringing the work under the direction of that Station. This year Muesanjala went from Ochileso to help Cingangu. They have built themselves good adobe houses just outside of the village and have begun a building for a school and church. At present they hold school and prayers in one of the villages, gathering in an onjango (the men's sitting place). The people have welcomed these teachers and some are learning to read and to know the Way of Life. These teachers are not paid but have been given a few tools with which they can support themselves while they carry on school and services. I was very glad to see the work in this out-station and left feeling that it pays to give one's life to the training of native teachers. They are the ones who must reach the Angola population. The sad part is that so few have the desire to give themselves to this work. Pray that the Holy Spirit may be poured out on our native Christians so that they may be led into such service for their Master.

We left Onoma on Friday morning and after two hard days of travel arrived here Saturday afternoon and received a cordial welcome from the natives. After spending a week in getting settled[,] we began schools. I have about one hundred children in the morning school, with six young men who I trust will be prepared to take charge when we leave. Ten or twelve weeks is too short, though, to give them the training they need. Our work is very much the same as last year and[,] as I wrote you fully then[,] I would only repeat now. We expect to return to Kamundongo in September. Miss Redick left us last Monday, but we hope we may have other company during our stay here.

With Christian love, and always with prayer for you all,
I am
Yours in His service,
Nellie J. Arnott

House Building in Africa

From *Mission Studies*, Children's Work Section, August 1910

Perhaps some of the children will be interested to know how the natives build their houses. Those who live on the Stations make sun-dried brick, of which they build, but most of the houses at the out-station are built in regular native style, except that they are usually larger than the regular native house.

After the house is staked out[,] the builder brings from the woods a lot of long, straight poles which he has cut down from time to time. These are inserted in the ground about twelve inches apart, leaving a space for a door, or possibly two doors, if the house is to have two rooms. When this is done, much smaller sticks, or split ones, but long and straight as can be found, are tied crosswise with bark string to the uprights, about ten inches apart. This is done both inside and outside and answers for [a] lath [i.e., a base for the mud plaster].

Then a roof is made. One end of the long sticks is tied to the top of the upright sticks, the other ends meeting at the peak. To these are also tied the small sticks crosswise. When this much is done[,] you see a lattice-work house. Long grass is then cut and brought in big bundles. They say a house full of grass is enough to thatch it. To thatch, the grass is tied in small bundles and then tied to the sticks on the roof very evenly and smoothly until it is covered. At the eaves it is cut straight, so that it looks very nice when finished.

After the thatching, mud is made and used to plaster the wall on the inside and outside, filling in the places between the sticks. To make the boards for the doors[,] a big tree is cut down. A short trunk will make only two boards, for the trunk is split slowly through the middle with a native ax, and then one board hewn out of each half. Of course, the boards are heavy and thick. Three good boards will make a door, and these are fastened together with cross pieces which are fitted into the boards and held by wooden pegs. You must remember there are no nails or hinges to be had.

For a hinge[,] a little piece of the inside extends at the top and bottom, and these act as joints which fit into sockets that are cut into the upper and lower frame boards of the door. For a knob[,] a small hole is made in the side of the door and through it is put a piece of bark string or hide, well knotted at each end, so that it cannot be pulled through. Those who have locks buy them from the traders.[47]

For a window[,] perhaps a space ten by eight inches will be left unmudded. The floor is made even and wet and then it is pounded until, when dry, it is hard and smooth. Thus the African house is built without any cost to the builder, aside from his labor[,] and the noise of the hammer, saw and plane is never heard.

Extracts from a Letter from Miss Nellie J. Arnott

From *Life and Light for Woman*, September 1910
Extracts from a letter from Miss Nellie J. Arnott, dated Bailundu, Africa, May 13, 1910:—

I am spending this week at Bailundu on my way back to Kamundongo. When Dr. Hollenbeck went to Ciyaka to annual meeting, he took my carriers so I could return. I think God did use me while I was at Ciyaka, and some village people whom I visited became much interested, and I might have done more, but it seemed best not to start what they would be unable to carry on when left alone. It was a case of not doing all one could and would like to for fear the work would become too large to be handled. When will our churches awaken to their opportunities and let the work grow as fast as it can?[48]

One reason I am returning now, it seemed best that Miss Stimpson and I spend a few months at Gamba again this dry season. So, after a couple of weeks at Kamundongo, we expect to go over there as we did last year. Miss Reddick [sic] is planning to be with us there part of the time.

Mr. Stover reached Ochileso sick, so they sent for Dr. Hollenbeck, who has been to see him. He is much better. Mrs. Stover went last week to be with him there until permission is received for his return here to Bailundu.[49] They are letting him back by inches it seems to us. But we are glad he is permitted to be so near. Miss Stover is doing very good work here and, of course, has the language already.

Mrs. Webster's schools are very good—the best I have seen in Africa. I am taking points.[50] She closes this month.

I came up from Ciyaka with Mr. Woodside, who had been there to annual meeting. We made it [in] four days' travel. I am spending this week here visiting. Monday Dr. Hollenbeck and I will start for Kamundongo and get home Friday of next week.

Mr. Sanders spent the month of April at Gamba and received eighteen into the church while there.[51]

Our Station is undergoing some changes at present which may give use some new opportunities of service. As soon as our plans are fully set in order[,] I hope to write a general letter telling about our hopes and aims.[52]

I am glad you are to be at Edinburgh.[53] The Misses Melville expect to be present. I should like to be there myself, but I expect there will be other good things when I go home.[54]

A Missionary Symposium: Miss Nellie J. Arnott, Benguella, Africa

From *Life and Light for Woman*, April 1911

At our annual meeting in July it was decided that someone should go to Ciyaka Station for a few months to be with Mrs. Ennis. I was the one chosen, so the middle of November I left my Kamundongo work and started on my way there. I was five days going to Bailundu, and although it was rainy, I really enjoyed the travel.[55]

I had some of our Olutu out-station boys as carriers and they were very attentive to my wants besides being good tepoia carriers. I spent nine days in Bailundu, including Thanksgiving Day.[56] The schools there are very good, which speaks well for their teacher, Mrs. Webster.

On the journey from Bailundu to Sacikela[,] the last two days the path was among the mountains and very pretty. A short distance after leaving camp the last morning we came upon the fresh tracks of two lions which followed beside the path for a long distance. The boys said that it 'made fear' but I wished I might view the lions themselves on some distant hill.[57]

This Station, Sacikela, is in Ciyaka district. It was started in 1905 by Dr. Wellman and Mr. Ennis. Two years ago, Mr. Wellman had to go home on account of ill health and since then the Ennises have been here alone. They have a dear little boy, Merlin, Jr., who is now two years old.[58]

Their house is built on the side of Mt. Elende, a fine old mountain. Below us is the valley, with mountains all around, except toward the west where through the break we can see peaks eighty miles away. The sunsets are often very beautiful.

I did not begin my work in Sacikela till the first of January when I took charge of the Station school. It is held afternoons with about thirty men and boys in attendance. It seems like play after the large schools we had in Ngamba,[59] but I am able to give them more individual attention, and I make the hours as long as possible. I have a Sunday-school class of young boys, and sometimes on Sunday afternoons, I take the meeting for the eight women and girls who are living on the Station. Mrs. Ennis has a daily school with them mornings, and Mr. Ennis has a school every afternoon at the nearest village.

We have spent three days each month in visiting different groups of villages about two hours distance from here. We take beds, tents, food box[es], and set up a village of our own within easy reach of all the villages.[60] Mr. Ennis has the people gather near the tents for meetings, which are held two each day, one in the morning about eight o'clock and the other about five in the afternoon. Sometimes the attendance is good, but often small when one considers the number of people in these villages. They know nothing of God and His word, and of our Saviour Jesus Christ. They are living in the depths of heathenism, worshiping devils and believing in witchcraft and fetishes.[61] I wish you could watch some of their faces when being told for the first time of the story of Jesus. They do not understand much, but they are interested and we can only pray that God will bless His word. Some from the villages have been coming to the Sunday services. Pray, dear friends, that the seed sown in this way may grow. Sunday afternoons I have

Figure 12: Camping scenes, 1911. Courtesy of The Bancroft Library, University of California, Berkeley.

been going to a small group of villages about an hour's walk from here. Lately I have ridden in a tepoia for it gives me more time, as the boys can carry me so much more quickly than I can walk. Besides, walking in these native paths under the tropical sun is not easy. Last Saturday I held three meetings in as many villages. At two of them there was an attendance of over forty, in the other only a few.[62]

Thursday afternoons, Mrs. Ennis goes to the village in which Mr. Ennis has school and holds a meeting with the women. As yet there is no church organized at this Station but there are several who are ready for church membership. Mr. Ennis hopes a church may be organized sometime this year. There has been a request for some time that another missionary be appointed to this Station, but there seem to be so few who want to come to Africa. Will you not all pray that someone may soon be led to offer himself for Africa?

I have not told you of the death of Cituvika. I have often mentioned his name in my letters for he was one of the oldest members of our Kamundongo Church, and the teacher at our Owayanda outstation. His face and life gave every evidence of a Spirit-filled life and he was one of the best Christians I ever knew. He said one time that when he was unable to sleep nights he thought out the Bible lesson he expected to teach the next day and prayed for those in his school. Many of the natives feel that they owe their conversion to him, and Mr. Sanders leaned on him more than any other in our church, so his loss is very greatly felt. He leaves a wife, an earnest Christian, and two children.[63] Sakulumb[u], the teacher in our Kamundongo schools[,] has been chosen to take Cituvika's work at Owayanda and seems to be doing well.[64] He was one of Cituvika's children in the faith and received much of his training under him. Pray for him.

Notes

1. Another version of this article appeared in the January 1908 edition of *Mission Studies* under the title of "A Trip to an African Woman's Conference." The two texts are virtually identical, except that the *Life and Light* account includes several sentences not in *Mission Studies*.

2. See discussion of the annual Women's Conferences in Chapter 2. Arnott does not discuss the conference itself in this account, perhaps because she thought the audience would find the journey itself more interesting, and/or because her continuing difficulty with the language prevented her from participating fully in sessions with Umbundu women. She admitted in her

diary after the 1906 conference that meetings with the women missionaries "have been a real blessing to me but [I] have gotten nothing out of the Umbundu meetings" (July 15, 1906).

3. This comment provides a rare example of Arnott's acknowledging a problem about which she wrote more openly in her diaries—the challenge of finding any quiet, personal time away from the constant stress of her daily work.

4. The printed article has a spelling error in this sentence, using "Unbundu."

5. Umbundu men and women were known for their ability to sing in harmony from a young age. Some converts associated their conversion to Christianity with hearing the beautiful hymns which the missionaries sang. Nellie Arnott's own skill as a singer, developed in her youth, would have been a considerable asset to her mission work. One of her treasured possessions, which she brought home and saved for her grandchildren, was a hymnal, with words in both English and Umbundu. See Fig. 16 below and also Mary Floyd Cushman, *Missionary Doctor*, 132–34.

6. Arnott spells the name of this station "Ohualondo"; apparently the editor misread her handwriting.

7. The "English Mission" stations in central Angola were Ocilonda and Ohualondo, run by missionaries of Christian Churches in Many Lands, commonly called the Plymouth (or Christian) Brethren.

8. Arnott incorrectly spells the surname of George R. and Elizabeth Murrain, who were from Georgetown, in the region of Demerara, British Guiana (now Guyana). They went to Angola in 1891. George Murrain was known for his medical knowledge in treating tropical fevers (Tucker, *Tucker Treasury*, 111). A number of families in the Demerara area (including the Murrains) were descendants of slaves brought from Central Africa; the region furnished a number of Brethren missionaries to Angola. George Murrain served in Angola until his death in 1924, and Elizabeth Murrain until her death in 1946 (Stunt, et al., *Turning the World Upside Down*, 245, 382–83).

9. Arnott was likely thinking of her teaching at AMA schools in making her recommendation for Jack Murrain. Arnott reported in her diary (Oct. 23, 1909) that the four oldest Murrain children were in school in South Carolina.

10. One of the most demanding aspects of a foreign missionary wife's role was entertaining large groups of colleagues. Along those lines, Nancy Henderson-James, the daughter of Lawrence Henderson (who served in Angola decades after Arnott left), noted that her family's home in the port town of Lobito felt like a hotel, and that her mother (Muriel "Ki" Henderson) was

often exhausted from providing accommodations for arriving and departing missionaries. Interview, August 31, 2005. See also Nancy Henderson-James, *At Home Abroad: An American Girl in Africa* (Austin, TX: Plainview Press, 2009), 69-80.

11. The correct spelling is "Gamba." Arnott's readers would have understood that protecting this woman was especially important since she was married to a Christian and was herself in a catechumen's class; that is, undergoing a probationary period in preparation to become a church member.

12. In this passage about a woman originally purchased as a slave in the "interior" (likely eastern Angola or the Belgian Congo), Arnott shows the potential of the "girls' compound" for protecting such women. Later in her mission service, she reiterated similar reasons for needing a Girls' Boarding School. These arguments would have had strong appeal to her audience, for whom "rescuing" women was central to mission work. (See Chapter 2.)

13. Arnott frequently wrote in her diary about her struggles to learn Umbundu, a situation which made her doubt her effectiveness as a missionary. For example, she noted on New Year's Eve, 1906, "Another year is drawing to a close. . . . I feel my life amounts to nothing. I am just holding on the ropes[,] seems to me[,] & being no real blessing to anybody." As late as February of 1909, she was still not fluent. In a letter to Reverend James Barton at ABCFM headquarters in Boston, she reported: "I am now well in my fourth year on the field and I have every reason to thank God for leading me here. My only sorrow is my slow progress in the language. I have sought to be faithful in the study of it. Perhaps there have been times, especially during the two years Miss Stimpson was in America, when I have let other things put it to the side. But I had been here such a short time when she left, that I did find it hard to do all that fell into my hands to do, and keep the language study first. I never realized it before coming to the field, but evidently I have not a good memory. I am seeking to train it in every way possible and am daily reading and studying in the language. I trust some day to be able to use it as I long to, although my progress may be slow" (Nellie J. Arnott to James L. Barton, February 25, 1909. ABCFM Papers, Vol. 15, reel 164, Pitts Theological Library, Emory University). Arnott did continue to work on language study, eventually becoming so fluent that she sometimes slipped into the local language in her diary, using a combination of English and Umbundu.

14. At Oberlin, Arnott had studied the kindergarten movement's new approaches for teaching young children.

15. As Arnott's comments here suggest, the preparation of printed materials was crucial to increasing conversions.

16. Whereas in the early stages of the American foreign mission movement, single women were barred from overseas postings, by the early twen-

tieth century, mission organizations like Arnott's were encouraging such assignments, especially in locations where schools, medical facilities, and related social services had been established.

17. The last two paragraphs of this essay also appear in the *Life and Light* version of Arnott's report on the woman's conference she attended in the summer of 1907. Such transpositions of material demonstrate the role that editors back home in the U.S. played in shaping, as well as circulating, the stories of mission women overseas.

18. "Interior" here refers to the midwestern United States.

19. The best available copy of this article contains several words rendered illegible because of holes in the paper. As indicated by our bracketing, we have inferred what likely appeared in the original copies.

20. "Mission bands" were children's organizations in Congregational churches; they studied foreign missions and supported them with small gifts such as the box of beads mentioned here.

21. Just after Arnott's letter, this article lists study questions, presumably to enhance children's understanding of her report. The "Quiz On Our Lessons" offers these questions: "Where is Kamundongo? Who is our Missionary there? How large a school has she there? Why do not the African children go to school on rainy days? What do the little ones do in school? The older ones? Tell about their Christmas feast. Do you think if the missionaries stay with them they will learn to use knives and forks and live as we do? Will you pray for them as Miss Arnott asks you to do?"

22. Although Arnott's diary indicates she often found living in such close quarters with Sarah Stimpson to be frustrating, having her colleague away on furlough presented another problem—coping with heightened loneliness and homesickness for family and friends in the U.S.

23. Throughout her time in Africa, Arnott campaigned for additional women missionaries to be sent to the highlands region, so that increased supervision of outstation schools being run by local teachers would be possible.

24. These excerpts are from a letter Arnott wrote to Dr. James L. Barton of the ABCFM in Boston, Feb. 25, 1909. ABCFM Papers, Vol. 15, reel 164, Pitts Theological Library, Emory University.

25. The name of this outstation is typically spelled "Owayanda."

26. Usually, Arnott's publications use the spelling "Kamundongo." Arnott was the sole missionary at the outstation of Olutu from January 23, 1909, until March 3, 1909. According to her diary, she taught children's classes, held women's meetings, instructed Sunday school teachers, held Bible

lessons for some of the men, and helped Sakamana, the Umbundu minister, prepare his sermons.

27. In most of Arnott's published materials, "Fumika" is the spelling used. Such variations in spelling may be due to editors' difficulty reading Arnott's handwriting. However, Arnott herself is not always consistent in her spellings.

28. This heading appears to have been added by someone in the ABCFM office.

29. Nellie J. Arnott to James L. Barton, October 5, 1909, ABCFM Papers, Vol. 15, reel 164. Pitts Theological Library, Emory University. Rev. James Levi Barton graduated from Middlebury College and Hartford Theological Seminary. He served as an ABCFM missionary in Turkey, where he founded Euphrates College in Harput. In 1892, he became Foreign Secretary of the ABCFM, a position which he held until 1927. Active in philanthropy, Barton was the author of works about missions, about his experiences in Turkey, and about his involvement in Near East relief efforts after World War I. He died in 1936 at age 81. Biographical information is in Fred Field Goodsell, *James Levi Barton: Dynamic World Christian Statesman* ([Boston:] Congregational Christian Historical Society, 1964); a biographical sketch by David M. Stowe is in Anderson, *Biographical Dictionary of Christian Missions*, 46.

30. Arnott infrequently refers to the ruling government of the Portuguese in her writing. Here, where she is making requests to an ABCFM official for reinforcements and also justifying the request she and Sarah Stimpson have made to work alone in Gamba, the discussion of politics seems more suitable to her, apparently, than when she is writing to women supporters. Government officials perhaps thought that a move of the Kamundongo station to Gamba would excessively extend the mission's influence. In any case, refusing to allow a move to Gamba reinforced the authority of the Portuguese. A similar situation existed in the Congo, where the government denied requests for new Protestant mission stations in order to curtail their activity (Grant, *Civilised Savagery*, 46).

31. Frederick T. Lane, from Hounslow Heath in England, served in Angola's Plymouth Brethren missions from 1889 to 1929 (Stunt, et al., *Turning the World Upside Down*, 379, 626).

32. Arnott's Reports of the Kamundongo School for 1906, 1907, and 1908 are in ABCFM Papers, Vol. 14, reel 163. ABCFM authors like Arnott used a technique similar to reports on AMA-sponsored schools, where she had worked in the southern U.S. More specifically, AMA reports invoked rhetorical markers to convince potential supporters that black students were interested in and capable of learning—i.e., that investments made in schools

in the post-Civil War South would pay dividends. When writing about her students in Angola, Arnott sometimes employed parallel language designed to show readers at home that the work with African learners was progressing well and therefore worthy of continued support.

33. Arnott became increasingly convinced that local teachers were worthy colleagues, essential to the missionary enterprise and capable of doing quality teaching. The scrapbook she prepared during her post-missionary years in California contains numerous marginal notes referencing the work of Angolans who had studied with her and who later became teachers themselves. For example, in her "Ideal Scrapbook," she pasted a January, 1946, publication entitled "An African Pastor and His Wife Go to Their New Field," which appeared in *The Missionary Monthly* in January 1946. On page 12 of the report, beside a picture labeled "Pastor Enoque Gomes Sacamana and his wife Laurinda Lucia," Arnott has written "Were both my helpers."

34. The progression Arnott describes of moving from oral recitation around short texts written on the blackboard to study in primers and, eventually, to Bible reading was a pattern also being followed in some schools within the U.S. This sequence harkens back to nineteenth-century New England one-room schoolhouses, whose curriculum became the basis for much of the teaching for black children that was delivered by white, middle-class women journeying south after the Civil War to teach the freedmen and their children.

35. By the time this article appeared, Cituvika had died. (See Arnott's letter of October 1909 on the missionaries' mourning his loss but supporting Sakalumbu as his replacement.) Lag time between a missionary's submitting material and publication of a magazine like *Mission Studies* was so long that having outdated information like this portrait of Cituvika still at work was not uncommon. The image of a learning exchange cast as a domesticated act of shared fireside reading would have appealed to Arnott's audience in the U.S. There, throughout the nineteenth century, an ideology exalting maternal teaching as an avenue to sociopolitical influence played out in many narrative texts. See Robbins, *Managing Literacy, Mothering America*, 1–37. In the Angola mission setting of Arnott's day, the Umbundu teacher (whether in a traditional or a Christian community) was typically male rather than female, following local custom. (See Chapter 2.)

36. This location is usually spelled "Olutu."

37. Arnott's responsibilities were becoming increasingly administrative. This expansion of her duties beyond her own teaching to training and supervising other educators beyond her home station was paralleled by women missionaries working in other locations, such as Laura Haygood, who served in China. See Robbins, *Managing Literacy, Mothering America*, 215–24, on

this professionalization process as occurring throughout the mission movement.

38. A traditional Umbundu community was divided into family sections with houses for a leader's several wives located near his main house. Christian settlements, in contrast, were laid out with straight streets and houses for nuclear families. (See Chapter 2.) Such an arrangement thus drew attention to the "cleanliness and order" of the Christian village (Cushman, *Missionary Doctor*, 66, 104). It also distinguished a town in which monogamous families were the norm from one in which more than one wife was common; thus the "Christian village" marked what Mary Floyd Cushman called "The New Life."

39. Fumika's "Matthew" was his Umbundu translation of that book of the Bible.

40. Cloth was one staple of exchange used by such colonial powers as the Belgians in their interactions with local Africans, who in the Congo region not far north of Arnott's station were often cheated out of land and rights to rubber harvesting by wily European (and American) traders. See Hochschild, *King Leopold's Ghost*, 158–208.

41. When Portuguese authorities blocked the plan to move the Kamundongo station to Gamba, the missionaries responded by spending several months each year in the new location. Arnott and Stimpson went to teach in Gamba over the objections of some of the male missionaries, though with the support of Rev. Sanders. (See Chapter 3.)

42. We have been able to identify several "general letters" that Arnott sent to the ABCFM during her time in Africa, but some are unaccounted for. The report she describes as having sent in March of 1910 is one for which we have not found a copy. The letter reproduced here was pasted in one of Arnott's scrapbooks (*Ideal Scrapbook*, box 2 of NJADP).

43. Foreign missionaries routinely complained about the difficulty of finding time to write home. As Patricia Hill has noted, organizations such as the ABCFM and the Congregational Woman's Board of Missions consistently pressured foreign missionaries to write home "where, after all, the letter reached a wider audience than the teacher's voice could among the heathen. The supporting societies in America obviously expected . . . that their missionaries would supply them as well as the heathen with spiritual blessings. The missionaries, on their side, considered writing letters to auxiliaries a drain on precious time that might otherwise be devoted to what they believed to be their real task; they had not left home and family in order to stir the sluggish spiritual senses of American women" (*The World Their Household*, 104). Arnott, an avid writer, was more willing than many mis-

sionaries to devote time to such correspondence, and her careful saving of her articles suggests she was proud of her writing.

44. Arnott's discussion of both the bicycle and the one-wheeled cart in this letter show that new modes of transportation were working their way even into the more remote sections of West Africa by this time.

45. Arnott's ranking of her preferences from among various means of transportation exemplifies a trend Sidonie Smith has traced in *Moving Lives: 20th-Century Women's Travel Writing* (Minneapolis: Univ. of Minnesota Press, 2001). As Smith has observed, increased access to modes of travel is a marker of modernity's growing influence on women's lives, including increases in "freedom and prowess." Smith sees early twentieth-century women's exercising choices about which means of travel to use as closely linked to their sense of identity (xi–xii). In that context, Arnott's preference for the tepoia over the cart, and the train over either one, situates her sense of herself as deserving to be properly transported. The "bush-car" is described by missionary Mary Floyd Cushman as a "one-wheeled vehicle with a sort of chair seat. There are iron handles in front and behind, which the carriers grasp," Cushman noted. "If the path is rough, so is the riding" (*Missionary Doctor*, 122).

46. Arnott associates her traveling to the falls with the type of African exploration that had been gendered as masculine by such popular authors as Henry Morton Stanley and David Livingstone. Still, as she points out, this exciting trip is gender-appropriate, since 1) she is following a route already tested out by her male colleague, Mr. Neipp; 2) she is accompanied by two lady companions, Miss Redick and Miss Stimpson; 3) these falls, though in a remote part of Africa, are cast as reminiscent of that familiar American watery tourist site, Niagara Falls. On the gender politics of travel by American women of Arnott's era, see Schriber, *Writing Home*, especially 1–11.

47. Here we can see Arnott's growing awareness of how the material culture around her at the ABCFM's West African mission outposts reflects the impact of cross-cultural interaction. In explaining "how the natives build their houses," Arnott also demonstrates specific examples of elements from western Euro-American domestic culture—e.g., locks—that were being taken on by the local community members, sometimes by adapting native materials and sometimes by seeking to acquire whites' goods. At the same time, as Arnott's lyrical closing sentence suggests, Umbundu culture retained many of its own markers, sometimes evident as much by what is *not* interpolated from white Euro-American models as from an overt choice to maintain local practices and structures. Specifically, by noting that "the noise of the hammer, saw and plane is never heard," Arnott separates the community where she is living from technological activity linked to American home-building. Despite the connections she highlights, her essay also shows that "House Building in Africa" is *not* the same as it would be in the U.S.

48. Arnott alludes to the frustration ABCFM missionaries in Angola felt at their numbers not being adequate to their duties. Their campaign for reinforcements was ongoing, but never as successful as they would have liked.

49. The original sentence reads: "Mrs. Stover went last week to to be with him. . . ." While Wesley Stover was on furlough to the U.S. (1908), the Portuguese government, apparently angry at his stand against the contract labor system, ordered him not to return. (See Chapter 2.) Portuguese authorities by May, 1910, had allowed him to travel to the Ocileso station, but not yet to his own post at Bailundu; he was approved to return there in June. See (above) Arnott's Circular Letter of August 5, 1910.

50. Throughout her teaching career, Arnott used observation in others' classrooms as a strategy for improving her own instructional techniques. Marion Webster, due to her abilities as a teacher and administrator, was eventually chosen to head the new Means School for Girls.

51. The original published manuscript says "Saunders," though Arnott most likely means her mission colleague "Sanders." The mention of Miss Reddick (rather than Redick) earlier in this same article suggests either that Arnott was lapsing into carelessness about spelling or that the editor who prepared this piece was less familiar than most with the cast of ABCFM characters in Angola—or both.

52. Arnott may be alluding to the upcoming campaign to promote start-up of a boarding school for Angolan girls.

53. The *Life and Light* article does not identify the person Arnott references as "you." She or he was likely a member of the ABCFM delegation to the World Missionary Conference in Edinburgh in June, 1910. For a guide to the records of this conference and information about its history, scope and Continuation Committees, see John L. Grillo and Ruth Tonkiss Cameron, "Finding Aid for world Missionary Conference Records Edinburgh, 1910." Missionary Research Library Archives, Section 12, Burke Library Archives, Union Theological Seminary, New York. http://www.columbia.edu/cu/lweb/img/assets/6398/MRL12_WMC_FA.pdf. For an analysis of the conference, see Brian Stanley, *The World Missionary Conference: Edinburgh 1910* (Grand Rapids: William B. Eerdmans, 2009). Stanley notes that Africa was "scarcely represented" at the conference except by "expatriate missionaries"; only one black African delegate was present (97-99).

54. Arnott was anticipating her upcoming furlough to the U.S.

55. Although Arnott found her occasional postings to outstations challenging, she did apparently appreciate the change in scene, according to a number of her diary entries.

56. Like other missionary writers, Arnott often used references to American holidays to help her readers contextualize chronology in her accounts.

57. Arnott's move to picture herself as unafraid of the wild animals—indeed, as eager to see them—signals her increasing self-confidence as a traveler through remote areas between mission stations.

58. Tragically, Merlin Ennis, Jr., died in Angola of an infection caused by a jigger bite, according to John Tucker. Deaths of missionary children were all too common. Tucker and his wife lost a child in Angola, as did Rev. and Mrs. Sanders, the Neipps, and the Fays (Tucker, *Tucker Treasury*, 78, 112; W.H. Sanders, "Reminiscences," 66 and 76).

59. Missionaries usually spelled this location "Gamba." In Umbundu, however, a preliminary sound, indicated by an "n" or "m" precedes b, d, and g; "Ngamba" thus represents local pronunciation (Cushman, *Missionary Doctor*, 131).

60. Original reads "tennis" instead of "tents" in this sentence.

61. Although Arnott had by this time developed an affection for many of the Africans with whom she worked on a daily basis, and although she had a far deeper understanding of local customs than during her first years in Africa, she continued to emphasize the superiority of Christianity as a value system and to characterize some local practices in negative terms as "heathen."

62. Significantly, by this time Arnott is comfortable preaching, on her own, in remote villages—a role that had for many years been reserved for male missionaries.

63. Arnott's highly positive character sketch of Cituvika extends her previous depictions of him and exemplifies a technique—creating particularized portraits of Christians with whom she worked—which she was using often in her published writing by this time. Emphasizing his teaching talents and religious commitment, Arnott individualizes Cituvika, distancing him from the stereotype "heathen" figure that dominated a good deal of her early writing from Africa. See earlier discussion of Cituvika's death in a letter written in fall of 1909.

64. Arnott's opening statement in this paragraph ("I have not told you of the death of Cituvika") would apply to general readers of the women's magazine where this article appeared, who would not have had access to her earlier letter reporting Cituvika's death to the ABCFM administration. In that previous report, she had spelled the name of his successor as Sakalumbu.

6 Cultivating Networks of Influence

After years of teaching in Portuguese West Africa, in early 1912 Nellie Arnott prepared to re-cross the Atlantic. Although furloughs represented a normal stage in a missionary's service, Arnott's plans for her trip back home included an innovative dimension—soliciting support for a proposed girls' boarding school. She would first make stops to visit institutions in southern Africa like the one she hoped to establish in Angola. Once in the U.S. again, she would take on the speaking engagements typical of returning ABCFM missionaries but, in doing so, would focus on generating funds for the new school.

Arnott's hesitancy to leave her longtime colleagues and students in Angola seemed to be tempered by a growing self-confidence about her upcoming role in the mission organization. Her letters to mission officials over the months of her speaking tour reflect an increased assertiveness and a persistent energy. Yet, soon after she reached California, she unexpectedly married Paul Darling. Given a commitment to the Angolan mission still evident in the writing published after her marriage, key questions about this stage of her career include these: What social forces led to her change in plans? In what ways did she view her marriage as consistent with or at odds with her mission service? How would she herself have characterized her links to the movement after her May 1913 wedding?

Whereas her personal reflections during the first continental and Atlantic crossings had conveyed worries about how she would manage the separation from friends and family, as she entered her marriage, she tried to reconcile this choice with the strong feelings she had developed for Umbundu people and for her work as a Christian teacher in the Angolan highlands. Having struggled so long to learn the Umbundu language, to mentor local students and teachers, and to assume a leadership position in the complex hierarchy of her mission community in Africa, she sought ways to stay connected to that part of her life. Still submitting mission-oriented stories for publication in the first period of her married life, she subsequently turned more attention to mothering her son and, later, her grandchildren. Meanwhile, she used her scrapbook collection to memorialize her time in Africa and to maintain records of the ongoing activities of ABCFM and Umbundu colleagues in the Angolan highlands. Her writing shifted from the extended reports, letters, and magazine accounts she had sent from Angola to penciled margin notes on the multifaceted accounts that she continued to accumulate in her scrapbooks, marking the lingering importance of the mission movement to her sense of self.

CIRCULAR LETTER #7 (TO FRIENDS AT OBERLIN COLLEGE)[1] AND THE BEGINNING OF A BOARDING SCHOOL IN WEST CENTRAL AFRICA

From *Mission Studies*, August 1911[2]

Kamundongo, Africa
Mar. 22, 1911.

Dear friends:

I find I have not written you a general letter since Aug. How quickly time passes! Then we were busy with the schools at Gamba. We returned here in September. The first part of Oct. the Station schools here were begun and they have continued with the exception of three weeks' vacation at holiday time. Miss Stimpson has the two afternoon schools and I have the children in the morning school.

The first of October Mr. and Mrs. Sanders went to Gamba and remained until just before Christmas. While they were away[,] Dr. Hollenbeck boarded with us and we had some company, but nevertheless we greatly missed Mr. and Mrs. Sanders and we were brought to realize how much they will be missed in the work and how lonely it will be while they are away for furlough. They expect to take the July English steamer so will be leaving us in less than four months.

Mr. Sanders was asked by the Mission to revise the Umbundu Vocabulary and to make an English-Umbundu [one]. The previous months and while at Gamba[,] he and Mrs. Sanders spent much of their time in collecting and proving words. Mr. Sanders made two copies of the Umbundu part on the typewriter. On their return[,] the English part was in readiness to be arranged alphabetically. Miss Bell of Cisamba was with us for a visit over the holidays[,] so we all went to work on the

Vocabulary, she making the copies on the typewriter while the rest of us arranged the words in order. When this was finished, we decided, as the book was so much needed and as we could have Miss Bell remain and help us, to print it here on the press. As the natives, who usually do the press work, make so many mistakes when they set up in English, we did all setting up ourselves, just completing the book of over six hundred pages last week. Now they are being bound and covered, Mrs. Sanders over-seeing and doing a large portion of the work. It was a big job for us[,] but we are delighted to have a good Vocabulary for study. Since we began this press work[,] most other work has been set aside, just the schools and services continuing.[3]

The week of Prayer was observed with a fair attendance. At the last communion service[,] nine were received into church membership, but much to our sorrow some of our old members have had to be suspended for one cause or another. Pray for these [so] that they may be brought into fellowship.

Some of you have known of my desire to open a Girls' Boarding School.[4] It is one of the needs that impressed me when I first came to Africa, and has grown upon me every year as being very necessary. Older girls have been gathered into compounds and given special attention, but they have lived largely as their mothers do. What I desire is to gather in girls of about ten years of age or younger and teach them to be more cleanly in their living and cooking.[5]

In November, with the approval of my fellow missionaries[,] a beginning was made with six girls.[6] They have a house with two half windows and two doors. In this they eat and sleep and spend their evenings. Nasiku, Cituvika's widow, sleeps with them and has prayers with them [in the] mornings. Their beds consist of a reed mat put on the floor, on top of which they spread the regular native sleeping mat and a cloth. Two girls sleep together and are covered with a blanket. They remove all their clothing and wear a white cloth for sleeping. The native usually wears his cloth day and night until worn out. Once a week they carry all of their sleeping cloths and any dirty dresses to the stream and wash them.[7]

There are a couple of tables in the room and to these they sit down and eat every morning and evening.[8] Some enamel plates, cups and spoons left over from a load sent out a few years ago have been put in use. I wish now we had more. Most of them had been given as Christmas and wedding presents. At noon they lunch on an ear of roasted corn, a few peanuts or a piece of squash. In the same yard near the sleeping house is a smaller house used for [a] kitchen. In this is a half window and a low shelf built up inside of adobe, also a table made of boxes, and I'm learning patience in trying to teach them to keep all pots, baskets, and dishes off of the floor. The native woman has everything on the floor around her fire. She sits down by the fire to prepare the evening meal and does not need to move until the next morning, for everything is in reach. When the mush and relish are ready she fills a basket with the mush and a clay dish with the relish and a child carries it to her husband at the onjango.[9] Then the children gather around her and they eat what is left. When finished, there is no table to unspread or dishes to wash. They are pushed aside for the dogs to lick and are not washed until used again. She will sit over the fire and snuff until sleepy, then clear a place to spread her mat and go to sleep.[10] This is just a glimpse of the raw native woman.[11] The girls are being taught to wash their dishes and pots after each meal and put things in order. How fast they [will] learn remains to be seen. Inborn habits cannot be changed in even a few years, so it seems best to begin with young girls and to keep them until married. It is hoped that then a few changes will appear in their own homes.

Dr. Hollenbeck had a field or large garden enclosed. This the girls are cultivating. The goats jumped walls some places and ate off their first planting and have continued destroying corn and beans now and then. [In] another year we hope to have all who own animals live across the stream, so [we] will not be troubled in this way.

At present there are nine girls, and [we] hope to gather in a few more. The present houses will not accommodate more than fifteen girls. The hope is[,] as soon as the money can be raised[,] to build a house to accommodate fifty or sixty girls.[12] Some has already been given for this purpose which I hope will increase until we have about one thousand dollars. That will build such a house as is needed, as well as provide a separate building for [a] kitchen, dining-room and store house. Some may think a thousand dollars a large sum, but we are looking to the future. In the past our African houses have been built for five hundred or a little over, but they require rethatching every few years, which is a great expense as well as hinders greatly in the work while it is being done. There are other improvements which might be made in building that were not possible a few years ago. These adobe walls need to be plastered with mud often and cause constant repairing around doors and windows, as they can not be built in them strongly. We are hoping for a tile or tin roof and possibly burnt brick walls. The first expense would be greater[,] but we would have a good building that would not constantly be under repair. There has already been rather heavy expense.

The first digging over of the garden has had to be done by men, as the work was too heavy for the girls. Then, of course, we cannot expect such young girls to raise enough to support themselves. It is expected when the work is established and some of the girls are older that they will be able to raise most of their food supply.[13] At present, I estimate that food, clothing and other expenses will average about ten dollars a year for each girl.

Thus far[,] through the goodness of friends[,] all expenses have been met[,] and it gives encouragement to press forward and to make the most of the present accommodations until there can be provided a building and compound as is desirable.

It is expected that parents and relatives will bring presents of food and cloth and so help in the work. The people here are interested[,] and many have spoken to me about taking their daughters. Some have helped this year in giving food.[14]

Last week a man from a village some distance away brought his son and daughter to remain with us. Dr. Hollenbeck expects to begin a work for boys very much along the same lines, but he is not ready to receive them yet. They both returned for the present as it seemed best for the girl to wait until her brother can also remain.

Miss Stimpson expects to continue having the older girls in her compound as in the past, and looks forward to receiving some of the new ones from the villages in the near future.

I believe the earlier we can separate the children from their own homes, villages and heathen influences, the better and stronger Christian men and women we will have.[15] The girls can be taught to cook some things better and differently, also to cultivate a larger variety of foodstuffs. At present, they cultivate few things aside from corn, beans and manioc.[16] They can be taught to wash, iron, make baskets [and] pots and to sew, aside from the regular school work.

This work presents large opportunities and possibilities[,] and I trust it will prove to be the answer to my prayers and will be the means of developing and enriching the lives of the African women.

Yours truly,
Nellie J. Arnott

Address—A.B.C. F. M
Benguella
Angola
Africa

Circular Letter #8[17]

Kamundongo, Saturday. Febry. 17–1912
By Nellie Arnott[18]

Doctor Hollenbeck returned from a visit at Gamba today. He reports that the work on the whole is in very good condition there. Nineteen were received into church-membership the last Sunday in Jan. There are now four outstation schools around Susua[,] the main settlement in Gamba, and a fifth about to be opened.

After our conference with Dr. Hollenbeck I have decided to go home by the way of the Cape visiting our Girl's Boarding Schools in Natal, so have written to engage passage on the Rapids leaving Lobita Bay the middle of April.[19]

Sunday. Feb. 25

It has been a red-letter day for Kamundongo. For some weeks back reports have come to us of more drinking among elders, and our Kamundongo church members. Dr. Hollenbeck has conferred with Miss Stimpson and myself and we all came to the conclusion that things could not go on. For a few weeks we have been having temperance Sunday School lessons and all the teaching and preaching as well as personal talks have aimed to bring them to desire a change in the church here. Today the time seemed ripe to allow them to express themselves and so a special meeting was called this afternoon. Some twenty-five, most of them church members, confessed to sins and the drinking of rum, and to smoking, saying they wished to give them up and asked for our prayers. There seemed to be deep feeling and a breaking up and a realization of the Spirit's presence such as I have never seen in any meeting in Africa. There were also five who made confession of Christ for the 1st time. We were there over two hours and a half, and it was a most precious time.[20]

Sun. Mar. 3

Another red-letter Sunday. At the morning service today nineteen[,] mostly boys and girls, made confession of Christ. Seven of the members were my own girls. How thankful I am. The attendance was better than usual and there is every evidence of the Spirit's special working among us.[21]

Sun. Mar. 10

Mr. Neipp came over from Cesamba [*sic*] on Thurs. to be with us for a few days and hold communion service with us.[22] We had a preparatory service Friday afternoon. Twelve had presented themselves for church membership and were received. Kayovo, my oldest girl, was among them. Also three who had been put on the suspension list were returned to fellowship.[23] The services of the day were very good and helpful.

Friday Mar. 22–1912

Yesterday I went to Wayanda outstation where Sakalumbu is the teacher and spent the afternoon in the schools. In the evening had prayers with them[,] after which we had a good sing. About a hundred are in the schools there. He holds the children's school in the early morning after their morning prayers together, which were over before I was up. About nine[,] I returned to the station.

This afternoon visited Kakoko Outstation. This village has moved to a new site not far from their old village. It was about an hour from the Station. Here the school is very much run down largely because we have been unable to give it much attention. I examined all, had a meeting with them, and told them they must hold a school every morning for the children, putting it in the care of a young man, who had been a helper in the Station school last year. At both these outstations the people are making good roads to the Station.

Tues Mar. 26th

In camp, near Belmont Fort.

I was late getting away this morning. All had been called out to work on the road so there were not many around when I left the house.[24] Some Olutu girls had come up to say good-bye, and also Fumika, one of the teachers. But when I reached the women, girls and children on the road the crying began, and they followed a long way. It was very hard indeed to leave them all. I can only commit them to Him each day who alone is able to strengthen them against the temptations that surround them.[25]

Camp Kakmana

We reached camp about one-thirty. It is near a lovely stream. We found a large caravan in camp, but they [gave] my carriers three or four huts. My tent is put across the road from the camp. Each afternoon I have spent in teaching reading and arithmetic to my carriers. Most of them are outstation men and are glad of such help. Have also led the prayers each evening. This evening the caravan in camp also gathered around the fire. They come from a village a day's distance from Bailundu, but have never heard the gospel. They were carrying loads from a white trader in their locality to another trader near Kamundongo. There were a dozen or more young girls in the caravan, who were finally persuaded to come to my tent and visit awhile after prayers. Just to think[,] they never have heard of Jesus and yet there are hundreds of such villages, yes, thousands scattered over Angola, where there are many such bright girls, who have never yet come in touch with the gospel. Tomorrow we will reach Bailundu.[26]

Easter Sunday: Bailundu[27]

Have been here all week and Mrs. Stover has kindly helped me with some sewing. Dr. Stover preached a clear sermon on the resurrection this morning. I enjoyed having the meeting with the girls this afternoon. The last Sunday I spent in the U. S. seven years ago was Easter Sun. Tomorrow I start on for Ciyaka.

Sunday Apr. 14 Ciyaka

I arrived here on Thurs and have enjoyed my visit with Mr. and Mrs. Ennis and Dr. and Mrs. Moffatt. The latter have been back a little over a month. Attended service and took the women in Sunday School. It is the last Umbundu teaching I am likely to do until my return. I do hope I will not forget the language.

Catumbella. April 16–1912

Dr. Moffatt has come to the Coast with me. We left Ciyaka about nine Monday morning. He in his new bush cart and I in my tepoia. Three hours brought us to Cuma where we took the train about two. I really felt sorry to leave the hammock and my carriers. We took an apartment which was very good indeed, but soon found a Portuguese with his two little girls were to have it with us.[28] The train went a very good speed until seven when we reached Cubal where it stopped for the night. There was a restaurant where we got quite a good dinner. We slept on the train and suffered with the heat. About seven in the morning we started on, the train passing through a very pretty mountainous country all day. Through the mountains that seven years before we had climbed and walked[,] though being carried partly in tepoia, then the only way to enter. Now the railway extends over two hundred miles. We reached Catumbella about five and are here at the house of our Portuguese Agent. Everything is very nice, but oh, it is hot. We hear that the steamer will be in at Lobita Bay tomorrow, so by this time tomorrow I will be on the ocean.

April 17th-Steamship Portugal

We left Catumbella this forenoon and came to Lobita Bay. It is now quite a port. There was an English freight steamer in port unloading railroad material. Quite a town is growing up and they are building a house for the Governor. Shortly after dinner the steamer arrived and we came aboard about three. I was given a cabin alone. Dr. Moffatt bid me good-bye and I am left alone, the only English speaking person [or] passenger.

Cape Town. April 22nd

We arrived here about five and I am at the Y.W.C.A. It is homelike and one feels among friends at once. What a blessing these associations are all over the world. I was sea-sick most of the way from Lobita Bay but on the whole got along nicely. I slept a great deal of the time. Have decided to stay a week in order to visit Wellington over Sun.

Wellington, Sun. April 28th

Came out here Thursday. I had met Miss Ferguson who has been the president so many years. She is now over seventy[-]four and does not teach any more. Has her own little dining room and how I have enjoyed the quiet meals with her and the visits. Dr. Bliss, who came out with Miss Ferguson in 1873[,] is the president of Huguenot College now. They have built up a wonderful institution and its earnest Christian graduates are making their influence felt all over South Africa as well as in many missionary centers. Dr. Andrew Murray is the founder and he is living here with two of his daughters. It was my privilege to meet him in his home yesterday and this evening he preached a strong simple sermon in Goodnow Hall. It has been a happy week and this my first Sunday in civilization a most blessed one. I wish all might read Dr. Murray's latest book "The State of the Church." It is splendid.[29]

Durban. May 5th

I left Cape Town last Tues. evening on the Edinburgh Castle. Had a good passage and reach[ed] here about noon today. Rev. Bridgman met me and I am in their home. Mrs. Bridgman, his mother, is here. She has been a missionary in Natal since 1860.[30] I have attended two native services, one this afternoon and one this evening. The work here reminds me of the work in the South under the American Missionary Association.[31] Durban is a city of about 60,000.

NOTE: I have wanted very much for some time back to send out another general letter, but have been unable to do so. So I decided it would be easier and perhaps just as interesting to you if I would make some copies from my diary. I began in Feb. and have brought you up to the present and I hope in a few weeks to send on this month's diary.

I might explain that when the American Board deputation visited our Mission last July and August that it was suggested that when I took my furlough it might be well for me to come to Natal on my way home and visit the Girl's Boarding Schools in this Mission.[32] So that is why I came this way, and am spending this month in Natal.

With Christian love,
Nellie J. Arnott

CIRCULAR LETTER #9

383 Burke Street
Youngstown, Ohio

Dear Friends—[33]

I believe I sent out my last general letter to you shortly before leaving Kamundongo. At the time I expected to go directly home, but just before leaving it seemed best for me to go to South Africa to visit the boarding schools under our Board there, so I sailed a little earlier than first planned, leaving Lobito Bay April 19th. I was five days in reaching Cape Town. I remained there a week spending four days of the time in Wellington, visiting a friend, Miss Ferguson, who has been president of the Huguenot College for many years. This is called the Mt. Holyoke of South Africa, a college for Dutch girls which was opened in 1873 through the efforts of Dr. Andrew Murray.[34]

From Cape Town I went to Durban, Natal, and spent five weeks in visiting three boarding schools.[35] These visits helped me very much in formulating my plans for opening a school in our own Mission. I was glad to meet all the missionaries who are working in these schools, and see the splendid work that they are doing. Let me say here that there is a great need of three or four good American teachers in these schools at the present time.

From Durban I took a trip up the East Coast of Africa, leaving Durban on the 14th of June, and after stopping at many ports along the coast[,] reached Port Said July 14th. From there I went to Cairo, where I spent four days. In Cairo I was much interested in seeing the work of the United Presbyterian Church. They have a splendid college for girls. I returned to Port Said, and sailed to Naples, and from Naples went overland to London, stopping in Rome, and a few days in Switzerland.[36] In London I spent a week visiting a friend, and sailed August 13th for Boston.

On my arrival in Boston I went to the home of Dr. E. E. Strong, who was one of the secretaries for so many years of the American Board. While I enjoyed being in their home, I greatly missed the best friend of our Mission, Mrs. Means, who had died in June. It was through the efforts of her husband largely that our West African Mission was opened, and all these years she has prayed for us, and been a friend to all the missionaries as no other person has. I asked myself many times, "Who is there to take her place, of interceding for missionaries and the work in West Africa?" I spent a week in Boston, and had some very nice visits with the Secretaries in the Board Rooms. From there I went to Clifton Springs, where I spent a week.[37] You will be glad to know that the Doctors at Clifton Springs consider me in a very good condition of health. I am now visiting my brother [Charles] here in Youngstown, and my future plans are rather unsettled. I may remain in the Central States until the last of October so as to attend the Annual Meeting of the Women's Board of the Interior, at Evanston, Ill.

For the present address me here, and any letters will be forwarded to wherever I may be.

Some of you know that our Mission has decided to open a Girls Boarding School, and that while I am home I hope to raise sufficient funds for the building, and the first year's running expenses.[38] Will you not unite with me in prayer that I may be guided aright, and that the hearts of those who are able to make offerings for this work may be opened to give[?] If you know of friends that might be interested in this effort[,] will you kindly let me know, and perhaps I can give them more definite information[?]

Yours with Christian love,
Nellie J. Arnott
Sept-17–12[39]

Letter to ABCFM Official Reverend James Barton: #2[40]

Youngstown, Ohio, September 7th, 1912

Dr. James L. Barton,
Congregational House,
Boston, Mass.

My dear Dr. Barton:

I arrived in Clifton Springs safely, and spent one week in the home of Dr. Sanders.[41] They have a cottage in the village, and are keeping house. They like this very much, and it certainly makes it very much more pleasant for their daughter Jenny.

You will be glad to know that on examination of blood, no malaria germs were in evidence. The Doctor thinks I am on the whole in very good condition, which he says is largely due to my long sea voyage. He says that did me more good than doctors and medicine. I am greatly relieved, to know the malaria is disappearing.[42]

I saw Dr. Tinker, the surgeon who operated on me nine years ago, and he said that I looked stronger and better than when I went out to Africa.[43]

I found that Miss Wingate had gone to Schenectady, so [I] remained in Clifton longer than I had intended.[44] She returned Tuesday evening, and I spent all day Wednesday in conference with her. She is somewhat doubtful whether the committee will feel like taking the responsibility of raising ten thousand dollars for the Girls' Boarding

School. She greatly desires that I remain for [the] Annual Meeting, which is held in Evanston, Ill., the last of October. I am considering doing this, and in the meantime may visit friends and relatives in the Middle States.

I trust the minutes of the Annual Meeting are in ere this.[45] I would like, if it is not too much trouble, to have you copy from the West African letters any items referring to the Girls' Boarding School. Have you received a detailed report of the Financial Committee? I wish I might have a copy of it. I find I have forgotten the name of those appointed as Trustees for the Girls' Boarding School. Have you any indications from the letters received whether they expect this ten thousand dollars at the beginning, or whether it is the amount to be raised for use in the completion of the School, some years hence?[46]

I received no other letters, aside from some from Miss Bell. She does not seem to be very well, and was finding the medical work very heavy. She said a report had reached them that Mr. and Mrs. Tucker were to arrive in the Melville party.[47] I understood that they were still in England.

I am at present here with my brother and sister, and may remain the next ten days or two weeks.
Yours most cordially,
Nellie J. Arnott
383 Burke St.

Letter to ABCFM Official Reverend James Barton: #3[48]

The Moody Bible Institute
Chicago, Ill.
Sept. 26—1912

Dr. James L. Barton
Congregational House
Boston, Mass.

My dear Dr. Barton:

I thank you for your letter of Sept. 11, which reached me before leaving Youngstown.

While at Youngstown I spoke in the Congregational church at their prayer meeting & the following week in the First Presbyterian

Church. It was in this church that I worked as Pastor's assistant for two years before going to Africa.

I made the acquaintance of Dr. Thomas, one of the members of our Board. He is a fine man and seems to be very much interested in our Girls' School & has promised a gift. I hope some of my rich Presbyterian friends may remember us also.

While here a few days, I am speaking in the Thanksgiving offering meetings of some of the churches. I go on to Fremont, Neb[raska] Mon. for their Branch Meeting & then will visit my brother [Edward] in S. Dak[ota], returning here Oct. 29–31 for the Annual meeting of the W.B.M.I.[49] Then I will go directly home where I hope to remain for a few months. You may address me care of the W.B.M.I. until Nov. 1st.

I thank you for the copy of Mr. Woodside's letter. He has written to Miss Wingate, so the ladies here have the action of the Annual Meeting in hand.[50] I hope a copy of the minutes will be sent to them.

I could not help but note the tone of Mr. Woodside's letter regarding Dr. Cammack's return. I cannot agree fully & still feel that they should be given another chance and hope things will turn out that way.[51]

So sorry to hear of the fire at Cisamba. It is a great loss & will make the year's work so hard for those who are there.[52]

After that revival at Kamundongo in Feb. there were some, who had fallen to drinking again. It does grieve me so much. But reports from Gamba & the Olutu outstations are good.

Most cordially yours,
Nellie J. Arnott

What it Means in Africa to the Mother and Child to be without the Christ Child[53]

(Copy of a Talk for Mission Supporters as Given by Nellie Arnott)

Our little black sister often enters upon life with a weak little body, especially so if the mother is young and she the first child. She may live a few weeks and then sicken and die or she may succeed in digesting the corn meal gruel and other foods her mother feeds her in addition to the breast, and begins her life of existence on her mother's back. She is carried back & forth to the field each day & while the mother stoops to hoe or pounds the corn[,] she rocks back & forth on her back.[54]

On her arrival she does not find a beautiful white wardrobe awaiting her. The African mother fears that any preparation may mean the death of her child, so not even a piece of clean cloth is ready[,] but she is wrapped up in any piece of cloth that is handy & usually goes with little aside from a string around the waist or a bead bracelet on the wrist until she is seven or eight years old.[55]

The child may be born in a mud hole as was the case I was called to once. The mother had a son of about seven years of age who was in the house when her pains began and as it is a native woman's custom never to ask her son to leave her presence, she was forced to go outside rather than bear her child in the child's presence. It had rained all day & about the house were the mud holes made by the pigs. She got around the corner of her house when the little one came. It was night & I was called to bring a lantern & to help her. I picked the little one up out of the mud & soon got the mother in the house near the fire. Although the baby was chilled through, he survived and the last I heard was a fine child.

One time I found a mother sitting on the ground with her month[-] old baby on her lap and beside her a pot of corn gruel. This she was stuffing with her finger down the throat of her baby. The little naked body was covered with the gruel & the baby would let out a cry of resistance every opportunity it could get.

Is it any wonder that many of the babies die leaving mothers with broken hearts and no comfort[?]

In times of sickness they turn to witch doctors who often torture them & require the payment of large sums. In death, they hold palavers seeking to find out the guilty party & then extort large fines from them.[56] They believe they are surrounded by evil spirits and that the spirits of the dead return & pursue them with trouble. In order to pacify them [the evil spirits], large offerings are made on the graves of the dead & to evil spirits.

As soon as the baby girls are old enough to walk, they follow their mothers to the fields & later you see them with hoes & their life of labor in the field & of pounding corn meal begins.

At the age of thirteen or fourteen she is bartered by her father to some man who can pay the price. She may be one of several wives.[57] The ceremony consists of feasting & dancing & when this is over she begins her work in the field & soon becomes a mother. One time I visited a woman who was rather young. She had a baby three months old.

She told me that she was the youngest wife of the old man, and that he had only five wives now, that three had left or been driven away.

Sunday, Church, School, with all they mean to us are unknown things to them.

I am now going to give you a few quotations from my journal which will show you the first steps taken by the missionaries in bringing the knowledge of the Christ Child to these women & children.[58]

"At the village I found a funeral. I went into the house and sat down a few minutes to talk with the women gathered there. The mother said she had buried seven children and had none left. I told her how it was possible to go to her children and meet them again. When I said we could not enter Heaven with our sins, that they must be forgiven by Jesus, she said several times, 'I have no sin.' I tried to tell her how we all had sinned & all needed a Saviour. Then I went in the yard and the women & children gathered around for our meeting. We sang 'The Light of the World is Jesus' & 'The Great Physician' and I gave them a little talk on the birth of Jesus."

"Yesterday I went to a group of villages and had three meetings. At the first there were about forty-five, mostly women & children. They have learned quite well, 'The Great Physician' & 'Jesus the Light of the World.' They listened well while I told them about John the Baptist & Jesus['] entrance upon his ministry. Showed the picture roll which they like so much & it gave me an opportunity to go over the lesson again.[59] One woman was all marked with red & white on her face and wore a charm on her neck which shows that she is doctoring with some witch doctor. At the second village there were about sixty[,] including a number of men who listened well. At the third village the meeting was small but there are two old women who appear very much interested."

"Today (Sun.) I asked some of the village women why they had not come to our services for two Sundays and they said two weeks ago they attended a witch doctor[']s ceremony at a distant village and that last week they lost count & did not know which day was Sunday."

"This afternoon went to Soma Kesenje's village. It rained all the way over. About thirty came and listened well. I told the story of the woman at the well & showed the picture.[60] There are several women that show a real interest. I was told today that one woman said she wasn't coming to the meetings any more lest she would come to truly believe."

"When we left the villages last Sat. we told them the next day would be Sunday and invited them to the services at the station. After we left[,] a man passed through their village & told them the next day would not be Sun. So Sunday morning we looked in vain for them, but Tues. morning about twenty appeared having come a distance of two hours['] walk over a high rocky mountain to attend service. So we dropped every thing and had a meeting with them on the front porch. We told them to return home & come again the fifth day which would be Sunday again. It is only as God's Spirit creates a hunger in their hearts for the Words, can we expect to see them. How important it is that we pray much."

LETTER TO ABCFM OFFICIAL
REVEREND JAMES BARTON: #4[61]

Nellie J. Arnott
Campbell, Calif.
Dec. 9—1912
Dr. James L. Barton,
Boston, Mass.

My dear Dr. Barton:

I have been wanting to write to you ever since my arrival home. Miss Wingate prevailed upon me to remain East until after the Evanston Annual Meeting so I spent the intervening time speaking at some meetings and making some visits among relatives and friends.

I reached here Nov. 4th and found my mother quite poorly with inflammatory rheumatism, and she doesn't seem to improve much although following carefully the Doctor's directions.

My father is well and at work every day. I do not find him changed any in his attitude toward missionary work, but says nothing against my return. My return next year seems to be a settled fact with them for which I am thankful. Mother has [been] a very sweet Christian spirit in regard to my work[,] which is a great comfort to me, but my heart often is burdened for my father's conversion and change of attitude.[62]

One of my brothers that I visited I found completely changed during my visit. He stood with my father against my entrance upon missionary work when we went out but during my visit he made a public testimony in the church the evening I spoke and said he had been wrong and hereafter I should have his hearty approval of my work. He has also written to father on the subject. So I see some of my prayers answered, for which I am thankful.

This is a very quiet little town, but convenient to San Jose. In the Campbell church we are fortunate in having Rev. Geo. Atkinson as pastor. His mother was one of our missionaries in India and lives here also. His brother is Dr. Atkinson in Turkey. So this is a real missionary church and we hear some very helpful sermons.

I wonder whether you ever received the minutes of our Annual Meeting. I never have and have wished very often that I might have the reading of them. From letters I have gathered some information. I understand that the Girls' Boarding School site is to be near the Institute, and that they consider that $10,000 is the amount to raise.[63]

The Executive Committee of the W.B.M.I. do not feel that they can take this on their list for 1913.[64] I cannot blame them for they are behind for 1912. They are giving me liberty to write letters and solicit anywhere and everywhere as long as I do not infringe on the treasuries of the Boards. I spoke to them about my desire to have the school called "The Means Memorial" or "The Jennie Means Memorial," but they said as she was not known among them, that it would mean nothing. Now if it is left to me to raise this money the best way I can, is there any objection to my calling our school by her name? Do you suppose there is some one there in the East who could make an effort for us among Mrs. Means' friends?

Yesterday I received a letter from Mrs. Cammack in which she told me the decision regarding their return.[65] I am sorry for I had hoped they would be given another opportunity. The mission must have taken another vote on them at the Annual meeting, for I understood that the vote taken before they left favored their return. I know there was some feeling because they left when the force was so short at Cisamba, but Dr. Hollenbeck told me that Mrs. Cammack's physical condition made it best for them to get home & from reports of her doctors it seems as though it is well they got here as soon as they did. Of course, I know there are many things against them[,] but they were certainly in a hard place and I did feel that perhaps another term would bring about better results.

Having been with Mrs. Cammack over two months in 1911[,] they know me pretty well & she has in this letter opened her heart to me. She seems to feel it keenly. I feel the need of wisdom in knowing how to reply to her in a way that will be best for all concerned and helpful to her.

I forgot to mention the other member of our present family, a sister, who is pursuing her studies in music. She is an earnest Christian and a great comfort to us all. I am keeping very well[; I] only wish we had it a little colder here. We have had frost & cold nights, but have had no rain yet.

With best wishes always,
Most sincerely,
Nellie J. Arnott

Circular Letter #10[66]

To the Friends of Mrs. Jane C. Means:

You all know that it was Dr. Means who made the investigation necessary and gave himself most assiduously to the work of carefully studying missionary work in Africa in preparation for the selection of the proper locality of our West Central Africa Mission which was opened in 1880.[67]

His wife shared with him the same loving interest and has[,] until God called her Home June 12, 1912, given to our Mission and each of its members her love and devotion and every month we have been cheered and encouraged by her loving letters.[68]

She was especially interested in a Girls' Boarding School and[,] knowing this, one of her dear friends sent, instead of flowers for Mrs. Means' casket[,] a gift towards starting a school as a memorial to her. I have written to the Mission and many have responded that they would love to have it called the Means Memorial, the name that has meant so much to us.[69]

Thus far the method of work among the girls has been to gather them into compounds, largely in order to provide a protected place from temptation for them to sleep. They have learned to read and write in the day schools. They have been taught some sewing. A few have been used as teachers in station schools. They are more cleanly in their person and dress better than the village girls. Many of those who have married from these compounds keep better homes than they would otherwise. But on the whole the filthy ways of living on the part of women is not much changed.

It has been the custom among the Ovimbundu for the women to do all the cultivating; therefore it cannot be expected that those girls, who must work in the fields a large part of the day, then pound corn [into meal] and prepare their food, have much alertness left for school in the late afternoon. As most of the girls live, aside from sleeping, in their own homes, they cultivate, prepare and cook their food as their mothers have done for years.[70]

The custom of the women, only doing the field work, has been hard to overcome, but now the Mission considers the time ripe to begin a Central Girls Boarding School, that will draw its pupils from all the stations. It is the purpose of this school to provide accommodations for about a hundred girls, and under the directions of missionary teachers, teach them better methods of cultivation, the preparation of these food stuffs in a cleanly way and the proper cooking of them, the care of baskets, pots and dishes and the keeping of a kitchen clean and in order. Teaching all to make the clay pots and baskets that now only a few of the women can make, and improve upon these arts.[71] Instructing them to make their own clothes, to care for and wash and iron them. Also teaching them the proper feeding, care and training of babies and children. And in addition to the manual labor and arts, give them such class-room and Bible instructions as will better fit them to be helpmates to their future husbands in their village and outstation work.[72]

The Woman's Board of the Interior has given me the liberty to present this need to the friends of our work. No church or individual should take away from their regular offering to the treasuries of our Boards in order to make an offering for this purpose, but let all who receive this statement of our need first of all pray that those who can may be led to offer an extra gift for this school, and let us all ask ourselves whether we cannot by a little self-sacrificing have a share in this blessed work.[73] Those wishing to make such an offering will please send it to, Mr. Frank Wiggin, 14 Beacon St., Boston, Mass. or Mrs. Mary C. Stevens, Secretary, Waynesboro, Va.

Our eyes are unto the Lord, above all let us pray for our African girls and that this effort to establish a school for them may be effectual and bring honor and glory to His name.

Most sincerely yours in our Master's work.

Nellie J. Arnott

Letter to ABCFM Official Enoch Bell: #1 [74]

Campbell, Calif.
Dec. 28- 1912
Mr. Enoch F. Bell,
Boston, Mass.

My dear Mr. Bell:

Your letter of the 16th was received a few days ago and the one of the 19th yesterday. I thank you for the copy of the minutes of our Annual Meeting. They will be useful for reference.

I am very glad that the Cammack case is to be reopened and I earnestly pray that God's will regarding them may be made very clear.

I doubt very much, from all I can gather from letters, that there was a vote taken again at Ndondi.[75] If there was one taken, why was it not recorded in the minutes?[76] I think Dr. Woodside's letter was the result of his impressions while at Ndondi.

Yes, I know there is some just criticism, but during my stay with them July 6th to Sept. 13th, 1911, I was constantly brought to believe that much of it would be removed did he use more freely the language. Will he return with a set purpose to make good in the language, he will be able to overcome much criticism along other lines.

As to doing more for the general work of the station, it must be remembered that he was handicapped in many lines. He has done much in improving the health conditions at Cisamba and would they carry out his suggestions in some of the other stations it would be well. I heard the Cisamba elders give their praise for the ways in which he had helped them in agricultural lines.

Dr. Cammack is progressive along many lines and has some very good ideas that will be advantageous to our work when the Mission [moves to] carry them out.

His attitude toward the natives, much of it is because he has been unable to speak & understand in the language as he should, and then again—there are difficulties at Cisamba with the natives. Several recent letters show difficulties there in discipline as serious as when Dr. Cammack was there. There has been so much of disunion there that one cannot wonder at this condition. Dr. Cammack is ready to follow the decision of the majority in all station matters and in dealing with the natives but we all know that station meetings are unknown at Cisamba.[77]

I believe that this doubtful position regarding their return will result in a real spiritual blessing to them. While with them I often felt that they showed a far greater readiness to forgive and overlook wrong than I could have done in their circumstances. I had some very profitable talks with Mrs. Cammack along spiritual lines, both about the work & personal. She craved Christian fellowship that was greatly lacking at that station.

The Mission as a whole may be sorry to have them returned, I do not know, but I for one consider that there are many admirable things in them both and should be sorry to have them dropped.

I did not for one moment think or expect that in giving the name "Means" to our Boarding School that it would call for any fund from their family.[78] It was not in the light of financial advantage that the name is suggested, but just because of all Dr. and Mrs. Means have been to our Mission. I am sure there are others who want to share with me the feeling that every effort made in the establishment of that school, is to perpetuate the memory of our beloved friends.

I just thought that if this was made known among their friends that there might be those who would like to make offerings, but I realize that the large gifts must be found elsewhere.

We are having a very cold winter in this part of Calif. Many complain but I would welcome snow.

Father and Mother reached their fortieth anniversary the 26th.

Sincerely yours,

Nellie J. Arnott

Letter to ABCFM Official Enoch Bell: #2[79]

Campbell, Calif.
Feb. 13—1913
Rev. Enoch F. Bell,
Boston,
Mass.

My dear Mr. Bell:

I have just been away for over a week helping out in some meetings. Attended the Northern Branch meeting at Alameda, the Mt. Hebron mid winter meeting in San Francisco & yesterday spent the day at Santa Cruz with Dr. Tenney & Dr. Chambers.[80] Splendid reports come from the Institute meetings they have had up the coast. Mrs. Cowles is just fine.

I am grateful for your letter of the 3rd of Jan. I didn't realize I had been so slow in replying. I appreciate having a copy of the letter addressed to the Mission regarding the future of Kamundongo. I do think the only place for the press is at the Institute site & for the present Mrs. Sanders is the best one on the field to take charge of it. Dr. Sanders ought to press forward the translation of the Old Test[ament] as the Mission has asked him to do. We ought to have his good Umbundu, in as much work of this kind as possible. But it seems to me the Institute should look for a <u>man</u> trained & fitted to take charge of the Press including book binding & ability to train the natives in this work. This is too much work to ask of Mrs. Sanders.[81]

I hate to see Kamundongo given up. Seems to me the property is too valuable with all those fruit trees & the R.R. drawing nearer. I still feel that there are possibilities there if the right man was at liberty to carry them out.[82] Dr. Hollenbeck writes that he is tired of holding on & of this indecision. He wants it <u>settled</u> one way or the other.

Dr. Sanders['] last letter is most encouraging. He had been at Gamba & received thirty-two into the church[,] one of the number being old Chief Kapitango.[83] Surely great praise is due Dr. Sanders in the way those Kamundongo men carry out that Gamba work. Being with him from the time they were young lads they have imbibed his spirit & are carrying out that work with great credit. It ought to bring him much joy.

I have not yet heard of the result of the meeting in the Cammack case.

Have been looking daily for news of the arrival of Mr. & Mrs. Ennis. Seems to me that book of A. G. Hogg[,] "Christ's Message of the Kingdom[,]" would be a fine one to put in their hands.

Very cordially yours,
Nellie J. Arnott

Letter to ABCFM Official
Reverend James Barton: #5[84]

Campbell, Cal.
Mar. 7- 1913
Rev. James L. Barton, D.D.
Boston, Mass.

Dear Dr. Barton:

A letter from Mr. Bell reached me a couple of days ago. I am very glad to know that Dr. and Mrs. Cammack are likely to be returned. I feel sure they will prove to be such workers as Africa needs. I have several letters from Africa received today. They show that there is growth in outstations but some instances of sin among some church members in three of the Stations. I am so sorry. It makes me feel more strongly than ever how much those native Christians need to be upheld by the prayers of the Church at home.[85]

I have just returned from Los Angeles. I went down with Dr. Tenney for the Santa Barbara Institute meeting and while in Los Angeles spoke in a couple of the churches and at one of the Ladies Missionary Societies.

While there I met a Miss Nellie Tracy, who is at present Educational Secretary in the Y.W.C.A. She tells me her application is in, but she is engaged to a young man who is a Presbyterian and his application is in their Board. They first applied, I believe through the Student Volunteer. He does not graduate for a year yet. [He] is taking a course in some line of Manual Arts. But she is ready to go out now and would like to be studying the language. They are quite ready to go to Africa or anywhere they are most needed and under either Board.[86] I liked her very much and thought of the need of such workers in our new Institute.

And now you will be surprised to know that I have become engaged to a Mr. Paul L. Darling and will find it necessary to withdraw from active service in Africa. Mr. Darling and his people are friends since girl-hood days. He has at different times desired to marry me, but until the present I have never felt I really wanted to do so.

We regret very much the situation in which this places the Mission. In view of the present effort to open a girls' boarding school, the great need of missionaries, my own knowledge of the language, and keen desire to see the girls' school established, it has been very difficult for us to come to this decision.[87] But it has been very carefully and prayerfully considered from all sides by both of us and we believe we are acting according to God's best will for our lives.

Mr. Darling is a Christian business man and in sympathy with all lines of missionary and church work and will be one with me in every effort to do all we can for Africa. He has wished for some years that he was fitted for such work, so as to devote his life to Africa with me. But his training has been only in business lines, aside from taking a few terms of work in the Chicago Bible Institute for the purpose of better fitting himself for Sunday School and church work.[88]

I do not wish you to think for one moment that I had any intention of reaching this decision this year, for I did not[;] I fully intended to return and give my life to Africa. I want to keep informed of every part of the work and prove to be a blessing to them although I am in the home land.[89] I want the Board and Mission to inform me of all their needs for they will ever find us ready to do all in our power.

Most sincerely yours,
Nellie J. Arnott

Letter to ABCFM Official Enoch Bell: #3[90]

Campbell, Cal.
Apr. 5—1913

Rev. Enoch F. Bell,
Boston, Mass.

My dear Mr. Bell:—

Your letters of March 17th & 26th are at hand. For these and your hearty congratulations, I thank you.[91]

I am indeed glad that the Prudential Committee has authorized the return of Dr. & Mrs. Cammack to the field. I am sure they will prove to be good workers and I hope the Mission will receive them kindly and give them a place. They are certainly needed with the small force of workers that are on the field.

I am sorry Miss Stover has had to leave a year earlier than she expected & that Mrs. Webster had to leave earlier in order to travel with her. I trust Miss Stover will find that her furlough will bring back to her good health so that she can return to Africa after her furlough. With Mr. & Mrs. Bell's leaving this year[,] it leaves Bailundu in great need. I hope Dr. [Fred] Stokey will soon be there to help them out.

In my last letter I referred to Miss Helen [Nellie] Tracy of Los Angeles who is looking forward to entering foreign work. The young man to whom she is engaged is Mr. Hoist and he is preparing to teach manual training. He still has one more year. Her application is in the American Board but his in the Presbyterian Board as he applied through the Student Volunteer. If he is as fine a man as she is a woman I feel sure they would make splendid workers for our Institute.

Letters in from the Mission bring good news on the whole. Miss [Mabel] Woodside seems to be improving in health.

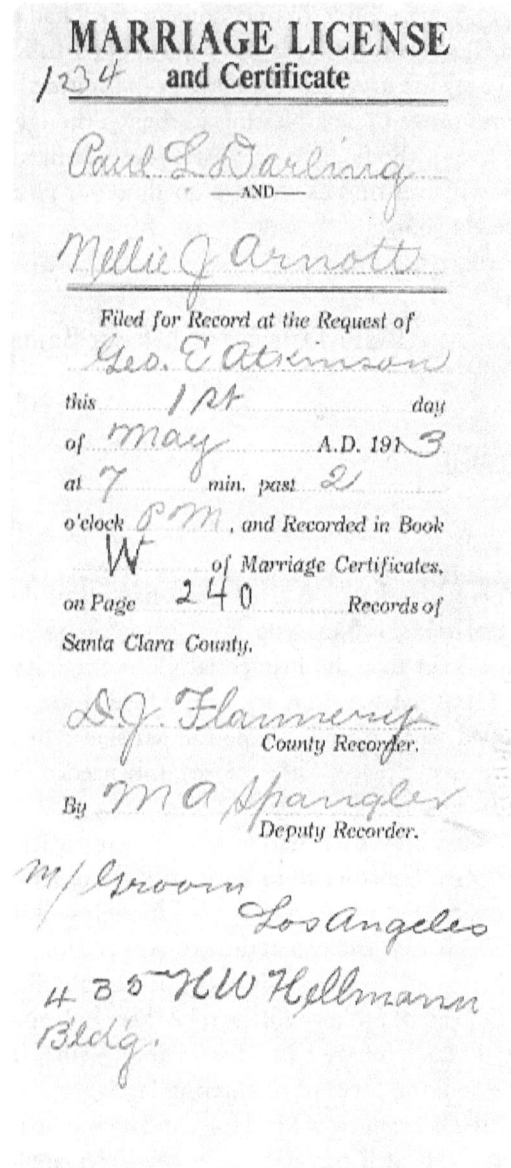

Figure 13: Marriage license of Nellie Arnott and Paul Darling. Courtesy of Mary Darling Caris, San Francisco, CA.

I understand that the Canadian Society stood ready to back up the Institute financially, but Dr. Sanders writes that they are not to take any further steps at Dondi until the money was in hand.[92] I thought there was some $10,000 ready to be used at Dondi. Will you please inform me as I wish to be able to present the situation correctly as I have opportunity[?] Again they decided to carry the new press to Kamundongo, so that looks as though Kamundongo is not to be given up. They say last year[']s report showed too good a work to be closed. I suppose you have had the reading of it. I do think it a good report. Am glad Dr. Hollenbeck is making an effort with the boys in Boarding School lines.

I smile at a statement in Dr. Sanders['] letter regarding the Girls' Boarding School. "If they were not so set against having it here, it would have a fairer chance of beginning soon." He has always been so against Kamundongo as the site for any school but I guess Dr. Hollenbeck's improvements in agricultural lines changes the food situation there.[93] I do believe a mistake will be made if Kamundongo is not selected for a Boarding School site for either boys or girls.

Until some $5,000 is in view[,] not much head way can be made in the Girls' Boarding school and I hope by then some one will be in view to take my place. Seems to me an experienced woman is needed or the appointment of one of the lady missionaries on the field, letting a younger & new missionary step into the place made vacant in the Station. I wish it were possible to secure Mrs. Read or Mrs. Wellman for that place.[94]

It has been suggested by some in the mission that I remain in [the] U.S. longer than I planned in order to raise the money, so it looks as though they considered the money more important than my presence on the field. If this money can be raised, & I mean to put forth every effort possible, & if one or two missionaries can be found to return with Mrs. Webster, then I believe the Girls' Boarding School can move forward.[95]

There is very little interest in our African work here on the coast, but I hope as my home is to be at Los Angeles, that I shall be able to make friends for Africa and the Board.

Very sincerely,
Nellie J. Arnott[96]

A Visit to an African Village

From *Mission Studies*, Children's Work Section, May 1913[97]

Let us visit an African village only a half-hour's walk from one of our mission stations. After a short walk through some brush[,] we must cross a small stream on a couple of wabbly sticks (be careful you do not get your feet wet), then climb a low hill, walk through the woods, over another stream, up another hill, and we are at the village. It is enclosed with a stick fence, and each household has its yard and little garden enclosed with stick fences, so that as we enter the village we follow a zigzag path between the stick fences. Gates open from these paths into the yards.

Finally we come out into an open space and here on patches of green grass we find little children unclothed, or partly clothed, playing. Some men are sitting by whittling out hoe handles or big mush spoons. Others are sewing[;] a couple more are making a sleeping mat out of some coarse grass, some are smoking and talking and one man is having his hair cut with a knife very much like our paring knives.

Nearby is a building made of sun-dried brick with half windows and a door. This is the school house, for at this village they have a school, although it has had little influence on the fathers and mothers.[98] As we draw near, the children will run and bring us low stools, and when we are seated each person will come in front of us and say "Kalunga, kalunga," and we must reply with the same words. So if fifty people speak to us, how many times will we say that word? That is the way they greet us.

Very soon an old blind man will greet us and then he will say, "Shall I sound the drum and call the people to school?" We will say "Yes," and then a boy will bring to him a drum which he will hold between his knees[,] and looking upward into the blaze of the sun he will pound the drum with the palm of his hands and fingers and really make music, for he can play it better than one will often hear.

This drum is made from a log about three or four feet long that has been hollowed out and over one end stretched a piece of hide on which is smeared wax. If the drum does not speak well[,] he will warm this end over the fire.

This drum can be heard long distances, so very soon we will see the women and girls coming in from their fields bringing on their heads baskets filled with foodstuffs and on top of this large bundles of firewood. They carry their baskets to their houses and then very soon all gather in the school house. The older ones will bring their stools to sit on[;] the other children will sit on the dirt floor. They will not have their regular school today, as the Ondona (white lady) has not been to see them for a long time, so she will read and talk with them. They will sing several songs that you know, only you will not understand the words.

Their language is very different from ours and if you wish to speak to them[,] you must study several months and learn to speak to them in their own language. Before the missionaries went to their country[,] they did not have a written language or any books. How would it seem never to have a story book[?] Or a Sunday school, paper, or a Bible? Would you like to live where there were no books?

The pioneer missionary, Dr. Sanders, had to learn from their language as best he could and then write down every word he heard, until he and other missionaries who followed him have translated into their language parts of the Bible, a hymn book, the "Pilgrim's Progress" and other books.[99] Do you wonder at these boys and girls being thankful that missionaries came to them and that now many of them can read the stories of Jesus?

But as to our visit. After our songs and reading and talk and prayer we will close the meeting. If we have some of the Sunday school picture cards to give the children[,] they will be glad. They like those with the pictures of Jesus best of all. The women will hurry to their kitchens to get ready the evening meal of mush and beans[,] and we will stroll around and visit in the yards.

{Continued}

A Visit to an African Village (Continued)

From *Mission Studies*, Children's Work Section, June, 1913

Here is a woman who sometimes comes to church. She has a daughter about twelve years old and she has engaged her to be married to a young man in the village. We have heard that the girl is subject to temptations, so suggest to the mother that she allow her to come and sleep in our girl's compound on our mission station. After much persuasion[,] she consents, and for a few months the girl is happy at being with the missionaries. Then the mother, fearful lest her daughter is getting too old, takes her back, and in a short time has her married and she goes to live with her mother-in-law. Although she is small and young, she must now work a large field, pound corn into meal, cook and raise a family.

In the next yard we enter we find another mother who has a young daughter. She has been given to a Portuguese trader, who saw her and

AFRICAN GIRLS POUNDING MEAL.

Figure 14: Cipuku and Nakalu, with Arnott's notation: "My Girls, 1905–1912." Courtesy of The Bancroft Library, University of California, Berkeley.

wanted her as his wife. Of course, the man paid a lot of cloth and rum for the girl as a dowry.[100]

In the next yard is a man who attends school and church. He has two wives who are often quarreling and making trouble. He would like to be a Christian, but he likes his beer too well and does not want to give up the extra wife.

Here is a woman we know very well. She was one of the wives of the old chief who ruled this village so many years, but died a few years ago. She has a son and four daughters. The eldest is Cipuku, and as we walk home I will tell her history.[101]

Before her father died and when Cipuku was about thirteen[,] she began attending the station school and sleeping in the girl's compound so as to be away from the evil influences of the village. Her father did not like this, so [he] engaged her to a village man of very bad habits, but, as the young man kept the old chief supplied with rum, he liked him.[102] One day Cipuku came to the teachers in tears and asked them to deliver her from being married to this man. They told her they would do all they could for her, and finally that engagement was broken.

A Christian young man wanted to marry Cipuku, so he paid the village man the amount of dowry he had paid out and the engagement was settled. After this Cipuku came and lived in the girls' compound all the time. She was an earnest girl and often went with one of the teachers to help in conducting women's and children's meetings in the villages. After a couple of years she was married to the Christian young man, who had become a teacher in the station school. He was such a good teacher that a year later, when one of the outstation teachers died, he was sent to take his place.[103] Now they live at this outstation and Cipuku helps her husband in the school. They have a little son, and are loved and respected by the people.[104]

After Cipuku was married, the heathen mother said she was going to keep her other three daughters with her and not let them go to the station, as the teachers would not let them marry until they were old women! The African women want their daughters to marry when they are young girls. How would you like to cultivate a field of corn and beans, pound corn into meal, get wood and water and cook for a man while you were still a young girl, say only fourteen years old? That is what many young African girls have to do.

Very soon Kanjala, Cipuku's youngest sister, began staying with her and attending the station school. Then we heard that Kayovo, the next girl younger than Cipuku, was being led into evil ways at the village, so the teachers talked with her and she, too, decided to come and stay in the girls' compound. But the mother was troubled, and so, against her daughter's wish, engaged her to a man at the village. He drank and had bad habits, but nevertheless the mother was anxious to have Kayovo married. The man built a small house of sticks and mud, and one time when he was away as a carrier he sent word that on his return he would be married and that the mother was to get Kayovo home and have her ready.

Unknown to the teachers, one day the mother succeeded with threatening words to get Kayovo back to the village. But a few days later, when the young man returned, Kayovo came to the teachers and told them all and asked that they save her from the marriage. They promised to do all they could if she would stay in the compound.

Then the brother came and by main force took her part way back to the village, but Kayovo got away and returned. He was very angry and talked shamefully to the teachers. The next morning the old mother came and, standing at the gate, talked with abusive words to the teacher and to her daughter, who was pounding corn in the yard. The next week on the day her brother was married, and which was to be the day of Kayovo's marriage, she thanked the teachers for their protection. The teachers paid back the amount of dowry the young man had paid, so now the mother is unable to engage her again.

Nalungu, the only one remaining, had also been engaged by her mother, and when she saw that Kayovo was free[,] she also came and asked to stay on the station.

What we needed was a girls' boarding school into which we could put these sisters and some other young girls who needed to be provided with a home, but do you know there is not a girls' boarding school in the whole mission?

But now, just as soon as enough money can be raised, we hope to put up some buildings that will accommodate about 100 girls and have a girls' boarding school to which each station can send girls for teaching and training. Would you not like to have a part in this work?[105]

The Need of a Girls' Boarding School in West Central Africa

From *Mission Studies*, April 1914

Mission Studies editor's note: Mrs. Darling spent seven years in the West Central African Mission as a missionary of the WB.M.I. She is now living in California.

As we Young People are supporting two of our missionaries in West Central Africa, we are acquainted more or less with the work that is being done among the girls.[106]

In each of the five stations the missionary teachers have girls' compounds where girls live and attend the station day schools. Some of the girls come from distant heathen villages, others from outstation schools, and some are the daughters of native Christians, who want them to receive the best training there is to be had.

Having the girls together in these compounds gives the missionary opportunity to direct them in their fields and gardens, the preparation and cooking of food, the care of their bodies and clothing, and enables her to teach them many things that cannot be touched upon in the day schools.

The girls are very happy and grateful for the opportunities offered them. Great improvement is manifest in the homes of the women who once lived in these compounds and are now married.

Those of you who were interested in the Kamundongo girls under Miss Arnott's care will be glad of a bit of news from them received in recent letters from Miss Stimpson, who now has these girls in charge.

The older girl, Kayovo, has married one of the station boys and they have charge of an outstation school. She is helping her husband in every way possible, teaching others to read, although she is not a very good reader herself. Pray for these young people, who are working alone and surrounded by every heathen influence.

Another one of the girls, Margareta, died during the summer. She was a good Christian and loved by all.

Other girls have been received into the compound, so that now Miss Stimpson has twenty-four girls under her care. As a number of these girls are very young, they are unable to do very much to support themselves, so must be supported from gifts received from friends in this country. Here are a few sentences from Miss Stimpson's last letter which will show you the burden she is carrying and how much money and prayer is needed for this work. She writes: "I do wish some one would send more money for the girls' account, for they have a debt and I do not see how I can carry the expense of them myself. I do not like the thought of sending them home again, but it will have to be done unless help comes from somewhere. I cannot stand having a debt on hand. Do you not know of some ladies who could take the support of some girls? I am sure there are some who are able to give ten dollars a year. I don't think ten dollars a year is too much for a girl."[107]

This station work for the girls is very necessary and should have our support in every way, but at the same time we must remember that the money sent for it is an "extra" and will not help on the regular Board work.

But all the missionaries realize that these station compounds are not giving the girls sufficient training, so an effort is being made to establish a Central Girls' Boarding School. In this will be received girls from the different stations' compounds and they will be given an all round training which will fit them to be such wives and mothers as the Ovimbundu people so much need.

So let us do all we can for these girls. Both phases of the work need our immediate help. Are there not some of us who can adopt one of these girls and so enable her to be kept in the compound, costing us only ten dollars a year? And perhaps others of us can help in raising money for the buildings for the Central Girls' Boarding School? We can *all* pray for this work, our missionaries and our black sisters across the ocean.

Chief Kanjundu's Death

From *Mission Studies*, April 1914

Those of us who are interested in the West African Mission are familiar with the name Soma Kanjundu.[108] For years he has been the chief of the Ciyuka district, near the Chisamba Mission Station.

Some years ago he brought his fetishes to be burned, put away all of his wives but one, and became a Christian. He built a church and school house in his village, and there the men, women and children gathered daily in their respective sessions and learned to read. The chief himself became a pupil and, although quite old, learned to read the Bible for himself.

Every morning and evening the whole village gathered in the church for family prayers. Sundays the regular services of morning worship, Sunday school, women's prayer meeting and children's meeting, were conducted. The attendance at Sunday morning service would be from five to eight hundred.

Then one day the chief was arrested under false charges and for two years he was in prison. He bore all his persecution and imprisonment with true Christian courage, ever bearing witness to all about him of Christ, and like Daniel, he prayed to his God and read the Word. Finally he was acquitted and returned to his village, with the testimony that God had answered prayer and brought about his liberty.

On his return from his imprisonment he gave all his slaves their liberty, although since being a Christian he had treated them as children rather than slaves. And now our last African letters bring us news of his death.

Miss Bell of Chisamba writes thus:[109] "You will be sorry to know that Chief Kanjundu is dead. When he left Ciyuka on the 10th of October, he was poorly. Miss Melville thought it was pneumonia, and after a week had passed, urged him to go to Dr. Hollenbeck at Kamundongo. He went, and his lung cleared nicely, but his strength was not equal to the strain, and on Saturday, at eleven in the evening, he died. His carriers and friends started at once for Ciyuka. Nearing there at time of service, they sent messengers to the elders *only*, and no one knew until service was over that he was dead."

"When the messenger arrived here, we sent for Lumbo, and he sat a while, just dumb, and then we had prayer.[110] I led in the Umbundu and Mr. Tucker in English. Then Lumbo went and told the people of the station."

"Mr. [L. Gordon] Cattell made a box, or coffin, Monday morning, and the chief's people covered it with black cloth."

"Mr. Sanders arrived from Kamundongo Monday, and the funeral was Tuesday, Mr. Sanders conducting the service, as Mr. Tucker cannot yet undertake more than simple reading."

"It is a hard blow to Ciyuka district, for he was a much esteemed ruler by all. It will bring out the best in the Christians, we hope. Poor people, they are sorely stricken."

His Christian influence was felt throughout the whole mission, and he was loved by all. Let us pray that the Spirit may fill the one who shall be appointed to take his place as it did Chief Kanjundu.

Foreign Mission Work from a California Home

Published well after her marriage, Arnott's narrative on "Chief Kanjundu's Death" signals the shift in her role in the mission movement from teacher overseas to supporter at home. Alluding to Miss Bell's letter, Arnott (now Mrs. Paul Darling) positions herself in much of this piece as a reporter providing information secondhand rather than writing based on personal experience. Yet, in other parts of the story, Arnott maintains her familiar stance as an informant with insider expertise, for she recounts a backstory about Kanjundu's conversion, his influence on others, and the testing of his commitment through persecution borne "with true Christian courage." Thus, the idealized Christian death of Kanjundu marks both change and continuity for his village far away in Angola and also for Arnott herself. Closing the text with her own commentary after quoting from Miss Bell's correspondence, Arnott salutes Kanjundu as a role model and expresses hope that "the Spirit may fill the one who shall be appointed to take his place." Associating herself implicitly with Kanjundu and his leadership, she envisions the ongoing progress of mission service—as both the converted African chief and the dedicated missionary teacher enter new realms of Christian identity while others prepare to carry on the movement's agenda.

Nellie Arnott could see a fruition of her own personal work abroad with the opening of the Means School for girls located in Dondi just across the Kutatu River from the Currie Institute for boys. Construction of the first buildings, the girls' dormitories, took place during 1916–1917 under the direction of Arnott's friend Dr. William Cammack; the first dean was missionary Marion M. Webster, with initial teaching staff (including Sarah Stimpson) drawn from the mission stations.[111] Echoing the goals that Arnott described in her fund-raising letters (as well as attitudes of that day regarding appropriate women's roles), Means School would, according to missionary John Tucker, "fit its girls to be real forces for good in the villages to which they will go, to be worthy companions for their husbands, to care properly for their children." Twenty-five years after Arnott left Angola, the school boasted some 300 students who followed a four-year course, including domestic science, teaching, and evangelism.[112]

Long after her marriage, Arnott continued to take a keen interest in Means School, pasting postcards, missionary writing, and photographs about it in her scrapbooks. One such memento was a Christmas card she received in 1937 with a photo of Means students neatly lined up in their Westernized school uniforms and with the caption "Happy Girlhood."

As noted in an earlier discussion of this text in Chapter 3, such artifacts are highly complex records whose representations of Umbundu people and their experiences certainly cannot give us a clear sense of how the "objects" of the mission enterprise—in this case, the school's students—would have felt about its curriculum and its larger goals. Would they have affirmed the card's message? In a larger sense, how would they have characterized the work Nellie Arnott did in their homeland or the longer-term effects of her missionary group's interventions in their local culture?

The very limited inferences we can draw today around such questions must acknowledge multiple strands of interpretation outlined by Jeffrey Cox in a discussion of competing explanatory narratives linked to the mission movement. On the one hand, Cox observes, numerous interpretations of missionaries situated in colonized settings depict them negatively—as either bumbling figures whose humanitarian aims are guided by limited understanding of cultural difference and imperial power or as complicit agents whose role in the oppression of colonized peoples must be unmasked. On the other hand, however, Cox argues that increased attention should be paid to the work of pre-

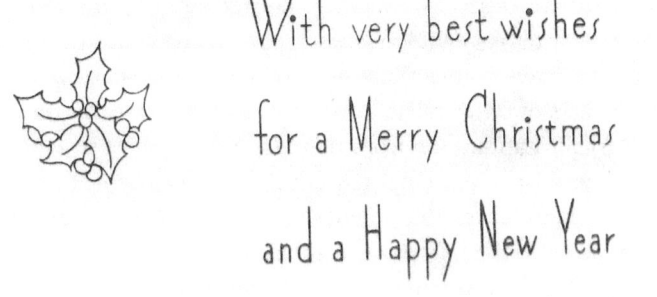

Figure 15. 1937 Christmas card from Means School. Courtesy of The Bancroft Library, University of California, Berkeley.

vious eras' missionaries at the interpersonal level, where relationships, over time, could become less one-sided and more mutually affirming. In particular, he proposes, the views of "non-Western Christians" who chose to seek "'sympathy and congruence'" with missionaries should be taken into account.[113]

Signs that some of Arnott's former students would have viewed their sustained contact with her along those lines recur throughout her personal records. In scrapbook articles depicting Umbundu teachers she had trained, in photographs of former mission student Jonas Soma's progress through Tuskegee Institute, and in letters from young people still studying in Angolan schoolrooms where she had taught, we can see her influence. As late as 1935, in fact, Arnott received a letter sent to "Dona Nele," signed "Yoano," and composed entirely in Umbundu—moves reflecting confidence that Arnott had remained committed to those she had known at her station and would still be able to draw upon the language she had struggled so hard to learn.[114]

As we begin positioning her public writing in relation to her personal archive, we must continue to explore the connections between the published materials she produced originally for a U.S.-based audience of mission movement supporters and the texts she composed later, over time, primarily for her own use and memory. Ultimately, we can see, the hallmark of all her compositions and the strongest affiliation she has is with her colleagues in the mission movement. It is for them that she originally wrote and through them that she maintained her self-positioning as an active agent in a worldwide endeavor, a role she had claimed via her service overseas and her publications about that work. In page after page of Arnott's scrapbooks, we see evidence of her efforts to maintain connections with that far-flung network of colleagues. Images of other missionaries are drawn both from their time at West African stations and from their activities in later years, including retirements and occasional reunions. Similarly, while some items of their correspondence offer updates on events in Angola, others, like a postcard sent from Elizabeth Campbell in 1937, focus more on the friendships still being maintained years after shared service overseas. (See figure 5 in Chapter 2.)

In that context, even as we recognize the contradictions and troubling issues embedded in a document like the Means School Christmas card, we can safely speculate that Mrs. Paul Darling likely viewed its "Happy" characterization as applying, most of all, to her own past sojourn in Africa. After all, through the social communities that experience had provided for her, with both Umbundu people and missionaries, her time in Africa was central to her self-definition. The multilayered texts she composed within her scrapbooks and the care with which she maintained her personal records of service in Angola clearly demonstrate that the mission endeavor remained a touchstone in her life.

Notes

1. This letter is in the C.N. Pond Papers, Oberlin College Archives. A cover letter dated April 3 to Mrs. [Harriet Perkins] Pond indicates that Arnott was extremely busy, but very happy in her work as she prepared for Rev. and Mrs. Sanders to leave on furlough: "Day after tomorrow I go to Olutu for a three weeks stay. The schools have needed to be visited for a long time and this is the first opportunity. So you can guess I'm busy. Tomorrow must pack up bed, box up clothing books etc., food box for three weeks, besides get some letters ready for the mail which comes in a few days. But I love it all. We shall miss the Sanders and it makes me want to go too, but it seems best I wait another year." The opening line of this text uses the term "general letter," a phrase Arnott sometimes employed to designate a circular letter being sent to a large audience.

2. Only part of the letter was published in *Mission Studies* with the title listed here: "The Beginning of a Boarding School in West Central Africa." The article was evidently reprinted, as missionary John T. Tucker quotes information from it in his *Drums in the Darkness*, 143, citing as his source an Arnott publication in the issue of *Canadian Congregationalist* dated November 23, 1911. We include the full text of the general letter.

3. The printing of translations and educational materials in Umbundu had become a major enterprise at Kamundongo, as noted in Chapter 2. According to an article in *Missionary Herald*, the new vocabulary contained "648 pages, 400 of them giving Umbundu-English and 248 English-Umbundu words," considerably expanding an earlier volume compiled by William E. Fay ("An Umbundu Vocabulary," September 1911, 383). For the new volume, as Arnott reports, Rev. and Mrs. Sanders spent much time not only in collecting new words, but also in "proving" them—that is, establishing accurate English equivalents. Books printed at the Sarah H. Bates Memorial Press at the station were used by Plymouth Brethren missions as well as by the ABCFM. Sarah Sanders, who operated the mission press, trained Umbundu men as printers (Tucker, *Drums in the Darkness*, 92). Norman Etherington discusses the crucial role that preparing and printing materials in local languages played in the instruction (and acculturation) of local people in Kwazulu-Natal, beginning as early as the 1830s. Etherington argues that we should recognize not only the importance of language and writing in this effort but also "the material paraphernalia that marked the evangelical enterprise as distinctively as the colonial state was marked by the pass, the police register, and the tax collector's receipt book" (37). "The Missionary Writing Machine in Nineteenth-Century Kwazulu-Natal," in *Mixed Messages: Materiality, Textuality, Missions*, ed. Jamie S. Scott and Gareth Griffiths, 37-50 (New York: Palgrave, 2005).

4. This sentence begins the portion of the text published in *Mission Studies*.

5. "Cleanly" is a highly coded word in this context of Christian missionary work. As in benevolent outreach and Christian missions within the U.S., cleanliness here connotes both physical hygiene and social traits that were thought to promote enhanced morality through the conversion process. Women missionaries of Arnott's generation often came to focus more on social service issues such as healthy management of food, maintenance of clean water, and medical techniques than on spiritual training. However, they also associated the development of "clean" social practices with the acquisition of Christian beliefs and virtues. The plethora of "before" and "after" photographs of "heathen" and "Christian" women in missionary publications illustrates this ideology. See Dana L. Robert's discussion of the "Christian home" as a model for African women. "The 'Christian Home' as a Cornerstone of Anglo-American Missionary Thought and Practice," in Robert, *Converting Colonialism*, 134–36, 141–42.

6. Missionary John Tucker, who arrived in Angola in 1913, credits Arnott with creating the first "hostel for girls" in Angola at Kamundongo. This was the nucleus of the Girls' Boarding School. Helen Melville later began a similar facility at the Cisamba station (*A Tucker Treasury*, 114, 199).

7. Arnott's detailing the girls' efforts to regularly wash their "sleeping cloths" and dresses picks up on the code of cleanliness, thereby signaling to her white middle-class readers that these young women are worthy of support.

8. Sitting at a table to eat and using western utensils provide additional evidence of the "civilization" process.

9. The "onjango" was the Umbundu men's meeting house. (See Chapter 2.) By this time, Arnott was slipping individual Umbundu words into her accounts, especially when there was not an English synonym.

10. Both men and women traditionally smoked tobacco and used snuff, but in the Christian villages, tobacco and alcohol were prohibited (Cushman, *Missionary Doctor*, 109). Hambly provides information on methods of preparing snuff and on varieties of pipes for smoking (*Ovimbundu of Angola*, 151–52).

11. Phrases like "raw native women" may be attributable in part to Arnott's understanding the expectations of her reading audience, but they also demonstrate that her sense of cultural hierarchy persisted well beyond the period in her posting to Africa when she had developed some appreciation for local customs. In this case, one reason behind the use of this phrase would be to distance the girls Arnott is teaching from what they would otherwise become.

12. Arnott has structured her account to include a vision of the boarding school—with its American middle-class domestic ideology—being "built" at the end of the article. Given her arguments to show the need for the school, she could hope that readers would support the ambitious number of "fifty or sixty" students for enrollment. The *Mission Studies* article ends with this sen-

tence. The editors' choice (or Arnott's decision?) to cut the piece at this point is somewhat surprising. However, mission magazine stories generally avoided making requests for a particular amount of funds or giving a specific budget justification, opting instead for less explicit expressions of need.

13. Arnott reminds her audience that Umbundu women were skilled agriculturalists. Arnott envisioned the students' putting these abilities to use in supporting the school "family." Agricultural work was incorporated into the programs of some other ABCFM girls' schools, such as Inanda Seminary in South Africa; there, according to Dana Robert, students "raised one-third of their own food" ("The 'Christian Home,'" 156).

14. Umbundu Christians generally built their own schools, receiving little or no assistance from mission funds. Gifts of food and cloth (used as a medium of exchange) thus contributed to support of the school (Tucker, *Angola: Land of the Blacksmith Prince*, 52).

15. Tabitha Kanogo points out in "Mission Impact on Women in Colonial Kenya" (in Bowie, Kirkwood and Ardener, *Women and Missions*), that such segregation of young girls often "alienated them from village life" and sometimes caused them to become "misfits in their own societies" (169–70).

16. Arnott uses the spelling "mandioc" in her original text. David Livingstone critiqued this carbohydrate staple of Angolans' diet: "The chief object of agriculture is the manioc, which does not contain nutriment sufficient to give proper stamina to the people." But he also acknowledged its appeal: "They subsist chiefly on the manioc, and, as that can be eaten either raw, roasted, or boiled, as it comes from the ground; or fermented in water, and then roasted or dried after fermentation, and baked or pounded into fine meal; or rasped into meal and cooked as farina; or made into confectionary with butter and sugar, it does not so soon pall upon the palate as one might imagine, when told that it constitutes their principal food. The leaves boiled make an excellent vegetable for the table; and, when eaten by goats, their milk is much increased. . . ." (*Missionary Travels and Researches in South Africa*, 78). Wilfrid Hambly gives details on methods that Umbundu women used to prepare manioc; each of five varieties had a different technique (*Ovimbundu of Angola*, 146–47). Manioc (sometimes called yucca or cassava) could also be used to make a tapioca-like seasoning as well as an alcoholic beverage.

17. This typewritten text is held at The Bancroft Library in Arnott's papers. Unlike many of the circular letters appearing in this edition, this composition was not written in one of her surviving notebooks, but rather has been filed in a folder for box 2 of the collection, labeled "Loose letters and other items from scrapbook, 1910–1943." Also unlike some circular letters, this text does not include a list of recipients. Its date and content indicate that Arnott prepared this piece in the early stages of her journey home to the U.S. Though Arnott's note at the end of the circular letter says she "made copies"

from her diary, she did not copy the diary verbatim. Rather, she deleted information, sometimes combined several entries, and occasionally added editorial comments.

18. Arnott has written "By Nellie Arnott" in ink below the typewritten title and date for this account. Other than her signature here, the rest of the text is typewritten on thin paper.

19. Most accounts by members of Arnott's team and their successors use "Lobito" as the spelling.

20. In her diary entry for February 25, Arnott carefully listed each individual's name, followed by, in Umbundu, the sin confessed; e.g. "Cipeta[,] ocimbombo." *Ocimbombo* was a native alcoholic drink, which Hambly describes as "strongly intoxicating"; it was made of corn, germinated and cooked for several days (Hambly, *Ovimbundu of Angola*, 149).

21. In her diary, Arnott lists the "boys and girls" by name. The letter omits a passage from her diary (March 1) in which she spent the evening talking with five of the young women. "They all have expressed a desire to confess Christ, & I have been trying to make them realize what it means. . . . May these dear girls ever be kept in the path of righteousness & never yield to the many temptations around them." While Arnott was thrilled at "the spirit they manifest," her worry that they did not really understand the commitment which "confession of Christ" implied is evident in the diary, especially since she was leaving Angola and could no longer counsel the young women. Not surprisingly, the circular letter underscores a celebratory message rather than Arnott's fears.

22. This location is usually spelled "Cisamba" or "Chissamba" by Arnott and others.

23. Arnott consistently refers to young women like Kayovo, who had lived with her in Kamundongo, as her "girls." Though her tone seems patronizing to us today, for Arnott's original readers the term could have indicated that she felt a close attachment to the young women she had been teaching, as well as pride in their learning. The three church members who were "on the suspension list" had been cited for drinking alcohol.

24. Umbundu men and sometimes women were subject to perform public labor for the Portuguese government; as the Benguela railroad extended into the highlands, such laborers constructed roads connecting towns to the rail line. In this instance, the Portuguese at Fort Belmont (or Belmonte) would likely have been using Umbundu women and children to help maintain or improve the road to the fort (Heywood, *Contested Power in Angola*, 38–40; Mastrobuono, "Ovimbundu Women," 61–65).

25. In her diary, Arnott expresses considerable anguish about leaving the young women, but also elation at the prospect of her furlough: "My girls

followed a long way crying & I too want to cry when I think of them. I'm really glad to be off for my vacation & I hope I can drop all care & really rest & enjoy every day" (March 26, 1912).

26. Arnott was at this camp on March 29. Her diary entry is somewhat different in tone from the letter: "We found a large caravan in camp before us. My tent is across the road from them. . . . Read with the boys & caravan. They are heathen of the heathen. Have never heard the Words before. The girls came to my tent afterwards for a visit & are such nice looking bright girls. Makes the heart ache & I wish I could go to their village. They say their villages are very large. Trust the words will linger in their hearts & I pray the Father to send some one to them."

27. Easter Sunday was April 7. Arnott's diary describes her week in Bailundu between March 30 and April 7.

28. Arnott adds in her diary a detail which would have shocked her readers: "There are a Portuguese & his two little girls by some black woman he has left in the interior."

29. Huguenot College (originally Huguenot Seminary), founded in 1874 in Wellington, Cape Colony, South Africa, was the oldest mission college affiliated with Mount Holyoke College. Rev. Andrew Murray raised money for the school and Mount Holyoke graduates Abbie Ferguson and Anna Bliss were the academic heads; the school became a college in 1899. Huguenot Seminary Papers are in the Mount Holyoke Archives; a description of the collection and historical information are at http://asteria.fivecolleges.edu/findaids/mountholyoke/mshm237.html.

Andrew Murray's book is *The State of the Church: A Plea for More Prayer*, originally printed by the World Missionary Conference (Edinburgh: 1910) and later reissued by J. Nisbet & Company in London.

30. Laura Nichols Bridgman, a graduate of Mt. Holyoke College, was the widow of Henry Martyn Bridgman; they joined the Zulu Mission in Natal in 1860. Their son, Rev. Frederick B. Bridgman, was born in Natal in 1869. Educated at Oberlin College, he and his wife, Clara Davis Bridgman, returned to South Africa in 1897. Their mission in Durban marked the first time that ABCFM missionaries in Africa had worked in a large urban center. The Bridgman Family Papers are in the Oberlin College Archives; biographical information is at http://www.oberlin.edu/archive/holdings/finding/RG30/SG349/biography.html.

31. Arnott here references her own past experiences as a teacher for the AMA in the southern U.S.

32. The American Board deputation was sent to Africa in 1910, under the leadership of Cornelius Patton, to gather information about mission stations and make recommendations for the future. Rev. Frederick Bridgman

accompanied Patton on his visit to Angola. Their report is in C.H. Patton and Frederick B. Bridgman, *Report of the Deputation to the West Central Africa Mission* (Boston: ABCFM, 1911). See also Soremekun, "History of the American Board Missions," 150–52. An account of Patton's journey in Africa entitled *The Lure of Africa* was reissued in 2006 (New York: Cosimo, orig. pub. 1917).

33. By now, Arnott was sometimes typing her circular letters rather than handwriting them in the carbon-paper copybooks she had used earlier in her overseas posting. This letter is one of several Arnott saved herself; currently it is filed in a folder labeled "Loose letters and other items from scrapbook, 1910–1943" for box 2 of NJADP.

34. Mount Holyoke College in Massachusetts was well known as one of the major suppliers of women missionaries and was also admired for its rigorous academic program.

35. Arnott was especially impressed by the program of Inanda Seminary in Natal (now KwaZulu-Natal). She described her stay there in her diary, May 8–14, 1912. The seminary was founded in 1869 by the ABCFM to educate the daughters of African Christians. The curriculum emphasized gender-specific courses, "stressing subjects that would equip students for a life of domesticity." The institution's philosophy was that a female graduate would be a "helpmate to her husband as well as a good Christian mother" and would be equipped to "control her own domain," that is, her home (Hughes, "A Lighthouse for African Women," 197, 203). See also Hlongwane, "The Role of Inanda Seminary," especially 13–15.

36. Arnott's diaries exude enthusiasm over sights she saw during this phase of her journey home—a stage only briefly mentioned here. The difference in focus between the diary and her public writing around this time is linked, of course, to awareness of her audience's interests and to the rhetorical strategies missionaries used when depicting themselves so as to promote the larger mission cause.

37. The itinerary reverses key stages in the U.S.-based portion of her original trip to Africa back in 1905.

38. During Arnott's first months back in the U.S., as she made her way from the east toward the west coast, she concentrated on fundraising, particularly by talking to women's groups.

39. Arnott typed this text, as she did most of her general letters during the last stage of her mission service, but signed and dated it in her own handwriting.

40. Nellie J. Arnott to James L. Barton, September 7, 1912. ABCFM Papers, Vol. 19, reel 168, Pitts Theological Library, Emory University. This letter covers some of the details in circular letter #9, but for a different audience.

41. Dr. Joseph Sanders, brother of Arnott's colleague in Africa, had hosted her before she sailed from Boston in 1905.

42. Malaria was a relatively common problem among missionaries serving overseas during this era.

43. Arnott's posting to Africa had been delayed due to her medical exam's indicating she did not meet the ABCFM health requirements. Tinker performed a surgical procedure considered successful at the time, evidently to correct a uterine condition. (See Chapter 1, note 18).

44. Marcia D. Wingate was Secretary of the WBMI, 1881–1914. She had "training in business," and Grace T. Davis, historian of the organization, credited Wingate with bringing professional management to the WBMI office (*Neighbors in Christ*, 168, 172).

45. That is, the minutes should have reached the ABCFM office by the time of Arnott's writing.

46. Polite but persistent, Arnott's questions here seek access to information and thus also to social power.

47. The Tuckers were John Taylor Tucker, a Canadian Congregational missionary, and his wife Mabel. As noted in Appendix 2, John Tucker wrote widely about his experiences in Angola and about the history of ABCFM missions there.

48. ABCFM Papers, Vol. 19, reel 168, Pitts Theological Library, Emory University. Arnott continued her correspondence with ABCFM officials as she made her way to California. She sent this letter from Moody Bible Institute, which she had attended as part of her preparation for her overseas posting.

49. Arnott's combining of visits to family members with mission business was typical of workers on furlough. Missionaries used networks of friends and family to identify potential donors. Meanwhile, supporters often provided a place to stay for workers on furlough, at "home" in the U.S. but generally without a home of their own.

50. The "ladies" Arnott references are women who led the WBMI in Chicago.

51. Arnott voices her opinion with confidence—even assertiveness. Her tone is far different than what she had used in letters earlier in her foreign missionary career. Arnott commented on the situation of Dr. William Cammack and his wife, Dr. Libbie Cammack, in several letters to Dr. Barton. See her letter of December 9, 1912.

52. The fire at Cisamba was not the work of an arsonist, as were those at Kamundongo early in Arnott's service. Rather, the wind spread a small fire to some 40 buildings at the station (Tucker, *Drums in the Darkness*, 89). Tucker reported that *Soma* Kanjundu sent 500 "bundles of grass" to use in

"re-thatching," as well as "large quantities of bark string" to bind the grass. In addition, Kanjundu sent his "imported bed, mattress and chairs" for use of the missionary women, whose furnishings had burned (111).

53. This handwritten piece pasted in Arnott's scrapbook of clippings (in NJADP) apparently records the text for one of her talks to mission supporters. Arnott's diary indicates that she gave such presentations during her cross-country tour. Arnott also gave two addresses to the Annual Meeting of the WBMI in Evanston, Illinois, in October of 1912. Annie E. Nourse, in "Minutes of the Forty-Fourth Annual Meeting, *Annual Report of the Woman's Board of Missions of the Interior, 1912* (Chicago: WBMI, [1913]), reported that before Arnott's first talk, she sang "Jesus Loves Me" in Umbundu, with a children's group joining her in the chorus (80). Arnott then "showed [the audience] a snuff box used by the native women and gave a graphic picture of the raw African village and the effect of the first hearing of the 'Jesus story.'" In her second talk, Arnott "took us through the day's round of an African mother's life, and spoke eloquently of the need of a girls' boarding school" (86). Assuming this material originally served as lecture notes, we have corrected spelling and punctuation as needed for clarity. The strike-out in the opening paragraph duplicates Arnott's handwritten substitution of "life of" with "existence."

54. In this piece, pitched to gain sympathy and thus to promote donations, Arnott pictures this method of carrying babies as burdensome and primitive. However, her granddaughter Mary Caris showed us family photographs of Arnott (then "Grandma Darling") using the same approach to carry her grandchild in the family's California yard.

55. One sign of the distance between "heathen" depravity and "Christian" culture had long been measured in clothing practices. Arnott taps into this expectation here by depicting young Africans as naked and therefore uncivilized.

56. In traditional Umbundu culture, all death was regarded as unnatural; the spirit of the deceased was thought to know who had caused its death. In an elaborate ceremony, the corpse, swathed in a cloth and suspended from a pole held by two men, was questioned as to who had caused the death. The corpse was believed to cause the men holding it to move backwards (not guilty) or forwards (guilty) as names were suggested. Arnott described such a ceremony in detail in her notebook titled "Happenings in Africa," dated "Olutu, Feb. 1909." The person identified as the guilty party would, according to Arnott, "be called on to pay to the relatives of the one dead a fine, perhaps a goat, a pig or ox." William H. Sanders and John Tucker also wrote about such ceremonies; both of them argued that there was consensus among Umbundu leaders beforehand as to the guilty party, with the corpse "instructing"

its bearers accordingly (Sanders, "Reminiscences," 109–10; Tucker, *A Tucker Treasury*, 123–24).

57. For some Umbundu women, an early marriage offered status and protection; others might seek out the mission stations to avoid an unwanted marriage (Mastrobuono, "Ovimbundu Women," 85–86). Though the missionaries consistently opposed men having multiple wives, not all Umbundu women were similarly inclined, as noted in Chapter 2.

58. Arnott appears to be quoting from several different diary entries. The particular journal from which these excerpts came is not in Arnott's papers and has not been located. Her diary for 1910, which consists of very short entries, records several visits to the settlement headed by *Soma* Kesenje, located near the Ciyaka station where she taught January through April; she also taught there in 1911.

59. Mission magazines frequently include reports on the success of this technique and requests for correspondents to send more of the pictures or funds to purchase picture books.

60. The account of the meeting of Jesus and the Samaritan woman at the well is in John 4:6–42.

61. Nellie J. Arnott to Dr. James L. Barton, December 9, 1912. ABCFM Papers, Vol. 19, reel 168, Pitts Theological Library, Emory University. At this point in her correspondence with ABCFM officials, Arnott still envisions herself as returning to her mission post. Arnott's continuing efforts to rally family members' support for her foreign mission service—clearly reflected in this letter—are noteworthy given her eventual decision to stay in the U.S. and marry her long-time beau Paul Darling

62. Arnott's father had opposed her accepting the assignment to Portuguese West Africa. Throughout her stay in Africa, Arnott's diary contains references to her concern that her father had not committed himself to Christianity.

63. As in her previous letter to Barton, Arnott seeks access to official ABCFM correspondence. Her inability to obtain an entrée to this important source of information is clearly frustrating to her, especially in light of the fundraising duty she has taken on. Though initially Kamundongo was discussed as the site of the Girls' Boarding School, it was located near the boys' school, the Currie Institute, at Dondi (sometimes called Kachivungo).

64. Failure to claim a spot on the WBMI's approved list of projects—and associated access to funds from the general campaign—would have been a significant blow to Arnott's plans.

65. The Cammacks had been deemed unfit to return to foreign mission work by a vote taken at the Annual Meeting of the West Central Africa mission. Decisions of the Annual Meeting could be overridden by the Prudential

(Executive) Committee of the ABCFM. Arnott's defense of the Cammacks indicates an assumption that her career in Africa gave her influence with Boston officials. Well aware of the desperate need for trained medical personnel in Angola, she may have thought it foolish to turn away two physicians who wished to return to the field.

66. One typed version of this letter is pasted into Arnott's clippings scrapbook, where she has written in a 1912–13 date designation. Another copy, with only slightly different wording, is available in the ABCFM Papers, Vol. 19, reel 168, Pitts Theological Library, Emory University. The version reproduced here includes the additional text typed in at the close of the letter in the copy Arnott pasted into her personal scrapbook.

67. Arnott references the process through which the ABCFM selected the highlands of Portuguese West Africa as a promising site for mission work.

68. Arnott here adopts a familiar argument in foreign mission literature—that women supporting the movement from home through their reading and writing played a crucial role in the movement.

69. Arnott evidently hopes that the Means name will encourage additional donations for establishment of the school.

70. The Umbundu woman controlled the distribution of her crops, deciding whether or not there was surplus to barter, and she thus had notable economic power. (See Chapter 2.) ABCFM missionaries recognized women's crucial role in Umbundu society, but, in writing for a home audience, tended to stress their hardships. Cushman, *Missionary Doctor*, 72–78, and Sanders, "Reminiscences," 77–78, offer perceptive comments on women's responsibilities.

71. Umbundu women were skilled in making pottery and baskets. Cushman describes these crafts in *A Missionary Doctor*, 141–45. Arnott brought a collection of baskets to the U.S.; her granddaughter, Mary D. Caris, later donated these to the Lowie Museum of Anthropology (now Phoebe A. Hearst Museum of Anthropology) at UC-Berkeley.

72. The order of presentation Arnott uses for the curriculum positions practical "life training" goals ahead of direct instruction in the Bible and Christian beliefs. Arnott's typical reader might assume that the girls should master domestic skills before taking on Bible instruction to support their husbands' Christian work.

73. Arnott carefully navigates the political minefield around fundraising. By this time, many mission organizations were discouraging efforts to attract donations for "specials," i.e., for individual projects in particular foreign locations, and were instead emphasizing fundraising for central organizations such as the WBMI. Arnott has gained permission from her superiors to seek donations for her pet project—but on condition that she cast these contribu-

tions as extras, beyond what supporters would normally give to the governing boards.

74. Nellie J. Arnott to Mr. Enoch F. Bell, December 28, 1912. ABCFM Papers, Vol. 19, reel 168, Pitts Theological Library, Emory University. Bell was Assistant Secretary of the ABCFM.

75. Usually this station site is referenced as "Dondi," but "Ndondi" is a more accurate reflection of its pronunciation in Umbundu, in which Arnott had become fluent.

76. Arnott here implies that any action taken outside of the normal governance procedures would be unethical and thus not appropriate; her questioning of a male official demonstrates her confidence that her seven years in Angola had made her valuable enough to the organization that she should speak forcefully.

77. Arnott here asserts the authority of on-site experience—something not available to Bell or his colleague Barton, or to other U.S.-based ABCFM officials, for that matter. As early as October 1905, Arnott had commented in her diary about the "lack in spiritual things" at Cisamba and said that she felt "more & more grateful that my station is Kamundongo." She evidently believed that management of the Cisamba station, under the leadership of the Canadian Congregational Foreign Missionary Society, was ineffective, contributing to the Cammacks' difficulties.

78. We infer from this comment that Arnott has elicited a negative reaction to her exploratory queries, in a previous letter, about the possibility that using the Means name could be an asset in fundraising.

79. Miss Nellie J. Arnott to Reverend Enoch F. Bell, February 13, 1913. ABCFM Papers, Vol. 19, reel 168, Pitts Theological Library, Emory University. Signing this letter "cordially," Arnott nonetheless continues to push the administration on several points where she feels her experience-based views should be taken into account.

80. Reverend H. Melville Tenney was the Secretary of the District of the Pacific Coast of the ABCFM.

81. Although Arnott does not say so at this point, diary entries composed after her marriage indicate that she made a sustained effort to persuade her husband to be a candidate for the position of printer at the mission station. Paul Darling was never convinced. Shortly before World War I, a trained printer, James Hunter, went to Angola to assist Sarah Sanders, but after Hunter died while on a hippopotamus hunt and his wife went on furlough, Mrs. Sanders resumed her duties. In 1921, when Mrs. Sanders was no longer able to keep up with the physical demands of the job, the press moved to Dondi (Tucker, *Drums in the Darkness*, 92–93). See also "Getting a Printer for West Africa," *Missionary Herald*, May 1915, 232–33.

82. Arnott implies that having the "right man" is not enough; the Board also needs to allow its leaders in the field to do their work without excessive interference.

83. One of Arnott's early letters in 1905 (Circular Letter #5) asks supporters to pray that Kapitango might join the church; that he finally did so would be noteworthy for her readers.

84. Nellie J. Arnott to Reverend James L. Barton, March 7, 1913. ABCFM Papers, Vol. 19, reel 168, Pitts Theological Library, Emory University. With its announcement that she will not be returning to Angola, this letter marks a major turning point in Arnott's career—and her correspondence.

85. Considering the surprising information Arnott is about to reveal—that she will be marrying and remaining in California—her touting the potential value of home-based support for the mission movement is understandable.

86. Perhaps Arnott is hinting that she can be replaced with Nellie Tracy, whom she has just praised.

87. Arnott's careful recitation of arguments favoring her return to Africa implies that she and Paul Darling had considered the pros and cons of their marriage in both personal and institutional contexts. Her diary suggests that she felt as much distress at ending her mission service as she had felt in leaving Paul for Africa in 1905. Arnott accepted Paul's proposal on March 1; her entry on March 7 shows her anguish: "These are days of suffering in spite of the inner joy. To withdraw from the Mission nearly kills me."

88. This brief character sketch of her fiancé could be designed to illustrate his potential value to the movement through his business skills.

89. Arnott here calls upon the very argument she has used so often when writing to U.S.-based mission movement supporters—that a dedicated Christian living "in the homeland" can be as valuable as a worker posted overseas.

90. Nellie J. Arnott to Reverend Enoch F. Bell, April 5, 1913. ABCFM papers, Vol. 19, reel 168, Pitts Theological Library, Emory University. Despite her resignation via the previous letter, Arnott continues to make specific recommendations as to how the work in Angola should continue.

91. Apparently, rather than criticize her decision not to return to her post in Africa, Bell has taken the more magnanimous stance to which Arnott alludes here.

92. Arnott refers to the Congregational Foreign Missionary Society of British North America, or "Canadian Society," which, at this time, operated the Cisamba (Chissamba) station in Angola under the auspices of the ABCFM. The Canadian Congregationalists in Angola began to operate separately from the ABCFM in 1926, after the formation of the United Church of Canada. See Paul Byam, "New Wine in A Very Old Bottle: Canadian Protestant Missionaries as Facilitators of Development in Central Angola,

1886–1961" (PhD diss., University of Ottawa, 1997), 60–64. Byam notes that by the early 1920s, tension had developed between the American and Canadian groups over funding and administration of the Currie Institute and Means School (62).

93. Arnott's portrayals of her colleague Sanders have been so glowing over the years that even this slight hint that she may have been frustrated by his failure to support her boarding school plans is striking.

94. Arnott refers to former Angola missionaries Annie Williams Read and Lydia Isely Wellman. Read had left Angola several years before Arnott arrived. After the death of her missionary husband while they were on furlough, Annie Read did not return to Angola. John Tucker describes her as a "brilliant linguist," so it would not be surprising for Arnott to suggest Read be recalled to service (Tucker, *Tucker Treasury*, 113). See Appendix 2 for information on Lydia Wellman.

95. As with her subtle reference to Rev. Sanders earlier in this letter, Arnott's restrained complaint here is telling: perhaps her colleagues' pushing her to a role as fundraiser versus the one with which she was more familiar—teacher and administrator—helped nudge her toward the altar.

96. This may be Arnott's final letter to the ABCFM—at least under her maiden name. In May of 1913, she married.

97. Given the time lags between initial composition and publication in a mission movement magazine, Arnott may well have written this article while she was still planning to return to Africa. In any case, by the time it appeared in *Mission Studies*, she had accepted Paul Darling's proposal.

98. Arnott here taps into a familiar strategy of mission movement rhetoric—distinguishing between the young generation, who may be relatively likely to convert, and their parents and grandparents.

99. Commenting on the influence that their readings in mission schools have had on many African authors, Ngũgĩ wa Thiong'o singled out the very texts Arnott references here as pervasive: "The early practitioners of the African novel, particularly in South Africa, were products of missionary educational institutions and they were more likely to have been exposed to Bunyan's *Pilgrim's Progress* and the King James or Authorized version of the bible than to Tolstoy, Balzac or Dickens" (Ngũgĩ, *Decolonizing the Mind*, 69). As noted in the introduction, Ngũgĩ has been especially critical of colonial educational institutions—including mission schools—whose curricular programs were delivered in the language of the imperial power. Though he might appreciate the efforts of Arnott's mission group, the ABCFM, to learn the local language in Angola and to teach in Umbundu (including providing instructional texts in that language), Ngũgĩ could still point to dimensions of this pedagogy that were constraining: "The printing press, the publishing houses and the educational context . . . were controlled by the missionaries and the colonial admin-

istration," to the extent that reading opportunities were tightly managed "so as not to expose the young minds to dangerous, undesirable and unacceptable moral and political influences" (69).

100. Arnott carefully navigates controversies associated with white women's advocacy for African girls' rights. On the one hand, she points to local customs promoting early marriage; on the other, she invokes the practice of transferring young girls into the hands of Portuguese traders, who essentially "bought" their wives through payments of rum and/or cloth. Although Arnott refrains from direct condemnation of these practices in the early part of this narrative, the Christian alternatives she depicts later in the essay are clearly cast as preferable.

101. Arnott focuses her readers' attention on a particular individual rather than offering only a generalized discussion about young African girls. She draws on the interconnected stories of these sisters to build a cluster of examples. Arnott's diaries and journal include a number of affectionate entries about Cipuku. For example, she wrote in her diary (July 13, 1908) about her disappointment that she could not be present when Cipuku joined the church and that she missed Cipuku and her sister Nakalu "very much" when they left the mission station to live with their husbands following their marriages on June 10, 1908. Though Nakalu is clearly identified in Arnott's diaries as Cipuku's sister, she is not named in this article; possibly her name is spelled as Nalungu here. For more on Cipuku and her family, see Chapter 2.

102. Cipuku's father, Mueno, the headman or *sekulu* of the village of Cisanje, died without converting to Christianity (Arnott's diary, Nov. 10 and 18, 1906).

103. Cipuku's husband was Sakalumbu, who took over outstation work upon the death of Cituvika. (See Chapter 5.)

104. Arnott presents Cipuku in this passage as the ideal Umbundu Christian woman, assisting her husband in the teaching of a new generation of Christians. Deborah Gaitskell found a similar development in South African mission literature; stories of "saintly *indigenous* Christians, worthy products of mission education" [emphasis in original] began to appear in the late nineteenth century, taking their place alongside portrayals of missionary heroines. "Women and Education in South Africa: How Helpful Are the Mission Archives?" in Bickers and Seton, *Missionary Encounters*, 120.

105. Arnott has repeatedly used rhetorical questions in this article to invite young readers to engage with the experiences of the children about whom she writes.

106. Now Mrs. Darling, Arnott uses a different stance than in earlier pieces of her published writing, where she wrote from the perspective of someone living in the culture she was describing.

107. In previous publications, Arnott generally avoided appeals for specific amounts of money—asking instead for "help" and leaving it to readers to infer that cash donations would be most useful. Here, however, she [or the editor] quotes from Sarah Stimpson, whose more overt approach may be a reflection of their personality differences, but could also relate to the pressures Stimpson would be feeling about working alone now that Arnott was gone.

108. *Soma* "Hosi" Kanjundu was the first royal leader in the highlands to become a Christian. (See Chapter 2.) When a destitute Portuguese trader accused Kanjundu of burning the European's house down—the trader evidently angered at Kanjundu's stand against rum—Kanjundu was taken to the coast for trial. Rev. Sanders accompanied him as a pledge to the Portuguese that Kanjundu would not try to escape. ABCFM missionaries pressured colonial authorities and eventually Kanjundu was freed; however, his health never fully recovered after his imprisonment (Sanders, "Reminiscences," 124–25; Tucker, *Drums in the Darkness*, 108–10, 113).

109. As in the essay on "The Need of a Girls Boarding School," which appeared in the same month's issue of *Mission Studies*, Arnott relies here on correspondence from a former colleague to provide content for her writing. While not on the scene herself, Arnott is able to draw on her knowledge of the Angola mission to contextualize Diadem Bell's report. Intriguingly, Arnott did not continue submitting regular contributions to the mission periodicals after these 1914 pieces appeared. Although her scrapbooks show that she avidly read about work at her former posting, and although she kept up regular correspondence with her friends there and arranged to see them when they were on furlough, Arnott apparently ended her career as a published author. Given the energy she had devoted to her writing during her time in Africa, this change is somewhat surprising, especially since mission magazines routinely printed contributions from movement supporters in the U.S. We can speculate that the demands of middle-class American family life—eventually including motherhood—took their toll, but we should also note that her new form of composing—scrapbook-making—may have been a more appealing type of writing for someone whose most exciting experiences were now a part of memory rather than daily life.

110. Lumbo was the Umbundu minister at the Cisamba station and as such was the one asked to relate the news of Kanjundu's death. His father, Sanembelo, had been an early Christian convert at Cisamba, and Lumbo himself was "a man loved by all for his steadfast character and solid counsel," according to John Tucker (*Drums in the Darkness*, 81; *Tucker Treasury*, 63).

111. Tucker, *Tucker Treasury*, 198–200, describes the early history of Means School. He also provides a history of the Currie Institute, which opened in 1914 under his leadership (183–95). Tucker lists members of the

Institute's first class, which included Enoque Gomes Sacamana, Arnott's assistant teacher at Kamundongo (187).

112. Tucker, *Drums in the Darkness*, 134; Heywood, *Contested Power in Angola*, 106. The gender-based curricula at Means School and Currie Institute featured agricultural education for boys and domestic education for girls. Fola Soremekun criticizes this "Tuskegee model" as contributing to the conversion of Umbundu men from traders to sedentary farmers. By the 1920s, both missions and colonial authorities supported this goal, which, he argues, came at the expense of Umbundu autonomy and traditional life ("Religion and Politics in Angola," 369–70, 375–76). The large mission complex at Dondi, including the two schools, a church, hospital, and seminary, was virtually destroyed during the 1975–2003 Civil War in Angola, a time when American Congregational (United Church of Christ) and United Church of Canada missionaries were forced to leave the country (Joyce Myers-Brown, interview with Ann Pullen, September 21, 2005). Members of the Evangelical Congregational Church of Angola, along with former missionaries, are raising funds to rebuild school facilities. Photos showing some of the buildings as they appeared originally, and as they are now, appear on the website of the Angola Memorial Scholarship Fund: http://www.angolamsf.org/. A UCC missionary, Donna Dudley, recently returned to Angola for the first time since the Civil War (Cally Rogers-Witte, e-mail to Ann Pullen, December 12, 2008).

113. Jeffrey Cox, "Master Narratives of Imperial Missions" in Scott and Griffiths, *Mixed Messages: Materiality, Textuality, Missions*, 4-18. Cox draws on Edward Said for the idea that "Within the contact zones may be found ... 'an experience of imperialism that is essentially one of sympathy and congruence, not of antagonism, resentment, or resistance.'" Cox himself notes that, in this context, "Missionaries were often important and respected figures in non-Western Christian communities, and in some cases also in non-Western, non-Christian communities" (14).

114. Yoano to Dona Nele [Nellie Arnott Darling], 20 January 1935, "Loose Letters, 1910-1943," box 2 NJADP. "Dona Nele" was a nickname (roughly, "teacher Nellie") that had been given to Arnott while she was in Angola. In her article on "A Visit to an African Village," also in this chapter, Arnott suggests another potential translation for "dona," sometimes spelled "ndona": "white lady."

Appendix 1
Mission Publications' Editing of Arnott's Writing

Whenever Arnott's writing about her foreign mission work was published, it first passed through an editorial process that positioned her work within the highly evolved institutional context of her sponsoring organizations. Indeed, by the time Arnott had arrived in Africa, women's foreign mission movement publications had developed a whole set of rhetorical conventions that she had been well trained to follow through her own reading of similar texts in the years before her posting. Thus, Arnott's own familiarity with missionary publications guided her choices about what and how to report to her readers. However, women editors at home also left their mark on her texts, to varying degrees, partly depending upon the particular venue where a report was appearing.

Below, we provide two examples of this editorial process in action, from different positions on the continuum of intervention and reshaping. In the first case, excerpts from a story in *Mission Studies*, we see very few differences between the published piece and Arnott's own handwritten circular letter from the same time period. In the second case, a section of the 1907 annual report of the WBMI on the work of its women missionaries, we can note how a U.S.-based editor could incorporate material from a faraway writer like Arnott into a broader argument supporting the movement's overarching agenda.

For the 1907 publication, some of Arnott's reportage was folded into a larger essay on the WBMI's program in Africa; the presentation of her particular experiences was used to bolster the organization's goal of building commitment among supporters. Interestingly, even in this piece where her voice is somewhat subsumed into another's, some of Arnott's strengths as a writer remain evident. Her eye for detail, her appealing characterizations of the children she served, and her emphasis on her own activities as consistent with American middle-class women's idealized social role would all have resonated with mission movement enthusiasts. We can readily surmise that the annual report author's choice to quote repeatedly from Arnott's writings was calculated for maximum appeal.

The article entitled "Benguella" appeared in the February 1906 issue of *Mission Studies*. Drawn from a circular letter Arnott had begun writing on July 11, 1905, the magazine version of this material does not differ significantly from her round-robin, handwritten text. Looking at the close matches and the slight alternations between the two pieces, therefore, we gain a window into the editing process whereby Arnott's writing for a relatively small audience (the recipients of her circular letters) was polished for a larger readership through the editorial intervention of the mission movement's periodical managers. Characterizing the shifts in her text, we note that most involve straightforward changes like replacing her use of "&" with "and," standardizing her punctuation patterns (such as adding commas for appositives and some numerals), and adjusting capitalization choices. In the places where her diction is revised, we see that the editing process honors her voice, content focus, and tone, opting for changes at the word (rather than the sentence or paragraph) level in ways that do not alter her overall message. One inference we might draw from comparing the two versions of this account is that Arnott's writing reached her magazine readers with only minor editorial interventions in between. This observation, in turn, underscores both her skill as an individual writer for this particular audience and the familiarity both readers and authors would have had, by this time, with the genre-based expectations associated with missionaries' reports for home-based readers.

To highlight the editorial process in action, in our partial transcript of the "Benguella" article below, we have placed the sites of textual intervention in bold for ease of comparison with the circular letter that appeared earlier in this volume.

Benguella

Benguella, W. C. Africa,
July 11, 1905.

We landed in Benguella June 20th and have been detained here longer than we expected on account of the steamer we came on from

Lisbon being unable to bring all of our goods. So we have had to wait here for the next steamer, which arrived here last Sunday, being nearly a week late. They have been unloading the last two days **and** we hope to get everything through the custom[deleted hyphen]house during the next two days. If so, we will start on our journey up country the last of the week. We feel that we have much to be grateful for in the safe arrival of our goods, as the steamer, "The Benguella," had a fire in the hold for three days on the way down. Some 14,000 volume of cargo were burned, but ours are unhurt.

Benguella is a town of about 2,000 inhabitants, 600 of them being white. It is spread out over a large area, with many large open spaces. There are a very few straight streets, but what there are, **are** very wide. It looks as though each one had chosen his place to build without regard to streets. There are no sidewalks, but all walk in the middle of the street. There is very little traffic outside of carriers. The governor of Benguella district lives here **and** his jurisdiction extends over Bihé, the district in which we live. Of course he has a nice place, **and** then the **manager of the telegraph,** Mr. Kitchen, has a very nice place. He is English, **and** we have enjoy**ed** taking tea with him several afternoons since being here. There are two hotels, several shops **and** a few other **very good** buildings. There is also a **well built** jail, hospital, custom house and a **large** market place.

We visited the market this morning. It is a large square, fenced in with a high iron fence. There are two long sheds, one on either side, extending across it. They just spread out a piece of cloth **on the ground** and on this they put their meats, mandioc, beans, eggs, etc. Women with their babies sit around selling what they can from their baskets. It is all so dirty that one feels as **though he** never could eat some things again. Some have bundles of sticks, others baskets of charcoal. As we were leaving several came up **with baskets** on their heads, **in each of which** was one very large fish just brought from the ocean. Here **they** cut them up **and** sold them piece by piece.

Some of the women in this district wear a very large collar. Two of the women in the market had these on, and Mr. Sanders asked one of them if I might lift her collar. I did so, and it weighs fully ten pounds. Mr. Sanders says some of them are larger **and** weigh even more. It is about five inches in diameter **and** is made of strings **and** strings of small beads that have been matted together with palm oil, dirt, etc., and then all bound together with bands of brass or iron so that it is solid like a stone. It cannot be taken off and they wear it night and day. At night the wearer pushes it up as far as she can on her neck and uses it as a pillow.

Across the corner from **where** we are boarding is a large public garden. It is fenced in with an iron fence and in the center is a fountain from which the women get water in large cans. These they carry on their heads to the remotest parts of the garden **and** water the plants and trees. Every morning we can see them sweeping the paths with **brushes and** making a great dust. Here they do not need any signs, "Keep off the grass," as there is no grass in all Benguella. The plants and trees in the garden are very pretty. At present the oleanders are in bloom **and** a few pretty roses, as well as other varieties of flowers. I am sure the boys **and** girls would think some of the trees here very strange, for they not only send roots down into the ground, but many of them send long roots out on their branches.

Today, July 14th, Mrs. Sanders and I took a walk in one of the **streets. We** found a washing of clothes spread out on the ground to dry. **Near by** was a pig wandering around. It is very seldom one sees a **clothesline** here and much of the washing is done in the ocean. We have been told that the "Ambaca," the steamer **on which** we came, on its return took 150 "contracted laborers" to St. Thomas island to work on the coco plantations. I am very sorry we missed seeing them embark. As I told you in a previous letter, these "contracted laborers" are really slaves. They have been bought or captured in the far interior of Africa **and** are tied or chained together **and** brought to the coast **and** sold to some plantation owner.

[Note: There are no notable differences beyond this point in the two texts.]

Africa: West Central Africa, Kamundongo

From *Annual Report of the Woman's Board of Missions of the Interior*, 1907[1]

[To distinguish the editor's words from Arnott's, we show the editor's comments in **bold**.]

Miss Nellie Arnott, **our newest misionary** [sic] **in Africa, writes at the end of her first year,** "I have kept well and happy, with the exception of bitter hours over the language." **The longing to speak to the** natives on the things most precious to her heart is sometimes almost too great to be borne.

Miss Arnott has become very much interested in the work of the out station schools.[2] Beginning with December she began teaching the children the Christ-child stories and with the help of pictures tried to have them get hold of the real Christmas thought. "On Christmas Day I had all the children on the Station here for a feast. Seventy-two children sat down at tables in the yard." Each child was given a dish of mush and a dish of meat and of beans. Some red and white beads were given to each little girl and they had enough Perry pictures of the Christ child to give each child one.[3]

Mrs. Sanders has charge of the Mission Press at this Station and much of Miss Arnott's time is occupied in helping her. With only a small printing press to do the work and the folding, pasting and covering of the books done by hand, we can imagine the amount of work necessary to get out a thousand copies of Genesis. A revised edition of the Primer of 1,200 copies, one thousand copies of Luke and two thousand copies of the hymn book are some of the other items. How much it means to these people to have the Scriptures and other books in their own language!

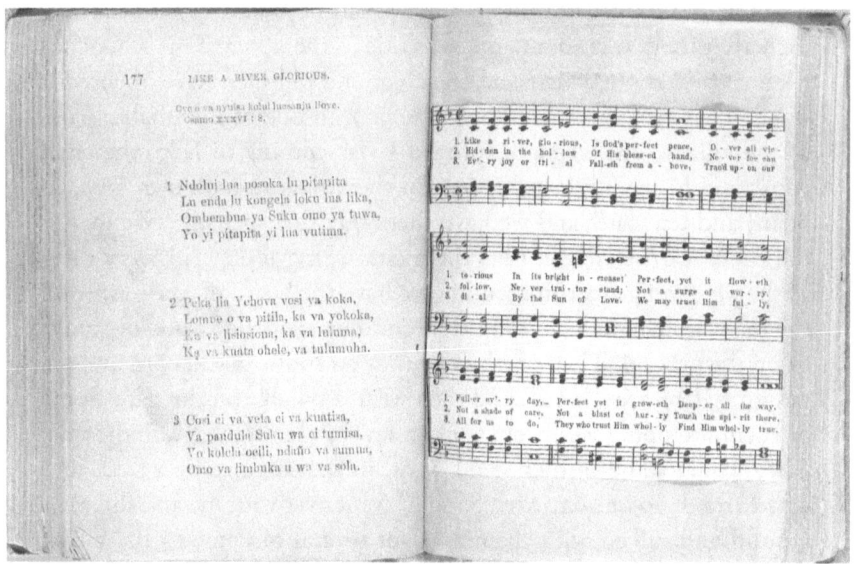

Figure 16: Page of English-Umbundu Hymnal. Courtesy of The Bancroft Library, University of California, Berkeley.

Many cases of sickness have occurred among the natives and there is a great temptation to return to the heathen practices of superstition. Some yield to the pressure of relatives, but most of the Christians remain firm in resisting.[4] The need of a physician is felt here as at other stations.

Nine members were received into the church here the first of the year.

In June of this year, Miss Arnott wrote of her work, "There are about twenty girls here most of the time and they are all more or less under my care. Many of my evenings are given to them. Sometimes they sew, other evenings we have meetings or study the Sunday school lessons or sing.

From the last of September until the first of June most of my time and strength is given to the schools. The children's school is in the mornings and the school for girls and women in the latter part of the afternoon. I am very much thankful I have the children's school as work with them is very interesting and promising and as I gain a better use of the language, there are many ways in which I hope to improve the schools."

This description of the work in one of the out-stations is interesting, as it shows the methods employed to bring knowledge to these heathen and darkened minds. "Two of our boys have carried me over each afternoon. It is about an hour's ride in the *tepoia*. This school has been started about a year and the chief and old men have opposed it some. They have been holding the school in one of the smaller parts of the village, but when they heard I was coming to help, the chief consented to having it in his part of the village. I took over a blackboard and ten slates and we have them buy their pencils.[5] We met in the center of the village, near the men's sitting room. It is very dirty as the pigs and goats run around. We have the board on the fence and the men, women and children sit around on blocks of wood or stools, or on the ground. Then one by one they go to the blackboard and are taught syllables and words and then write a syllable on the slate. Some of them are doing very well. Only a few of the women would come. They would stand in their gates or off in the distance by a fence and acted afraid. So one day Mrs. Sanders went over with me and she went around and talked with them and got several to come to the blackboard. So little by little they must be won until in time they will come to our services here. The teacher at Unyunya goes over on Monday and remains until Saturday. He has prayers with them every evening and morning and also has school in the morning. Next season I hope to have blackboard and slates so as to supply our other schools."

This outstation work is very encouraging. Mr. Sanders had recently visited a number of them. Miss Arnott writes, "One of the strong Christians in one of these stations lost his wife a short time ago. While Mr. Sanders was there he came to him and said now that he was free to go, he had been thinking much of his village where his relatives lived. He said they had heard the Word only a very little and that now he would like to go to them and teach them and see whether they would not accept. Of course, Mr. Sanders encouraged him to go to them by all means, so Saturday he came here and has been with us over Sunday. This morning he started toward his old village where he hopes to remain and teach them. It makes our heart glad whenever we see a desire to spread the Word of Life."

The work in this part of the Dark Continent is slower and results are less apparent than in some of our older missions, where the people are more developed intellectually.[6] But these devoted missionaries are seeing the fruit of their labor and patient endurance and we rejoice with them.

Notes

1. Miss A.G. Marchant, "Africa: West Central Africa, Kamundongo." *Annual Report of the Woman's Board of Missions of the Interior* 39 (Chicago: Woman's Board of Missions of the Interior, 1907), 48–50. The WBMI's annual reports summarized the status of mission work at the numerous foreign stations supported by the Board. Accordingly, these reports synthesized submissions from women missionaries whose writings could also be used as articles for magazines such as *Mission Studies*. In this case, Miss Marchant, author of the 1907 annual report on African missions, draws from material submitted by Nellie Arnott to create a portrait of the women-run elements in the work at Kamundongo. We have not located the the original of Arnott's letter upon which this report is based.

2. This report uses three different spellings: "out station" (two words, as here) and later "out-stations" and still later "outstation" (one word).

3. Besides offering its catalog, the Perry Pictures company also published *Perry Magazine*, which published contextualizing stories about some of the company's pictures and advertised the array of available images as suitable for both classroom teaching and home decoration. For examples of

images and of information on sizes, prices, and ordering processes, see *Perry Magazine* 5 (September 1902), the back pages' ads (beginning at page iv).

4. Many of the Christians were pressured by their non-Christian relatives to turn away from mission medical practices and return to remedies suggested by traditional healers. Such pressure was particularly likely in the case of sick children who did not improve under missionaries' care (Cushman, *Missionary Doctor*, 59–62). The Kamundongo mission station did not have a physician assigned to the station in 1907; Arnott and the other ABCFM women mission workers nursed ill children and adults as effectively as possible.

5. Mission stations in Angola often operated small commissaries for local Christians so as to keep them away from stores run by Portuguese traders who sold rum (Soremekun, "American Board Missions in Angola," 128).

6. Miss Marchant, the editor, referred to areas such as Turkey, China, Japan and India, where the WBMI first sent missionaries. In keeping with Social Darwinist theories current at the time, leaders of the WBMI assumed that African societies were not as highly developed as those in many other areas of the world. Grace T. Davis, author of a history of the WBMI, for example, argued that the Angola mission faced problems "quite different" from "other of our mission fields" in that potential Christian leaders had experiences limited by "a short period at school and the primitive conditions of the African bush" (*Neighbors in Christ*, 154).

Appendix 2
ABCFM Missionaries in Angola

In her publications, Arnott frequently refers to missionaries who worked in Portuguese West Africa. The list below contains biographical sketches for those who served under the auspices of the ABCFM during Arnott's era. Chapter endnotes provide information on major Angola missionaries affiliated with other religious groups as well as on mission officials working in the U.S.

The main sources for the list below are ABCFM Vinton Book I, Africa, Asia, Papal Islands, ABC 90.5, Vol. I,*99M66, 8–10, and ABCFM Vinton Book IV, 1885–1910, ABC 90.5, Vol. 4, *99M66, 22–33, ABCFM Archives, Houghton Library, Harvard University. The Vinton Books are online at http://www.14beacon.org/resources/vinton. For dates of service, the "Substation List" (279-83) in American Board of Commissioners for Foreign Missions, Papers of the American Board of Commissioners for Foreign Missions . . . Guide to the Microfilm Collection supplemented data in the Vinton Books. Additional sources are indicated in the entries. Vinton Books and other sources sometimes spell names inconsistently. The spellings of names below come from the missionaries' own signatures submitted with West Central Africa Mission annual reports to the ABCFM. In some cases, we have modernized spellings of locations for clarity. We indicate each person's primary appointment site, but missionaries frequently were reassigned to other stations, sometimes for months, to cover for someone on furlough or to perform special duties.

Bell, Diadem. Born October 12, 1870, in Milton, Queens County, Nova Scotia, Diadem Bell left for Angola in 1902 to join the Canadian Congregational mission station (under the ABCFM) at Cisamba. She served in Angola until 1922 and died in Coburg, Ontario, in 1923.

Bell, Lena Grace Hiller. Born January 9, 1876, in Ithaca, NY, Lena Hiller married William Clark Bell in Ithaca in 1897 and went with him to Angola to join the Philafrican Liberators' League Mission, aiming to aid freed slaves in Angola. This group was founded by Swiss linguist Héli Chatelain. After leaving that mission, she received an appointment from the ABCFM to the Bailundu station in 1907. She left Angola in 1936 and died in Stanford Hospital, CA, in 1946.

Bell, William Clark. Born July 27, 1872, in Lockport, NY, William Bell graduated from Cornell University in 1897 and attended Moody Bible College. He and his wife, Lena, went to Africa to join the Philafrican Liberators' League mission under Héli Chatelain. He left that group after a brief time and volunteered at the ABCFM station at Cisamba. He was officially commissioned by the ABCFM in 1907 and worked at the Bailundu station. Known for his skill in agricultural methods, he served in Angola until 1936. He died in Claremont, CA, February 19, 1942 (Tucker, *Tucker Treasury*, 184–86, 194).

Figure 17: Photo album page with Bailundu (Bailundo) scenes and missionary photos. Courtesy of The Bancroft Library, University of California, Berkeley.

Cammack, Sarah Libbie Seymour, M.D. Born March 7, 1875, in Iowa City, IA, Libbie Seymour studied medicine at the State University of Iowa and married William Cammack in 1906. Shortly thereafter they embarked to do medical work in Angola at the Cisamba station. She retired in 1923 due to ill health.

Cammack, William, M.D. Born March 27, 1880, in Salem, IA, William Cammack graduated from the State University of Iowa and studied medicine there and at Northwestern University. He left for Angola in 1906, serving at Cisamba with his wife, Libbie. In 1923 he retired from mission service and moved to Florida due to his wife's ill health.

Campbell, Elizabeth B. Born June 17, 1869, in Luncoe County, Ontario, Elizabeth Campbell studied at Collingwood Collegiate Institute and taught school for 12 years before leaving for Angola in 1902. She served at Cisamba with Canadian Congregational missionaries. This station operated under the ABCFM until 1926 when its operation was placed under the United Church of Canada. Campbell served at Cisamba until 1934 and died in Toronto in 1951.

Currie, Amy Johnston. Born in Dublin, Ireland, in 1861, Amy Johnston was educated in Dublin and came to the U.S. in 1889. She left for Angola in 1893 and married Walter Currie there in 1894. She returned to the U.S. in 1911 and died in 1928.

Currie, Walter Thomas. Born July 27, 1858, in Toronto, Walter Currie was a graduate of McGill College (1885) and Congregational College, Montreal. He was the first of a group of missionaries in the Congregational Foreign Missionary Society of British North America, or "Canadian Society" (which worked under the auspices of the ABCFM), to go to Angola. He departed for the field in 1886 with his first wife, Clara Wilkes Currie, who died shortly after their arrival. In 1894 he married his missionary colleague Amy Johnston. Currie established the Cisamba (or Chissamba) mission station, where he served until 1911. Currie Institute (for boys) was named in his honor when it opened in 1914. He died in 1915 at his home, which he called "Chissamba," near Victoria, British Columbia. John Tucker wrote about Currie's life in *Currie of Chissamba*.

Ennis, Elisabeth Logan. Born March 8, 1881, in Hortonville, WI, Elisabeth Logan studied at Lawrence University, the University of

Oregon and Wellesley College. She married Merlin Ennis in 1907 and went with him to Angola. She left missionary service in 1945 and died in Cambridge, MA, in 1961.

Ennis, Merlin. Born January 29, 1874, in Douglas (Marquette County), WI, Merlin Ennis graduated from Beloit College in 1900 and Yale Divinity School in 1903. He left for Angola shortly after graduation from Yale. He returned to the U.S. in 1906 to marry Elisabeth Logan, who went with him to Africa. With Frederick Wellman, he founded the "Sacikela" mission station in the Ciyaka region at the base of Mt. Elende. (The station was variously called Ciyaka or Elende as well as Sacikela.) Ennis retired from missionary service in 1945 and died in 1964 at the home of his daughter in Marblehead, MA. Ennis was the author of *Umbundu: Folk-tales from Angola*. Further information about Ennis is on the Beloit College website: https://campus.beloit. edu/archives/documents/archival_collections/alumni/merlin_ennis

Fay, Annie M. Kimball. Born in Flatbush, NY, November 26, 1860, and trained as a kindergarten teacher, Annie Kimball married William E. Fay in March of 1886. They left for Angola a short time later, serving at Bailundu. She began the first kindergarten for Umbundu children. She left Angola in 1907 due to her husband's ill health and did not return to Africa after his death. She died in Milford, OH, in 1952 (Remick, "American Influence on the Education of the Ovimbundu," 65, 93).

Fay, William E. Born in Louisville, KY, November 8, 1855, William Fay was a graduate of Marietta (Ohio) College (1878) and Oberlin Theological Seminary (1881). He arrived at Bailundu in Angola in 1882 but returned to the U.S. in 1884 with Wesley Stover after an Umbundu group robbed them and drove them from the station. He conferred with the ABCFM and returned to Angola in 1886 after marrying Annie M. Kimball. Fay left Angola in early 1907 due to ill health and died in Oberlin, OH, in October of that year. Fay had studied treatments for tropical diseases and, though not a trained physician, was respected for his wide medical knowledge (Remick, "American Influence on the Education of the Ovimbundu," 65, 93).

Hollenbeck, Henry Stanley, M.D. Born May 22, 1878, in Sheldon, IA, Henry Hollenbeck studied at Beloit College and graduated from Iowa State University in 1902. He received his medical degree from

Northwestern University in 1907. He left for Angola in 1909, studying for a term at the London School of Tropical Medicine en route. He was stationed at Kamundongo during Arnott's service. Hollenbeck was a member of the Phelps-Stokes Commission that produced the report *Education in Africa: A Study of West, South, and Equatorial Africa by the African Education Commission, under the Auspices of the Phelps-Stokes Fund and Foreign Mission Societies of North America and Europe* prepared by Thomas Jesse Jones. He left Angola service in 1942 and died in Chicago in that year.

Melville, Helen Jane. Born October, 1864, in Toronto, Helen Melville went to Angola in 1893. She served at the Cisamba station with a group of Canadian Congregational missionaries. When that station passed from the ABCFM to the United Church of Canada in 1926, she continued to serve with that board. A trained nurse, she returned to Canada after her service overseas (Tucker, *Drums in the Darkness*, 84).

Melville, Margaret (Maggie) Walker. Born July 11, 1867, in Toronto, Margaret Melville studied at Parkdale Model School and Normal School and in 1895 went to join her sister Helen at the Cisamba station in Angola. She wrote Umbundu primers in reading and arithmetic for use in mission schools. She left the field in 1924 and died in Toronto in 1925 (Tucker, *Angola: Land of the Blacksmith Prince*, 148).

Miller, Janette Estelle. Born September 19, 1879, in Hancock (Houghton County), MI, Janette Miller took courses at the Chicago Theological Seminary and worked at the Detroit Public Library before going to the Ocileso (Chilesso) station in Angola in 1910. She resigned from the ABCFM mission in 1929 and eventually opened her own orphanage in Angola. She died in 1969. On her career, see Elizabeth Ellen Rohan's "Imagined Communions: One Woman's Spiritual Journey."

Moffatt, Robert G. Robert Moffatt, a Canadian born in Huron County, Ontario, was one of the early staff members with Walter Currie at Cisamba, where he was employed as a teacher of industrial trades. He returned to Canada in 1899 due to ill health. He later received medical training at Western Reserve Medical College in Cleveland and was accepted as an ABCFM missionary in 1911. He served in Angola with his wife, Mary, until 1917 (Tucker, *Tucker Treasury*, 112). *Missionary Herald* profiled Moffatt in "To West Africa" in August 1911.

Neipp, Fredericka Heinrich. Born March 21, 1870, in Bergzabern, Rheinland Pfalz, Germany, Fredericka Heinrich married Henri Neipp in Benguela in 1899 and served briefly in the mission of the Philafrican Liberator's League. She joined the ABCFM mission in Bailundu and served in Angola until 1936. Returning to the U.S. because of ill health, she died in Wellesley, MA, October 23, 1936.

Neipp, Henri A. Born July 1, 1874, in Neuchâtel, Switzerland, Henri Neipp came to the U.S. in 1894 and studied at Gordon Bible College in Boston. In 1898 he went to Angola to join Héli Chatelain's Philafrican Liberators' League Mission. He rather quickly left Chatelain's mission and joined the ABCFM station at Bailundu. Known for his manual skills, he was the inventor of the "bush car," a conveyance with one wheel that Umbundu carriers could move much more quickly than a *tepoia*. He served in Angola until 1941 (Henderson, *Church in Angola*, 60; Tucker, *Tucker Treasury*, 112–13).

Redick, Emma Cecilia. Born August 19, 1872, in Galion, OH, Emma Redick graduated from Mansfield (Ohio) High School and studied at Oberlin College. She taught at Tougaloo University (an AMA institution in MS) for five years before going to Angola in 1900. Assigned to the Ocileso (Chilesso) station, she served in Angola until 1940. She died in Corunna, MI, in 1959 (WBMI, *Miss Emma Redick, Ochileso, Africa*).

Sanders, Sarah Bell. Born July 10, 1862, in Radrum, County Monaghan, Ireland, Sarah Bell studied at Oberlin College and went to Angola in 1887. She and William H. Sanders married in Angola in 1893. Assigned to the Kamundongo station, she was a close colleague of Nellie Arnott. She was in charge of the ABCFM printing press in Angola and spent much of her time supervising the printing of Umbundu translations of Bible books, hymns, and other materials. She served in Angola until 1930 and died in Wilmington, DE, in 1959 (Tucker, *Tucker Treasury*, 185).

Sanders, William Henry. Born March 2, 1856, in Tillipally, Jaffna, Ceylon (Sri Lanka), where his father, Rev. Marshall D. Sanders, and mother were ABCFM missionaries, William Sanders graduated from Williams College (1877) and the Theological Institute of Connecticut (1880). One of the first three ABCFM missionaries in Angola, he married his colleague Mary Jane Mawhir in Angola in 1882. After her death

Appendix 2

Figure 18: Dr. and Mrs. Sanders, Marshall and Danforth, 1912. Coutesy of The Bancroft Library, University of California, Berkeley.

in 1891, he married Sarah Bell Sanders. Assigned to the Kamundongo station, he served in Angola until 1930. He was known for developing an Umbundu Vocabulary. He died in 1947 at Wilmington, DE. His "Reminiscences" of Angola are in the ABCFM papers in the Houghton Library at Harvard University, as is a collection of letters written by Minnie (Mary Jane) Mawhir Sanders (Tucker, *Tucker Treasury*, 109).

Stimpson, Sarah. Born in Mittineague (West Springfield), MA, December 6, 1865, Sarah Stimpson studied at the Chicago (Moody) Bible Institute. Prior to going to Angola, she taught in Meridian, MS, in an American Missionary Association (AMA) School, where she met Nellie Arnott. Stimpson went to the Kamundongo station in Angola in 1898 and urged Arnott to join her there. She left Angola in 1918 and died in Boston in January 1919.

Stover, Bertha Bennett Dodge. Born February 4, 1852, in Milton, IL, Bertha Dodge married Wesley Stover in 1880 and went to Angola in 1882. The Stovers were among the earliest missionaries at the first ABCFM station in Angola, Bailundu. She left service in Angola in 1920 and died in Claremont, CA, in 1951.

Stover, Helen Hurlburt. Daughter of Bertha and Wesley M. Stover, Helen Stover was born at Benguela, Angola, on May 6, 1883. She studied at Oberlin College and graduated from the Baptist Hospital Training School for Nurses in Chicago. After graduation she joined her parents at the Bailundu station (1908), where she ran the dispensary. She left Angola in 1920 with her parents and died in Claremont, CA, in 1960.

Stover, Wesley Maier. Born November 28, 1850, in York, PA, Wesley Stover was a graduate of Oberlin College (1878) and Oberlin Theological Seminary (1881). He married Bertha B. Dodge in 1880, and they went to the recently-established Bailundu station in Angola in 1882. The Portuguese believed that he had helped the Umbundu cause in the Bailundu Revolt of 1902 and, when he went on furlough to the U.S. several years later, he was forbidden to rejoin the mission. After the intervention of the U.S. Ambassador to Portugal, he was allowed to return in 1910. Stover translated many works into Umbundu. He left Foreign Service in 1920 and died in Claremont, CA, in 1922 (Tucker, *Tucker Treasury*, 110).

Tucker, John Taylor. Born in Fremington, Devon, England, John Tucker was educated at Congregational College in Montreal. Sent to Angola under the auspices of the Canadian Congregationalists, he arrived there in 1913 with his wife, Mabel. After Mabel Tucker's death in 1920, he married his colleague Leona Stukey in 1922. He was first principal of the Currie Institute at Dondi. He led in the formation of the Aliança Evangélica de Angola and by 1949 was representative to the Portuguese government for all of the Protestant missions in Angola. Tucker died in 1958. He wrote extensively about his years in Angola, including *Currie of Chissamba*; *Angola: Land of the Blacksmith Prince*; *Drums in the Darkness*; and *A Tucker Treasury: Reminiscences and Stories of Angola, 1883–1958*. Personal information is in *A Tucker Treasury*, and a biographical sketch by Norman E. Thomas is in Anderson, *Biographical Dictionary of Christian Missions*, 683. A collection of Tucker's correspondence and research material is in the United Church of Canada Archives at Victoria University, Toronto.

Webster, Marion Murchie. Born November 6, 1863, in Walton, Huron County, Ontario, Marion Murchie studied at Northwestern College, Naperville, IL. In 1887 she married Ardell Henry Webster, M.D., and they immediately left for Angola. Dr. Webster died in Benguela in 1889. Marion Webster chose to continue her work at the Bailundu station. She became the first Dean of Means Memorial School for Girls when dormitories were constructed in 1916–1917 on land adjoining Currie Institute. She left Angolan service in 1933 and died in Los Angeles in 1952 (Tucker, *Tucker Treasury*, 199).

Wellman, Frederick Creighton, M.D. Born in Fredonia, KS, January 3, 1871, Frederick Wellman graduated from Chicago Theological Seminary in 1895 and from Kansas City Medical College. He went to Angola in 1896. With Merlin Ennis, he founded the Sacikela mission station in the Ciyaka district. Official ABCFM records state that he was released from service in 1909 due to ill health. John Tucker, however, reports that he was released because he "strayed from the way" and left his wife (*Tucker Treasury*, 112). Wellman himself claims that he left Angola because of disagreements with mission staff, whom he characterizes as a "set of American puritans" based on their opposition to Umbundu customs such as the drinking of alcoholic beverages and polygyny (*Life Is Too Short*, 62-70). Wellman returned to the U.S., where he divorced Lydia Wellman. He lived a colorful life after changing his name to Cyril Kay-Scott. He was the partner of novelist Evelyn Scott. He died in 1960. For information about his relationship with Evelyn Scott, see http://www.lib.utk.edu/spcoll/online/texdisp.htm. His rather self-serving autobiography, *Life Is Too Short*, was published under the name C. Kay-Scott.

Wellman, Lydia Isely. Born in St. Joseph, MO, May 19, 1869, Lydia Isley studied at Kingfisher College and Chicago (Moody) Bible Institute, marrying Frederick C. Wellman in 1894. They departed for Angola in 1896. She returned to the U.S. and was released from service in 1909. She and Frederick Wellman were the parents of novelists Paul and Manly Wade Wellman. She died in Wichita, KS, in 1948.

Woodside, Emma Dreisbach. Born in Circleville, OH, November 5, 1861, Emma Dreisbach studied at Northwestern College in Illinois and married Thomas W. Woodside in 1882. They went to Angola in 1888, serving at first at the Bailundu station and later at Ocileso (Chilesso). She left Angola in 1919 and died in Hudson, IL, in 1951. Thomas and Emma Woodside's daughter Mabel served in Angola as well (1912–1917); she married her mission colleague Dr. Fred Stokey in 1913 and died in 1917 (Tucker, *Tucker Treasury*, 62).

Woodside, Thomas W. Born December 25, 1852, in Brookville, Ogle County, IL, Thomas Woodside graduated from Northwestern College, Naperville, IL, in 1878 and from Union Biblical Institute in 1880. He went to the Bailundu station in Angola in 1888. During Arnott's time in Angola, he was at Ocileso (Chilesso). Though he did not have formal training, he served as the dentist for Angola mission stations according to Arnott's diaries. He left the field in 1919 due to ill health and died in Winter Park, FL, in 1929.

Appendix 3
Image Citations and
Explanatory Context

Given their complex contexts of creation, circulation, and preservation, each of the illustrations in this book of Nellie Arnott's public writing could easily merit its own detailed analysis.[1] Most of the images we selected for this edition came from the elaborate scrapbooks and photo albums Arnott used to memorialize her experience as a foreign missionary. Through Arnott's careful thematic sequencing of pictures and other materials, we can see that she continued to relish composing texts about her experience. From numerous chronological markers (such as handwritten captions on photos of retired missionaries with whom she had served decades earlier), we can infer that much of Arnott's scrapbook-making actually occurred many years after her teaching career in Angola. Her notations also indicate that one audience she envisioned for these texts was her grandchildren, as some captions reference them via labels of Arnott herself as "grandma."

Overall, the social intervention Arnott aspired to through her scrapbook-keeping built upon and extended the writing she had done for larger, more public audiences during her foreign mission service. Taken together, as recent work by scholars such as Ellen Gruber Garvey have shown, such multifaceted personal compositions are certainly deserving of analyses far more sustained than we can carry out in our current project, which has focused on Arnott's earlier, more "professional" writing.[2] Nonetheless, in the comments below about each of this book's illustrations, we hope to characterize the cultural context behind these images as well as to suggest the rich possibilities for additional research based in Arnott's personal compositions.

Front Cover

Arnott penciled in a note, "Grandma's station, 1905–1912," below this photo from one of her albums. Likely clipped from a mission magazine, the image also carries a printed caption: "Group of Kamundongo church members, West Central Africa," which Arnott hand-dated "1905." Citation: Fig. 10 verso (left center). Kamundongo Church Members. Vol. I Scrapbook. *Nellie Jane Arnott Darling Papers, 1905–1943*. The Bancroft Library, University of California, Berkeley, BANC MSS 92/901z, box 2 v. 1.

Figure 1, Introduction

This page from one of Arnott's albums focuses on Kamundongo, her primary mission station. According to Arnott's handwritten captions, the individual images here include "Kamundongo Church in process of building—1905" (top left); "Ombambi—a deer in the garden" and "Ombambi—the pet" (bottom left); "Church and schoolhouse, Kamundongo" (center); and "Lucy" and "Nellie," Anglicized names for two of Arnott's students, (top right). Nellie was Arnott's namesake, as she noted in her diary entry of July 16, 1905. (Arnott acquired her own Umbundu nickname that she translated as "teacher Nellie.") As an example of how these images raise as many questions as they answer, we might ask how young "Nellie" acquired and used the doll she holds here and what she might tell us today about Arnott's activities as a mission teacher. Citation: Fig. 24 recto. Six Photographs of Kamundongo. Photograph Album. *Nellie Jane Arnott Darling Papers, 1905–1943*. The Bancroft Library, University of California, Berkeley, BANC MSS 92/901z, box 3.

Figure 2, Introduction

Arnott has labeled this photograph "Nellie Arnott, Grandma, 1905-1912." The dates mark her time in Angola. In designating herself as both "Nellie Arnott" and "Grandma," she links her term of service to both her maiden name and her later role as a grandmother. Nellie Arnott (who does not dub herself "Mrs. Paul Darling" here) seems to want to ensure her grandchildren's appreciation of this aspect of her past. Also noteworthy is Arnott's decision not to identify others in this photograph. Postcolonial critics often remark on the tendency in colonial discourse to leave indigenous people unnamed. Here, how-

Appendix 3 291

ever, Arnott also renders her missionary colleague Sarah Stimpson anonymous, though we can deduce Stimpson's identity from other records, including photos elsewhere in Arnott's scrapbooks. Citation: Fig. 21 recto. Nellie Arnott Grandma 1905-1912. Photograph Album. *Nellie Jane Arnott Darling Papers, 1905–1943*. The Bancroft Library, University of California, Berkeley, BANC MSS 92/901z, box 3.

Figure 3, Chapter 1

Arnott's careful recording of "Now I Lay Me Down to Sleep, in Umbundu" was included in one of her letters to her grandchildren. Arnott explained that she learned the prayer as a child while visiting her grandparents and taught it to her "two little brothers Ed and Jimmie." She continued, "[L]ater on [I] went to Africa and taught the Umbundu children the prayer that all children love." Citation: Letter #1, Nellie A. Darling to Mary and Truman, n.d. Personal collection of Mary Darling Caris, San Francisco, CA.

Figure 4, Chapter 1

Based on a very similar image of Nellie Arnott, which she hand-dated 1898, this photo was probably made at the same time (shortly before the death of James Arnott on December 31, 1898). It shows Arnott's sister Myrtle, seated in front; Arnott seated between her parents, Philander and Martha Arnott; and her youngest brother Charles standing at left. Arnott's brother standing at right is likely Edward, with James ("Jimmie") seated at the right. Citation: Family Photograph. Personal Collection of Mary Darling Caris, San Francisco, CA.

Figure 5, Chapter 2

These maps and a postcard, pasted on the second page of Arnott's photo album, she likely intended to provide geographic information for her grandchildren. The top left map depicts the regions of southern Africa, with Arnott's mission station at Kamundongo designated in Bihé. The right top map shows American Board stations in Angola and was apparently produced after the mid-1920s, when the Kamundongo station (and the Cisamba station) came under the management of the United Church of Canada. The ABCFM established its mission station at Galangue in 1923; work in the coastal city of Lobito also began in the early 1920s (Henderson, *Church in Angola*, 79–80, 82–83). The hand-drawn map in the lower right provides a high level of detail, designating Catholic and Protestant mission stations, major towns, Portuguese forts, a "waggon road" and the caravan route (which Arnott and Reverend and Mrs. Sanders had followed on their journey inland from Benguela in 1905). The postcard, mailed from Toronto in 1937, was from Arnott's colleague Elizabeth Campbell, who had recently retired from Angola service. In her message, Campbell mentions "seeing Miss [Helen] Melville often." Arnott's scrapbook includes a number of similar postcards suggesting that she, like Elizabeth Campbell, cherished her friendships with mission colleagues and remained in touch with them long after she married Paul Darling. Citation: Page 2. Maps and Postcard of Africa. Photograph Album. *Nellie Jane Arnott Darling Papers, 1905–1943*. The Bancroft Library, University of California, Berkeley, BANC MSS 92/901z, box 3.

Figure 6, Chapter 2

Arnott's labels for these photos of the Woman's Conference at Bailundu in 1911 indicate that they depict "The Deputation's Welcome" (top left) as well as Umbundu delegates (top right) and missionary delegates (bottom right). Arnott has written on her own picture (second from left, top row of missionary photo) "Ondon Nele." The term "ondon" (usually spelled *ondona* or *ndona*) was generally used as a title for a white female teacher. "Nele" was the Umbundu spelling of Nellie. For a photo of missionary delegates to the 1907 Woman's Conference, see Chapter 4. Citation: Page 30. Photographs of delegates at Bailundu. Photograph Album. *Nellie Jane Arnott Darling Papers, 1905–1943*. The Bancroft Library, University of California, Berkeley, BANC MSS 92/901z, box 3.

Figure 7, Chapter 3

Nellie Arnott used this "duplicating book" to compose her first set of circular letters for mission supporters at home in the U.S. She has written a note at the top of the tablet naming its contents "Letters Nos. 1, 2, 3, 4, 5," and she also lists the dates for the individual letters as follows: "1. May 3, 1905; 2. May 13, 1905; 3. June 6, 1905; 4. June 22, 1905; 5. July 11, 1905." An additional notation near the bottom of the tablet designates these pieces as "Letters written by Nellie J. Arnott who became Mrs. Paul L. Darling May 13, 1913 and became *Grandma*

Appendix 3 293

Darling Mar. 21, 1930." (Other records, including her marriage license and her diary, give a different date—May 1—for Arnott's wedding.) Citation: Standard Series Duplicating Book, Cover. *Nellie Jane Arnott Darling Papers, 1905–1943*. The Bancroft Library, University of California, Berkeley, BANC MSS 92/901z, box 1.

Figure 8, Chapter 3

This picture of Nellie Arnott (left) in a tepoia and Mrs. Elisabeth Ennis on a bush-cart (sometimes called a "bush-car") was originally published in a mission magazine and later saved in Arnott's photo album. On a duplicate photo preserved in one of Arnott's scrapbooks (vol. 1, box 2), she dated the picture 1910 and noted that it was made in front of the gate to her yard. Arnott experimented with several modes of transportation for travel within Angola and by the time she went on furlough could use the new railroad for much of her trek back to the coast from the interior. Most of her travel during her service involved walking, particularly to outstations, though for some vacation trips she and her colleagues went in groups with carriers toting the supplies. Citation: Page 44 top left. Two modes of travel 1909. Photograph Album. *Nellie Jane Arnott Darling Papers, 1905–1943*. The Bancroft Library, University of California, Berkeley, BANC MSS 92/901z, box 3.

Figure 9, Chapter 3

This photograph of Arnott was taken not long before the initial journey to her overseas posting and was published with a 1905 *Missionary Herald* article ("New Recruit for Africa," 267) announcing her departure for Angola. The ABCFM relied on images like this one to help cultivate supporters' close identification with particular missionaries as familiar friends. This photograph also appeared with an article titled "Kamundongo, West Central Africa," published in *Mission Studies* (April 1906); Arnott pasted that article in her scrapbook with the handwritten notation "Grandma Darling to Mary & Truman." Citation: "Miss Nellie J. Arnott." Ideal Scrapbook. *Nellie Jane Arnott Darling Papers*, 1905–1943. The Bancroft Library, University of California, Berkeley, BANC MSS 92/901z, box 2 v. 2.

Figure 10, Chapter 4

These four photos illustrate Umbundu life in the Chilesso (Ocileso) region of Andulu. In the bottom right photo, two women are standing in front of a thatched-roof structure. On their heads they carry large baskets of corn from their fields; the women would have grown the corn as well as made the baskets. (Cushman, *Missionary Doctor*, 141–42, contains detailed information on the preparation of grass for baskets and procedures for weaving them.) The woman on the right is carrying a child who is secured on her back by a long length of cloth. The top left photo, Arnott noted, depicts "An Ondulu [Andulu] Chief and His Family." The bottom left shows women hulling the corn and is very similar to the one of Cipuku and Nakalu included in Chapter 6. Corn that had been soaked overnight was pounded in a wooden mortar with a long wooden pestle. Missionary Mary Floyd Cushman explained that two women often pounded together and that the process had to be done very skillfully "so as not to break up the kernels, but only to get the hulls off," which then had to be "winnowed out . . . on a reed tray" (Cushman, *Missionary Doctor*, 76). The top right photo (of very poor quality) pictures women "Pounding on the Rocks," according to Arnott's note, that is, performing the final step of preparing the corn, taking the hulled kernels and pounding them into meal to be used in cooking. Citation: Fig. 44 recto. Four Photographs of Cilesso. Photograph Album. *Nellie Jane Arnott Darling Papers, 1905–1943*. The Bancroft Library, University of California, Berkeley, BANC MSS 92/901z, box 3.

Figure 11, Chapter 5

The Woman's Conference in 1907 was held at the Plymouth Brethren mission station at Ohualondo. Arnott is pictured standing on the top row, second from the right. The woman seated in the middle is likely Plymouth Brethren missionary Elizabeth Murrain. Arnott also included in her album a photo of the Umbundu delegates to this conference. Citation: Top left image from Fig. 46 recto (right). Missionary delegates at Ohualondo conference. Photograph Album. *Nellie Jane Arnott Darling Papers, 1905–1943*. The Bancroft Library, University of California, Berkeley, BANC MSS 92/901z, box 3.

Figure 12, Chapter 5

This set of photos depicts a typical camp where ABCFM missionaries stayed while traveling between stations or visiting rural settlements. Arnott labels the photos with phrases such as "An Afternoon in Camp"

Appendix 3 295

(second from left, top). Though individuals are difficult to distinguish in the small images, Arnott is likely the woman pictured in the middle of this photo. Other scenes show activities such as "Evening Meal in Camp." Arnott appears to be the left of the two women in this photo. In "Awaiting the Loads" (middle photo, bottom row), there is a large banner, such as the missionaries might have used at their meetings to illustrate a Bible story. Fig. 20 recto. Ten Photographs of Camping Scenes, 1911. Photograph Album. *Nellie Jane Arnott Darling Papers, 1905–1943*. The Bancroft Library, University of California, Berkeley, BANC MSS 92/901z, box 3.

Figure 13, Chapter 6

This copy of the marriage license of Nellie Arnott and Paul Darling indicates that Arnott's friend Reverend George Atkinson performed the ceremony, which was held at her parents' home in Campbell, CA, on May 1, 1913. Arnott's diary notes that the house was "well-decorated" and that guests included, in addition to her parents, her sister Myrtle, Paul Darling's mother, and family friend Leila Dodson (Diary, May 1, 1913). Citation: Marriage License of Nellie J. Arnott and Paul L. Darling, May 1, 1913. Personal Collection of Mary Darling Caris, San Francisco, CA.

Figure 14, Chapter 6

Arnott's diaries and public writings often contained information about Cipuku and her family. In this photo, Cipuku and her sister Nakalu are pounding corn to remove hulls from the kernels. (See discussion of Figure 10 above.) Arnott's reference to them as "My girls" may have been intended to signal her close relationship to them as teacher and friend. After Arnott left Angola, Cipuku had a daughter that she and her husband Sakalumbu named "Nele" in Arnott's honor. Arnott recorded in her diary (Dec. 29, 1913) that, sadly, the baby lived only a few weeks. (See also Chapter 2.) Citation: Bottom right image of Fig. 10 verso. Kamundongo Scenes. Vol. I Scrapbook. *Nellie Jane Arnott Darling Papers, 1905–1943*. The Bancroft Library, University of California, Berkeley, BANC MSS 92/901z, box 2 v. 1.

Figure 15, Chapter 6

This Christmas card from Means School (from one of Arnott's albums) portrays students in white dresses, posed in a neat line with their books. The notation, "Angola . . . Happy Girlhood," may not be Arnott's handwriting, but she would probably have shared the statement's sentiment. Though Means School followed a Western model of education critiqued by some scholars today, Arnott would have affirmed its goal of teaching young women to become role models in Angola's Christian communities and would have been proud of her contributions to its founding. Citation: Fig. 32 recto. "Christmas Card 1937." Photograph Album. *Nellie Jane Arnott Darling Papers, 1905–1943*. The Bancroft Library, University of California, Berkeley, BANC MSS 92/901z, box 3.

Figure 16, Appendix 1

The printing press at Arnott's mission station played a key part in efforts to Christianize the local population. Besides the ambitious project of creating a vocabulary of English/Umbundu words, publications included this dual-language hymnal. Nellie Arnott shared with many of her Angolan students a love of and a talent for singing hymns. The Portuguese government would eventually mandate that instruction in mission schools be given in that European language rather than in Umbundu. Arnott reported in her diary (April 7, 1907) that she "spent the evening at Mr. Sanders['s] folding on the hymn book"; on June 2 she noted that the "hymn books are just finished so now we will have the covers to put on." Citation: English-Umbundu Hymnal. *Nellie Jane Arnott Darling Papers, 1905–1943*. The Bancroft Library, University of California, Berkeley, BANC MSS 92/901z, box 2.

Figure 17, Appendix 2

This page from one of Arnott's albums blends photographs of mission houses in Bailundu with images of missionaries who served there. Arnott's handwritten captions identify the structure at upper left as "Mrs. Bell's house" in 1909 and the one at upper right as "Mrs. Webster's house" in 1911. She labels the photos of missionaries as follows, left to right: the Bell family, Mrs. Stover, Helen Stover (Mrs. Stover's daughter), and Mrs. Webster. Helen Stover is shown with a child identified elsewhere in one of Arnott's scrapbooks as Madelina

Bonga. Citation: Page 34. Mr. and Mrs. Bell and Mrs. Stover. Photograph Album. *Nellie Jane Arnott Darling Papers, 1905–1943.* The Bancroft Library, University of California, Berkeley, BANC MSS 92/901z, box 3.

Figure 18, Appendix 2

Although she frequently interacted with other Protestant missionaries serving in her region, the team members at Kamundongo were Arnott's closest colleagues. Here pictured are Reverend and Mrs. Sanders, who accompanied Arnott on her initial journey to Angola, and their two children, Marshall and Danforth, who (as typical in missionaries' families) spent many years away from their parents while being educated in the U.S. Arnott's handwritten notation dates the photo from 1912, though it may have been taken in the early 1900s. Citation: Dr. and Mrs. Sanders, 1912. Fig. 2 verso. Photograph Album. *Nellie Jane Arnott Darling Papers, 1905–1943.* The Bancroft Library, University of California, Berkeley, BANC MSS 92/901z, box 3.

Notes

1. For an example of the kind of productive analysis that images associated with colonial contexts can generate, see the opening discussion of Chapter 2, "Culture and Rule: Theories of Colonial Discourse," in Nicholas Thomas's *Colonialism's Culture,* 33–37.

2. On the social role of scrapbook making and its longstanding appeal, see Ellen Gruber Garvey, "Scizzoring and Scrapbooks: Nineteenth-Century Reading, Remaking, and Recirculating," in *New Media, 1740–1915,* ed. Lisa Gitelman and Geoffrey B. Pingree, 207–28 (Cambridge, MA: MIT Press, 2003). See also Garvey's "Imitation is the Sincerest Form of Appropriation," *Common-place* 7, no. 3 (April 2007). http://www.common-place.org/vol-07/no-03/garvey/.

Bibliography

Manuscript Collections, Family Papers and Institutional Records

American Board of Commissioners for Foreign Missions Archives (ABC 1–91). Houghton Library, Harvard Univ. By permission of the Houghton Library, Harvard Univ. and by Wider Church Ministries of the United Church of Christ. Cited after the first reference as ABCFM Archives.

American Board of Commissioners for Foreign Missions. Papers of the American Board of Commissioners for Foreign Missions. Unit 1–6 [microform]. (Woodbridge CT: Research Publications, 1983–1985). Pitts Theology Library, Emory Univ. Originals held at Houghton Library; referenced in this edition by permission of the Houghton Library, Harvard Univ. and by Wider Church Ministries of the United Church of Christ. Cited after the first reference as ABCFM Papers.

American Board of Commissioners for Foreign Missions. *Papers of the American Board of Commissioners for Foreign Missions: Documents Administered by the Houghton Library of Harvard University; Also includes individual reel units from 1-6; Guide to the Microfilm Collection.* Woodbridge, CT: Research Publications International, 1994.

Ancestry.com. http://www.ancestrylibrary.com/search/ for Darling, Paul L. (birthplace Iowa), Darling, Paul L. [Jr.] (birthplace California) and Jas. R. Patten (birthplace Maine).

Caris, Mary Darling. Private Family Papers.

Chickasaw County, Iowa. Death Index and Record Book, 1898.

—. *Atlas of Chickasaw County, Iowa, Containing Maps, Plats of the Townships* ..., 1892.

—. Town Lot Deed and Mortgage Records, 1892–1902.

Chickasaw County Genealogical Society, "School Censuses: New Hampton, 1900–1901," 1998.

Clerk's Record Book, 1866–1913, First Congregational Church, Nashua, Iowa.

Darling, Nellie Jane Arnott Papers, 1905–1943. BANC MSS 92/901 z. Bancroft Library, Univ. of California, Berkeley. Cited after the first reference as NJADP.

Darling, Nellie Jane. Death Certificate. Los Angeles (CA) County, 7069–412.

Darling, Truman Christopher, Private Family Papers.

Grillo, John L. and Ruth Tonkiss Cameron, "Finding Aid for World Missionary Conference Records Edinburgh, 1910." Missionary Research Library Archives, Section 12, Burke Library Archives, Union Theological Seminary, New York.

Pond, C. N. (Chauncey Northrop), 1841–1920. Papers, 1852–1920, OCA 30/42, Series I: Correspondence of Foreign Missionaries, Collected and Received by Chauncey N. Pond, Oberlin College Archives.

Arnott's Writings Published in this Edition

Arnott, Nellie J. "Africa." *Life and Light for Woman*, February 1909, 93–94.

—. "The Beginning of a Boarding School in West Central Africa." *Mission Studies: Woman's Work in Foreign Lands*, August 1911, 240–41.

—. "Benguella." *Mission Studies: Woman's Work in Foreign Lands*, February 1906, 48–50.

—. [Circular Letter #1; May 3, 1905], in "Letters Written by Nellie J. Arnott, Who Became Mrs. Paul L. Darling, May 13, 1913." Standard Series Duplicating Book. In NJADP.

—. [Circular Letter #2; May 13, 1905], in "Letters Written by Nellie J. Arnott, Who Became Mrs. Paul L. Darling, May 13, 1913." Standard Series Duplicating Book. In NJADP.

—. [Circular Letter #3; June 6, 1905], in "Letters Written by Nellie J. Arnott, Who Became Mrs. Paul L. Darling, May 13, 1913." Standard Series Duplicating Book. In NJADP.

—. [Circular Letter #4; June 22, 1905], in "Letters Written by Nellie J. Arnott, Who Became Mrs. Paul L. Darling, May 13, 1913." Standard Series Duplicating Book. In NJADP.

—. [Circular Letter #5; July 11, 1905 and August 10, 1905], in "Letters Written by Nellie J. Arnott, Who Became Mrs. Paul L. Darling, May 13, 1913." Standard Series Duplicating Book. In NJADP.

—. [Circular Letter #6]. A.B.C.F.M., Benguella, Africa, August 5, 1910, in Ideal Scrapbook. In NJADP.

—. [Circular Letter #7]. Dear Friends, March 22, 1911, C.N. (Chauncey Northrop) Pond Papers, 1852–1920, OCA 30/42, Series I: Correspondence of Foreign Missionaries, Collected and Received by Chauncey N. Pond, Oberlin College Archives.

—. [Circular Letter #8]. Kamundongo, Saturday. Febry 17–1912, in "Loose Letters and Other Items from Scrapbook, 1910–1943." In NJADP.

—. [Circular Letter #9]. 383 Burke St., Youngstown, Ohio [September 17, 1912], in "Loose Letters and Other Items from Scrapbook, 1910–1943." In NJADP.

—. [Circular Letter #10]. To the Friends of Mrs. Jane C. Means [1912–1913], in Ideal Scrapbook. In NJADP. Similarly-worded copy in ABCFM Papers, 15.1: Western Africa, Vol. 19, African Mission, 1910–1919, Letters, A-M, Part I, A-E, reel 168, Pitts Theological Library, Emory Univ.

—. "Extracts from a Letter from Miss Nellie J. Arnott, Dated Bailundu, Africa, May 13, 1910." *Life and Light for Woman*, September 1910, 430–31.

—. "A Glimpse at an African School." *Life and Light for Woman*, March 1910, 143–44.

—. "House Building in Africa." *Mission Studies: Woman's Work in Foreign Lands*, August 1910, 248–49.

—. "Inland in a Tepoia." *Life and Light for Woman*, March 1906, 137–41.

—. "Kamundongo. No II." *Mission Studies: Woman's Work in Foreign Lands*, May 1906, 134–36.

—. "Kamundongo and Vicinity." *Mission Studies: Woman's Work in Foreign Lands*, May 1910, 144–45.

—. "Kamundongo, West Central Africa." *Mission Studies: Woman's Work in Foreign Lands*, April 1906, 103–05.

—. Letter to Enoch F. Bell, December 28, 1912. ABCFM Papers, 15.1: Western Africa, Vol. 19, Africa Mission, 1910–1919, Letters A-M, Part I, A-E, reel 168, Pitts Theological Library, Emory Univ.

—. Letter to Enoch F. Bell, February 13, 1913. ABCFM Papers, 15.1: Western Africa, Vol. 19, Africa Mission, 1910–1919, Letters A-M, Part I, A-E, reel 168, Pitts Theological Library, Emory Univ.

—. Letter to Enoch F. Bell, April 5, 1913. ABCFM papers, 15.1: Western Africa, Vol. 19, Africa Mission, 1910–1919, Letters A-M, Part I, A-E, reel 168, Pitts Theological Library, Emory Univ.

—. Letter to James L. Barton, Feb. 25, 1909. ABCFM Papers, 15.1, Unit 2, Vol. 15, West Central Africa, 1900–1909, Documents and Letters, A-E, reel 164, Pitts Theological Library, Emory Univ.

—. Letter to James L. Barton, October 5, 1909. ABCFM Papers, 15.1, Western Africa, Vol. 15, West Central Africa, 1900–1909, Vol. 2, Documents and Letters, A-E, reel 164. Pitts Theological Library, Emory Univ.

—. Letter to James L. Barton. September 7, 1912. ABCFM Papers, 15.1: Western Africa, Vol. 19, Africa Mission, 1910–1919, Letters A-M, Part I, A-E, reel 168, Pitts Theological Library, Emory Univ.

—. Letter to James L. Barton, September 26, 1912. ABCFM Papers, 15.1: Western Africa, Vol. 19, Africa Mission, 1910–1919, Vol. 2, Letters A-M, Part I, A-E, reel 168, Pitts Theological Library, Emory Univ.

—. Letter to James L. Barton, December 9, 1912. ABCFM Papers, 15.1: Western Africa Vol. 19, Africa Mission, 1910–1919, Letters A-M; Part I, A-E, reel 168, Pitts Theological Library, Emory Univ.

—. Letter to James L. Barton, March 7, 1913. ABCFM Papers, 15.1: Western Africa, Vol. 19, Africa Mission, 1910–1919, Letters A-M, Part I, A-E, reel 168, Pitts Theological Library, Emory Univ.

—. Letter to Judson Smith, October 4, 1905. ABCFM Papers, 15.1, Unit 2, Vol. 15: West Central Africa, 1900–1909, Documents and Letters, A-E, reel 164, Pitts Theological Library, Emory Univ.

—. "Letter from Miss Arnott." *Life and Light for Woman*, September 1909, 430–31.

—. "A Letter from Miss Nellie J. Arnott, Kamundongo, January 27, 1908, To the Children of the Interior." *Mission Studies*, October 1908, 111–13.

—. "Miss Nellie Arnott Writes from Kamundongo, Africa, September 3, 1908." *Life and Light for Woman*, February 1909, 93–94.

—. "Miss Nellie J. Arnott, Benguella, Africa." [Sub-section in "A Missionary Symposium".] *Life and Light for Woman*, April 1911, 189–90.

—. "News from Kamundongo." *Mission Studies: Woman's Work in Foreign Lands*, May 1908, 106–07.

—. "A Trip to an African Woman's Conference." *Mission Studies: Woman's Work in Foreign Lands*, January 1908, 22–23.

—. "A Trip to the Woman's Conference in the West Central Africa Mission." *Life and Light for Woman*, January 1908, 43–45.

—. "A Visit to an African Village." *Mission Studies: Woman's Work in Foreign Lands*, May 1913, 150–51.

—. "West Central African Mission—Fresh Interest." *Missionary Herald*, June 1909, 261.

—. "What it Means in Africa to the mother and child to be without the Christ Child," in Ideal Scrapbook, [1912–13?]. In NJADP.

Darling, Nellie Arnott. "Chief Kanjundu's Death." *Mission Studies: Woman's Work in Foreign Lands*, April 1914, 118–19.

Darling, Mrs. Nellie Arnott. "The Need of a Girls' Boarding School in West Central Africa." *Mission Studies: Woman's Work in Foreign Lands*, April 1914, 119–21.

—. "A Visit to an African Village, Continued." *Mission Studies: Woman's Work in Foreign Lands*, June 1913, 184-86.

Interviews

Abaidoo, Samuel. Interview by Ann Pullen and Sarah Robbins, June 25, 2008.

Ashley, Kathleen Henderson. Interview by Ann Pullen and Sarah Robbins, February 3, 2005.

Caris, Mary. Interview by Sarah Robbins, November 23, 2003.
Darling, Christopher [Truman]. Interview by Sarah Robbins, November 22, 2003.
Henderson, Muriel (Ki). Interview by Sarah Robbins and Ann Pullen, August 31, 2005.
Henderson-James, Nancy. Interview by Sarah Robbins and Ann Pullen, August 31, 2005.
Myers-Brown, Joyce. Interview by Ann Pullen, September 21, 2005.

ADDITIONAL WORKS CITED OR CONSULTED

"Additional Locals." *Nashua* (IA) *Reporter.* April 5, 1900, 6. http://www.ancestry.com/
Adeney, Miriam. "Do Missions Raise or Lower the Status of Women? Conflicting Reports from Africa." In Robert, *Gospel Bearers, Gender Barriers,* 211–22.
"Africa: Folks and Famine in Angola." *Missionary Herald,* June 1916, 288.
"Africa: He Likes His Job." *Missionary Herald,* August 1916, 369–70.
"Africa: Two by Two in Kamundongo." *Missionary Herald,* May 1915, 238–39.
"An African Pastor and His Wife Go to Their New Field." *The Missionary Monthly,* January 1946, 12.
Ajayi, J. F. Ade. *Christian Missions in Nigeria, 1841–1908.* Evanston: Northwestern Univ. Press, 1965.
Alcoff, Linda. "Speaking for Others." In Roof and Wiegman, *Who Can Speak?,* 97–119.
Alexander, Caroline. *One Dry Season: In the Footsteps of Mary Kingsley.* New York: Knopf, 1990.
Allman, Jean, Susan Geiger and Nakanyike Musisi, eds. *Women in African Colonial Histories.* Bloomington: Indiana Univ. Press, 2002.
Anderson, Benedict. *Imagined Communities: Reflections on the Origin and Spread of Nationalism.* London: Verso, 1991.
Anderson, Gerald H., ed. *Biographical Dictionary of Christian Missions.* Grand Rapids: William B. Eerdmans, 1998.
Angola Memorial Scholarship Fund: http://www.angolamsf.org/.
Arnold, David and Robert A. Bickers. "Introduction." In Bickers and Seton, *Missionary Encounters,* 1–10.
Arnot, Frederick Stanley. *Garenganze: Seven Years' Pioneer Mission Work in Central Africa.* London: Hawkins, 1889.
—. "Journey from Natal to Bihé and Benguella." *Proceedings of the Royal Geographical Society and Monthly Record of Geography* 2 (February 1889): 65–82.

Atkinson, Fred W. "The Educational Problem in the Philippines." *The Atlantic Monthly* 89 (March 1902): 360–65.
Ayandele, E. A. *The Missionary Impact on Modern Nigeria: 1842–1914: A Political and Social Analysis*. London: Longman, 1996.
Bassnett, Susan. "Travel Writing and Gender." In Hulme and Youngs, *Cambridge Companion to Travel Writing*, 225–41.
Bays, Daniel H. and Grant Wacker, eds. *The Foreign Missionary Enterprise at Home: Explorations in North American Cultural History*. Tuscaloosa: Univ. of Alabama Press, 2003.
Bebbington, D.W. "Atonement, Sin, and Empire, 1880–1914." In Porter, *The Imperial Horizons of British Protestant Missions*, 14–31.
Bender, Gerald J. *Angola under the Portuguese: The Myth and the Reality*. Trenton, NJ: Africa World, 2004.
Bendroth, Margaret Lamberts and Virginia Lieson Brereton, eds. *Women and Twentieth-Century Protestantism*. Urbana: Univ. of Illinois Press, 2002.
Bhabha, Homi K. *The Location of Culture*. London: Routledge, 1994.
Bickers, Robert A. and Rosemary Seton, eds. *Missionary Encounters: Sources and Issues*. Richmond, Surrey: Curzon, 1996.
Birmingham, David. *Empire in Africa: Angola and Its Neighbors*. Athens: Ohio Univ. Press, 2006.
—. "Themes and Resources of Angolan History." *African Affairs* 73, no. 291 (1974): 188–203.
Blunt, Alison. *Travel, Gender, and Imperialism: Mary Kingsley and West Africa*. New York: Guilford, 1994.
Bowie, Fiona. "The Elusive Christian Family: Missionary Attempts to Define Women's Roles; Case Studies from Cameroon." In Bowie, Kirkwood and Ardener, *Women and Missions*, 145–64.
—. "Introduction: Reclaiming Women's Presence." In Bowie, Kirkwood and Ardener, *Women and Missions*, 1–19.
Bowie, Fiona, Deborah Kirkwood and Shirley Ardener, eds. *Women and Missions: Past and Present. Anthropological and Historical Perceptions*. Providence, RI: Berg, 1993.
Brandt, Deborah. *Literacy in American Lives*. Cambridge: Cambridge Univ. Press, 2001.
Bratton, J. S. "Of England, Home and Duty: The Image of England in Victorian and Edwardian Juvenile Fiction." In MacKenzie, *Imperialism and Popular Culture*, 73–93.
Bridges, Roy. "The Christian Vision and Secular Imperialism: Missionaries, Geography, and the Approach to East Africa, c. 1844–1890." In Robert, *Converting Colonialism*, 43–59.
Bridgman Family Papers. Biographical Profile. Oberlin College Archives. http://www.oberlin.edu/archive/holdings/finding/RG30/SG349/biography.html

Briggs, Laura, Gladys McCormick, and J. T. Way. "Transnationalism: A Category of Analysis." *American Quarterly* 60, no. 3 (September 2008): 625–48.
Bruner, Edward. *Culture on Tour: Ethnographies of Travel*. Chicago: Univ. of Chicago Press, 2005.
Bundy, David. "William Taylor." In Anderson, *Biographical Dictionary of Christian Missions*, 660.
Butler, Judith. *Gender Trouble: Feminism and the Subversion of Identity*. New York: Routledge, 2006.
Byam, Paul. "New Wine in a Very Old Bottle: Canadian Protestant Missionaries as Facilitators of Development in Central Angola 1886–1961." PhD diss., Univ. of Ottawa, 1997.
Cadbury, William A. *Labour in Portuguese West Africa*. 2nd ed. London: G. Routledge and Sons, 1910; New York: Negro Univ. Press, 1969.
Campbell, Mary Baine. "Travel Writing and its Theory." In Hulme and Youngs, *Cambridge Companion to Travel Writing*, 261–78.
Campbell, Miss Elizabeth. "Extracts from a Personal Letter of Miss Elizabeth Campbell of Bailundo, Africa." *Light and Life for Woman*, December 1913, 539–40.
Cayton, Mary Kupiec. "Canonizing Harriet Newell: Women, the Evangelical Press, and the Foreign Mission Movement in New England, 1800-1840." In Reeves-Ellington, Sklar and Shemo, *Competing Kingdoms*, 69–93.
Césaire, Aimé. *Discourse on Colonialism*. Trans. Joan Pinkham. New York: Monthly Review Press, 2000.
—. *Notebook of a Return to the Native Land*. Trans. Clayton Eshleman and Annette Smith. Middleton: Wesleyan Univ. Press, 2001.
Chidester, David. *Savage Systems: Colonialism and Comparative Religions in Southern Africa*. Charlottesville: Univ. Press of Virginia, 1996.
Chikueka, Maria Chela. *Angola Torchbearers*. Toronto: Chela Book Group, 1999.
—. *The Trail of My Life Journey*. Toronto: Chela Book Group, 1999.
"The Children for Whom We Work." *Mission Studies: Woman's Work in Foreign Lands*, February 1908, 36–37.
"Children's Work: Miss Arnott's School." *Mission Studies: Woman's Work in Foreign Lands*, November 1909, 344.
Childs, Gladwyn Murray. *Umbundu Kinship & Character: Being a Description of the Social Structure and Individual Development of the Ovimbundu of Angola, with Observations Concerning the Bearing on the Enterprise of Christian Missions of Certain Phases of the Life and Culture Described*. London: Oxford Univ. Press, 1949.
Chipenda, Eva de Carvalho. *The Visitor: An African Woman's Story of Travel and Discovery*. Risk Book Series. Geneva, Switzerland: World Council of Churches, 1996.

Clark, Francis E. "A Quarter-Century of Christian Endeavor." *Outlook* 82 (January 13, 1906): 80–87.
Clifford, James. *Routes: Travel and Translation in the Late Twentieth Century.* Cambridge, MA: Harvard Univ. Press, 1997.
Coble, Christopher, "The Role of Young People's Societies in the Training of Christian Womanhood (and Manhood), 1880–1910." In Bendroth and Brereton, *Women and Twentieth-CenturyProtestantism,* 74–92.
—. "Where Have All the Young People Gone? The Christian Endeavor Movement and the Training of Protestant Youth, 1881–1918." DTh diss., Harvard Divinity School, 2001.
Comaroff, John L. "Images of Empire, Contests of Conscience: Models of Colonial Domination in South Africa." In Cooper and Stoler, *Tensions of Empire,* 163–97.
Comaroff, John L. and Jean Comaroff. *Of Revelation and Revolution, Vol. II: The Dialectics of Modernity on a South African Frontier.* Chicago: Univ. of Chicago Press, 1997.
Cooper, Frederick. *Colonialism in Question: Theory, Knowledge, History.* Berkeley, Univ. of California Press, 2005.
Cooper, Frederick and Ann Laura Stoler, eds. *Tensions of Empire: Colonial Cultures in a Bourgeois World.* Berkeley: Univ. of California Press, 1997.
Cox, Jeffrey. "Master Narratives of Imperial Missions." In Scott and Griffiths, *Mixed Messages,* 4-18.
"Current Topics." *Mission Studies: Woman's Work in Foreign Lands,* August 1911, 1.
Cushing, Mrs. Otis. "What the Children are Doing." *Mission Studies: Woman's Work in Foreign Lands,* March 1912, 74–75.
Cushman, Mary Floyd, M. D. *Missionary Doctor: The Story of Twenty Years in Africa.* New York: Harper & Brothers, 1944.
Davis, Grace T. *Neighbors in Christ: Fifty-Eight Years of World Service by the Woman's Board of Missions of the Interior.* Chicago: Woman's Board of Missions of the Interior, 1926.
De Gruchy, John W. "'Who Did They Think They Were?': Some Reflections from a Theologian on Grand Narratives and Identity in the History of Missions." In Porter, *The Imperial Horizons of British Protestant Missions,* 213–25.
Depestre, René and Aimé Césaire, "An Interview with Aimé Césaire." Translated by Joan Pinkham. In *Discourse on Colonialism,* 81–94.
DeRogatis, Amy. *Moral Geography: Maps, Missionaries, and the American Frontier.* New York: Columbia Univ. Press, 2003.
Dias, Jill R. "Famine and Disease in the History of Angola. 1830–1930." *The Journal of African History* 22, no. 3 (1981): 349–78.

Diawara, Manthia. "Reading Africa through Foucault: V. Y. Mudimbe's Reaffirmation of the Subject." In McClintock, Mufti and Shohat, *Dangerous Liaisons*, 456–67.
"Digest of Recent Letters." *Mission Studies: Woman's Work in Foreign Lands*, April 1909, 101.
Dorsett, Lyle W. *A Passion for Souls: The Life of D. L. Moody*. Chicago: Moody Publishers, 1997.
"Dr. Stover at Bailundu." *Missionary Herald*, September 1910, 379.
"Dr. Stover Returns to His Field." *Missionary Herald*, March 1910, 100.
Duffy, James. *A Question of Slavery*. Cambridge: Harvard Univ. Press, 1967.
Dunch, Ryan. "Beyond Cultural Imperialism: Cultural Theory, Christian Missions, and Global Modernity." *History and Theory* 41 (October 2002): 301–25.
E. J. "A Sketch of the West Central African Mission." *Mission Studies: Woman's Work in Foreign Lands*, February 1912, 43–44.
Elphick, Richard. "Evangelical Missions and Racial 'Equalization' in South Africa, 1890–1914." In Robert, *Converting Colonialism*, 112–33.
Ennis, [Elisabeth] Mrs. Merlin. "African Witchcraft." *Mission Studies: Woman's Work in Foreign Lands*, October 1910, 317–19.
—. *The Hope of Glory: An Account of the Work of the West Central Africa Mission of the American Board for the year 1916–1917*. Kamundongo: Sarah H. Bates Memorial, 1917.
—. "So Our Missionaries Write: Mrs. Merlin W. Ennis, Sachikela, West Africa." *Missionary Herald*, July 1925, 348.
—. "The Umbundu Baby and Its Mother." *Light and Life for Woman*, September 1914, 390–96.
—. "West Central African Mission: A Cry for Help." *Missionary Herald*, October 1910, 459–60.
—. "Women's Names Among the Ovimbundu of Angola." *African Studies* 4, no. 1 (March 1945): 1–8.
Ennis, Merlin. "An African Church for Africans." *Missionary Herald*, September 1939, 30–32.
—. "Letters from the Missions, West Central African Mission: Progress at Kamundongo." *Missionary Herald*, January 1905, 243.
—. "Prospecting Around Chiyaka." *Missionary Herald*, April 1910, 156–59.
—. *Umbundu: Folk-Tales from Angola*. Boston: Beacon, 1962.
Etherington, Norman. "The Missionary Writing Machine in Nineteenth-Century Kwazulu-Natal." In Scott and Griffiths, *Mixed Messages*, 37-50.
Evans, Julie, Patricia Grimshaw, David Philips and Shurlee Swain. *Equal Subjects, Unequal Rights: Indigenous Peoples in British Settler Colonies, 1830–1910*. Manchester: Manchester Univ. Press, 2003.
Falola, Toyin. "Missionaries and Domestic Slavery in Yorubaland in the Nineteenth Century." *Journal of Religious History* 14 (1986): 181–92.

Fanon, Frantz. *Black Skin, White Masks*. London: Pluto, 1952.
—. *A Dying Colonialism*. New York: Grove, 1965.
—. *The Wretched of the Earth*. New York: Grove, 1965.
"A Fatal Accident." *Weekly Nashua Post*, January 12, 1899, 1.
Fay, Miss Louise B. "Africa's Need." *Light and Life for Woman*, February 1904, 89–91.
"Field Notes: Furtherance and Hindrance (West Central African Field)." *Missionary Herald*, January 1910, 31–32.
Fitzpatrick, Kristin. "American National Identify Abroad: The Travels of Nancy Prince." In Siegel, *Gender, Genre, and Identity in Women's Travel Writing*, 263–78.
Flemming, Leslie. "A New Humanity: American Missionaries' Ideals for Women in North India, 1870–1930." In *Western Women and Imperialism: Complicity and Resistance*, edited by Nupur Chaudhuri and Margaret Strobel, 191-206. Indianapolis: Indiana Univ. Press, 1992.
Fowler, Corinne. "The Problem of Narrative Authority." In Siegel, *Gender, Genre, and Identity in Women's Travel Writing*, 210.
Freire, Paulo. *Education for Critical Consciousness*. New York: Seabury, 1973.
Gaitskell, Deborah. "Crossing Boundaries and Building Bridges: The Anglican Women's Fellowship in Post-Apartheid South Africa." *Journal of Religion in Africa* 34, no. 3 (2004): 266–97.
—. "Devout Domesticity? A Century of African Women's Christianity in South Africa." In Walker, *Women and Gender in Southern Africa to 1945*, 251–72.
—. "Housewives, Maids or Mothers: Some Contradictions of Domesticity for Christian Women in Johannesburg, 1903- 1939." *Journal of African History* 24, no. 2 *The History of the Family in Africa* (1983): 241–56.
—. "Power in Prayer and Service: Women's Christian Organizations." In *Christianity in South Africa: A Political, Social, and Cultural History*, edited by Richard Elphick and Rodney Davenport, 253–67. Berkeley: Univ. of California Press, 1997.
—. "Rethinking Gender Roles: The Field Experience of Women Missionaries in South Africa." In Porter, *The Imperial Horizons of British Protestant Missions, 1880–1914*, 131–57.
—. "Women and Education in South Africa: How Helpful Are the Mission Archives?" In Bickers and Seton, *Missionary Encounters*, 114–27.
Garvey, Ellen Gruber. "Imitation is the Sincerest Form of Appropriation." *Common-place* 7, no. 3 (April 2007). http://www.common-place.org/vol-07/no-03/garvey/
—. "Scizzoring and Scrapbooks: Nineteenth-Century Reading, Remaking, and Recirculating." In *New Media, 1740–1915*, edited by Lisa Gitelman and Geoffrey B. Pingree, 207-28. Cambridge, MA: MIT, 2003.
Gaunt, Mary. *Alone in West Africa*. London: T.W. Lowrie, 1912.

Gengenbach, Heidi. "'What My Heart Wanted': Gendered Stories of Early Colonial Encounters in Southern Mozambique." In Allman, Geiger and Musisi, *Women in African Colonial Histories*, 19–47.

George, Rosemary M. "Homes in the Empire, Empires in the Home." *Cultural Critique* 26 (1993–94): 95–127.

Gere, Anne Ruggles. *Intimate Practices: Literacy and Cultural Work in U. S. Women's Clubs, 1880–1920*. Urbana: Univ. of Illinois Press, 1997.

—. "Kitchen Tables and Rented Rooms: The Extracurriculum of Composition." *CCC: College Composition and Communication* 45 (February 1994): 75–92.

Gere, Anne Ruggles and Sarah R. Robbins. "Gendered Literacy in Black and White: Turn-of-the-Century African-American and European-American Club Women's Printed Texts." *Signs* 21 (Spring 1996): 643–78.

"Getting a Printer for West Africa." *Missionary Herald*, May 1915, 232–33.

Goodsell, Fred Field. *James Levi Barton: Dynamic World Christian Statesman*. [Boston]: Congregational Christian Historical Society, 1964.

Grant, Kevin. *A Civilized Savagery: Britain and the New Slaveries in Africa, 1884–1926*. New York: Routledge, 2005.

Greetham, D. C. *Scholarly Editing: A Guide to Research*. New York: Modern Language Association, 1995.

Grimshaw, Patricia. *Paths of Duty: American Missionary Wives in Nineteenth-Century Hawaii*. Honolulu: Univ. of Hawaii Press, 1989.

Hall, Catherine. *Civilising Subjects: Colony and Metropole in the English Imagination, 1830–1867*. Chicago: Univ. of Chicago Press, 2002.

—, ed. *Cultures of Empire: A Reader: Colonizers in Britain and the Empire in the Nineteenth and Twentieth Centuries*. Manchester: Manchester Univ. Press, 2000.

—." Introduction." In Hall, *Cultures of Empire*, 1–36.

Hambly, Wilfrid D. *The Ovimbundu of Angola*. Chicago: Field Museum of Natural History, 1934.

Hanley, Mark. "Revolution at Home and Abroad: Radical Implications of the Protestant Call to Missions, 1825–1870." In Bays and Wacker, *The Foreign Missionary Enterprise at Home*, 44–59.

Hardage, Jeanette. "The Legacy of Mary Slessor." *International Bulletin of Missionary Research* 26, no. 4 (2002): 178–81.

Hardesty, Nancy A. "The Scientific Study of Missions: Textbooks of the Central Committee on the United Study of Foreign Missions." In Bays and Wacker, *The Foreign Missionary Enterprise at Home*, 106–22.

Harris, Susan K. "Mark Twain's America: Race, Religion, and American Identity in the Annexation Debates of 1899." Manuscript in Progress, Univ. of Kansas.

—. "Mark Twain and America's Christian Mission Abroad." In *A Companion to Mark Twain*, edited by Louis J. Budd and Peter Messant, 38-52. New York: Wiley-Blackwell, 2006.

—. "Women, Anti-imperialism and America's Christian Mission Abroad: The Impact of the Philippine-American War." In *Becoming Visible: Women's Presence in Late Nineteenth-Century America*, edited by Janet Floyd, Alison Easton, R.J. Ellis and Lindsey Traub, 307-26. Amsterdam: Rodopi, 2010.

Hastings, Adrian. "Were Women a Special Case?" In Bowie, Kirkwood, and Ardener, *Women and Missions*, 104–25.

Haygood, Laura A., "Relation of Female Education to Home Mission Work." In *Life and Letters of Laura Askew Haygood*, edited by Oswald Eugene Brown and Anna Muse Brown, 89-95. Nashville: Smith and Lamar, 1904.

Heintze, Beatrix. "In Pursuit of a Chameleon: Early Ethnographic Photography from Angola in Context." *History in Africa* 17 (1990): 131–56.

Henderson, Lawrence. *Angola: Five Centuries of Conflict*. Ithaca: Cornell Univ. Press, 1979.

—. *The Church in Angola: A River of Many Currents*. Cleveland: Pilgrim, 1992.

—. *Galangue: The Unique Story of a Mission Station in Angola Proposed, Supported and Staffed by Black Americans*. New York: United Church Board for World Ministries, 1986.

Henderson, Muriel W. "One Birthday to Another." (Typescript memoir in possession of Muriel W. Henderson, Chapel Hill, N.C.).

Henderson-James, Nancy. *At Home Abroad: An American Girl in Africa*. Austin, TX: Plain View Press, 2009.

—. "Diving In." In *Uprooted Childhoods: Memoirs of Growing up Global*, edited by Faith Eidse and Nina Sichel, 161-76. Yarmouth, ME: Intercultural, 2004.

Hennessy, Rosemary. "Subjects, Knowledges, . . . And All the Rest: Speaking for What?" In Roof and Wiegman, *Who Can Speak?*, 137–49.

Heywood, Linda M. *Contested Power in Angola, 1840s to the Present*. Rochester: Univ. of Rochester Press, 2000.

—. "The Growth and Decline of African Agriculture in Central Angola, 1890–1950." *Journal of Southern African Studies* 13, no. 3 (1987): 355–71.

—. "Slavery and Forced Labor in the Changing Political Economy of Central Angola, 1850–1949." In *The End of Slavery in Africa*, edited by Suzanne Miers and Richard Roberts, 415-36. Madison: Univ. of Wisconsin Press, 1988.

—. "Towards an Understanding of Modern Political Ideology in Africa: The Case of the Ovimbundu of Angola." *Journal of Modern African Studies* 36, no. 1 (1998): 139–67.

Heywood, Linda M. and John Thornton. "Demography, Production and Labor: Central Angola, 1890–1950." In *African Population and Capitalism: Historical Perspectives*, edited by Dennis D. Cordell and Joel W. Gregory, 241–54. Boulder, CO: Westview Press, 1987.

Hill, Patricia R. *The World Their Household: The American Woman's Foreign Mission Movement and Cultural Transformation, 1870–1920*. Ann Arbor: Univ. of Michigan Press, 1985.

Hlongwane, Lynette. "The Role of Inanda Seminary in the Education of Africa Girls in South Africa: A Report of Graduates' Views." EdD diss., Teachers College, Columbia Univ., 1998.

Hochschild, Adam. *King Leopold's Ghost: A Story of Greed, Terror, and Heroism in Colonial Africa*. Boston: Houghton Mifflin, 1998.

Hollenbeck, Henry S. "Africa: The Boys at Kamundongo." *Missionary Herald*, December 1917, 579–80.

—. "Africa: The Boys of Kamundongo." *Missionary Herald*, August 1916, 370–72.

—. "Africa: A Kamundongo Conference." *Missionary Herald*, May 1918, 225–26.

—. "A Coveted Opportunity." *Missionary Herald*, May 1910, 221–22.

—. "Kandala." *Missionary Herald*, February 1925, 70.

—. "A Sample Cry from the Field," *Missionary Herald*, August 1918, 360–62.

—. "So Our Missionaries Write: Henry S. Hollenbeck Kamundongo, West Africa." *Missionary Herald*, July 1925, 349.

"Home and Abroad." *Nashua* (IA) *Reporter*. October 16, 1902, 8. http://www.ancestry.com/

Howard, J. Keir. "Arnot, Frederick Stanley, Open Brethren (Christian Missions in Many Lands, Central Africa (present day Democratic Republic of Congo, Angola and Zambia)." *Dictionary of African Christian Biography*. http://www.dacb.org/stories/demrepcongo/arnot_stanley.html.

Huber, Mary Taylor and Nancy C. Lutkehaus, eds. *Gendered Missions: Women and Men in Missionary Discourse and Practice*. Ann Arbor: Univ. of Michigan Press, 1999.

—. "Introduction: Gendered Missions at Home and Abroad." In Huber and Lutkehaus, *Gendered Missions*, 1–38.

Hughes, Heather. "'A Lighthouse for African Womanhood': Inanda Seminary, 1869–1945." In Walker, *Women and Gender in Southern Africa to 1945*, 197–220.

Huguenot Seminary Papers, 1874–1978, Finding Aid. MS 0550. Mount Holyoke College Archives and Special Collections. http://asteria.fivecolleges.edu/findaids/mountholyoke/mshm237.html.

Hulme, Peter and Tim Youngs, eds. *The Cambridge Companion to Travel Writing*. Cambridge: Cambridge Univ. Press, 2007.

Hunt, Nancy Rose, Tessie P. Liu and Jean Quataert, eds. *Gendered Colonialisms in African History*. Oxford: Blackwell, 1997.
Hunter, Jane. *The Gospel of Gentility: American Women Missionaries in Turn-of-the-Century China*. New Haven: Yale Univ. Press, 1984.
—. "Women's Mission in Historical Perspective: American Identity and Christian Internationalism." In Reeves-Ellington, Sklar and Shemo, *Competing Kingdoms*, 19–42.
Hutchison, William R. *Errand to the World: American Protestant Thought and Foreign Missions*. Chicago: Univ. of Chicago Press, 1987.
Ireland, Alleyne. "The United States in the Philippines." *The Atlantic Monthly* 94 (November 1904): 575–94.
Jackson, Gregory S. "'What Would Jesus Do?' Practical Christianity, Social Gospel Realism, and the Homiletic Novel," *PMLA* 121, no. 3 (May 2006): 641–61.
Jacobs, Sylvia M. "African-American Women Missionaries and European Imperialism in Southern Africa, 1880-1920." *Women's Studies International Forum* 13, no. 4 (1990): 381-94.
—, ed. *Black Americans and the Missionary Movement in Africa*. Westport: Greenwood, 1982.
—. "Three African American Women Missionaries in the Congo, 1887-1899: The Confluence of Race, Culture, Identity, and Nationality." In Reeves-Ellington, Sklar and Shemo, *Competing Kingdoms*, 318–41.
Jameson, Fredric. *The Political Unconscious: Narrative as a Socially Symbolic Act*. Ithaca: Cornell Univ. Press, 1981.
Jenkins, Ruth Y. "The Gaze of the Victorian Woman Traveler." In Siegel, *Gender, Genre and Identity in Women's Travel Writing*, 15–30
Johnston, Anna. *Missionary Writing and Empire, 1800–1860*. Cambridge: Cambridge Univ. Press, 2003.
Johnston, May J. "A Trip to Kamundongo and Ochileso." *Mission Studies: Woman's Work in Foreign Lands*, October 1908, 307–10.
Jones, Jacqueline. *Soldiers of Light and Love: Northern Teachers and Georgia Blacks, 1865–1873*. Chapel Hill: Univ. of North Carolina Press, 1980.
Jones, Thomas Jesse. *Education in Africa: A Study of West, South, and Equatorial Africa by the African Education Commission, under the Auspices of the Phelps-Stokes Fund and Foreign Mission Societies of North America and Europe*. New York: Phelps-Stokes Fund, 1922.
"Kandundu." *Missionary Herald*, November 1907, 528.
Kanogo, Tabitha. "Mission Impact on Women in Colonial Kenya." In Bowie, Kirkwood, and Ardener, *Women and Missions*, 165–86.
Kay-Scott, C[yril] [Frederick Creighton Wellman]. *Life Is Too Short: An Autobiography*. Philadelphia: J.B. Lippincott, 1943.
Kincaid, Jamaica. *A Small Place*. New York: Farrar, Straus and Giroux, 2000.

"Kindergarten in Bailundu." *Light and Life for Woman*, October 1904, 473–75.
Kingsley, Mary Henrietta. *Travels in West Africa: Congo Francais, Corsico and Cameroons*. London: Macmillan, 1897.
Kirkwood, Deborah, "Protestant Missionary Women: Wives and Spinsters." In Bowie, Kirkwood and Ardener, *Women and Missions*, 23–42.
Korte, Barbara. *English Travel Writing from Pilgrimages to Postcolonial Explorations*. Translated by Catherine Matthias. Reprint, London: Macmillan, 2000.
Kramer, Paul. "Empires, Exceptions, and Anglo-Saxons: Race and Rule between the British and United States Empires, 1880–1910." *Journal of American History* 88 (March 2002): 1315–55.
Kriel, Lize. "From Private Journal to Published Periodical: Gendered Writings and Readings of a Late Victorian Wesleyan's 'African Wilderness.'" *Book History* 11 (2008): 169–98.
Labode, Modupe. "From Heathen Kraal to Christian Home: Anglican Missionary Education and African Christian Girls, 1850–1900." In Bowie, Kirkwood and Ardener, *Women and Missions*, 126–44.
—. "'A Native Knows a Native': African American Missionaries' Writings About Angola, 1919-1940." *The North Star: A Journal for African American Religious History* 4, no. 1 (2000): 1-14.
Laszlo, Andreas E. *Doctors, Drums, and Dances*. Garden City, NY: Hanover House, 1955.
Lazreg, Marnia, "Decolonizing Feminism." In Oyěwùmí, *African Gender Studies*, 67–80.
Leake, Mrs. Joseph B., "Africa: West Central Africa." *Fortieth Annual Report of the Woman's Board of Missions of the Interior, 1908*. Chicago: WMBI, [1909], 46–47.
—. "Africa: West Central Africa." *Thirty-Eighth Annual Report of the Woman's Board of Missions of the Interior, 1906*. Chicago, WBMI, [1907], 28–29.
—. "Africa: West Central Africa." *Thirty-Seventh Annual Report of the Woman's Board of Missions of the Interior, 1905*. Chicago: WBMI, [1906]. 31–33.
LeRoy, James A. "Our Spanish Inheritance in the Philippines." *The Atlantic Monthly* 95 (March 1905): 340–46
—. "Race Prejudice in the Philippines." *The Atlantic Monthly* 90 (July 1902): 100–17.
Lewis, Desiree. "African Gender Research and Postcoloniality," in Oyěwùmí, *African Gender Studies*, 382–83
Livingstone, Dr. David. *The Life and African Explorations of David Livingstone*. St. Louis: 1874. Reprint, New York: Copper Square, 2002.

—. *Missionary Travels and Researches in South Africa: Including a Sketch of Sixteen Years' Residence in the Interior of Africa*. 2 vols. London: 1857. Reprint, New York: The Narrative, 2001.

L.L. "At Kamundongo." *Mission Studies: Woman's Work in Foreign Lands*, August 1908, 251–52.

Loomba, Ania. *Colonialism/Postcolonialism*. 2nd edition. New York: Routledge, 2005.

Love, Eric T.L. *Race Over Empire: Racism and U.S. Imperialism, 1865–1900*. Chapel Hill: Univ. of North Carolina Press, 2004.

Lutkehaus, Nancy C. "Missionary Maternalism: Gendered Images of the Holy Spirit Sisters in Colonial New Guinea." In Huber and Lutkehaus, *Gendered Missions*, 207–36.

Mackenzie, Jean Kenyon. *Black Sheep Adventures in West Africa*. Boston: Houghton Mifflin, 1916.

MacKenzie, John M., ed. *Imperialism and Popular Culture*. Manchester: Manchester Univ. Press, 1986

—. "Missionaries, Science, and the Environment in Nineteenth-Century Africa." In Porter, *Imperial Horizons*, 106–30.

—. *Propaganda and Empire: The Manipulation of British Public Opinion, 1880–1960*. Manchester: Manchester Univ. Press, 1984.

Marchant, Miss A.G. "Africa: West Central Africa." *Thirty-Ninth Annual Report of the Woman's Board of Missions of the Interior, 1907*. Chicago: Woman's Board of Missions of the Interior, [1908], 47–50.

Marshall, David B. *Secularizing the Faith: Canadian Protestant Clergy and the Crisis of Belief, 1850–1940*. Toronto: Univ. of Toronto Press, 1992.

Mastrobuono, Luisa. "Ovimbundu Women and Coercive Labour Systems: 1850–1940: From Still Life to Moving Pictures." Master's thesis, Univ. of Toronto, 1992.

Maughan, Steven. "'Mighty England Do Good': The Major English Denominations and Organisations for the Support of Foreign Missions in the Nineteenth Century." In Bickers and Seton, *Missionary Encounters*, 11–37.

McAllister, Agnes. *A Lone Woman in Africa: Six Years on the Kroo Coast*. New York: Eaton & Maius, 1896.

McClintock, Anne. *Imperial Leather: Race, Gender and Sexuality in the Colonial Contest*. New York and London: Routledge, 1995.

McClintock, Anne, Aamir Mufti, and Ella Shohat, eds. *Dangerous Liaisons: Gender, Nation, and Postcolonial Perspectives*. Minneapolis: Univ. of Minnesota Press, 1997.

McCulloch, Merran. *The Ovimbundu of Angola*. Ethnographic Survey of Africa: West Central Africa, Part II, edited by Daryll Forde. London: International African Institute, 1952.

McEwan, Cheryl. "Encounters with West African Women: Textural Representations of Difference by White Women Abroad." In *Writing Women and Space: Colonial and Postcolonial Geographies*, edited by Alison Blunt and Gillian Rose, 73–100. New York: Guilford, 1994.

Means, Mrs. J. O. [Jane]. "Congregational Missions in West Central Africa." *Light and Life for Woman*, June 1906, 253–56.

Memmi, Albert. *The Colonizer and the Colonized*. Boston: Beacon, 1991.

—. *Decolonization and the Decolonized*. Translated by Robert Bononno. Minneapolis: Univ. of Minnesota Press, 2004.

"Merlin E. Ennis." Beloit Archives. Beloit College Library. https://campus.beloit.edu/archives/documents/archival_collections/alumni/merlin_ennis

Miller, Janette. "The Need of the Hour in West Central Africa." *Mission Studies: Woman's Work in Foreign Lands*, June 1912, 169–70.

—."The Ombala of Ondulu." *Mission Studies: Woman's Work in Foreign Lands*, November 1912, 335–36.

—. "A Zoo in Africa." *Mission Studies: Woman's Work in Foreign Lands*, September 1912, 282–83.

Mills, Sara. *Discourses of Difference: An Analysis of Women's Travel Writing and Colonialism*. New York: Routledge, 1993.

"Miss Arnott Tells of Work." *New Hampton* (IA) *Gazette*, October 31, 1912, 1.

"Miss Arnott's School." *Mission Studies: Woman's Work in Foreign Lands*, November 1909, 344–45.

"Miss Nellie Arnott left for New Hampton Saturday." *Weekly Nashua* (IA) *Post*, October 31, 1912, 1.

"A Missionary Conference in West Central Africa." *Mission Studies: Woman's Work in Foreign Lands*, November 1912, 333–34.

Mohanty, Chandra Talpade, "Under Western Eyes: Feminist Scholarship and Colonial Discourses." In McClintock, Mufti, and Shohat, *Dangerous Liaisons*, 255–77.

Montgomery, Helen. *Western Women in Eastern Lands: An Outline Study of Fifty Years of Women's Work in Foreign Missions*. New York: Macmillan, 1910.

M.P.H.L. "Miss Nellie Arnott, the Children's Missionary." *Mission Studies: Woman's Work in Foreign Lands*, October 1910, 350–51.

"Mr. Arnott of Deerfield Was in Town." *Weekly Nashua* (IA) *Post*, September 23, 1886, 8.

"Mrs. Stover Back at Work." *Missionary Herald*, September 1909, 371.

Murray, Andrew. *The State of the Church: A Plea for More Prayer*. Edinburgh: World Missionary Conference, 1910.

Neipp, Rev. H.A. "Letters from the Missions, West Central Africa Mission: Good News from Ochilseo." *Missionary Herald*, May 1907, 243–44.

"Nellie Arnott and Edna Heald Left Monday Evening for Savannah." *Weekly Nashua* (IA) *Post*, September 27, 1894, 8.
Nevinson, Henry W. *A Modern Slavery: With an Introduction by Basil Davidson.* New York: Harper, 1906. Reprint, London: Harper & Bros. Background Books, 1963.
"New Recruits." *Missionary Herald*, November 1906, 525.
Nfah-Abbenyi, Juliana Makuchi. "Gender, Feminist Theory, Post-Colonial Writing." In Oyěwùmí, *African Gender Studies—A Reader*," 259–76.
Ngũgĩ wa Thiong'o. *Decolonising the Mind: The Politics of Language in African Literature.* Portsmouth: Heinemann, 1981.
———. *The River Between.* Berkshire: Cox & Wyman for Heinemann, 1965.
Nnaemeka, Obioma. "Bringing African Women into the Classroom: Rethinking Pedagogy and Epistemology." In Oyěwùmí, *African Gender Studies: A Reader*, 51–66.
Nourse, Annie E. Minutes of the Forty-Fourth Annual Meeting. *Forty-Fourth Annual Report of the Woman's Board of Missions of the Interior, 1912.* Chicago: WBMI, [1913], 78–89.
"Our Field Workers: Georgia," *American Missionary*, February 1895, 54 and 77.
"Our Field Workers: Georgia." *American Missionary*, February 1896, 45 and 70.
"Our Field Workers: Mississippi." *American Missionary*, March 1898, 20 and 29.
"Our Literature," *Mission Studies*, September 1910, 310.
"Out of Doors Where Our Boys and Girls Are Working: Africa." *Mission Studies: Woman's Work in Foreign Lands*, February 1909, 36.
Oyěwùmí, Oyèrónké, ed. *African Gender Studies: A Reader.* New York: Palgrave Macmillan, 2005.
"P. Arnott Was in Town." *Weekly Nashua* (IA) *Post*, October 28, 1886, 8.
Pascoe, Peggy. *Relations of Rescue: The Search for Female Moral Authority in the American West, 1874–1939.* New York: Oxford Univ. Press, 1993.
Pattison, Vane A. "History of Education in Chickasaw County, Iowa." Master's thesis, Univ. of Iowa, 1939.
Patton, C. H. *The Lure of Africa.* 1917. Reprint, New York: Cosimo, 2006.
Patton, C.H., and Frederick B. Bridgman. *Report of the Deputation to the West Central Africa Mission.* Boston: ABCFM, 1911.
"Paul Darling Came Home Saturday." *Weekly Nashua* (IA) *Post*, June 2, 1893, 8.
"Paul Darling of Julien." *Weekly Nashua* (IA) *Post*, August 4, 1893, 8.
Peel, J.D.Y. "Problems and Opportunities in an Anthropologist's Use of a Mission Archive." In Bickers and Seton, *Missionary Encounters*, 70–94.
———. *Religious Encounter and the Making of the Yoruba.* Bloomington: Univ. of Indiana Press, 2003.

Perry Magazine 5, no. 1 (September 1902).
"Plan of Work for Mission Bands of the W.B.M.I." *Mission Studies: Woman's Work in Foreign Lands*, February 1909, 42.
Pollock, Sarah. "An African Story." *Mission Studies*, March 1911, 89–90.
Porter, Andrew. "'Cultural Imperialism' and Protestant Missionary Enterprise, 1780–1914." *Journal of Imperial and Commonwealth History*, 25, no. 3 (1997): 367–91.
—, ed. *The Imperial Horizons of British Protestant Missions, 1880–1914*. Cambridge: William B. Eerdmans, 2003.
Pratt, Mary Louise. *Imperial Eyes: Travel Writing and Transculturation*. 1st ed. London: Routledge, 1992.
Predelli, Line Nyhagen and Jon Miller. "Piety and Patriarchy: Contested Gender Regimes in Nineteenth-Century Evangelical Missions." In Huber and Lutkehaus, *Gendered Missions*, 67–112.
Pullen, Ann, Sarah Robbins, and students. Women's Work in the Long Nineteenth Century. http://www.kennesaw.edu/hss/wwork/.
Ranger, Terence. "Europeans in Black Africa." *Journal of World History* 9, no. 2 (1998): 255–68.
"Recruit for Africa." *Missionary Herald*, June 1905, 267.
Redick, Emma C. "Vacation Days at Ochileso." *Light and Life for Woman*, October 1910, 473–75.
"Re-enforcement for Bailundu." *Missionary Herald*, June 1908, 261.
Reeves-Ellington, Barbara, Kathryn Kish Sklar and Connie A. Shemo, eds. *Competing Kingdoms: Women, Mission, Nation, and the American Protestant Empire, 1812-1960*. Durham: Duke Univ. Press, 2010.
Remick, John Erni. "American Influence on the Education of the Ovimbundu (the Benguella and Bié Highlands) of Angola, from 1880-1914." PhD diss., Miami Univ., 1976.
"Retroversion of the Uterus." Medline Plus U.S. National Library of Medicine and the National Institutions of Health. http://www.nlm.nih.gov/medlineplus/ency/article/001506.htm.
Riggs, Arthur Stanley. "A Letter from the Philippines." *The Atlantic Monthly* 92 (August 1903): 256–66.
Richardson, Joe M., *Christian Reconstruction: The American Missionary Association and Southern Blacks, 1861–1890*. Athens: Univ. of Georgia Press, 1986.
Robbins, Sarah. *Managing Literacy, Mothering America: Women's Narratives on Reading and Writing in the Nineteenth Century*. Pittsburgh: Univ. of Pittsburgh Press, 2004.
—. "*Woman's Work for Woman:* Gendered Print Culture in American Mission Movement Narratives." In *Women in Print: Essays on the Print Culture of American Women from the Nineteenth and Twentieth Centuries,*

edited by James Danky and Wayne Wiegand, 245-74. Univ. of Wisconsin Press, 2006.

Robert, Dana L. *American Women in Mission: A Social History of Their Thought and Practice.* Macon: Mercer Univ. Press, 1996.

—. "The 'Christian Home' As a Cornerstone of Anglo-American Missionary Thought and Practice." In Robert, *Converting Colonialism,* 134-65.

—, ed. *Converting Colonialism: Visions and Realities in Mission History, 1706-1914.* Cambridge: William B. Eerdmans, 2008.

—, ed. *Gospel Bearers, Gender Barriers: Missionary Women in the Twentieth Century.* American Society of Missiology Series, No. 32. Maryknoll, New York: Orbis, 2002.

—. "Introduction." In Robert, *Converting Colonialism,* 1-20.

—. "Introduction: Historical Themes and Current Issues." In Robert, *Gospel Bearers, Gender Barriers,* 1-28.

Robertson, Elizabeth. *Mary Slessor: The Barefoot Missionary.* Edinburgh, Scotland: NMS, 2001.

Rohan, Elizabeth [Liz] Ellen. "Imagined Communions: One Woman's Spiritual Journey." PhD diss., Univ. of Illinois, 2002.

Rohan, Liz. "One Woman's Battle for God: Literacy, Modernity and the Turn-of-the-Twentieth Century American Women's Missionary Movement." *Le Fait Missionaire* 18 (July 2006): 45-71.

Romero, Patricia W. *Women's Voices on Africa: A Century of Travel Writing.* Princeton: Markus Wiener, 1992.

Roof, Judith and Robyn Wiegman, eds. *Who Can Speak?: Authority and Critical Identity.* Urbana: Univ. of Illinois Press, 1995.

Rosenberg, Emily S. "Rescuing Women and Children." *Journal of American History* 89 (September 2002): 456-65.

Ross, Andrew C. "Christian Missions and Mid-Nineteenth-Century Change in Attitudes to Race: The African Experience." In Porter, *The Imperial Horizons of British Protestant Missions,* 85-105.

—. *David Livingstone: Mission and Empire.* London: Hambledon & London, 2002.

Samuels, Michael. *Education in Angola, 1878-1914: A History of Culture Transfer and Administration.* New York: Teachers College Press, 1970.

Sanders, Frank Knight. "Impressions of the Angola Jubilee." *Missionary Herald,* September 1930, 331-33.

Sanders, Mrs. William H. [Sarah]. "Missionary Letters: West Africa." *Light and Life for Woman,* April 1909, 168-69.

Sanders, [William]. "Letters from the Missions, West Central Africa: From Kamundongo." *Missionary Herald,* December 1905, 644-45.

Sanders, William H. "Reminiscences." American Board of Commissioners for Foreign Missions Archives, 1810-1961. ABC 76:2, Personal Papers. Houghton Library, Harvard Univ.

Sanneh, Lamin. *Encountering the West: Christianity and the Global Cultural Process: The African Dimension.* Maryknoll, NY: Orbis, 1993.
Satre, Lowell J. *Chocolate on Trial: Slavery, Politics & the Ethics of Business.* Athens: Ohio Univ. Press, 2005.
Sawicki, Jana. *Disciplining Foucault: Feminism, Power, and the Body.* New York: Routledge, 1991.
Schriber, Mary Suzanne. *Writing Home: American Women Abroad, 1830–1920.* Charlottesville: Univ. Press of Virginia, 1997.
Scott, Anne Firor. *Natural Allies: Women's Associations in American History.* Urbana: Univ. of Illinois Press, 1991.
Scott, Jamie S. and Gareth Griffiths, eds. *Mixed Messages: Materiality, Textuality, Missions.* New York: Palgrave Macmillan, 2005.
Sedgwick, Ellery. The Atlantic Monthly *1857–1909: Yankee Humanism at High Tide and Ebb.* Amherst: Univ. of Massachusetts Press, 1994.
Semple, Rhonda Anne, *Missionary Women: Gender, Professionalism and the Victorian Idea of Christian Mission.* Rochester, NY: Boydell, 2003.
Seton, Rosemary, "Open Doors for Female Labourers: Women Candidates of the London Missionary Society, 1875–1914." In Bickers and Seton, *Missionary Encounters,* 50–69.
Sharpe, Jenny. *Allegories of Empire: The Figure of Woman in the Colonial Text.* Minneapolis: Univ. of Minnesota Press, 1993.
Siegel, Kristi, ed. *Gender, Genre, and Identity in Women's Travel Writing.* New York: Peter Lang, 2004.
—. "Intersections: Women's Travel and Theory." In Siegel, *Gender, Genre and Identity in Women's Travel Writing,* 1–14.
Simpson, Mark. *Trafficking Subjects: The Politics of Mobility in Nineteenth-Century America.* Minneapolis: Univ. of Minnesota Press, 2005.
Sinor, Jennifer. *The Extraordinary Work of Ordinary Writing: Annie Ray's Diary.* Iowa City: Univ. of Iowa Press, 2002.
Smalley, Martha Lund. *Guide to the Frank Knight Sanders Papers.* Record Group No. 122. Yale Univ. Library, Divinity Library Special Collections. http://drs.library.yale.edu:8083/fedora/get/divinity:122/PDF.
Smith, Judson Papers (Description). Collection 173. Billy Graham Center Archives. Wheaton College. http://www.wheaton.edu/bgc/archives/GUIDES/173.htm#3.
Smith, Sidonie. *Moving Lives: Twentieth-Century Women's Travel Writing.* Minneapolis: Univ. of Minnesota Press, 2001.
"Some West African Curios." *Missionary Herald,* November 1907, 527.
Soremekun, Fola. "The Bailundu Revolt, 1902." *African Social Research* 16 (1973): 447–73.
—. "A History of the American Board Missions in Angola 1880–1940." PhD diss., Northwestern Univ., 1965.

—. "Religion and Politics in Angola: The American Board Missions and the Portuguese Government, 1880–1922." *Cahiers d'études africaines* 11, no. 3 (1971): 341–77.

—. "Trade and Dependency in Central Angola: The Ovimbundu in the Nineteenth Century." In *The Roots of Rural Poverty in Central and Southern Africa*, edited by Robin Palmer and Neil Parsons, 82–95. Berkeley: Univ. of California Press, 1977.

Spurr, David. *The Rhetoric of Empire: Colonial Discourse in Journalism, Travel Writing, and Imperial Administration*. Durham: Duke Univ. Press, 1993.

Stanley, Brian. *The Bible and the Flag: Protestant Missions and British Imperialism in the Nineteenth and Twentieth Centuries*. Leicester: APOLLOS, 1990.

—. "Some Problems in Writing a Missionary Society History Today: The Example of the Baptist Missionary Society." In Bickers and Seton, *Missionary Encounters*, 38–49.

—. *The World Missionary Conference: Edinburgh 1910*. Grand Rapids: William B. Eerdmans, 2009.

Stevens, Michael E. and Steven B. Burg. *Editing Historical Documents: A Handbook of Practice*. Walnut Creek: Altamira, 1997.

Stimpson, Sarah. "Missionary Letters: West Africa." *Light and Life for Woman*, April 1909, 168.

—. "The Work of African Christians in Susua." *Light and Life for Woman*, January 1913, 137–41.

Stoler, Ann Laura. "Carnal Knowledge and Imperial Power: Gender, Race, and Morality in Colonial Asia." In *Gender at the Crossroads of Knowledge: Feminist Anthropology in the Postmodern Era*, edited by Micaela di Leonardo, 51-101. Berkeley: Univ. of California Press, 1991.

—. "Making Empire Respectable: The Politics of Race and Sexual Morality in Twentieth-Century Colonial Cultures." In McClintock, Mufti, and Shohat, *Dangerous Liaisons*, 344–73.

Stoler, Ann Laura and Frederick Cooper, "Between Metropole and Colony: Rethinking a Research Agenda," In Cooper and Stoler, *Tensions of Empire*, 1–56.

Stover, Bertha D. *Women of West Central Africa*. Chicago: Woman's Board of Missions of the Interior, n.d., ca. early 1900s.

Stover, Helen. "What I Do and What I Should Like to Do." *Mission Studies: Woman's Work in Foreign Lands*, February 1912, 55.

Stover, [Wesley]. "Letters from the Missions, West Central African Mission: A Bright Outlook." *Missionary Herald*, January 1905, 30.

Strong, William E. *The Story of the American Board: An Account of the First Hundred Years of The American Board of Commissioners for Foreign Missions*. Boston: Pilgrim, 1910.

Stunt, William T., A. Pulleng, A. Pickering, G.P. Simmons, D.K. Boak, S.F. Warren. *Turning the World Upside Down: A Century of Missionary Endeavour.* Eastbourne, Sussex: Upperton, 1972.

Swan, Charles A. *The Slavery of to-Day or the Present Position of the Open Sore of Africa.* Glasgow: Pickering & Inglis, [1909?].

Sweet, Leonard I. *The Minister's Wife: Her Role in Nineteenth-Century American Evangelicalism.* Philadelphia: Temple Univ. Press, 1982.

"Thank Offerings for Our Work: Miss Arnott's Schools." *Mission Studies: Woman's Work in Foreign Lands,* September 1909, 282.

Thomas, Nicholas. "Colonial Conversions: Difference, Hierarchy, and History in Early Twentieth-century Evangelical Propaganda." In Hall, *Cultures of Empire,* 298–328.

—. *Colonialism's Culture: Anthropology, Travel and Government.* Princeton: Princeton Univ. Press, 1994.

Thomas, Norman E. "John Taylor Tucker." In Anderson, *Biographical Dictionary of Christian Missions,* 683.

Thorne, Susan. "Missionary-Imperial Feminism." In Huber and Lutkehaus, *Gendered Missions,* 39–66.

"To West Africa." *Missionary Herald,* August 1911, 338.

Trinh, T. Minh-ha. *Woman, Native, Other: Writing Postcoloniality and Feminism.* Bloomington: Indiana Univ. Press, 1989.

Tucker, John T. *Angola: The Land of the Blacksmith Prince.* New York: World Dominion, 1933.

—. *Currie of Chissamba (Herald of the Dawn).* Toronto: United Church of Canada, 1945.

—. *Drums in the Darkness.* New York: George H. Doran, 1927.

—. *A Tucker Treasury: Reminiscences and Stories of Angola, 1883–1958. Selected and Prepared by Catherine Tucker Ward.* Winfield, British Columbia: Wood Lake, 1984.

Tucker, Leona Stukey. "The Divining Basket of the Ovimbundu." *The Journal of the Royal Anthropological Institute of Great Britain and Ireland* 70, no. 2 (1940): 171–201.

Tyrrell, Ian."Woman, Missions, and Empire: New Approaches to American Cultural Expansion." In Reeves-Ellington, Sklar and Shemo, *Competing Kingdoms,* 43–68.

—. *Woman's World, Woman's Empire: The Woman's Christian Temperance Union in International Perspective, 1880–1930.* Chapel Hill: Univ. of North Carolina Press, 1991.

"An Umbundu Vocabulary." *Missionary Herald,* September 1911, 383.

Urban-Mead, Wendy. "Dynastic Daughters: Three Royal Kwena Women and E.L. Price of the London Missionary Society, 1853–1881." In Allman, Geiger and Musisi, *Women in Colonial African Histories,* 48–70.

—. "An Unwomanly Woman and Her Sons in Christ: Faith, Empire, and Gender in Colonial Rhodesia, 1899-1906." In Reeves-Ellington, Sklar and Shemo, *Competing Kingdoms*, 94-116.
Von Rohr, John. *The Shaping of American Congregationalism*. Cleveland: The Pilgrim, 1992.
Walker, Cherryl, ed. *Women and Gender in Southern Africa to 1945*. Cape Town: D. Philip, 1990.
"The Way Our Missionaries Travel." *Mission Studies: Woman's Work in Foreign Lands*, April 1910, 119.
Webster, Marion M. "Extracts Taken from a Letter by Mrs. M. M. Webster, Dated Bailundu, West Central Africa, January 17, 1905." *Light and Life for Woman*, April 1905, 287–88.
—. "A New Enterprise in West Central Africa," *Mission Studies: Woman's Work in Foreign Lands*, July 1912, 204.
—. "West Central African Mission: Fields White—Laborers Few." *Missionary Herald*, July 1909, 310.
Wellman, Mrs. F.C. [Lydia], "Letters from the Missions, West Central Africa Mission: Gains at Kamundongo." *Missionary Herald*, June 1904, 243–44.
—. "Letters from the Missions, West Central African Mission: In Spite of Obstacles." *Missionary Herald*, July 1907, 346–48.
Wellman, Sam. *Mary Slessor: Queen of Calabar*. Uhrichsville, Ohio: Barbour, 1998.
"West Central African Mission: Broadening the Field." *Missionary Herald*, May 1909, 215–18.
"West Central African Mission: Recent Observations." *Missionary Herald*, December 1909, 550.
Wexler, Laura. *Tender Violence: Domestic Visions in an Age of U.S. Imperialism*. Chapel Hill: Univ. of North Carolina Press, 2000.
Wheeler, Douglas and C. Diane Christensen. "To Rise with One Mind: The Bailundo War of 1902." In *Social Change in Angola*, edited by Franz-Wilhelm Heimer. 54–92. Munich: Weltforum Verlag, 1973.
Willis, Justin. "The Nature of a Mission Community: The Universities' Mission to Central Africa in Bonde." In Bickers and Seton, *Missionary Encounters*, 128–52.
Wollons, Roberta. "Travelling for God and Adventure: Women Missionaries in the Late 19th Century," *Asian Journal of Social Science* 31, no. 1 (2003): 55–71.
Woman's Board of Missions of the Interior. *Miss Emma C. Redick, Ochileso Africa: Missionary of the Congregational Endeavor Societies of Kansas*. Chicago: Woman's Board of Missions of the Interior, n.d. [early 1900s].
Woodside, Mrs. T. W [Emma]. "A Summer Conference of Ovimbundu Women." *Light and Life for Woman*, June 1913, 255–59.

Woodside, Thomas W. "Is the African Worthwhile?" *Missionary Herald*, July 1908, 320–21.

—. "Letters from the Missions, West Central African Mission: From Ochileso." *Missionary Herald*, December 1905, 644.

—. "Letters from the Missions, West Central African Mission: The New Station—Ochileso." *Missionary Herald*, April 1905, 197.

—. "Letters from the Missions, West Central African Mission: Ochileso, The New Station." *Missionary Herald*, July 1905, 358–59.

—. "A New Man in West Africa." *Missionary Herald*, April 1908, 175–76.

—. "West Central African Mission: Spontaneous Growth." *Missionary Herald*, June 1910, 276–77.

Yoano to Dona Nele [Nellie Arnott Darling], January 20, 1935. "Loose Letters, 1910-1943," box 2, NJADP.

Yohn, Susan M. *A Contest of Faiths: Missionary Women and Pluralism in the American Southwest*. Ithaca: Cornell Univ. Press, 1995.

—. "'Let Christian Women Set the Example in Their Own Gifts': The 'Business' of Protestant Women's Organizations." In Bendroth and Brereton, *Women and Twentieth-Century Protestantism*, 213–35.

Youngs, Tim. "Africa/ The Congo: The Politics of Darkness." In Hulme and Youngs, *Cambridge Companion to Travel Writing*, 156–73.

Index

Abaidoo, Sam, 132–133
Abbott, Lyman, 28
ABCFM. *See* American Board of Commissioners for Foreign Missions
acculturation, xviii, 130, 183, 255
agriculture, 47, 257
Alcoff, Linda: *Speaking for Others*, xxvi–xxvii, xli
Aliança Evangélica de Angola, 286
Alpern, Sara, 138
Ambaca, The, 147, 151–153, 159, 178–179, 274
American Baptist Home Missionary Society (ABHMS), 16
American Board of Commissioners for Foreign Missions (ABCFM): deputation to Angola, 226, 259–260; history, 23–25, 31, 33, 175, 291; missions in Africa, xxii, xxxiii, xxxv, 33, 180, 257, 259, 291; Nellie Arnott's relationship with, xv–xvi, xxv, xxxvii, 9, 11, 26, 71, 75, 79, 83–84, 103–107, 211, 215, 265; relations with Portuguese, xviii, xx, xxiii–xxiv, 32, 38-40, 52, 65, 269; Prudential Committee, 51–52, 241, 263–264; secretaries, 51–52, 104, 140–141, 174, 211, 227; women missionaries of, xli, 80, 98, 113, 117, 127–128, 130, 264. *See also* names of ABCFM secretaries
American Freemen's Union Commission (AFUC), 16
American Missionary, The, 15–16
American Missionary Association (AMA), xv, 7–9, 13, 16, 21, 23, 53, 82, 208, 212, 226, 259, 284–285
Anderson, Benedict, 123
Anderson, Rufus, 52
Antler, Joyce, 138
Ardener, Shirley, xl, 64, 68, 121, 130, 257
Arnold, David, 114
Arnot, Frederick Stanley, 76–77, 119, 155, 177, 180
Arnott, Martha Patten, 4, 10, 233, 291, 295
Arnott, Charles, 9, 140, 227, 291
Arnott, Edward, 10, 230, 291
Arnott, James, 10, 18, 291
Arnott, Myrtle, 10, 235, 291, 295
Arnott, Philander, 4, 9–10, 233, 263, 291
Atlantic Monthly, The, 74, 116
authorial agency, xviii, xxv–xxvi
Ayandele, E.A., xl, 65

Bagster, Walter Weldon, 143, 175, 180
Bailundu Mission Station (ABCFM), 33, 43, 57, 61, 98,

325

125, 161, 164–167, 180, 200, 204–205, 215, 224, 241, 259, 280–288, 292, 296
Bailundu Revolt, 35–37, 39, 58–59, 61–62, 180, 286
Barton, James L., 17, 19, 104–105, 181, 194, 209–211, 228–230, 233–234, 238–240, 260, 263, 265–266
Bassnett, Susan, 120
Beach Institute (Savannah, GA), 7, 53
Bebbington, D.W., 54
Bell, Diadem, 200, 218–219, 229, 250–251, 269, 279
Bell, Enoch F., 104, 237–241, 265, 266
Bell, Lena Grace Hiller, 200, 241, 280, 296
Bell, William Clark, 200, 241, 280
Belmonte, Fort (Portuguese), 34, 37, 180, 223, 258
Bendroth, Margaret Lamberts, 15
Benguela Railroad, 34, 37, 156, 177, 224–225, 239, 258
Benguela (Benguella), Angola, xxxiii, 85–86, 119, 137, 147, 150–152, 156–159, 272–274; Nellie Arnott's visits to, 157–159, 273–274
Berlin Conference of 1884-1885, 34
Bickers, Robert A., 18, 54, 63, 66, 114, 268
Bié (Bihé), Angola, 33–35, 57, 76, 98, 119, 151, 154, 157, 165–166, 171, 186, 273, 291
Birmingham, David, 58–59
Blunt, Alison, 120, 126
Boston: Nellie Arnott's visits to, 140–141, 227
Bowie, Fiona, xxiv, xl, 64–68, 121, 130, 257

Brandt, Deborah, xxxvii
Bratton, J.S., xliii
Brereton, Virginia Lieson, 15
Bridges, Roy, xxiii, xl
Bridgman, Frederick B., 226, 259–260
Bridgman, Laura Nichols, 226, 259
Bruner, Edward, xlii
Bryan, Charles Page, 149
Bundy, David, 57
Burg, Steven B., 135
Burtt, Joseph, 179
bush-car (cart), 78, 201, 214, 224, 293
Byam, Paul, 266

Cabinda, 152, 176
Cadbury Brothers Ltd.: William Cadbury, 37, 59–60, 159, 179
Cameron, Ruth Tonkiss, 215
Cameroon, xxiv, 64–67
Cammack Case, 106, 237, 239
Cammack, Sarah Libbie Seymour, 234–235, 238, 240–241, 261, 263–265, 281
Cammack, William, 200, 230, 237–238, 240, 252, 261, 263–265, 281
Campbell, CA, 10–11, 240–241
Campbell, Elizabeth B., 166, 254, 281, 292
Canadian Congregational Foreign Missionary Society, 33, 122, 179, 243, 255, 261, 265–266, 279, 281, 283, 286
caravans, trading, 34, 38, 48, 50, 86, 102, 117, 160, 164–166, 179–180, 224, 259, 292
Caris, Mary Darling, xxxvi, 13–16, 19, 175, 242, 262, 264, 291, 295
carriers (porters), 42, 48, 117, 154,

Index

157–165, 179–180, 184, 200–201, 204–205, 214, 224–225, 250, 273, 284, 293
Catholic missions, Angola, 33–34, 38, 57, 292
Catholicism: anti-Catholic sentiment, 28, 54, 149–150
Catumbella, Angola, 161–162, 179, 225
Cayton, Mary Kupiec, 127
Césaire, Aimé, xxi–xxii, xxxviii–xxxix; *Discourse on Colonialism* and *Notebook of a Return to the Native Land*, xxi
Chatelain, Héli, 57–58, 61, 280, 284
Chickasaw County, IA, 4, 14, 18
Chidester, David, 64
Chikueka, Maria Chela, 63, 113, 131–132; *The Trail of My Life Journey*, 113
Childs, Gladwyn Murray, xxxiii, xliii, 51, 60, 63, 68
Chilesso Mission Station. See Ocileso Mission Station
Chilonda. See Ocilonda
Chipenda, Eva de Carvalho, xx, xxxviii, 63, 112–113, 131–132; *The Visitor: An African Woman's Story of Travel and Discovery*, 112–113
Chissamba Mission Station. See Cisamba Mission Station
Christensen, C. Diane, 58–59, 62, 111
Christian Churches in Many Lands, 33, 208. See also Plymouth Brethren
Christian Endeavor Society, 5–7, 14–15, 27, 54, 176
Christmas, 75, 90, 110, 164, 190, 196, 210, 218–219, 252, 254, 275, 296

Church Missionary Society (CMS), xxiii
Cipuku, 46–50, 67, 95, 111, 123, 247, 268, 294–295
circular letters, xiv, xvi, xxx, xxxv, 18–19, 59, 68, 72, 104, 135–137, 140, 143, 147, 152, 157, 176, 200, 215, 218, 222, 227, 235, 257, 260, 266, 272, 292. *See also* Substitute Circle
Cisamba Mission Station (ABCFM), 33, 57–58, 161, 180, 186, 200, 219, 223–234, 237–238, 250, 256, 258, 265–266, 269, 279–281, 283, 286, 291
Cisanje outstation, 43, 64, 183, 191, 197, 268. *See also* Mueno
Cisanji district, 163, 165, 178
Cituvika: death of, 50, 197–198, 216, 219; death of, 50, 195, 207, 212, 268
Ciyaka (Sachikela) Mission Station (ABCFM), xxxi, 33, 200, 204–205, 224, 263, 282, 287
Ciyuka district, 39, 250, 251. *See also* Kanjundu
Clark, Francis E., 27, 54
Clemens, Samuel L. (pseudo. Mark Twain): *King Leopold's Soliloquy*, 36, 59
cocoa: cultivation of, 36–37, 46, 151, 153, 159, 179, 274
Collins, Frank, 51
colonial discourse, xix, xxx, 31, 94–97, 99, 102, 290
colonialism, xix–xxii, xxxvii–xxxix, 29, 31, 39–40, 96–97, 115–116, 126, 132
Comaroff, Jean and John L., 29, 40, 55, 62
Congo Reform Association (CRA), 36, 59

Congo River, 153, 154, 176
Congregational Church, xiii, 5–9, 14, 16, 21, 23, 28, 33, 37, 55, 61, 92, 112–113, 132, 140, 144, 210–211, 213, 228–230, 266, 270, 281, 286; Commission Creed of 1883, 23
Conrad, Joseph: *Heart of Darkness*, 75
contract labor, 18, 28, 36–37, 39, 46, 59–60, 66, 176–179, 215. *See also* slavery
conversion story, 94, 97. *See also* narrative conventions
Cooper, Frederick, xix, xxxviii, 55–56, 131
Cordell, Dennis D., 61
cultural relativism, 97, 101
curriculum, 6, 49, 84, 86, 110, 126, 132, 212, 252, 260, 264
Currie Institute, 252, 263, 267, 269, 270, 281, 286–287
Currie, Amy Johnston, 161, 179, 281
Currie, Walter Thomas, 33, 57–58, 161, 179–180, 281, 283, 286. *See also* Canadian Congregational Foreign Missionary Society
Cushman, Mary Floyd, 49, 55, 64, 67–68, 181, 208, 213–214, 216, 256, 264, 278, 294

Daniels, Charles H., 16–17, 51, 53
Danky, James, xxxvii
Darby, John Nelson, 57
Darling, Harriet, 7, 295
Darling, Paul L., xxviii, xxxvi, 3, 7, 11–15, 19, 107–108, 110, 123, 175, 217, 240, 242, 251, 254, 263–267, 290, 292–293, 295; marriage to Nellie Arnott, 11, 19, 106–107, 240, 242, 293, 295
Darling, Paul L., Jr., 12, 19
Darling, Truman Christopher, 3–4, 13–16, 108, 181, 218, 289, 291
Davenport, Rodney, 63
Davis, Grace T., 18, 101, 126, 261, 278
Decolonising the Mind, xxi, xxiii, xxxix, xli, 123. *See also* Ngũgĩ Wa Thiong'o
Demerara (Guyana), 184, 208
Diawara, Manthia, xxxix
discourse community, 80
discursive gaps, xviii, xxix–xxxii, xxxv, 87, 96, 102, 105
domestic literacy narratives, 83, 94
Dorsett, Lyle, 16, 51, 175, 176
Dunch, Ryan, 30, 56

editorial technique: Modern Language Association (MLA), American Association for State and Local History (AASLH, 135, 137; Modern Language Association (MLA), American Association for State and Local History (AASLH), 135
Elende, Mt., 205, 282. *See also* Ciyaka Mission Station
Elphick, Richard, xxxvii, 55, 63
empire-building, xviii, xix, 40
Ennis, Elisabeth Logan, xxxi, 56, 97–99, 101, 117, 125, 186, 200, 205–207, 224, 239, 281–282, 293
Ennis, Merlin, xxxi, 68, 125, 166–168, 171, 200, 205–207, 216, 282, 287
Ennis, Merlin, Jr., 216
equivalency, rhetorical linking of missionaries and their readers, 93

Index

Etherington, Norman, 255
Evans, Julie, xxxviii

Falola, Toyin, 65, 66
Fanon, Frantz: *The Wretched of the Earth*, xxi, xxxix, 124
Fay, Annie M. Kimball, 49, 68, 282
Fay, William E., 255, 282
Ferguson, Abbie Park, 226–227
fetishes, 94, 109, 172, 182, 206, 250
Figg, Frank, 184, 186
fires: Kamundongo, xiii, 37, 60, 156, 167, 171, 178; Cisamba, 230, 261
Fitzpatrick, Kristin, 117
foreign missions, xxx, xxxiii, xxxvii, 26–27, 53, 74, 103, 116, 145, 176, 210
Foucault, Michel, xxv, xxxix, xli
Fowler, Corinne, 109, 130
Freedmen's Aid Society (FAS), 16
Freire, Paulo, xviii, xxxvii
Fumika, 94, 192, 193, 197–198, 211, 213, 223
fundraising, xxix, xxxii, 5, 11, 70, 107–108, 122, 243, 248–250, 260, 264–267

Gaitskell, Deborah, 58, 63, 121, 127, 268
Gamba district: schools, 105, 128, 137, 183, 190–198, 200–201, 204, 206, 209, 211, 213, 216, 218, 222, 230, 239
Garenganze (Katanga), 119, 156, 177. *See also* Arnot, Frederick Stanley
Garvey, Ellen Gruber, 289, 297
Gaunt, Mary: *Alone in West Africa*, 77, 120
gender-based curricula, 270

gendered writing, xv–xvi, 91
genre patterns, xvi–xviii, xxvi, xxix, 72, 75, 77, 83, 93, 96, 102, 108, 117, 121, 272
Girls' Boarding School, 12, 209, 218–219, 222, 228–229, 234–236, 238, 243, 248–250, 255–256, 263, 269; beginning of, xxx, 11, 24, 47, 50, 95, 107, 110, 215, 217, 227, 240, 248, 256, 262–263, 267; fundraising for, 107, 243, 248–250. *See also* Means Memorial School
Goodsell, Fred Field, 211
governor, Portuguese (Angola), 35, 273
Grant, Kevin, 55
Greetham, D.C., 137
Gregory, Joel W., 61
Griffiths, Gareth, 255, 270
Grillo, John L., 215
Grimshaw, Patricia, xxxviii, 62

Hall, Catherine, 55–56, 115
Hambly, Wilfrid D., 63, 65, 67, 178–179, 256–258
Harper's Monthly Magazine, 36–37, 118, 159, 179
Harris, Alice and John, 59
Harris, Susan K., 27, 54, 116
Hastings, Adrian, 64, 130
Hawaii, American missionaries in, 27, 54, 61
Hawksley, Alice, 145, 175, 179
Haygood, Laura, 53, 121, 213
healer, traditional, 44, 64, 77, 231–232, 278
Heart of Darkness. See Conrad, Joseph, 75
"heathen": Nellie Arnott's use of term, xxx–xxxi, 29, 47, 74, 93, 97, 102, 163–164, 166, 189, 206, 216, 221, 247–248, 256, 259

Henderson, Lawrence, xxiii, xliii, 52, 113, 174, 209
Henderson, Muriel (Ki), xxiii, 113, 127, 132, 209
Heywood, Linda M., 58–61, 65–66, 177, 179–180, 258, 270
Hill, Patricia, 25–26, 213
Hlongwane, Lynette, 130, 260
Hochschild, Adam, 18, 59, 213
Hollenbeck, Henry Stanley, 118, 195, 199–200, 204, 218, 220–222, 234, 239, 243, 250, 282
Howard, J. Keir, 119
Hualondo. *See* Ohualondo
Huber, Mary Taylor, xxxviii, 66
Hughes, Heather, 130, 260
Huguenot College, 226–227, 259
Hulme, Peter, 117, 120
Hunt, Nancy Rose, xl
Hunter, Jane, xxxvii, 125
Hutchison, William R., xxxvi, 51–52, 116

imagined communities, 93
imperialism, xviii–xxi, xxiii–xxiv, xxvii, xxxvii, xl–xli, xliii, 21, 28, 30, 32, 38, 40, 54, 62, 74, 75, 79, 94, 101–102, 116, 118, 121, 126, 129, 131, 252, 267, 270
In His Steps. See Sheldon, Charles, 7
Inanda Seminary, 11, 19, 111, 130, 257, 260
indigenous peoples, xxiii–xxiv, xxxviii, xl, 29, 32, 41, 56, 63, 96, 123, 130, 290

Jacobs, Sylvia M., xxxvii
Jameson, Fredric, xvii, xxxvii
Jenkins, Ruth Y., 129
jigger bites, effects of, 169, 216

Johnston, May J., 85, 96
Jones, Jacqueline, 13, 16
Judson, Adoniram, 103

Kamundongo Mission Press, 108, 188, 255, 275
Kamundongo Mission Station (ABCFM), 142, 162, 171, 181, 186–188, 239, 265, 278, 283–285; church, 192, 195, 207, 222, 262, 290; fires, xiii, 37, 60, 156, 167, 171, 178; girls' housing, 129, 187, 209, 247, 258; mission buildings and grounds, 167, 172; Nellie Arnott's arrival at, 166; proposed move to Gamba, 192–194, 198–199, 211, 213; school, 196, 211
Kanjundu, 65, 94, 123, 261–262, arrest of, 39, 61, 94, 123, 269; death of, 39, 61, 250–251, 269
Kanogo, Tabitha, 130, 257
Kapitango, 162, 172, 182, 239, 266
Kay-Scott, Cyril. *See* Wellman, Frederick Creighton
Kimbundu, xliii, 132, 177
kindergarten teaching, 26, 49, 68, 175, 179, 199, 209, 282
Kindergarten Training School, Oberlin College, 10
Kingsley, Mary Henrietta, 79, 127
Kirkwood, Deborah, xl, 64, 68, 121, 130, 257
Kramer, Paul, 54

Labode, Modupe, 68, 121, 130
Lamson, Kate, 128
Lane, Frederick T., 195, 196, 211
Larymore, Constance, 79
Lazreg, Marnia, 131
Leake, Mrs. Joseph B., 89–90,

121–122
Leopold II, King of the Belgians, 18, 36, 59, 119, 177, 213
Lewis, Desiree, 124
Life and Light for Woman, xiv, 63, 67, 69, 71, 77, 91, 94, 114, 120, 162, 183, 191, 193, 196, 204–205, 207, 210, 215
Lisbon, Portugal: Nellie Arnott's visit to, 146-151
literacy network: children's roles in, 71, 80
literacy practices, xv–xvi, 6, 70, 80
Liu, Tessie P., xl
Liverpool, England: Arnott's visit to, 85, 141, 143, 146, 151
Livingstone, David: *Missionary Travels and Researches in South Africa, The Life and African Explorations of David Livingstone*, 76–77, 117, 214, 257
Loanda. *See* Luanda
Lobito, Angola, xxxix, 156, 208–209, 225, 258, 291; Nellie Arnott's visits to, 156, 225
London: Nellie Arnott's visits to, 143–146, 227
London Missionary Society, xlii, 18, 53, 76, 107, 118
Loomba, Ania, xxxvii
Love, Eric, 28, 54
Luanda, Angola: Nellie Arnott's visit to, 153–156, 177
Lumbo, 156, 195, 199, 251, 269
Lutkehaus, Nancy C., xxxviii, 66
Lynch, Grace, 141

MacKenzie, John M., xxxvi, xliii, 55, 119, 129, 133
Manifest Destiny, 27
Marchant, A.G., xxx, xlii, 277–278
Marshall, David B., 57, 174, 284, 297
Mastrobuono, Luisa, 63, 65–67, 179, 258, 263
McAllister, Agnes, 124
McClintock, Anne, xxxix, xli–xlii
McEwan, Cheryl, 79, 120
Means Memorial School, 19, 110, 130, 174, 215, 234–236, 238, 243, 252, 254, 267, 269–270, 287, 296; beginning of, 226–229, 234–236, 238, 243, 248–249, 256, 262, naming of, 234–236, 238
Means, Jane C., 19, 68, 140, 174, 227, 234–235, 238
Means, John O., 24, 174, 235
Melville, Helen Jane, 205, 229, 250, 256, 283, 292
Melville, Margaret (Maggie) Walker, 56, 205, 229, 283
Memmi, Albert: *The Colonizer and the Colonized*, xxi, xxxix, 124
Meridian, MS: Nellie Arnott's teaching in, 9, 23, 80, 285
Methodist Episcopal Mission, Luanda, 33, 57, 155, 177
Miers, Suzanne, 59
Miller, Janette Estelle, 25, 56, 123, 128, 283
Miller, Jon, 66
Miller, Samuel, 180
mission discourse, 74, 95, 113, 115, 123
mission service: gender roles, 103–106; motivation for, 11, 25–26, 53
Mission Studies: Woman's Work in Foreign Lands, xiii, xxx, xxxvi, xlii, 12, 46, 49, 55, 61, 66–71, 77, 82, 84–85, 91–94, 114, 116–117, 120–123, 167, 172–173, 178, 181–182, 187, 189, 197, 203, 207, 212, 218,

244–245, 248, 250, 255–256, 267, 269, 271–272, 277, 293
Missionary Herald, The, xiii, 16, 55, 61, 71, 80–81, 91, 120, 192, 255, 265, 283, 293
Moffatt, Robert, 224–225, 283
Mohanty, Chandra Talpade, xlii
Montgomery, Helen Barrett, 53
Moody (Chicago) Bible Institute, 9, 16, 21, 23, 26, 51, 82, 174–176, 229, 241, 261, 285, 287
Moody, Dwight L., 16, 23, 175
Morel, Edmund D, 36. *See also* Congo Reform Association (CRA)
Morgan, G. Campbell, 144
Mueno, 43–46, 64, 268
Mufti, Aamir, xxxix, xli–xlii
Murrain, George R. and Elizabeth, 184–186, 208, 294
Murray, Andrew, xliii, 60, 226–227, 259
Murrian. *See* Murrain, George R. and Elizabeth
Myers-Brown, Joyce, 270

narrative conventions, 83, 94, 96, 123
Nashua, IA, 5–7, 19, 14–15, 18–19, 80, 175; *Weekly Nashua Post*, 7, 14–15, 18–19
Négritude, xxi, xxxix
Neipp, Fredericka Heinrich, 171, 284
Neipp, Henri A., 195, 201, 214, 223, 284
neo-colonialism, xxxviii
Nevinson, Henry W., 36–37, 59–61, 63, 176, 178–180. See also *Harper's Monthly Magazine*
New Hampton, IA, 10, 14, 19
New Woman, 119

Newell, Harriet, 103, 127
Nfah-Abbenyi, Juliana Makuchi, xl
Ngũgĩ Wa Thiong'o: *The River Between, Decolonising the Mind*, xx–xxii, xxxi, xxxviii–xli, 95, 123, 267
Nnaemeka, Obioma, 64

Oberlin College, 10, 56, 179, 218, 255, 259, 284, 286
Ochileso (Chilesso). *See* Ocileso
Ocileso (Chilesso) Mission Station (ABCFM), 57, 85, 96, 125, 161, 169, 181, 189, 194, 200–204, 215, 283–284, 287–288, 294
Ocilonda Mission Station (Plymouth Brethren), 33, 184, 186, 202, 208
Ohualondo Mission Station (Plymouth Brethren), 33, 57, 184, 186, 208, 294
Olosoma, 34, 38, 60. *See also* Umbundu rulers
Olutu outstation, 52, 129, 183, 192, 197–198, 205, 211–212, 223, 230, 255, 262
onjango (community house), 29, 172, 202, 220, 256
ordinary writing, 70
Orientalism, xix
Outstations, 87–89, 171, 184, 186, 199, 202, 240, 277; schools, 87–89, 183, 187–189, 191–193, 196–197, 199, 201–202, 224, 243–245, 275–277
Ovimbundu, xxxiii, xiii, 21, 28, 33, 36, 42, 46, 50–51, 64, 99, 125, 177, 236, 249. *See also* various topics listed under Umbundu
Owayanda outstation, 47, 183,

Index

192–193, 197, 207, 210, 223
Oyěwùmí, Oyèrónké, xl, 64, 124, 131

Packard, Luther N., 5–6
Palmer, Robin, 58
Parker, Joseph, 144
Parsons, Neil, 58
Pascoe, Peggy, 66
Patton, Cornelius H., 259
Pawns, 44–46, 66
pedagogy, Nellie Arnott's, 31, 49, 84, 95, 113, 190, 224, 267, 283
Peel, J. D. Y., 41, 56, 60, 63–64
Periodicals, xiii, xv, xxxiv–xxxv, 12, 69, 72, 77, 91, 129, 135, 269
Perry pictures, 275
Perry, Elisabeth Israels, 138
Philafrican Liberators' League Mission, 57, 280, 284
Philippines, American role in, xx, 27, 54, 74, 116
Philips, David, xxxviii
plantations, Portuguese, 36–37, 46, 151, 159, 180, 274
Plymouth Brethren: missions in Angola, 33, 37, 57, 119, 155, 177, 180, 184, 202, 208, 211, 255, 294
Pollock, Sarah, 17, 51, 53
Polygamy, 64, 98. *See also* polygyny
Polygyny, xxii, 44–45, 50, 64–65, 97–98, 123, 172, 287
Pond, Harriet Perkins, 179, 255
Populist Party, 23
Porter, Andrew, xxiv, xl, xlii, 30–31, 56
Portugal: colonial administration in Angola, xliii, 21, 28, 34, 37, 39, 59, 61, 149, 154, 177, 194, 215, 225, 258, 286, 296

Portuguese West Africa, xiv, xxxiii, xxxiv, 3, 11, 18, 26, 52, 59, 139, 179, 217, 263–264, 279
postcolonial theory, xx–xxi
Pratt, Mary Louise, 72, 115
Predelli, Line Nyhagen, 66
prisoners, Portuguese, 154
public writing, xiv, xvi–xviii, xxv, xxix, xxxv, 60, 67, 70–72, 74, 77, 101, 112, 135, 137, 139, 254, 260, 289, 295

Quataert, Jean, xl

racial essentialism, 27, 97
racial hierarchies, xxxix
Ranger, Terence, xl, 62
Ray, Annie, 70, 114
Read, Annie Williams, 243, 259, 267
Redick, Emma Cecilia, 56, 89, 93, 125, 161, 170–171, 201–202, 204, 214–215, 284
Reeves-Ellington, Barbara, xxxvii, 52, 54, 125, 127
Remick, John Erni, 68, 282
reports, mission movement, xlii, 72, 121–122, 262, 274, 277
rhetorical agency, xxv. *See also* authorial agency
Richardson, Joe, 53
Robbins, Sarah, xxxvi, 13, 15, 19, 114, 121–123, 127, 133, 212–213
Robert, Dana L., xxiii, xxxvii, xxxix–xl, 25, 126, 257
Roberts, Richard, 59
Rochelle, France: Nellie Arnott's visit to, 143, 146
Rohan, Elizabeth (Liz) Ellen, 25, 53, 122–123, 128, 283
Romero, Patricia, 78, 115, 120
Roof, Judith, xli

Index

Rosenberg, Emily, 66
Ross, Andrew C., xxix, 118
Royal Geographic Society, xl, 177
rubber trade, 18, 34, 58, 159, 165, 179, 187, 213
rum trade, 278

Sacamana, Enoque Gomes. *See* Sakamana
Sacikela (Ciyaka) Station, 33, 205, 282, 287. *See also* Ciyaka (Sachikela) Station
Sakalumbu, 47–50, 68, 195, 212, 216, 223, 268, 295
Sakamana (Enoque Gomes Sacamana), 52, 129, 192–193, 197, 211–212, 270
Samuels, Michael, 177
Sanders, Frank Knight, 141, 174
Sanders, Joseph A., 10, 18, 141, 174, 228, 261
Sanders, Sarah Bell, xxviii, 31, 87–89, 140–143, 146, 149–154, 158, 165–166, 171, 173, 183, 186, 187–189, 191, 193, 200, 216, 218, 239, 255, 265, 274–276, 284, 292, 297
Sanders, William Henry, xxv, 18–19, 24, 31, 35, 56–57, 61, 80, 125, 128, 141, 143, 149–150, 158–159, 161, 164, 166–167, 171–174, 180, 186, 189–199, 204, 207, 218, 239, 242–243, 251, 262, 273, 277, 284, 296
Sanneh, Lamin, 30, 56
Saõ Tomé, 36–37, 59–60. *See also* St. Thomas Island
Satre, Lowell J., 59, 60, 179
Sawicki, Jana, xxvi, xli
Schriber, Mary Suzanne, 77, 96, 97, 98, 119, 124, 214
Scobie, Ingrid Winther, 138
Scott, Jamie S., 255

scrapbooking, 12–13, 69, 108–110, 254, 269, 289, 297
Semple, Rhonda Anne, xxxii, xlii, 17, 53, 107, 114, 123, 127–128
Seton, Rosemary, 18, 53, 63, 66, 114, 128, 268
Sheldon, Charles: *In His Steps*, 7
Shemo, Connie A., xxxvii, 52, 54, 125, 127
Shields, Louise Raven, 155, 177
Shohat, Ella, xxxix, xli, xlii
Siegel, Kristi, 77, 117, 119, 129–130
Sinor, Jennifer, 70, 114
Sklar, Katherine Kish, xxxvii, 52, 54, 125, 127
slavery, 11, 18, 24, 36–37, 44–45, 48, 55, 60, 65–66, 78, 151, 156, 159, 166, 174, 178–180, 208–209, 250, 274; domestic, 45–46, 48, 59, 65–66, 94, 98, 123, 250. *See also* contract labor
Slessor, Mary, 79, 120
Smalley, Martha Lund, 174
Smith, Judson, 18, 104, 141, 169, 174, 181
Smith, Sidonie, 214
Social Darwinism, 27, 278
Social Gospel movement, 23
Soma, Jonas, 111, 254
Soma, 39, 233, 250, 261, 263, 269. *See also* Umbundu rulers
Soremekun, Fola, 52, 57–62, 125, 174, 178, 180, 182, 260, 270, 278
Spurr, David, xx, xxxviii, 96
St. Thomas Island, 36, 147, 151–153, 159, 274. *See also* Saõ Tomé
standpoint epistemology, xxv–xxvi
Stanley, Brian, 51, 55, 63, 215
Stanley, Henry Morton, 75, 117,

Index   335

214
Stevens, Michael E., 135
Stimpson, Sarah, xxv, xxviii,
   9–10, 48, 56, 80, 82, 89,
   93, 104–106, 124, 128, 142,
   156, 164–168, 170–173, 178,
   183, 187–188, 191–201, 204,
   209–214, 218, 221–222, 249,
   252, 269, 285, 291
Stokey, Fred, 241, 288
Stoler, Ann Laura, xli, 55, 56
Stover, Bertha Bennett, 97–98,
   100–101, 103, 124–125, 178,
   200, 204, 215, 224, 286, 297
Stover, Helen Hurlburt, 204, 241,
   286, 297
Stover, Wesley Maier, 39, 58,
   61, 200, 204, 215, 224, 282,
   285–286
Stowe, David M., 211
Strong, Elnathan E., 140, 142
Strong, William E., 52
Stunt, William T., 57, 208, 211
Substitute Circle. *See also* circular
   letters, 9, 11, 24, 72, 141–142
Sunday School, xvi, xxxi, xxxv,
   4–7, 15, 70, 173, 187, 192–193,
   199, 211, 222, 224, 241, 245,
   250, 276
Swain, Shurlee, xxxviii
Swan, Charles: *The Slavery
   of Today*, 37, 60, 66, 154,
   177–178. *See also* Cadbury
   Brothers Ltd

Taylor, William, 57
Tenney, H. Melville, 239–240,
   265
tepoia, 84, 86, 117, 160–161,
   164–165, 183, 201, 205, 207,
   214, 225, 276, 284, 293
Thomas, Nicholas, xix, xxxviii,
   96, 123, 124, 297

Thornton, John, 60–61
Torrey, Reuben L., 16, 23, 146,
   176
travel writing, xxxiv, 72, 73,
   75–77, 79, 83, 92, 94, 96, 106,
   108, 117, 119–120, 129
Trinh, T. Minh-ha, 41, 62
Tucker, John T.,19, 39, 42, 56, 58,
   61, 63–67, 122, 130, 180, 208,
   216, 229, 251–252, 255– 257,
   261–262, 265, 267, 269–270,
   280–288
Tuskegee Institute, 111, 254
Twain, Mark. *See* Clemens, Samuel L. (pseudo. Mark Twain),
   36, 54, 74, 116
Tyrrell, Ian, 54

U.S. Expansionism, 21
Umbundu Christians, 24, 60,
   125, 183, 187, 195, 209, 257;
   regional identity, 32, 60. *See
   also* Umbundu settlements:
   Christian
Umbundu (language): Nellie Arnott's study of, xxxi, 90, 162,
   170, 209, 224; instruction in,
   30, 84, 172, 276; Umbundu-
   English Vocabulary, 31, 218,
   255, 285
Umbundu rulers (*olosoma*), 34–35,
   38–39, 58, 60, 233, 250,
   261–263, 269
Umbundu settlements: Christian, 29, 38, 50, 55, 197, 213,
   256; traditional, 29, 55, 98,
   172–173, 213, 244
Umbundu trade system, 34, 38,
   48, 58, 60–61, 165, 179
Umbundu traditional social practices: education, 49; religious
   rituals, 43–44, 49, 117. *See also*
   healer, traditional; Umbundu

women

Umbundu women: as pawns, 44–46, 65–66; child care, 48–49; food preparation, 67, 100, 190–191, 220, 222, 257, 275, 294–295; gender roles, 47–48, 50, 67–68, 99–100, 161, 247; marriage customs, 44, 47, 50, 64, 66–67, 247–248, 263, 268; skill in agriculture, xxxi, 47–48, 50, 67, 100, 236, 257. *See also* polygyny

United Church of Canada, 57, 58, 266, 270, 281, 283, 286, 291

Urban-Mead, Wendy, 52

vernacular: literacy in, 30–32

Von Rohr, John, 23, 51–52, 54

Walker, Cherryl, 58

WBMI. *See* Woman's Board of Missions of the Interior

Webster, Marion Murchie, 89, 125, 161, 204–205, 215, 241, 243, 252, 287, 296. *See also* Means Memorial School

Wellman, Frederick Creighton, 35, 171, 205, 282, 287

Wellman, Lydia Isley, 186, 243, 287

West Central African Mission, xxxiii, 9, 35, 63, 80, 82, 98, 114, 125, 140, 183, 192, 235, 248, 260, 279

Wheeler, Douglas, 58–59, 62, 111

Wiegand, Wayne, xxxvii

Wiegman, Robyn, xli

Willis, Justin, 66

Wingate, Marcia, 229–230, 233, 261

witchcraft, practice of, xxiii, 58, 86, 117–118, 123, 206

Wollons, Roberta, 130

Woman's Board of Missions (Boston), 25, 174, 213

Woman's Board of Missions of the Interior, Chicago (WBMI), xxx, xlii, 9, 17–18, 25–26, 51, 71, 88–92, 98, 100, 107, 126, 136, 173, 230, 234, 237, 261–264, 271, 277–278, 284; reports, 92, 121–122, 274, 277

Woman's Conferences (Angola), 42–43, 63, 69, 114, 183–184, 207, 292, 294

women donors, xxxv, 93

Women's Christian Temperance Union (WCTU), 27, 54

Woodside, Thomas W., 200–201, 204, 230, 288

Woodside, Emma Dreisbach, 42, 170, 201, 287

Woodside, Mabel (Stokey), 243, 287–288

World Missionary Conference, Edinburgh (1910), 205, 215, 259

Yohn, Susan M., 115, 129

Young Women's Christian Association (Y.W.C.A.), 225, 240

Youngs, Tim, 117, 120

About the Authors

Sarah Robbins is the Lorraine Sherley Professor of Literature at Texas Christian University and the author of *Managing Literacy, Mothering America* (Pittsburgh Press, 2006), which won a Choice award from the American Library Association. She is also the author of *The Cambridge Introduction to Harriet Beecher Stowe* (Cambridge, 2007).

Ann Ellis Pullen, is Professor of History, Emerita, at Kennesaw State University, where she chaired the Department of History and Philosophy and the Women's Studies Program. She has authored articles on the early twentieth-century interracial movement in the U.S. South in a variety of publications.

Photograph of Ann Ellis Pullen and Sarah Robbins. Courtesy of University Relations Photography, Kennesaw State University..

www.ingramcontent.com/pod-product-compliance
Lightning Source LLC
Chambersburg PA
CBHW020635230426

43665CB00008B/176